Canadian Novelists and the Novel

Canadian Novelists and the Novel

Edited by

Douglas Daymond and *Leslie Monkman*

Borealis Press
Ottawa, Canada
1981

259757|000

The Publishers gratefully acknowledge the support of the Ontario Arts Council and the Canada Council.

Canadian Cataloguing in Publication Data
Main Entry Under Title:

Canadian novelists on Canadian fiction

ISBN 0-88887-047-7 bd. ISBN 0-88887-049-3 pa.

1. Canadian fiction (English) — History and criticism — Addresses, essays, lectures. I. Daymond, Douglas, 1940-   . II. Monkman, Leslie, 1946-

PS8187.C36   C813'.009   C79-090030-0
PR9192.2.C35

Borealis Press Limited
9 Ashburn Drive
Ottawa, Canada K2E 6N4

Printed and bound in Canada.

Table of Contents

Part 3
The Rise of Realism

Part 4
Regionalism and Nationalism

Part 5
The Contemporary Novel

Introduction

> Time and again I am forced to the conclusion
> that if we want intelligent comment about writing
> and the temperament of writers, we are more likely
> to get it from writers themselves than from critics.
>
> Robertson Davies, « La Littérature Engagée »

From the early nineteenth century to the present, English-Canadian novelists have contributed to the critical discussion of the possibilities and challenges of novel-writing in Canada. Although the earliest novel with a Canadian setting, Frances Brooke's *The History of Emily Montague* (1779), was written by an author who brought a lively intelligence to the art of dramatic criticism, no record of her views on fiction has survived. In the early nineteenth century, however, the novel emerges in Canada as an indigenous genre, and with its appearance begins a parallel tradition of novelists articulating their aims and ideals, their frustrations and their failures.

Canadian Novelists and the Novel provides a selection of views by major English-Canadian novelists of the last one hundred and fifty years concerning the theory and practice of their art. Texts have been reprinted as they originally appeared with the exception of cases where obvious typographical errors and inconsistencies have been corrected. The selections have been arranged into five chronological parts, each part prefaced by a comment on the state of the novel by the arguably major critic of the period. This method and arrangement suggest at least some elements of the critical context in which the novelists of each era have worked as well as the extent to which they share, amplify and extend the critical preoccupations of their time. As the selections follow the development of English-Canadian fiction from its beginnings to the present, they reveal both the diversity and the continuity in the novelists' views of their art.

Part 1

David Chisholme begins his review of Julia Catherine Hart's *St. Ursula's Convent* (1824) by noting that only the book's claims as the first novel by a Canadian-born writer have induced him to consider the book in his journal. In the sub-title to Hart's novel, "Scenes From Real Life," he finds the promise of an antidote to "those light, amatory, and romantic tales, which . . . are daily issuing from the press," but he expresses disappointment at the scarcity of such scenes and points out that, although novels may inculcate virtue in their readers, morality may be served more directly by other literary forms.[1]

Novelists of the period also insistently link moral utility with realism in fiction. Hart argues that the characters of *St. Ursula's Convent* are not "mere creature[s] of imagination" and identifies *Tonnewonte* (1825) as a work whose "pages will not be found detrimental to the great cause of religion and morality" as it describes "some of the causes of the spirit of emigration . . . and also the general habits prevalent in many of our new settlements." John Galt's *Bogle Corbet* (1831) also focuses on characters and conditions associated with immigration to North America, and in his *Autobiography* (1833), Galt identifies the novel as a "literary essay," "a guide book," and as "an attempt to embody facts and observations, collected and made on actual occurrences." Although he admires the "recreative stories" of Sir Walter Scott, Galt insists that his own "parables in which the moral [is] more valuable than the incidents [are] impressive" should not be seen as rivals to the "unapproachable excellence" of Scott's romances. Scott's work remains popular throughout the nineteenth century, but the documentary realism identified by Galt as central to his own aims offers an alternative mode that influences novelists' discussions of fiction more directly.[2]

In his introduction to the 1851 edition of *Wacousta*, John Richardson explicitly expresses his indebtedness to Scott's North American heir, James Fenimore Cooper, and acknowledges that, apart from its basis in Pontiac's conflict with British forces in 1763, "all else is imaginary" in *Wacousta*. Yet he outlines in realistic detail the historical background to his novel and defends the book at length against isolated charges of improbability and geographical error. If accuracy and precision concern Richardson in this introduction, his choice of epigraphs for *Ecarté* (1829) more than twenty years earlier reveals a concern with instruction that presumably would have found favour with David Chisholme:

> "His very faults shall afford amusement, and under
> them he may, without the formality of a
> preceptor, communicate instruction."
> Preface to 1st Ed. *Disowned*

> "In a *novel*, not professing to be a mere *tale*,
> (with which it is often confounded, but from
> which, I think, it should be carefully distinguished),
> the materials for interest are not, I apprehend,
> to be solely derived from a plot."
> *Ibid*.[3]

Whatever the verdict of most of his contemporaries and of later generations of readers, Richardson's emphasis repeatedly falls on realism and instruction rather than on the place of his fiction in the tradition of romance.

2

Thomas Haliburton and Susanna Moodie affirm a relationship between realism and moral instruction even more explicitly. In *Nature and Human Nature* (1855), Haliburton's Sam Slick finds his models for "holding up the mirror" in the eighteenth-century novels of Smollett and Fielding where "men and women were taken from real life." Arguing that the novelist need not "go searching about for strange people or strange things," Sam asserts that he has offered a picture of the times that both entertains and instructs. Moodie feels less comfortable than Haliburton with the novels of Fielding and Smollett but, in "A Word For the Novel Writers" (1851), acknowledges their importance as realistic reflections of their age. If Chisholme doubts the efficacy of fiction as a vehicle for morality, Moodie insists that novel-readers may "be induced to listen to precepts of religion and virtue when arrayed in a more amusing and attractive garb, and enforced by characters who speak and feel like themselves." Thus novelists become "missionaries" and "heaven inspired teachers."

Despite his reservations concerning the success of Hart's novel in terms of documentary realism and moral usefulness, Chisholme recognizes the importance of the novel as "the first effort to cultivate a barren field." With colonial deference, the preface to *St. Ursula's Convent* modestly identifies the novel as an "incipient attempt" that must inevitably suffer from comparison with Hart's European models; nevertheless, the author hopes for support from her countrymen. In the dialogue that serves as an introduction to *Tonnewonte*, Hart addresses a North American rather than a British American audience and argues strenuously that North American novelists may acknowledge the "great geniuses" of Europe but must not be intimidated by the tradition established by those writers; she insists on the need for a native literary tradition, a conviction echoed by her contemporary novelists and their successors.

Throughout his work, John Richardson laments the failure of Canadians to honour and to support their men of letters and repeatedly contrasts the population of his own "matter-of-fact country" with the "reading people" of the United States. Although he views the novelist's talent as a "mere incidental gift" and "the creation of fiction as far below the arts of mechanical creation," Richardson echoes Chisholme and Hart in stressing the importance of literature to the evolution of a nation. His description in *Eight Years in Canada* (1847) of the financing of *The Canadian Brothers* (1840) anticipates a concern with practical considerations relating to copyright, pirated editions and American competition that has preoccupied Canadian novelists from Susanna Moodie to Matt Cohen.

Forty years after the publication of *St. Ursula's Convent*, Rosanna Leprohon, in her preface to *Antoinette de Mirecourt* (1864), reiterates the need for an indigenous literature. However, unlike her predecessor, Leprohon could add:

> More than one successful effort towards the
> attainment of this object has been made within
> the last few years, and more than one valuable
> work, Canadian in origin, subject and sympathies,
> has been produced and published among us.[4]

Stressing realism, moral utility, an acknowledgement of old world models and resistance to commercial difficulties affecting the publication of novels, English-Canadian novelists, by Confederation, had moved beyond the "air of novelty" that Chisholme found in Hart's use of Canadian settings to more serious, substantial and successful explorations of the novel in a Canadian context.

Part 2

Goldwin Smith's identification of popular novels as "the bad tobacco of the mind" at first seems to echo the scepticism of David Chisholme's comments almost fifty years earlier. Smith, however, while criticizing inferior fiction, shares none of Chisholme's doubts concerning the ultimate potential of the novel. Honouring the centenary of Sir Walter Scott's birth, "The Lamps of Fiction" (1871) illustrates prevailing critical attitudes towards the novel in the latter half of the nineteenth century. Scott emerges as the novelist whose novels are moral without lapsing into moralizing, committed without giving way to prejudice and faithful to human nature without descending into "lewdness", "impurity" or "filth".

Despite his insistence on the moral function of the novel—a position reiterated in Gilbert Parker's contention that fiction must "play a higher and higher part in the moral welfare of the nation"— Smith writes disparagingly of "religious zealots" who use the novel as a means "of enlisting imagination, as they think, on the side of truth." Sara Jeannette Duncan also unhappily notes the pervasiveness of novels with "theological aims to serve" in British fiction of the 1880s. Charles Gordon, however, argues that the religious content of his novels not only fulfills a moral function but has also introduced a "vast host of religious folk" to the art of fiction.

Smith looks to fiction not for explicit moralizing but for strong characterization, and he finds the key to Scott's greatness as a novelist in his characters. James De Mille shares this view of character as "the dominant force in fiction," and Gilbert Parker discusses character as "a law set in motion." More specifically, Sara Jeannette Duncan identifies the emergence of a new kind of heroine in the novel, and Stephen Leacock joins her in noting a shift away from heroines who combined "an ideal beauty, an impeccable virtue, a modesty and an innocence that ran idiocy hard."

Discussion of morality and character in fiction frequently shifts to consideration of the respective merits of realism and romance. Thus, in his survey of fiction published in 1884, G. Mercer Adam laments the disappearance of "the good old romantic and imaginative novel" in terms reminiscent of Smith's lamps of "ideality" and "chivalry." In sharp contrast to the objective detachment of De Mille's discussion of "the real and the ideal," Adam savagely attacks "the intellectual vivisection methods of the American schools of James and Howells; or worse still, the loathsome realism and putridity of the school of Zola and France." Ironically, when Sara Jeannette Duncan reviews *An Algonquin Maiden* (1887), she explicitly attributes the romance of the novel to Adam's collaborator and lauds Adam for his realism.

No English-Canadian novelist was more directly affected than Duncan by the American writers whom Adam attacked. Her columns in *The Week* present informed and articulate discussion of the continuing debate on romance and realism even as she cautions against rigidity in definitions and forms. Like Duncan, Gilbert Parker recognizes that "no great and permanent work of fiction can properly or arbitrarily be labelled naturalistic, idealistic, romantic, realistic or symbolistic." Yet, in "Fiction—Its Place in the National Life" (1907), Parker's sympathies become clear as he identifies realism with photography, journalism with "hopeless" conclusions while associating romance with "the sweep of wide and powerful imagination, the rush of large ideas, the impact of great conflicting passions, the beauty of sacrifice, the celebration of simple and primitive emotions, the faith in the heart of the writer that good is the final goal of ill." The reappearance of the discussion of romance and realism in Stephen Leacock's *How to Write* (1943) indicates the continued importance of this debate for writers of this era.

Praising Scott's achievement, Goldwin Smith notes that "historical romance is a perilous thing," but writers such as William Kirby and Gilbert Parker regard this genre as an important forum for the fiction of a new nation. Kirby's letters indicate a self conscious awareness of setting a new direction for Canadian fiction in using the *ancien régime* of New France as the focus of *The Golden Dog* (1877). Twenty years later, Parker praises this novel as the "one really notable work of fiction" built on the legends and traditions of Canadian history —"a veritable mine of information and research, a powerful and admirable piece of romance, not the easiest in the world to read and yet one to which I wish to pay my earnest tribute."

Scott's influence is apparent in the vogue for historical romance, but the tradition of "local colour" fiction dating back to Galt and Moodie continues to preoccupy writers in this era. Emphasis on "scenes of real life" diminishes, however; writers such as Parker insist that fiction can never simply be a photographic reproduction or "transcript of life." Indeed, Parker sees "local colour" as "a perilous catchword which deludes the public and leads young writers to think that a phonograph

5

and a guidebook are the weapons of fame." In his autobiography, *Post-script to Adventure* (1938), Charles Gordon acknowledges his "photographic quality of mind" but stresses that the vitality of his fiction stems from other sources. Writers such as Gordon and L. M. Montgomery link "local colour" with sentiment as Montgomery's frustration at the failure of an American reviewer to appreciate the regional setting of *Anne of Green Gables* (1908) indicates. Not surprisingly, Stephen Leacock, the writer of the era who explicitly identifies realism with photography, explodes many of the sentimental conventions of "local colour" fiction with the irony of *Sunshine Sketches of a Little Town* (1912).

Another genre providing a new focus for the debate on romance and realism emerges in the animal stories of Charles G. D. Roberts and Ernest Thompson Seton. Stressing the new realism of the treatment of animals in fiction at the end of the nineteenth century, Robert's "The Animal Story" (1902) nevertheless identifies such fiction as "psychological romance" built "on a framework of natural science." In his view, fiction based on the observation of nature and its creatures retains the power of romance as "it frees us for a little from the world of shop-worn utilities," but it achieves this role of "potent emancipator" through a detailed observation and analysis of its natural subjects.

One concern which is not voiced by Smith in "The Lamps of Fiction" but which often recurs in discussions of fiction by novelists of the period concerns practical difficulties relating to publishing novels in Canada. Like Richardson, William Kirby finds in Canada a "hard practical country" and is apprehensive about the reception of "the first attempt in English to draw from the romantic history of New France the materials for a work of fiction." Sara Jeannette Duncan ponders the sources of "a very distinct and widespread animus against Canadian literary efforts" in general terms, but G. Mercer Adam is more outspoken and precise. The "Interregnum in Literature" (1884) that Adam identifies in the early 1880s has specifically identifiable sources in Canada: the excessive influence of inferior newspapers, the rise of materialism, the decline in educational standards and "the colonial status, and the anomalies of the literary copyright law which surrender the native book-market to the American publisher." In "Canadian Literature and Copyright" (1883), William Kirby analyzes discriminatory aspects of the Copyright Law of 1842 in detail and, along with Duncan, Adam and others, reiterates many of the frustrations expressed by Richardson and Moodie in the preceding era.

Part 3

In "The Canadian Novel Turns the Corner" (1935), William Arthur Deacon also locates practical obstacles to the emergence of

Canadian fiction in the colonial "habit of mind" of Canadians, the domination of the small Canadian market by British and American books and the failure of the Canadian public to support their own novelists. By 1927, however, Deacon sees the novel emerging into a new era with the publication of novels by Mazo de la Roche, Frederick Philip Grove, Laura Goodman Salverson and Morley Callaghan. The strengths of this new fiction include economy and concentration of expression, a greater sense of complexity in character and motive, more sophisticated craftsmanship in both style and structure, a new "candor" in subject matter and a greater "seriousness" in subject matter than Deacon perceived in earlier Canadian fiction.

Deacon praises the movement away from evangelical and didactic fiction of earlier eras. He fears, however, a movement to escapism which, by restricting its focus to the individual and the local, ignores the sweeping forces of change. Such fictions, in Deacon's view, unconsciously reflect Canadian apathy and an unwillingness to acknowledge the currents of change.

Both major novelists of the era share several of Deacon's views. In "The Novel" (1929), Frederick Philip Grove argues that the novel must deal "with *socially significant* things from the main stream of life," rooting "the crisis and the characters involved in it in the social conditions of the period." In "The Plight of Canadian Fiction" (1938), Morley Callaghan notes that only the novelist in search of quick popular success neither challenges nor disturbs his complacent reader; indeed, the demands of the Canadian market actively work against the innovations of an author who seeks to "look at reality with his own eyes and record adult experience in a fresh form he moulds for himself."[6] Thus the harsh view of Canadian readers voiced by Richardson in *Eight Years in Canada* is refocused almost one hundred years later by Grove and Callaghan.

Despite the lack of response to serious fiction noted by Callaghan, Deacon perceives in the work of these novelists and their contemporaries a new interest in "demonstrating life as it is through selective interpretation." He sees this shift from a "consciously moral (hence often priggish) attitude . . . to conscientious fidelity of portraiture" as a key development. Deacon harbours none of the reservations of the critics and novelists of the preceding era regarding the dangers of "photographic" realism and praises Bertram Brooker's "photographically accurate" depiction of a Manitoba town. Nor does he share the fears of many of his predecessors regarding the potentially sordid proclivities of realistic fiction.

Grove, in "Realism in Literature" (1929), attempts to counter what he views as the erring definitions of this term in relation to "frankness in matters of sex," and insists that "whatever exists is the legitimate subject of the literary artist, be he romantic or realist." Unlike Deacon, he argues against analogies between realism and photography on the grounds that while the camera records, the realist interprets, reproduces and "evokes an emotional reaction." Ultimately, for Grove, the terms "realist" and "artist" become synonymous insofar as both are related to "an emotional response to the outside world and to life, which is, as nearly as such things can be, a universal response."

If Grove defines realism primarily in relation to content and artistic perspective, Callaghan focuses more precisely on the stylistic elements of economy and concentration identified by Deacon. *That Summer in Paris* (1963) recalls Callaghan's rejection of "the escape into metaphor" and his recognition that the individual image must become the key to the perspective, content and structure of the modern novel.

At the end of this era in which Deacon sees the Canadian novel shifting into new directions, Philip Child, in "Fiction" (1938), isolates "the trend towards realism" as the signal development of the period. Anticipating later writers Child argues that the Canadian prairie "has proved the natural home of realism" as evidenced in the work of Robert Stead, Martha Ostenso and others. Child's discussion of Morley Callaghan's work reflects his interest in the development of urban realism, and he displays special interest in Grove as the novelist who frees Canadian fiction from the "strangling traditions" related to forbidden subjects.

Child, like Deacon, considers realism not only in relation to the aesthetics of the novel but also in relation to the emergence of a national literature. Early in his essay, he reiterates the problems so frequently identified in earlier eras as wórking against the emergence of distinctive fiction: colonial mentality, sparse population, foreign domination. In "The Future of the Novel in Canada" (1938), Bertram Brooker joins with Child and Callaghan in seeing these factors as part of a conservatism that has bred a fear of innovation and experiment among both writers and readers. Brooker, like his nineteenth-century predecessors, advocates the historical novel as a vehicle for the exploration of Child's "characteristic elements of Canadian life"; Child, however, despite being the author of one of the finest historical novels of the era, *The Village of Souls* (1933), simply amplifies Callaghan's arguments for realism: "the great novels of all lands have been written by realists and Canadians, too, must be realists if we are to develop a really national literature."

Part 4

Surveying Canadian fiction to the end of World War II, Desmond Pacey, in "The Novel in Canada" (1945), both echoes and qualifies many of the ideas and attitudes emerging in the work of Deacon and the novelists of the preceding era. Like them, he insists on a bond between the novelist and his society and argues that in Canada a culture characterized by isolation, diversity and conservatism has too often produced "either sugar-coated tracts or novels of escape." He acknowledges the efforts of writers such as Frederick Philip Grove, Irene Baird and Morley Callaghan "to wrestle in fiction with the complexities of contemporary Canadian society"; but in contrast to Deacon's announcement of a new era in fiction, Pacey cautions that "the end is not yet." In Pacey's opinion, Canada has not yet produced a novel that displays a "profound knowledge and understanding of Canadian society" while developing ideas that transcend national and temporal boundaries. Pacey feels that novelists enthusiastically praised by Deacon show significant potential but that Grove is too often "laboured," Mazo de la Roche sinks into "shallow romanticism" and Morley Callaghan is "often guilty of sentimentalism." Returning to the debate on romance and realism, Pacey notes the lack of novels dealing with contemporary life and identifies escapism as a weakness of both Canadian fiction and Canadian society.

Novelists such as Hugh MacLennan and Thomas Raddall are less critical than Pacey of the realism of their contemporaries and predecessors. In "The Literary Art" (1954), Thomas Raddall praises the movement of the novel away from "the stuffy prudery" of earlier decades but is less enthusiastic about the extremes of the new realism when manifested as a preoccupation with sordidness and evil. He quotes Stendhal's definition of the novel as "a mirror walking along the road" but, like Gilbert Parker and Goldwin Smith, emphasizes that the novelist does not simply reflect but selects and transmutes. Rejecting the novel that serves as a moral tract, Raddall insists, nevertheless, on the responsibility of the novelist "to give life its full value, an existence not without its crimes and follies but also with its noble themes of love and courage and self-sacrifice." Hugh MacLennan's "The Future of the Novel as an Art Form" (1959) also argues against a cynicism associated with the realistic novel. While acknowledging the technical advances in the art of fiction identified by Pacey, MacLennan moves cautiously in his acceptance of changing trends in fiction.

Like their predecessors at the turn of the century, the novelists of this era often focus on the creation of "vital and important characters" as the most important legacy of realism. In "The Bridge or the Stokehold? Views of the Novelist's Art" (1960), Ethel Wilson puzzles over the origins of a novel's characters and concludes that they must be grounded in the novelist's direct experience of the world while Ernest Buckler's "My First Novel" (1953) argues that vital and credible characters are the core around which a novel "accretes." Edward McCourt's "The Canadian Historical Novel" (1946) attacks the "romantic puppets" of most Canadian historical novels and calls for a sharper focus on the past.

Even as he acknowledges this escapist trend, McCourt expresses hope for the survival and development of the historical novel. Arguing the importance of meticulous research and imaginative recreation of the past, McCourt uses Sir Walter Scott as a point of reference seventy-five years after Goldwin Smith's tribute. Pacey, unlike McCourt, does not call for the development of historical fiction in new directions but for fiction reflecting the contemporary world. Echoing the sentiments of Goldwin Smith that in the historical novel "the fiction is apt to spoil the fact and the fact the fiction," Pacey sees too many writers escaping into costume novels, cutting themselves off from the "richest source of fictional material," direct observation of life.[7]

Although Pacey lacks confidence in the efficacy of historical fiction in defining a "national consciousness," he assumes both the possibility of a "national novel" and the need for such a work. Gwethalyn Graham argues a similar case in "Why Books Cost Too Much" (1947); however, Hugh MacLennan, although identified as "national novelist" during this period, insists in "Where is My Potted Palm" (1952) that the national novel is only a stage in the development of the novel in Canada. Discussing his first novel, *Barometer Rising* (1941), MacLennan recalls:

> When I first thought of writing this novel, Canada was virtually an uncharacterized country. . . . it seemed to me that for some years to come the Canadian novelist would have to pay a great deal of attention to the background in which he set his stories. He must describe, and if necessary define, the social values which dominate the Canadian scene, and do so in such a way as to make them appear interesting and important to foreigners. Whether he liked it or not, he must for a time be something of a geographer, an historian, and a sociologist, to weave a certain amount of geography, history, and sociology into his novels. Unless he did this, his stories would be set in a vacuum.

A decade later, MacLennan suggests that Canadian novelists need not "worry so much any longer about the problem of unfamiliarity." Contemporaries such as Wilson and Buckler similarly question the necessity for any self-conscious recognition of nationality.

Part of Pacey's preoccupation with the national novel stems from his conviction that the lack of a "strong national consciousness" is "a barrier to the production not only of national novels but also of strong regional ones." Reacting against the "regional idylls" of the turn of the century, Pacey argues that "a merely regional consciousness produces fiction that is provincial in the worst sense." A similar acknowledgement of the need for a strong regional consciousness "supplemented by an equally strong consciousness of the world beyond the region" underlies Edward McCourt's identification of the defining qualities of prairie fiction in *The Canadian West in Fiction* (1949).

The novelist's preoccupation with practical problems relating to the publication of novels gains fullest expression in this period in Gwethalyn Graham's discussion of the relationship between author, publisher and reader. In her view, residual colonialism deprives Canadian novelists of fair payment and thwarts literary development by discouraging imaginative publishing. Hugh MacLennan also points to practical problems related to the publishing of mass paperbacks and the rapid rise of creative non-fiction as competitor for the novel's role as mirror of life. Just as Leacock speculates on the competition provided for fiction by film, MacLennan looks at television as the medium that now attracts the public who once were devoted to the novel. Yet, despite the novel's loss of stature as popular art form, MacLennan remains confident that "no other form of entertainment . . . can offer the novel's peculiar combination of intellectual satisfaction and emotional catharsis."

Part 5

Like MacLennan, George Woodcock sees the development of radio, television and "reportage" significantly infringing on the novelist's territory. More crucial, however, is the shift of the novel away from the traditional form of a "more or less realist narrative with symbolic overtones" towards increasingly solipsistic explorations of the interior landscape of character and creator. "Don Quixote's Dilemma, or, The Future of Fiction" (1976) argues that pronouncements of the "death of the novel" in the 1950s and '60s were simply confirming the failure of modern novelists "to reconcile the solitudes of the mind and the abstractions which writers construct in such solitudes, with the facts of a world where no man is alone." In continuing to turn in upon itself, the modern novel became "sterile, a mirror without a looker." In parable, fable and the picaresque, Woodcock sees potential solutions to the novelist's dilemma as these forms reconcile subjective and collective truths through myth.

Woodcock sees the nineteenth-century tradition of the novel presenting "panoramic social tapestries" disappearing from most western literatures of the twentieth century. The novel's role as a "mirror of human existence" in a broad social context gives way to works of technical and psychological complexity that move in "an ever closer and more solipsistic circle of observation." That in Canada, in the 1940s and '50s, Hugh MacLennan "could attempt with some success the role of Balzac le Petit for an emerging nation" is a result of the "retarding influence of colonialism."

For Margaret Laurence, this acknowledgement of Canada's colonial inheritance is crucial to an understanding of the evolution of Canadian fiction, and in "Ivory Tower or Grassroots" (1978), she identifies MacLennan and his contemporaries as "the first generation of non-colonial Canadian writers." The natural allegiance of the contemporary Canadian novel, argues Laurence, is not with the fiction of Europe where she finds the "weariness, repetition, and even triviality" that characterize the "solipsistic" fiction identified by Woodcock; instead, along with the writers of third-world nations, Canadian novelists are striving "to find [their] own voices and write out of what is truly [theirs] in the face of an overwhelming cultural imperialism." Aligning this struggle of writers from third-world, post-colonial cultures with the efforts of contemporary women's movements, Laurence anticipates the examination of images of women in fiction in Margaret Atwood's "The Curse of Eve" (1978). Just as Atwood calls for the creation and acceptance of female characters who are fully human, "with all the individuality and variety that term implies," Laurence calls for the creation and critical acceptance of third-world literatures that capture the distinctive voices of these nations.

While Woodcock suggests that "history, for the twentieth-century novelist, has largely been an abstraction dwindling into meaninglessness beside the eternal moments of individual experience," Laurence and several of her contemporaries insist on an integral link between history and fiction as the novel of post-colonial cultures retains its traditional role in defining the past, present and future of a people. For Rudy Wiebe, "the stories we tell of our past are by no means merely words. They are meaning and life to us as *people*, as a *particular* people." Even as he chronicles his exhaustive research as contemporary historical novelist in "On the Trail of Big Bear" (1974), Wiebe insists that the problem for the novelist is not one of collecting information so much as it is daring "to fully contemplate" the implications of the uncovered "facts."

This acknowledgement anticipates Robert Kroetsch's insistence on the extent to which the very language that the English-Canadian uses conceals British or American experience. Just as Laurence stresses the need "to take the language and make it truly ours," "Kroetsch, in "Unhiding the Hidden" (1974), insists that "the process of rooting that borrowed word, that totally exact homonym, in authentic experience" is a truly radical one that the Canadian novelist must pursue. In the experiences of the protagonists in novels as diverse as Margaret Atwood's *Surfacing* (1972), Robertson Davies' *The Manticore* (1972) and Rudy Wiebe's *The Temptations of Big Bear* (1973), Kroetsch sees a pattern of individuals "demythologizing the systems that threaten to define them" just as their creators "uninvent" a world of imported and imposed meanings in order to "uncreate themselves into existence." Sheila Watson's *The Double Hook* (1959) emerges as a landmark of Canadian fiction within this context of "decreation" in "Death is a Happy Ending" (1978).

Woodcock insists that "every novel has first and last to justify itself as a statement concerning the lives of men; and the novelists who are his contemporaries echo his concern in the contexts of religion, politics or morality. Thus, Robertson Davies acknowledges himself as a moralist and his novels as "a moralist's novels." Laurence speaks of the emergence through her characters "of beliefs which cannot be didactic but which in the most profound way are both religious and moral." Mordecai Richler, in turn, cites George Orwell, in "Why I Write" (1970), as he argues that "any serious writer is a moralist"; and Hugh Hood identifies himself as a "moral realist" in "Sober Colouring: The Ontology of Super Realism" (1971).

The explicit acknowledgement of this moral responsibility may underlie and partially explain the identification of "a rather old-fashioned avant-garde" in the contemporary Canadian novel. Robert Kroetsch suggests that much contemporary fiction deals in "developments of plot, character and theme that, for all their contemporary trappings, are curiously reminiscent of the Victorian." In contrast to Woodcock's statement that "any significant writer" of the twentieth century has been experimental, stands Hugh Hood's insistence that he is not "in any way an experimental or advance guard writer." Rudy Wiebe continues the nineteenth-century concern for the historical novel; and Robertson Davies, despite the admiration for Beckett's *Molloy* (1955) expressed in "Experiment and The Antinovel" (1960), sees few writers as truly experimental and cautions against "the dangers of the avant-garde."

Yet the novels of these writers and their contemporaries pervasively reveal the influence of what Woodcock identifies as the primary sources for a revitalized tradition of the novel:

> The novelist has had to find another way than that of the socio-historical epic to cope with the fact that man is a member of a congregation of tribes as well as an individual. He has found it by wandering on the verges of those dubious sciences in which imagination and reason productively mingle, the misty frontiers of psychoanalysis and anthropology, where Jung and Fraser preside as vast presences, half-priest and half-poet, to offer the uniting images and myths.

In Davies' acknowledgement of the influence of Jung, Hood's identification of his complex use of Christian numerology and Kroetsch's use of "the myth-born picaresque of search and initiation," the Canadian novelist emerges as definably contemporary. As Woodcock speculates on the contemporary novelist's "imaginative realization of possibility" in "speculative utopianism," Kroetsch calls for critics able to acknowledge the novel as "the play of possible meanings; the text not as artifact but as enabling act. Not *meaning*, but the possibility of meanings."

Just as William Arthur Deacon saw the Canadian novel "turning the corner" in 1927, Matt Cohen's "The Rise and Fall of Serious CanLit" (1979) sees the years between 1969 and 1979 as "the time when the publishing of Canadian fiction came of age." Like the novelists of preceding eras, Cohen identifies major problems relating to the publishing industry in Canada and the survival of serious fiction. Given the pessimism of his outlook, confidence in the future of the novel in Canada can perhaps be based only on the recognition that it has not only survived in Canada but also evolved in a tradition spanning one hundred and fifty years.

Parallelling the evolution of the Canadian novel is a tradition of the novelists exploring the nature and craft of their art. Many of the selections in *Canadian Novelists and the Novel* reveal interest in issues which transcend national boundaries—the moral responsibility of the novelist, the debate on realism and romance and the specific problems relating to the craft of fiction. Identifiably national contexts, however, are apparent in the preoccupation with issues such as the role of the novel in a developing culture or the practical difficulties relating to the publication of fiction. In addition, several of the selections illuminate aspects of the work of the particular writer, either through the continuity or discontinuity evident between the novelist's theory and practice. Other comments serve to focus attention on characteristic attitudes and expectations of the novelists of particular eras, and comparison of views on theoretical or practical aspects of the novel by novelists as remote in time as William Kirby and Rudy Wiebe, Sara Jeannette Duncan and Margaret Atwood or Susanna Moodie and Robertson Davies suggest surprising parallels. Both individually and collectively, these selections demonstrate the unique perspectives of English-Canadian novelists on the Canadian novel from the early nineteenth century to the present.

Notes

Reference notes have been provided only for citations that do not appear in the selections of *Canadian Novelists and the Novel*.

1. A harsh review of *St. Ursula's Convent* in *The Canadian Magazine and Literary Repository* II, 12 (May, 1824) also invokes moral usefulness as a standard by which fiction must be measured. This harsh, anonymous review concludes: "for its utility we can say nothing".

2. See Elizabeth Waterston, "Canadian Cabbage, Canadian Rose," *Journal of Canadian Fiction*, II, 3 (Summer, 1973) 129-131.

3. [John Richardson], *Ecarté; or, The Salons of Paris* (London: Henry Colburn, 1829), n.p.

4. Rosanna Leprohon, *Antoinette de Mirecourt, or Secret Marrying and Secret Sorrowing. A Canadian Tale* (Montreal: Lovell, 1864), n.p.

5. Gilbert Parker, "The Canadian Author Talks on Literary Matters," *The Globe* (October 31, 1896), 13.

6. Responding to Callaghan's essay, Grove finds his evaluation too lenient in its appraisal of the Canadian public; his own view is that

the Canadian public is ignorant, cowardly and snobbish; it is mortally afraid of ideas and considers the discussion of first principles as a betrayal of bad manners .... This lack of mental aliveness is fundamental. Canada is a non-conductor for any sort of intellectual current.
"The Plight of Canadian Fiction? A Reply", *The University of Toronto Quarterly*, VII, 4 (July, 1938) 459.

7. In his autiobiography, Thomas Raddall, one of the writers praised by McCourt, argues against the views expressed by Pacey:

One or two reviewers of my work as a whole have remarked airily that my first three novels, all historical, were written as "escape literature" during the Second World War. ... The simple fact was that the historical novel had been widely read in North America ever since its renascence in 1933 with Hervey Allen's delightful *Anthony Adverse*. As I was interested in history, and writing novels for my living, I chose this very good genre for my first three books .... It was never my wish or intent to be a historical novelist or, for that matter, a sea novelist, a forest novelist, or any other stereotypist. From early days when I was writing for *Blackwood's* I went back and forth between present and past, between sea and forest, between humour and drama, seeking always to portray men and women in the scenes I knew and in the context of their times and circumstances.
In My Time: A Memoir (Toronto: McCelelland and Stewart, 1976) p. 238.

Part 1
The Pre-Confederation Novel

David Chisholme
c. 1796-1842

David Chisholme, born in Ross-shire, Scotland, came to Canada in 1822. In 1823 he became the first editor of the *Canadian Magazine and Literary Repository* and in subsequent years edited the *Canadian Review and Literary and Historical Journal* and then the *Montreal Gazette*. His publications include: *Annals of Canada* (1831), *The Lower Canada Watchman* (1829), and *Observations on the Rights of the British Colonies to Representation in the Imperial Parliament* (1832). [*St. Ursula's Convent: The First Canadian Novel*] appeared in the first issue of *The Canadian Review and Literary and Historical Journal* in July, 1824.

[*St. Ursula's Convent:*
The First Canadian Novel]

Had this not been the first native novel that ever appeared in Canada, we candidly admit, that no consideration could have induced us to give its title a place among our pages, and that to descend from the contemplation of the continued splendour which is shed around our imagination by the productions of the mightiest geniuses of the age, to the perusal of this tale of a nursery, would be more than a sufficient reason for ranking ourselves amongst the most idle of all readers of fiction. The truth of it is, that, whatever our present avocations may lead us for the future to do, we have never been accustomed to the perusal of many novels; and that it is the satisfaction which we have derived from falling in thus accidentally with a contemporary candidate for literary fame, and the hope, that, in our riper years, we may one day meet again on better terms to aid each other on our difficult path, we have in the present instance deviated from our ordinary conduct for the purpose of expressing in as gentle and impartial a manner as we are able, consistently with our duty, our opinion of the book before us. We must, in the first place premise, that we have not yet arrived at a satisfactory conviction of the utility of novel writing, especially of those light, amatory, and romantic tales, which, under this title are daily issuing from the press;

> Unfinished things one knows not what to call
> Their generation's so equivocal

and that until that is the case, we cannot help thinking, that the genius and talents of young writers, of both sexes, might be applied to much greater advantage to themselves and others in commencing their labours, by pursuing some more serious and important course in literature than *fiction*, the most alluring of all species of composition. We are far from insinuating that this kind of writing may not be made subservient to the highest sentiments of morality and virtue; for that a novel might be written so as to interest the heart in behalf of these principles of our nature, as much as any one has ever warped it to the side of vice, is a truth which no man will ever venture to call in question who has any knowledge of human nature; and Dr. Johnson himself has said, that these familiar histories may perhaps be made of greater use than the solemnities of professed morality, and convey the knowledge of vice and virtue with more efficacy than axioms and definitions. But what is the reason, we would ask, that the moment a person bent upon a literary course of life deems his acquirements of sufficient importance to administer to the instruction of others, that instruction is sent forth to the world in the form and style of a novel? In our opinion, it is just because this is the most hackneyed road in literature to public notoriety, and being so, and there being so many fellow-travellers equally reckless of the manner in which the journey is performed, if the gaol to which it leads afford but a temporary gratification to the pride and the vanity of the itinerant, they greedily embrace this as the only opportunity by which their limited talents are destined to be perpetuated. If this be true, with what assiduity ought all our young writers to beware of committing themselves? How many thousand paths are open for the exercise and display of their talents besides novel-writing! In the actual occurrences of life there is a natural beauty, as well as a moral principle which the invention of the highest genius can never equal; and in reflecting upon them, a feeling and generous mind, is often struck with awe and veneration at the happy or unfortunate results to which they lead in human affairs. As the recollection of these are as useful and important for the preservation of social and patriotic feelings, as the worshipping of their household gods by the ancients, we could wish that all young persons aspiring to the enviable rank of authorship, instead of distracting their minds for the purpose of drawing an unnatural and insipid picture of humanity by means of a tale of fancy in the form of a novel, would apply themselves with assiduity to collect the scattered fragments of what may have happened in real life, and by combining them with those scenes of rural beauty of which nature has, almost, in every country, been so profuse, present them to our view in the unassuming garb of facts, which must inevitably lead to some moral deduction.

The little volumes before us, are represented to be partly composed from "scenes in real life," and so far the author has fallen in with our views as to the *first* steps in literary composition; but these "scenes from real life" are apparently so few and so absolutely unnatural, that their effect is totally lost upon the reader. What would completely obviate our objection to the impropriety of young writers rushing at the first bound of their career upon the dark and intricate courses of fiction, is not the *mixture*, as it were, of real with imaginary transactions, but a thorough disregard of all fictitious matter, until both the taste and the mind of the writer have been formed by all that is beautiful in nature, and moral and virtuous in real life. We do not, indeed, say that the taste and the mind cannot arrive at this degree of perfection without the necessity of expatiating upon scenes of this description *in writing*, or in painting, for it is extremely possible to arrive at the highest attainments in taste and intellectual capacity without going through the drudgery of practical composition; but we are of opinion that no person can ever arrive at any thing like perfection in imaginary composition unless they have undergone a long and careful study of nature and the real transactions of human life. Hence the utility of commencing to describe the circumstance of real life, before launching forth on the intricate plots and winding details of fictitious composition. In all the works of nature simplicity makes an illustrious figure; but in those works of fiction which assume not nature for their guide, a corrupted taste will too soon become manifest:

> Poets like Painters, thus unskill'd to trace
> The naked nature and the living grace,
> With gold and jewels cover every part,
> And hide with ornament their want of art.

With respect, more particularly, to the volumes before us, we have every disposition to receive them with cordiality and respect. They are, as we have already said, the first Novel which Canada has ever produced, and the first sacrifice at the shrine of public opinion of a lady who is represented as only seventeen years of age at the time of writing them—two circumstances of themselves sufficient, in our opinion, to render them very interesting favourites with Canadian readers, whatever may be their demerits in talents and execution. We are bound to honour and respect the man who makes the first effort to cultivate a barren field, or tear up the briars of the wilderness, in order to render it subservient to the purposes of civilization, however rough and artless his first essay may be: so we are bound to hail with feelings of respect and gratitude the first literary genius who starts up among us, to chase away, in the words of our fair author, "a long night of ignorance and inaction," however manifold may be his failings. It is in this light alone, that we would bespeak the good will of our readers in favour of the little work before us, notwithstanding that it comes to our presence enveloped in swaddling-bands, which we greatly fear no age or maturity will completely relieve it from. We are sorry that we have neither talents nor room for presenting our readers with an outline of the story of the "Nun of Canada." The plot is by far too intricate in its details, and miserably destitute of that simplicity which leads us with pleasure into a more intimate view of the machinery by which the operations of an ordinary story are regulated. The truth is, that the incidents which give life to this Novel may be seen to equal advantage in any well kept parish register; for it is wholly made up of those never varying events which attend births, marriages, and deaths, among the higher and some of the middling ranks. Instead therefore of attempting to give a detailed account of the subject matter of this book, we shall only enter upon a few cursory observations regarding its execution, which we hope may be of service to our fair author in her future progress towards literary distinction, and refer our readers to the volumes themselves for more particular information; hoping there are but few of them who are not in possession of this firstling of our Canadian Novels.

Though we have said, that the manner in which the details of this story are constructed is devoid of simplicity, yet we do not hesitate to admit that the *language* in which it is composed, is distinguished both by simplicity and elegance of expression, and is void of meretricious drapery or affected splendour. If it betrays any thing of studied polish, it is to be attributed to the almost uniform preciseness of its periods. In justice, however, to our young and fair "unknown," we must acknowledge, that, in having adopted this conciseness of style, she has not fallen into obscurity, which is too frequently the case with writers who affect brevity of expression. It is true her sentences are not always so full and clear as we could wish; and in several places she betrays a neglect—we will not say an ignorance—of grammatical propriety. She not unfrequently uses a repetition of a word in the same short sentence; and altho' this cannot in every instance be avoided, though it sometimes contributes to beauty and energy of diction, it should not be arbitrarily indulged. She has likewise some favourite expressions of which she has, in the course of the work, made a hackneyed application; such as *"sublunary affairs, showering choicest blessings, choicest favours, breathless expectation,"* &c. All these, though very well applied in their respective places, are nevertheless not the most pleasing from their being too often brought upon the tapis. In the following phrase, "I would sooner die a thousand deaths," &c. the word *"sooner,"* employed in the sense of *rather*, does not seem admissible; nor does the term *"lively,"* intended as an epithet of *country*, appear altogether applicable. In the first chapter of this work, as the nurse and the mother—as the latter then supposed herself to be—of the suppositious Adelaide, are introduced discoursing of the bad state of the infant's health, the mother addresses the nurse with an exclamation pronounced in French, and which address she concludes by communicating her sentiments in English:—"Eh, mon Dieu Josette! what is the matter with Adelaide? I should not have known the child, had I seen her elsewhere." She replies in the like exclamatory way, concluding her address also in the English tongue:—"O Jesu Marie! you frighten me with your wild looks. Pray, *ma chere Dame* be not alarmed." Now this, in our judgement is incongruous in the extreme, that two persons supposed to be of the same nation, and capable of conversing in the same language, should talk together in the manner above described. But perhaps this mode of colloquial intercourse is not unusual with such Canadians as speak both English and French. On this hypothesis, our author may be justified in representing her characters discoursing as they are sometimes wont to do in life. Near the commencement of the sixteenth chapter, there is certainly, as the present reading stands a very great mistake. There mention is made of Lord Dudley and his sisters having entered into the room when Mr. Turnor, his sister Charlotte, and the supposed Mademoiselle Adelaide de St. Louis, were sitting. Had the affirmation been made of Lord Dudley and his sister, there would have been no mistake; because we find Lady Augusta was in company with her noble brother, but not Lady Louisa, as she was then called. Had that gay, witty, and talkative lady been present, it is natural to suppose she would not have remained silent through the whole chapter.

It is to be regretted that the fair writer did not allow herself a wider field in the work before us. By confining her labor within so circumscribed a sphere, she has deprived herself of the opportunity of exhibiting in her characters a greater variety, and of more fully depicting their manners, habits, passions, affections, sentiments, so that we might be enabled to judge, whether nature or education had the stronger influence upon their conduct. To speak, however, in the tone of candour and sincerity—*omnia non possumus omnes*—when we reflect on the narrow space, two small duodecimo volumes, to which she has confined the operations of a genius just beginning to expand itself, we cannot be otherwise than surprised that she has performed so much.

Her despatch is admirable, take it all in all; but shews itself no where to such advantage as in description, and moral illustration. As to the last mentioned circumstance, let it be observed, that she does not sicken us with the tedious verbiage of canting sentimentalists. To give an air of novelty to her work, she has in some degree effected her aim, by introducing Canadian scenery: still her Novel is far from being new, as we meet with many scenes and incidents of a similar complexion to those of hers in the writings of others of the Novel tribe. Though criticism might, if extended to its great rigour, raise numerous objections to this work, one truth is however clear in spite of criticism, that it is worthy of regard, particularly on account of the liberal, enlightened and philanthropic sentiments it conveys, and the pure, exalted ideas of morality and religion it suggests. From the example of Catharine, the good Nun, we learn submission to the will of Heaven, acquiescence in the Divine appointments, and an entire confidence in the aid and protection of Omnipotence. By her example we feel inspired with that fortitude and patience which eminently distinguish the true philosophy of the christian from the boasted wisdom of the stoic: Hence the ways of God to man are vindicated, and the fear of death subdued. Such is the doctrine recommended by the practice of the virtuous Catharine, the heroine of the story: it is she that "points the moral and adorns the tale."

In conclusion, we beg to assure the author of this work, that if in any instance we may be looked upon as having spoken of her production with undue severity, we cannot accuse ourselves of having overstepped the bounds of fair criticism. To censure works, not men, is the just prerogative of criticism; and accordingly we have endeavoured to avoid all personal censure; censuring with a view merely to find fault cannot be entertaining to any person of humanity; and of this also we acquit ourselves. We sincerely hope, however, that we shall soon again have the pleasure of meeting our fair author in some of her literary walks, though we, with equal sincerity, trust, that it will not be on the "novel track." We would, with due respect, rather submit to her consideration the properiety of perusing with care and attention the History of the British American Colonies, where she will find ample means for the further development of her talents, which, if properly cultivated, we would fain hope are destined to throw much interesting light upon the literature of Canada. If the transmission of a copy of this work could be of the slightest gratification to her, we can assure her, that nothing could afford us more pleasure; and that she has only, to direct how our wishes to oblige her can be accomplished.

1824

Julia Catherine Hart
1796-1867

Born in Fredericton, New Brunswick, Julia Catherine Beckwith moved with her family to Kingston, Upper Canada, in 1820. Two years later she married George Henry Hart, and in 1826 the couple moved to the United States where they remained until 1831 when they settled in Fredericton. Hart's novel, *St. Ursula's Convent; or, The Nun of Canada* (1824), was the first novel by a Canadian to be published in Canada. A second novel, *Tonnewonte; or, The Adopted Son of America*, was published in Watertown, New York, in 1825. A third novel, *Edith; or The Doom*, remains unpublished.

Preface
to
St. Ursula's Convent; or, The Nun of Canada Containing Scenes From Real Life

It is the natural course of all sublunary affairs to proceed from small beginnings, and to advance gradually towards perfection. Such has been the slow progress of improvement in British America, where, until lately, genius has slept through a long night of ignorance and inaction; and scarcely a dawn of literary illumination is yet discerned. Our incipient attempts, then, can hardly hope to enter into competition with the finished productions of the old world.

Yet there are lovers of literature, even in this country; and, among these, some have been found willing to give encouragement to a British American, on the threshold of her humble career of authorship.

Such liberal minds will, it is hoped, approve of whatever is meritorious in the following tale, and candidly excuse the defects a more experienced eye may perceive, in the first production of an author of seventeen, which was the writer's age when *St. Ursula's Convent* was written. It has lain by her sometime, circumstances having hitherto deferred its publication. Their encouraging liberality may incite her to future exertion, when her judgement shall have been matured, and her taste improved by experience.

It was in the delightful vale of Cornwallis, justly styled the Garden of Nova Scotia, that this work was commenced. It was continued in New Brunswick, the subject having been suggested to the author, during a residence in the Canadas.

To her friends in those Provinces she is under many obligations. They encouraged her in the prosecution of her work; and they now lend their support towards its public appearance.

Our country is gradually rising into notice. Our physical resources are great. Our population is increasing; and the time may come, when British America will be as noted in 'song' or 'deeds,' as any kingdom of Europe: but, to attain that eminence, she must cherish native genius in its humblest beginnings.

The author does not, indeed, flatter herself, that this juvenile performance will add to the celebrity of the country; but the fostering hand of public patronage if kindly extended to such a production, may elicit others of real and intrinsic merit.

The era, to which this story relates, was an eventful one, and may be reviewed with interest by many families, who, like the author, trace their descent in a manner similar to that of the principal personages of the tale.

Our readers, in these Provinces at least, may likewise be gratified with the assurance, that mother St. Catherine is not a mere creature of imagination, but had a real existence in Canada, and that even the name of her daughter is preserved. Can the patriotic Canadian, then, refuse a kind reception to his own kindred? No; it is to be hoped the lover of his country will receive *The Nun of Canada* with native hospitality and characteristic kindness.

To the reviewers of our parent country the author looks up with deference and hope. She trusts that their candour, should this home-bred production ever cross the Atlantic, will view the unpolished stranger with indulgence, although destitute of the elegance and refinement wich adorn the land of our forefathers.

1824

Introduction
to
Tonnewonte; or, The Adopted Son of America
A Tale Containing Scenes From Real Life

The sun had just completed his daily course, but his last rays, dimly flitting on the expanded sheet of water that formed the western boundary of our horizon, displayed a relief of light and shade, unrivaled in the best designations of art. The day had been warm, uncomfortably so; but a rising breeze restored the elasticity of the air, and revived the vigour of animated creation. The milk-maid sang blithely, as she poised her milk-pails. The plough-boy whistled as he drove the cattle to the watering-place. My host bustled in his farm yard; the good lady of the house was occupied with her children, and I seated myself in the piazza, enjoying the luxury of solitude, amidst the enlivened scenes of rural peace and plenty.

I was aroused from a deep abstractive fit of meditation, by the hoarse voice of our honest neighbour Noxbury, who, with a pipe in his mouth, was sitting not three paces distance from me.

'Bless me!' he cried, taking his pipe in his hand, 'what can thus so entirely occupy your mind? Here have I been this half hour endeavoring to attract your attention, but I could not obtain even so much as a nod of recognition.'

'Oh, your servant, Mr. Noxbury; I beg pardon, but my mind was indeed much occupied. My publisher has sent to me for a preface.'

'A preface! Why, then, you really intend publishing your manuscript?'

'You surprise me, sir; and what should prevent my publishing it?'

'Fate, my friend, fate, that destined your birth on the wrong side of the Atlantic. Are you not an American? Can you, then, hope to vie with a native of Europe?'

'You provoke my patience, Mr. Noxbury. Am I not a descendant of those same Europeans, whom you extol so highly?'

'And so are all Americans, Canadians, Nova-Scotians, New-Brunswickers, Yankees, &c. They all doubtless derive their descent from the natives of Europe; yet whoever heard of a *Shakespeare*, a *Racine*, a *Tasso*, a *Milton*, a *Corneille*, a *Hume*, a *Robertson*, an *Addison*, not to mention the immortal geniuses of the present day; who ever heard of one of those being born in America? And the best judges allow that the human race degenerates in America.'

'Great God! Can this be borne with patience? Can I who feel that vital spark, that emanation from the Deity, first breathed into man at his creation, raising me above all materiality, and bidding me, by the divine pursuit of knowledge, to imitate and follow in the paths of superior intelligences? Can it be told, that this divine emanation is confined to one particular spot of the earth? Mr. Noxbury, compare the rivers, the mountains, the lakes, and the plains of your native country; compare them with the stupendous works of Nature ever present in America, and then say, can 'man be the only growth that dwindles here?'

'Oh, pray descend from the clouds, my young friend,' cried our portly neighbour, laughing. 'It would be too fatiguing an excursion for me to follow you there. And now answer me in the language of common sense, can the literature of America be compared with that of Europe? and he exultingly laid an emphasis on the last sentence.

'No sir. I acknowledge in that respect, our present inferiority. The school-boy conning over his lesson, cannot in acquirements be compared with his preceptor; but may he not in the course of years, vie even with his teacher?—America is young, but is fast verging towards maturity; and the country that in its infancy produced a WASHINGTON, and a FRANKLIN, may in its riper years, become a luminary, whose effulgence shall extend to all parts of the globe.'

'And my young friend here, is to be the instrument to bring about this 'consummation devoutly to be wished?'

'Mistake me not, Mr. Noxbury. I am far from having the vanity to imagine my talents equal to those of many of my countrymen in all parts of North America. But still may I not endeavour to follow in the path of knowledge, and imitate, though at a humble distance, those great geniuses who have gone before us, whose mortal remains now lie mouldering in the dust, but who have left us transcripts of their minds, that will defy the power of the destroyer time, as long as any parts of our globe shall retain traces of civilization.'

'And so my young enthusiast, instead of devoting your time to some more lucrative employment, wherein, with proper industry, you might acquire a sufficiency of that desideratum of life, that magnet of attraction, cash, you mean to sacrifice all your powers of exertion to study, and authorship, for the chimerical prospect of at length obtaining a niche in the temple of renown?'

'If such were my design, sir, my choice might not be deemed singular. Even in America, are there not many living persons who are proofs, that the literary character of America is fast rising into eminence? How many men distinguished for their acquirements in literature? How many eminent for their skill in the arts and sciences, now residing in all our principal cities? Each of our learned professions also contains numbers celebrated for their knowledge and acquirements. Have we not eloquent orators in our senate, and some distinguished politicians in all departments of our government? Observe the general extent of information diffused among the mass of our population, and then blame a young American for an engrossing attachment to the pursuit of learning. I may at least endeavor to cultivate to the utmost, the capabilities bestowed on me by the hand of nature. I may be indefatigable in the pursuit of knowledge, and I trust that a discriminating and liberal public will receive my productions with indulgence; and then perhaps on a future day, I may produce a work more worthy of their encouragement, and more calculated to do honor to our native country.'

'But the critics, my friend?'

'Not even that formidable name shall deter me from submitting my intended publication to the inspection of my countrymen. Our reviews, Mr. Noxbury, are mostly conducted by men of candour and liberality, who will not expect perfection from a young and unknown author. I trust that my pages will not be found detrimental to the great cause of religion and morality. In my tale of 'Tonnewonte,' I have endeavored to describe some of the causes of the spirit of emigration so predominant among the citizens of America, and also the general habits prevalent in many of our new settlements. I wished to demonstrate the effect of education, and accidental circumstances, in forming the general and individual character; and, for the sake of contrast, have extended my plot to the old world. I wished, also, to shew the vital importance of correcting the violent temper, displayed by many children, before habit shall have formed these excrescences of the mind into inseparable parts of the personal character. I trust, Mr. Noxbury, that a liberal public will overlook many defects in the execution of my work, from a consideration of my motives, and by the encouragement bestowed on my attempt to please them, induce some Americans of superior talents, to devote their abilities to the general service and amusement of their countrymen.'

'Well, my young friend,' said our honest neighbour, rising and heartily shaking me by the hand, 'I will no longer exercise your patience by contradiction. Pursue the bent of your inclination, since such is your determination, and I sincerely wish you success in the path you have chosen. I fear I have detained you from writing your Preface; but, perhaps, if you were to commit our conversation to writing, it might serve you for an introduction.'

Upon further consideration of Mr. Noxbury's hint, I even concluded on following it; and so, Mr. Publisher, I send you this, instead of a Preface.

1825

John Galt
1779-1839

Born in Ayrshire, Scotland, John Galt first came to Canada in 1825, as a commissioner of the Canada Company, appointed superinten dent in 1826. He was recalled to England in 1829. Before coming to Canada, Galt had established a reputation as a novelist with works such as *The Ayrshire Legatees* (1821), *Annals of the Parish* (1821), and *The Provost* (1822). His experiences in Canada are reflected in two novels: *Lawrie Todd; or, The Settlers in the Woods* (1830); *Bogle Corbet; or, The Emigrants* (1831); and in his *Autobiography* (1833).

From
The Autobiography of John Galt
[Bogle Corbet]

. . . I do not propose in this section of my biography to give more than a sketch of the history of some of my literary productions, omitting those occasional contributions to periodical publications; but the next work to the history of the players was *Bogle Corbet*, suggested by my publishers to be a companion to *Lawrie Todd*; its fate, however, shows how little an author is capable of rightly appreciating his own works.

In *Bogle Corbet*, I was desirous to exhibit the causes which now, in this country, induce a genteeler class of persons to emigrate than those who may be said to have exclusively embarked before. I do not mean to say that the incidents described in that work, happen to the kind of persons in the condition of the hero, but I certainly intended to show the natural effects, in some degree, of introducing the cotton manufactures into Scotland, and the result of that kind of commerce which the late war, both in its republican and imperial stages, fostered; in this attempt I have not, in my own opinion, failed.

In one respect, *Bogle Corbet* is the most peculiar of all my literary essays; I had models for the principal characters in my eye, and in few have I been so uniformly successful in the portraiture. The persons in my view, have been delineated with considerable truth, but not always, I suspect, with that sort of felicity, which is necessary to render a book agreeable to the general reader. The work, however, is really worth more than it seems, for it is an attempt to embody facts and observations, collected and made on actual occurrences. Canada, indeed, must have altered rapidly, if Bogle Corbet be not a true guide to settlers of his rank.

The excursion to Jamaica is entirely fictitious, with the exception of one incident which actually occurred, to a playmate of my boyhood.

In drawing up the view of West Indian society, though it is altogether a combination of the fancy, it is done with solicitude and care. It does not appear to me that there is so much difference between the notion, which one class of persons in this country entertain, of the West Indies, from those of another, that one of them should not be correct; what I consider as the true state is described in the work, but it does not fall in with the popular ideas on the subject: I shall be glad, however, should I prove wrong in my conceptions, by the result of emancipating the slaves. I say this with the more particular emphasis, as I felt it to be a kind of duty, to old associations, to point out the evils that might arise, in my opinion, from giving liberty to the slaves, without due checks and restraints.

In fact, *Bogle Corbet* was intended by me to be a guide book, particularly in the third volume, and I have, in all my works, kept the

28

instructive principle more or less in view; probably by doing so, and restraining the scope of inventions entirely to probabilities, I may have failed to give as much entertainment as works, more strictly amusing with the same incidents, might have furnished, but I always did my best, and I only desire it may be remembered by my readers that, I had an object in view beyond what was apparent. I considered the novel as a vehicle of instruction, or philosophy teaching, by example, parables, in which the moral was more valuable than the incidents were impressive. Indeed, it is not in this age that a man of ordinary common sense would enter into competition, in recreative stories, with a great genius who possessed the attention of all, I mean Sir Walter Scott, who, without aspiring beyond the limits of romance writing, has attained such splendid pre-eminence, by the power and variety that appear in his productions, insensibly elevating the minds of his readers with topics, which, though not historically correct, wear yet such an air of life and probability, as to increase the pleasures of mankind.

Since I have introduced the illustrious name of that superb genius, with relation to the class of composition in which he can never be excelled, I may venture to express in what respects I not only consider him the first in his walk, but ranking with the greatest in any. As a poet, I do not think so much of him as many others do; he relates his semi-epics, certainly, with great beauty, a vivacity quite unexampled, and in many instances, he approaches that "fine frenzy" which distinguishes the genuine poet; all else that he has done, is only in respectable mediocrity; but in romance, he towers into unapproachable excellence . . . .

1832

John Richardson
1796-1852

Born in Queenston, Upper Canada, Major John Richardson fought in the War of 1812 at the age of sixteen and was a career soldier in the West Indies and Europe until 1837. He returned to Canada in 1838, but financial problems ultimately drove him to emigrate to New York in 1850. Richardson's novels include: *Ecarté; or The Salons of Paris* (1829); *Wacousta; or, The Prophecy* (1832); *The Canadian Brothers; or The Prophecy Fulfilled* (1840); and *Wau-Nan-Gee; or, The Massacre at Chicago* (1852). *Eight Years in Canada*, one of several autobiographical works by Richardson, was published in Montreal in 1847.

29

From
Eight Years In Canada
[The Novelist In Canada]

... Finding it impossible to procure a house in Amherstburgh, we made our dwelling of a den in Sandwich, a small village about twenty miles up the river, and the spot from which General Brock embarked on the occasion of the capture of the American fortress of Detroit, nearly opposite. The gable end of this house fronted the street, and was ornamented, at the angle of the sloping roof, with a suspicious looking projection and pulley that very much likened it to the residence of a hangman who does business on his own account. The two rooms below were just large enough to enable the body to be turned, without rubbing the coat or petticoat which covered that body against the white-washed, or rather yellow-washed, wall; but the twin brother, or twin sister, rooms above, it required some dexterity, and not a little practice in the art of dodging and stooping, to move in without bumpings innumerable on the cranium. In all, there were four rooms and an apology for a kitchen, the whole occupying the space of a moderate-sized drawing-room, and for this bountiful accommodation I was only charged at the moderate rate of forty pounds a year. Still, as it was the only house to be had, we were glad to have wherewithal to shelter our heads for the few months we purposed remaining.

The town and people of Sandwich, I found precisely in the same condition of apathy and poverty with those I had so recently quitted, so that I was glad to avail myself of all opportunities of crossing to the American shore, where I was much better known than in Canada, and where I ever experienced a hospitality and kindness which I can never forget. At Detroit, and in its immediate vicinity, was laid the chief scenes of my Indian tale of "Wacousta," and as the Americans are essentially a reading people, there was scarcely an individual in the place who was not familiar with the events described in it, while, on the contrary, not more than one twentieth of the Canadian people were aware of the existence of the book, and of that twentieth not one third cared a straw whether the author was a Canadian or a Turk. Nor is this remark meant to apply simply to the remote region I was now visiting, but to hundreds of the more wealthy classes in all sections of the province.

It has been the custom in all ages, and in all countries, for men of education and acquirement to join in testifying regard for their authors, however mediocre their talent; and even in the United States— the last country which has given birth to men of genius and literary accomplishments—we find the caterers to the republic of letters treated with that consideration, which the civilized world has agreed in according to them. In Canada, they have this yet to learn and practice. Not, be it remembered, that I accuse the whole of my country-men of being so absorbed in the pursuit of pounds, shillings, and pence, as to have utterly lost sight of the *convenances* of life. There has been one exception, and this I have the greater satisfaction in recording, because it occurs among those who, not being so richly endowed with the gifts of fortune, were the last to have been expected to take the initiative in the matter. The compliment conveyed to me through the following letter, which was sent to me while absent from Sandwich, is no doubt far beyond any incidental merit I may possess, still it is the only document indicative of honor or approval that I have ever received since my return to my native country. It is the only bays that has been offered to me in Canada, and I must be permitted to wear it, for when I die this book may survive me:—

GOSFIELD, *February 20th*, 1846.

SIR,—A Committee, composed of John Scratch, J. P.; Thomas Hawkins, M.D.; and Thomas Brush, Esquires, appointed to make all necessary preparations, in order to commemorate the battle of Point-au-Pelée Island, by a public dinner, request me to make known to you a hope that you will honor them with your presence on the 3rd of March next, at the Gosfield Hotel, yourself, Colonel John Prince, M.P.P., and the Reverend William Johnson, Rector of Sandwich, being invited as the guests of a highly respectable portion of your fellow subjects of the county of Essex.

The Committee would beg, through me, to inform you, that this small testimony of the esteem entertained for you by your grateful countrymen, is but another way of evincing their respect and admira-tion of the man of talent, the gallant soldier, and the accomplished gentleman.

For myself, accept of my warmest wishes for your future welfare, and rest assured that I shall ever feel proud, as an adopted Canadian, to hear fame distinguish the character of a gentleman who, by the splendor of his genius has shed an additional lustre on his native country.

I have the honor to remain, with high consideration, &c.

MAJOR RICHARDSON, Sandwich.   L. C. KEARNEY, Secy.

The above is certainly couched in strong language, and were it not, as I have already remarked, that it is the only document indicative of a desire to do honor to me in my native land, I should have hesitated to publish it. Let it not, however, be supposed, that it has had the slightest tendency to create in my mind any undue estimate of my "genius," as the letter flatteringly terms the pourtrayings of my pen. No man less than I do, possesses the vanity of authorship. I look upon the art of ingenious writing, not as a merit, but a mere incidental gift, for which one is more indebted to nature than to judicious application. The mechanic possesses the same in a variety of ways, and I regard the works of many of these with a wonder and admiration surpassing even those which are produced by a contemplation of the more elegant and accomplished arts of painting and sculpture, and yet I am familiar with the *chef d'œuvres* in both. Painting and sculpture are, after all, but imitations,—splendid, I grant, but still imitations. The exquisite beauty of the perfect human form is placed before the artist as a model, and the whole secret is to copy with accuracy and fidelity. I am far from wishing to convey a belief that nicety of execution, in those more refined occupations, does not require both inspiration and genius; but the inspiration is one of thoughts which are familiar to the mind, and the genius has a tangible foundation on which to build. But in mechanics how different! There is no model no design on which, or after which, to erect a structure. For instance, in the construction of the higher orders of mechanism, both of an ancient and modern date, what inexhaustible powers of imagination have been put forth in order to invent, combine, mould, harmonize, and finally give life and motion to that on which the eye has never hitherto gazed, and which has alone been woven on the labyrinthean meshes of the brain. Such have ever been my sentiments, such my views in regard to the relative bearings of the fine arts to the more complicated mechanics, and even at the hazard of being accused of having "no music in my soul," do I now avow them. Not, be it understood, that I look upon mechanics with anything approaching to the enthusiasm with which I have gazed on the breathing Venus de Medici in the Louvre, or the glowing Madonna of a Raphael; but because I conceive that there is more of absolute genius in one than in the other. If, therefore, I regard painting and sculpture as requiring far less ingenuity than certain complicated operations in mechanicism, how much less in the scale of comparison must I necessarily class literature, and particularly that lighter literature which is embraced in works of fiction. The power so to weave together the incidents of a tale that they may be made comprehensible and attractive to the reader, is a mere gift, which some persons possess in a greater or less degree than others; and can reflect no more credit upon him who is endowed with it, than can reasonably be claimed by any man or woman who has been, by nature, fortunately gifted with personal beauty and attraction superior to that enjoyed by the generality of their kind. A man who chances to possess this advantage, cannot write ill if he would; neither, if nature has been lavish of her bounties, and made him what is called a man of talent, can he employ that talent in a less luminous way, whether for good or evil, than nature herself has designed and willed. It costs him no effort, and therefore there cannot be said to be much merit.

These, then, being my honest impressions, it may be asked wherefore it is that I allude, in a spirit of censure and complaint, to the absence of honoring notice by their countrymen, of the literary effusions of the few Canadian writers we have? The answer to this is very simple: Because it is the custom of the civilized world, and has been such for ages; and however I may differ from that world in my estimate of the lighter literature of the day, still as *all* are agreed in rendering honor to those whom they have invested with an overrated merit, the exception is so gross and glaring as to form a proper subject for animadversion. Where nations unite among themselves to elevate their men of letters, and when it is universally admitted that their efforts reflect favorably upon the land of their birth, and tend to raise it in the scale of civilization, any deviation from a principle so sacred and acknowledged, can only be regarded as a slight, whether originating in ignorance or in wilfulness. True, I have elsewhere remarked that the Canadians are not a reading people. Neither are they: but yet there are many hundreds of educated men in the country, who ought to know better,—who possess a certain degree of public influence, and who should have been sensible that, in doing honor to those whom the polished circles of society, and even those of a more humble kind, have placed high in the conventional scale, they were adopting the best means of elevating themselves. England prides herself on her innumerable host of literary men; France, on hers; Scotland renders homage to the shades of Scott and Burns; Ireland boasts of the versatility of talent of her many eminent writers. Every nation in the Old World has done honor to the profession of letters, and the United States, in the New, glories, and justly glories, in the well-won reputation of her gifted Cooper; nay, if I mistake not, the land of recipiency of pollution and crime—New South Wales—has not shown herself so degraded as not to seek for honorable estimation, by producing and encouraging one or two native authors who have recently flourished amongst them.

Canada, alone, in the wide universe, forms the exception. The few men of talent who exist within her bosom, have never met with that attention which it is the pride of the nations to which I have alluded to bestow upon those who undertake to instruct, inform, or amuse their minds; and so far has this apathetic feeling been carried, that in my own case it was left to the people of the United States to inform them that they possessed a writer not less favorably known in Europe than among themselves, of whose existence they (the Canadians) were ignorant, and to whose success they were indifferent.

As this is the last time I shall ever allude to the humiliating subject, I cannot deny to myself the gratification of the expression of a hope, that should a more refined and cultivated taste ever be introduced into the matter-of-fact country in which I have derived my being, its people will decline to do me the honor of placing my name in the list of their "Authors." I certainly have no particular ambition to rank among their future "men of genius," or to share in any posthumous honor they may be disposed to confer upon them.

* * *

To my "Wacousta," I had written, but never published, a continuation of that tale under the title of "The Canadian Brothers," and as much of the action of this was laid in the same neighborhood, at a more recent period, I was strongly urged by my American friends to publish it forthwith. Having nothing else wherewith to occupy my time, I assented; but aware as I was of the great pecuniary responsibility of the undertaking in a country so indisposed to the encouragement of literature as Canada, where the chief sale of the work was to be looked for, I stipulated for a list of subscribers which should in part guarantee me from loss, even although I did not expect to derive much profit from the publication ... I actually obtained among a population little exceeding a million of persons, not less than two hundred and fifty subscribers—two thirds of whom even went so far as to take their books when published. The other third had been kind enough merely to lend me the encouragement of their names, and nothing, therefore, was more natural when called upon, to decline their copies—some under the pleas that the volumes, the price of which had been made known to them on subscribing—were too dear; some, that they had been too long delayed in the publication; and not a few, that they did not feel inclined to take them at that moment.

This complaint of the dearness of books is, *par parenthese*, one of the rich fruits springing from the outrageous system of piracy which prevails in the United States. Accustomed as the American bookseller is to pounce upon every new English publication, and to reprint from it forthwith, he is, of course, enabled to sell the work at very little more than the cost of the paper and printing, and, until very recently, these re-publications found their way into Canada, where they have naturally created a desire for cheap literature. That an author should be paid for the fruit of his brain, or indemnified for the hours of application devoted to his composition, are considerations foreign to their purposes. Provided they can obtain what they want at a reduced rate, they care little for the injustice done to those from the perusal of whose writings they profess to derive amusement and instruction. The law, however, as it now exists in Canada in regard to books, is such, that neither the English author nor the English publisher can sustain much harm. The first obtains the full value of his copyright, while the latter sells for the English market alone. He could not, and does not, expect to dispose of any part of his stock in the United States, and as the introduction of American reprints of English works into Canada, or any other British colony, is prohibited, these colonies must necessarily look to the English publisher alone for a supply. But in the case of one who does not dispose of his copyright, but publishes on his own account, and for a very limited market, it is unreasonable to demand that his books shall be sold at the same nominal price at which the American pirate can re-produce them, and without his enjoyment of any of the profit which accrues to the English author of previous remuneration for his labor, which is so much deducted from the profits of the publisher.

One advantage, however, and it is an important one which the British publisher derives from the recent interdiction of American reprints of the works of British authors into British colonies is, that where a colonial writer publishes in England, his works, if at all

34

valuable, become to the former, who has purchased all right in them, an increased source of profit, from the fact that no other has the privilege of competing with him in the colonial market. For instance, a book purporting, as this does, to treat of the manners, habits, political and moral character, of a colonial people, cannot fail to find readers among that people, not from any innate love of literature which may prompt them to the purchase, but because they will entertain an eager desire to know what is said and thought of them. Curiosity is a wonderful quickener of human impulses, and frequently accomplishes what, from the absence of better and more ennobling sentiments, is otherwise difficult of attainment . . . .

1847

Introduction
to
Wacousta; or, The Prophecy

This chapter, written eighteen years subsequent to the original publication of *Wacousta* in London, will be found unavoidably replete with egotism. By none will it be more readily pronounced such than by those who are most open to the charge themselves. Without its exercise, however, the object of this introduction would not be gained.

As the reader may be curious to know on what basis, and in what manner this story (of which I have certainly robbed that first of vigorous American Novelists—the "Last of the Mohicans" Cooper—which tale, albeit I have never read a novel by another author twice, I have absolutely devoured *three* times,) was suggested to me, and on what particular portions of History the story is founded, I am not aware that this introductory Chapter, which I have promised my Publishers, can be better devoted than to the explanation.

It is well known to every man conversant with the earlier History of this country that, shortly subsequent to the cession of the Canadas to England by France, Ponteac the great Head of the Indian race of that period, had formed a federation of the various tribes, threatening extermination to the British posts established along the Western Frontier. These were nine in number, and the following stratagem was resorted to by the artful chief to effect their reduction. Investing one fort with his warriors, so as to cut off all communication with the others, and to leave no hope of succor, his practice was to offer terms of surrender which never were kept in the honorable spirit to which the far more noble and generous Tecumseh always acted with his enemies, and thus in turn, seven of these outposts fell victims to their confidence

35

in his truth. Detroit and Michillimackinac, or Mackinaw as it is now called, remained, and all the ingenuity of the Chieftain was directed to the possession of these strongholds. The following plan, well worthy of his invention, was at length determined upon. During a temporary truce, and while, Ponteac was holding forth proposals for an ultimate and durable peace, a ball playing was arranged by him to take place simultaneously, on the common or clearing on which rested the forts of Michillimackinac and Detroit. The better to accomplish their object, the guns of the warriors had been cut short and given to their women who were instructed to conceal them under their blankets, and during the game, and seemingly without design, to approach the drawbridge of the fort. This precaution taken, the players were to approach and throw over their ball, permission to regain which they presumed would not be denied. On approaching the drawbridge, they were with fierce yells to make a general rush, and, securing the arms concealed by the women, to massacre the unprepared garrison. The day was fixed—the game commenced, and was proceeded with in the manner previously arranged. The ball was dexterously hurled into the fort, and permission asked to recover it. It was granted. The drawbridge was lowered, and the Indians dashed forward for the accomplishment of their work of blood. How different the result in the two garrisons! At Detroit, Ponteac and his warriors had scarcely crossed the drawbridge when to their astonishment and disappointment, they beheld the guns of the ramparts depressed—the artillerymen with lighted matches at their posts and covering the little garrison, composed of a few companies of the 42d Highlanders, who were also under arms, and so distributed as to take the enemy most at an advantage. Sullenly they withdrew, and without other indication of their purpose than what had been expressed in their manner, and carried off the missing ball. Their design had been discovered and made known by means of significant warnings to the Governor by an Indian woman who owed a debt of gratitude to his family, and was resolved, at all hazards, to save them. On the same day the same artifice was resorted to at Michillimackinac, and with the most complete success. There was no guardian angel there to warn them of danger, and all fell beneath the rifle, the tomahawk, the war-club, and the knife, one or two of the traders—a Mr. Henry among the rest—alone excepted.

It was not long after this event, when the head of the military authorities in the Colony, apprised of the fate of these defeated posts, and made acquainted with the perilous condition of Fort Detroit, which was then reduced to the last extremity, sought an officer who would volunteer the charge of supplies from Albany to Buffalo, and thence across the lake to Detroit, which, if possible, he was to relieve. That volunteer was promptly found in my maternal grandfather, Mr. Erskine, from Strabane, in the North of Ireland, then an officer in the Commissariat Department. The difficulty of the undertaking will be obvious to those who understand the danger attending a journey through the Western wilderness, beset as it was by the warriors of Ponteac, ever on the look out to prevent succor to the garrison, and yet the duty was successfully accomplished. He left Albany with provisions and ammunition sufficient to fill several Schenectady boats—I think seven—and yet conducted his charge with such prudence and foresight, that notwithstanding the vigilance of Ponteac, he finally and after long watching succeeded, under cover of a dark and stormy night, in throwing into the fort the supplies of which the remnant of the gallant "Black-watch," as the 42d was originally named, and a company of whom, while out reconnoitering, had been massacred at a spot in the vicinity of the town, thereafter called the Bloody Run, stood so greatly in need. This important service rendered, Mr. Erskine, in compliance with the instructions he had received, returned to Albany, where he reported the success of the expedition.

The colonial authorities were not regardless of his interests. When the Ponteac confederacy had been dissolved, and quiet and security restored in that remote region, large tracts of land were granted to Mr. Erskine, and other privileges accorded which eventually gave him the command of nearly a hundred thousand dollars—an enormous sum to have been realised at that early period of the country. But it was not destined that he should retain this. The great bulk of his capital was expended on almost the first commercial shipping that ever skimmed the surface of Lakes Huron and Erie. Shortly prior to the Revolution, he was possessed of seven vessels of different tonnage, and the trade in which he had embarked, and of which he was the head, was rapidly increasing his already large fortune, when one of those autumnal hurricanes, which even to this day continue to desolate the waters of the treacherous lake last named, suddenly arose and buried beneath its engulfing waves not less than six of these schooners laden with such riches, chiefly furs, of the West, as then were most an object of barter. Mr. Erskine, who had married the daughter of one of the earliest settlers from France, and of a family well known in history, a lady who had been in Detroit during the siege of the British garrison by Ponteac, now abandoned speculation, and contenting himself with the remnant of his fortune, established himself near the banks of the river, within a short distance of the Bloody Run. Here he continued throughout the Revolution. Early, however, in the present century, he quitted Detroit and repaired to the Canadian shore, where on a property nearly opposite, which he obtained in exchange, and which in honor of his native country he named Strabane—known as such to this day—he passed the autumn of his days. The last time I beheld him, was a day or two subsequent to the affair of the Thames, when General Harrison and Colonel Johnson were temporary inmates of his dwelling.

My father, of a younger branch of the Annandale family, the head of which was attained in the Scottish rebellion of 1745, was an officer of Simcoe's well-known Rangers, in which regiment, and about the same period, the present Lord Hardinge commenced his services in this country. Being quartered at Fort Erie, he met and married at the house of one of the earliest Canadian merchants, a daughter of Mr. Erskine, then on a visit to her sister, and by her had eight children, of whom I am the oldest and only survivor. Having a few years after his marriage been ordered to St. Joseph's, near Michillimackinac, my father thought it expedient to leave me with Mr. Erskine at Detroit, where I received the first rudiments of my education. But here I did not remain long, for it was during the period of the stay of the detachment of Simcoe's Rangers at St. Joseph that Mr. Erskine repaired with his family to the Canadian shore, where on the more elevated and conspicuous part of his grounds which are situated nearly opposite the foot of Hog Island, so repeatedly alluded to in *Wacousta*, he had caused a flag-staff to be erected, from which each Sabbath day proudly floated the colors under which he had served and never could bring himself to disown. It was at Strabane that the old lady, with whom I was a great favorite, used to enchain my young interest by detailing various facts connected with the siege she so well remembered, and infused into me a longing to grow up to manhood that I might write a book about it. The details of the Ponteac plan for the capture of the two forts were what she most enlarged upon, and although a long lapse of years of absence from the scene, and ten thousand incidents of a higher and more immediate importance might have been supposed to weaken the recollections of so early a period of life, the impression has ever vividly remained. Hence the first appearance of *Wacousta* in London in 1832, more than a quarter of a century later. The story is founded solely on the artifice of Ponteac to possess himself of these two last British forts. All else is imaginary.

It is not a little curious that I, only a few years subsequent to the narration by old Mrs. Erskine of the daring and cunning feats of Ponteac, and his vain attempt to secure the fort of Detroit, should myself have entered it in arms. But it was so. I had ever hated school with a most bitter hatred, and I gladly availed myself of an offer from General Brock to obtain for me a commission in the king's service. Meanwhile I did duty as a cadet with the gallant 41st regiment, to whom the English edition of *Wacousta* was inscribed, and was one of the guard of honor who took possession of the fort. The duty of a sentinel over the British colors, which had just been hoisted, was assigned to me, and I certainly felt not a little proud of the distinction.

Five times, within half a century, had the flag of that fortress been changed. First the lily of France, then the red cross of England, and next the stripes and stars of America had floated over its ramparts; and then again the red cross, and lastly the stars. On my return to this country a few years since, I visited those scenes of stirring excitement in which my boyhood had been passed, but I looked in vain for the ancient fortifications which had given a classical interest to that region. The unsparing hand of utilitarianism had passed over them, destroying almost every vestige of the past. Where had risen the only fortress in

38

America at all worthy to give antiquity to the scene, streets had been laid out and made, and houses had been built, leaving not a trace of its existence, save the well that formerly supplied the closely besieged garrison with water; and this, half imbedded in the herbage of an enclosure of a dwelling house of mean appearance, was rather to be guessed at than seen; while at the opposite extremity of the city, where had been conspicuous for years the Bloody Run, cultivation and improvement had nearly obliterated every trace of the past.

Two objections have been urged against *Wacousta* as a consistent tale—the one as involving an improbability, the other a geographical error. It has been assumed that the startling feat accomplished by that man of deep revenge, who is not alone in his bitter hatred and contempt for the base among those who, like spaniels, crawl and kiss the dust at the instigation of their superiors, and yet arrogate to themselves a claim to be considered gentlemen and men of honor and independence —it has, I repeat, been assumed that the feat attributed to him, in connexion with the flag-staff of the fort, was impossible. No one who has ever seen these erections on the small forts of that day, would pronounce the same criticism. Never very lofty, they were ascended at least one-third of their height by means of small projections nailed to them, for footholds for the artillerymen, frequently compelled to clear the flag lines entangled at the truck; therefore a strong and active man, such as Wacousta is described to have been, might very well have been supposed, in his strong anxiety for revenge and escape with his victim, to have doubled his strength and activity on so important an occasion, rendering that easy of attainment by himself, which an ordinary and unexcited man might deem impossible. I myself have knocked down a gate almost without feeling the resistance, in order to escape the stilettoes of assassins.

The second objection is to the narrowness attributed, in the tale, to the river St. Clair. This was done in the license usually accorded to a writer of fiction, in order to give greater effect to the scene represented as having occurred there, and of course in no way intended as a geographical description of the river, nor was it necessary. In the same spirit and for the same purpose, it has been continued.

It will be seen that at the termination of the tragedy enacted at the bridge, by which the Bloody Run was in those days crossed, that the wretched wife of the condemned soldier pronounced a curse that could not of course well be fulfilled in the course of the tale. Some few years ago I published in Canada—I might as well have done so in Kamtschatka—the continuation, which was to have been dedicated to the last King of England, but which, after the death of that monarch, was inscribed to Sir John Harvey, whose letter, as making honorable mention of a gallant and beloved brother, I feel it a duty to the memory of the latter to subjoin.*

The Prophecy Fulfilled, which, however, has never been seen out of the small country in which it appeared, Detroit perhaps alone excepted, embraces and indeed is intimately connected with the Beauchamp tragedy, which took place at or near Weisiger's Hotel, in Frankfort, Kentucky, where I had been many years before confined as a prisoner of war. While connecting it with *The Prophecy Fulfilled*, and making it subservient to the end I had in view, I had not read, or even heard of the existence of a work of the same character, which had already appeared from the pen of an American author. Indeed, I have reason to believe that *The Prophecy Fulfilled*, although not published until after a lapse of years, was the first written. No similarity of treatment of the subject exists between the two versions, and this, be it remembered, I remark without in the slightest degree impugning the merit of the production of my fellow laborer in the same field.

1851

*"GOVERNMENT HOUSE, FREDERICTON, N. B., *November 26th*, 1839.

"DEAR SIR,—I am favored with your very interesting communication of the 2d instant, by which I learn that you are the brother of two youths, whose gallantry and merits—and with regard to one of them, his sufferings—during the late war, excited my warmest admiration and sympathy; I beg you to believe that I am far from insensible to the affecting proofs which you have made known to me of this grateful recollection of any little service which I may have had it in my power to render them; and I will add that the desire which I felt to serve the father, will be found to extend itself to the son, if your nephew should ever find himself,under circumstances to require from me any service which it may be within your power to render him.

"With regard to your very flattering proposition to inscribe your present work to me. I can only say that, independent of the respect to which the author of so very charming a production as "Wacousta" is entitled, the interesting facts and circumstances so unexpectedly brought to my knowledge and recollection, would ensure a ready acquiescence on my part.

"I remain dear Sir, your very faithful servant,
(Signed)   "J. HARVEY.
"Major RICHARDSON, Montreal."

Thomas Chandler Haliburton
1796-1865

Thomas Chandler Haliburton was born in Windsor, Nova Scotia. He practised law in Annapolis Royal, was elected to Nova Scotia's House of Assembly in 1826, and later became a judge of the Court of

Common Pleas, a position he held until his appointment as judge of the Supreme Court of Nova Scotia in 1841. He remained in this post until 1856 when he moved permanently to England where he became a member of the British House of Commons. Among the first native-born Canadian writers to achieve an international reputation, Haliburton's success was largely the result of a single character, Sam Slick, who first appeared in a series of sketches published in Joseph Howe's newspaper, the *Novascotian*, in 1835. Sam Slick's adventures were expanded in seven subsequent volumes, including: *The Clockmaker; or, The Sayings and Doings of Samuel Slick of Slickville* (1836, 1838 and 1840); *The Attaché; or Sam Slick in England* (1843 and 1844); and *Nature and Human Nature* (1855).

From
Nature and Human Nature
Holding Up The Mirror

From Halifax to Cumberland, Squire, the eastern coast of Nova Scotia presents more harbours fit for the entrance of men-of-war than the whole Atlantic coast of our country from Maine to Mexico. No part of the world I am acquainted with is so well supplied, and so little frequented. They are "thar" as we say, but where are the large ships? Growing in the forest I guess. And the large towns, all got to be built I reckon. And the mines, why wanting to be worked. And the fisheries. Well I'll tell you, if you will promise not to let on about it. We are going to have them by treaty, as we now have them by trespass. Fact is, we treat with the British and the Indians in the same way. Bully them if we can, and when that won't do, get the most valuable things they have in exchange for trash, like glass beads and wooden clocks. Still, Squire, there is a vast improvement here, though I won't say there ain't room for more; but there is such a change come over the people, as is quite astonishing. The Blue-nose of 1834 is no longer the Blue-nose of 1854. He is more active, more industrious, and more enterprising. Intelligent the crittur always was, but unfortunately he was lazy. He was asleep then, now he is wide awake and up and doing. He never had no occasion to be ashamed to shew himself, for he is a good looking feller, but he needn't now be no longer skeered, to answer to his name, when the muster is come and his'n is called out in the roll, and say, "here am I Sirree." A new generation has sprung up, some of the drones are still about the hive, but there is a young vigorous race coming on who will keep pace with the age.

It's a great thing to have a good glass to look in now and then, and see yourself. They have had the mirror held up to them.

Lord, I shall never forget when I was up to Rawdon here once, a countryman came to the inn where I was, to pay me for a clock I had put off on him, and as I was a passin through the entry I saw the crittur standin before the glass, awfully horrified.

"My good gracious," said he, a talking to himself, "my good gracious, is this you, John Smiler, I havn't seen you before now, going on twenty years. Oh, how shockingly you are altered, I shouldn't a known you I declare."

Now, I have held the mirror to these fellows to see themselves in, and it has scared them so they have shaved slick up, and make themselves look decent. I won't say I made all the changes myself, for Providence scourged them into activity, by sending the weavel into their wheat-fields, the rot into their potatoes, and the drought into their hay crops. It made them scratch round I tell you, so as to earn their grub, and the exertion did them good. Well, the blisters I have put on their vanity, stung em so they jumped high enough to see the right road, and the way they travel ahead now is a caution to snails . . . .

I know they feel sore here about the picture my mirror gives them, and it's natural they should, especially comin' from a Yankee; and they call me a great bragger. But that's nothin' new; doctors do the same when a feller cures a poor wretch they have squeezed like a sponge, ruinated, and given up as past hope. They sing out quack. But I don't care; I have a right to brag nationally and individually, and I'd be no good if I didn't take my own part. Now, though I say it that shouldn't say it, for I ain't afraid to speak out, the sketches I send you are from life; I paint things as you will find them and know them to be. I'll take a bet of a hundred dollars, ten people out of twelve in this country will recognize Jerry Boudrot's house who have never entered it, but who have seen others exactly like it, and will say, "I know who is meant by Jerry and his daughter and wife; I have often been there; it is at Clare or Arichat or Pumnico, or some such place or another."

Is that braggin? Not a bit; it's only the naked fact. To my mind there is no vally in a sketch if it ain't true to nature. We needn't go searching about for strange people or strange things; life is full of them. There is queerer things happening every day than an author can imagine for the life of him. It takes a great many odd people to make a world; that's a fact. Now, if I describe a house that has an old hat in one window, and a pair of trousers in another, I don't stop to turn glazier, take em out, and put whole glass in, nor make a garden where there is none, and put a large tree in the foreground for effect; but I take it as I find it, and I take people in the dress I find em in, and if I set em a talkin I take their very words down. Nothing gives you a right idea of a country and its people like that.

There is always some interest in natur, where truly depicted. Minister used to say that some author (I think he said it was old Dictionary Johnson) remarked, that the life of any man, if wrote truly, would be interesting. I think so too; for every man has a story of his own, adventures of his own, and some things have happened to him that never happened to any body else. People here abuse me for all this, they say, after all my boastin' I don't do em justice. But after you and I are dead and gone, and things have been changed as it is to be hoped they will some day or another for the better, unless they are like their Acadian French neighbours, and intend to remain just as they are for two hundred and fifty years, then these sketches will be curious; and, as they are as true to life as a Dutch picture, it will be interestin to see what sort of folks were here in 1854, how they lived, and how they employed themselves, and so on.

Now it's more than a hundred years ago since Smollett wrote, but his men and women were taken from real life, his sailors from the navy, his attorneys from the jails and criminal courts, and his fops and fine ladies from the herd of such cattle that he daily met with. Well, they are read now; I have em to home, and laugh till I cry over them. Why? Because natur is the same always. Although we didn't live a hundred years ago, we can see how the folks of that age did; and, although society is altered, and there are no Admiral Benbows; nor Hawser Trunnions, and folks don't travel in vans with canvas covers, or wear swords, and frequent taverns, and all that as they used to did to England; still it's a pictur of the times and instructin as well as amusin. I have learned more how folks dressed, talked, and lived, and thought, and what sort of critters they were, and what the state of society, high and low was then, from his books and Fielding's than any I know of. They are true to life, and as long as natur remains the same, which it always will, they will be read. That's my idea at least.

Some squeamish people turn up the whites of their peepers at both those authors and say they are coarse. How can they be otherwise? society was coarse. There are more veils worn now, but the devil still lurks in the eye under the veil. Things ain't talked of so openly, or done so openly in modern as in old times. There is more concealment; and concealment is called delicacy. But where concealment is, the passions are excited by the difficulties imposed by society. Barriers are erected too high to scale, but every barrier has its wicket, its latch key, and its private door. Natur is natur still, and there is as much of that that is condemned in his books, now, as there was then . . . .

1855

Susanna Moodie
1803-1885

A sister of Catharine Parr Traill, Susanna Strickland was born in Suffolk, England. In 1832, a year after her marriage to J.W. Dunbar Moodie, she emigrated with him to a farm near Cobourg in Upper

Canada. Two years later, the couple moved to the backwoods near Peterborough where they struggled to establish a farm until 1839 when they moved to Belleville. Moodie's best-known works, *Roughing It in the Bush* (1852) and *Life in the Clearings* (1853), chronicle Mrs Moodie's struggles and responses during her early years in Canada. Her novels include: *Mark Hurdlestone*; *The Gold Worshipper* (1853); *Flora Lyndsay*; or, *Passages in an Eventful Life* (1854); *Geoffrey Moncton*; or, *The Faithless Guardian* (1855); and *The World Before Them* (1868). "A Word for the Novel Writers" first appeared in *The Literary Garland* in August of 1851 and was reprinted as part of *Life in the Clearings* in 1853

A Word for the Novel Writers

Fiction, however wild and fanciful,
Is but the copy memory draws from truth—
'Tis not in human genius to *create*—
The mind is but a mirror which reflects
Realities that are—or the dim shadows,
Left by the Past upon its placid surface,
Recalled again to life.

There are many good and conscientious persons, who regard novels and novel writers with devout horror—who condemn their works, however moral in their tendency, as unfit for the perusal of responsible and intelligent creatures, who will not admit into their libraries any books but those that treat of religious, historical, or scientific subjects—imagining, and we think very erroneously, that all works of fiction have a demoralizing effect, tending to weaken the judgment and enervate the mind.

We will, however, allow that there is both truth and sound sense in some of their objections; and that if a young person's reading is entirely confined to this species of literature, and that of an inferior class, a great deal of harm may be the result, as many of these works are apt to convey to them false and exaggerated pictures of life. Such a course of reading would have the same effect upon the mind, as a constant diet of sweetmeats would have upon the stomach; it would destroy the digestion, and induce a loathing for more wholesome food.

Still, the mind requires recreation as well as the body, and cannot always be engaged upon serious studies without injury to the brain, and the disarrangement of some of the most important organs of the body. Now, we think, it could be satisfactorily proved, in spite of the stern crusade perpetually waged against works of fiction, by a large portion of well-meaning people, that much good has been done in the world through their instrumentality.

Most novels, or romances, particularly those of the modern school, are founded upon real incidents; and like the best heads in the artist's picture, are drawn from life, and the closer the story or painting approximates to nature, the more interesting and popular will it become.

Though a vast number of these works are daily issuing from the British and American press; it is only those of a very high class that are generally read, and become as familiar as household words. The tastes of individuals differ widely on articles of dress, food and amusements; but there is a wonderful affinity in the minds of men as regards works of literature. A book that appeals to the passions and sentiments, if true to nature, must strike nearly all alike, and obtains a world-wide popularity; while the mere fiction sinks back into obscurity, is once read and forgotten.

The works of Smollet and Fielding were admirable pictures of society as it existed in their day; but we live in a more refined age, and few young people would feel any pleasure in the coarse pictures exhibited in those once celebrated works. The novels of Richardson, recommended by grave divines from the pulpit, as perfect models of purity and virtue, would now be cast aside with indifference and disgust. His characters are unnatural, and some of the scenes he pourtrays are highly immoral. But they were considered quite the reverse in the age he wrote, and he was looked upon as one of the great reformers of the vices of his time. We may therefore conclude, that, although repugnant to our tastes and feelings, they were the means of effecting much good in a gross and licentious age.

In the writings of our great modern novelists, virtue is never debased, nor vice exalted; but there is a constant endeavor to impress upon the mind of the reader, the true wisdom of the one, and the folly of the other. And where the author fails to create an interest in the fate of his hero or heroine, it is not because they are bad and immoral characters, like Lovelace in *Clarissa Harlowe*, and Lord B—— in *Pamela*; but that like Sir Charles Grandison, they are too good for reality, and their very faultlessness renders them, like the said Sir Charles, affected and unnatural. Where high moral excellence is represented as struggling with the faults and follies common to humanity; sometimes yielding to temptation, and reaping the bitter fruits; and at other times, successfully resisting the allurements of vice; all our sympathies are engaged in the contest, it becomes our own, and we follow the hero through all his trials, weep at his fall, or triumph at his success.

Children, who possess an unsophisticated judgment in these matters, seldom feel much interest in the model boy of a moral story. Not from any innate depravity which makes men prefer vice to virtue, for no such preference can exist in the human *mind*, no, not even in the perverted hearts of the very worst of men, but, because the model boy

45

is like no other boy of their acquaintance. He does not resemble them, for he is a piece of unnatural perfection, he neither fights nor cries, nor wishes to play when he ought to be busy at his lessons. He lectures like a parson, and talks like a book. His face is never dirty; he never tears his clothes, nor soils his hands by making dirt pies, or paddling in a puddle. His hair is always smooth, his face always wears a smile, and he was never known to sulk, or to say, "*I won't!*" The boy is a perfect stranger, they can't recognize his likeness, nor follow his example, and why? Because both are unnatural caricatures.

But, be sure, that if the naughty boy of the said tale, creates the most interest for his fate, in the mind of the young reader, it is simply, because it is drawn with more truthfulness than the character that was meant to be his counterpart. The language of passion is always eloquent, and the bad boy is drawn true to his bad nature, and is made to speak and act naturally, which never fails to awaken a touch of sympathy in beings equally prone to err. I again repeat, that few minds (if any) exist, that can find beauty in deformity, or aught to admire in the hideousness of vice.

There are many persons in the world who cannot bear to receive instruction when conveyed to them in a serious form; who shrink with loathing from the cant, with which, too many religious novels are loaded; and who yet might be induced to listen to precepts of religion and virtue, when arrayed in a more amusing and attractive garb, and enforced by characters who speak and feel like themselves, and share in all things a common humanity.

Some of our admirable modern works of fiction, or rather truths disguised in order to render them more palatable to the generality of readers, have done more to ameliorate the sorrows of mankind, by drawing the attention of the public to the wants and woes of the lower classes, than all the charity sermons that have been delivered from the pulpit.

Yes, the despised and reprobated novelist, by daring to unveil the crimes and miseries of neglected and ignorant men, and to point out the abuses which have produced, and which are still producing the same dreadful results, are missionaries in the cause of humanity, the real friends and benefactors of mankind.

The selfish worldling may denounce as infamous and immoral, the heart-rending pictures of human suffering and degradation, which the writings of Dickens and Sue, have presented to their gaze, and declare, that they are unfit to meet the eyes of the virtuous and refined, that no good can arise from the publication of such revolting details; and that to be ignorant of the existence of such horrors, is in itself a species of virtue.

Daughter of wealth, daintily nurtured, and nicely educated. "Is blindness virtue?" Does your superiority over these fallen creatures spring from any innate principle in your own breast, which renders you more worthy of the admiration and esteem of your fellows. Are not you indebted to circumstances for every moral quality that you possess?

You can feel no pity for the murderer, the thief, the prostitute; such people might aptly be termed the wild beasts of society; and, like them, should be hunted down and killed, in order to secure the peace and comfort of the rest. Well, the law has been doing this for many years, and yet the wild beasts still exist, and prey upon their neighbors. And such will be the case, until Christianity, following the example of her blessed founder, goes forth into the wilderness on his errand of mercy, to seek and to save that which was lost.

The conventional rules of society have formed a hedge about you, which renders any flagrant breach of morality very difficult, in some cases, almost impossible. From infancy the dread commandments have been sounding in your ears:—"Thou shalt not kill; Thou shalt not steal; Thou shalt not commit adultery;" and the awful mandate has been strengthened by the admonitions of pious parents and friends all anxious for your good.

You may well be honest, for all your wants have been supplied, and you have yet to learn, that where no temptation exists, virtue itself becomes a negative quality. You do not covet the goods which others possess. You have never looked down with confusion of face, and heartfelt bitterness, on the dirty rags that scarcely suffice to conceal the emaciation of your wasted limbs. You have never felt hunger gnawing at your vitals, or shuddered at the cries of famishing children sobbing around your knees for bread. You have dainties to satiety every day, and know nothing of the agonies of sacrificing your virtue for the sake of a meal. If you are cold, you have a good fire to warm you; a comfortable mansion to protect you from the inclemency of the weather, and garments suitable for every season of the year. How can you sympathize with the ragged, houseless children of want and infamy?

You cannot bear to have these sad realities presented to your notice. You blame the authors who point out the dreadful depravity which such a state of hopeless degradation is too apt to produce. You cannot read the works of Dickens and Sue, because these humane men bid you step with them into the dirty hovels of these outcasts of society, and see what crime really is, and all the miseries which ignorance and poverty, and a want of self-respect, never fails to bring about. You cannot step into the neglected abodes of these starving brothers and sisters, these forlorn scions of a common stock, and view their cold hearths, and unfurnished tables, their beds of straw, and tattered garments, without defilement, or witness their days of unremitting toil, and nights of unrest,—and worse, far worse,—to behold the evil passions and the crimes which spring from a state of ignorance, producing a moral darkness that can be felt. You are insulted and offended at being seen in such bad company; and cannot for a moment imagine that a change in your relative positions, could render you no better than them.

But, let me ask you candidly. Has not the terrible scene produced some effect? Can you forget its existence—its shocking reality? The lesson it teaches may be distasteful, but you cannot shake off a knowledge of its melancholy facts. The voice of conscience speaks audibly to your heart. That still small voice, that awful record that God has left of himself in every breast, and woe be to you when it ceases to be heard, tells you that you cannot, without violating the divine mandate, to love thy neighbor as thyself, now leave these miserable creatures to languish and die, without one effort made on your part, to aid in rescuing them from their melancholy fate. "But what can I do?" methinks I hear you indignantly exclaim: "Much," I reply; "Oh, how much?" You have wealth, which cannot be better bestowed than in applying a small portion of it to pay for the instruction of these poor creatures, in those divine laws which they have broken, and in leading them step by step into the paths of piety and peace which they have never known. Ignorance, the fruitful parent of all vice, has been the most powerful agent in corrupting these perishing creatures. Idleness has lent her part. Give them a knowledge of their unrecognized Christian duties and healthful employment, and these victims of over-population may yet prove beneficial members of that society by which they are only recognized as a blight and a curse.

In the very worst of these degraded creatures some good exists. A few seeds remain of divine planting, which, if fostered and judiciously trained, might yet bear fruit for heaven.

The authors, whose works you call disgusting and immoral, point out this, and afford you the most pathetic illustrations of its truth. You need not fear contamination from the vice which they pourtray. It is depravity of too black a hue to have the least attraction, even to beings only removed a few degrees from their guilt. Vice may have her admirers, when she glitters in gold and scarlet, but when exposed in filth and nakedness, her most reckless devotees shrink back from her in disgust and horror. Vice, without her mask, is a spectacle too appalling for humanity; it exhibits the hideousness, and breathes of the corruption of hell.

If these reprobated works of fiction can startle the rich into a painful consciousness of the wants and agonies of the poor, and make them, in despite of all the conventional laws of society, acknowledge their kindred humanity, who shall say that these books have been written in vain? For my own part I look upon these men as heaven inspired teachers, who have been commissioned by the great Father of souls, to proclaim to the world the wrongs and sufferings of millions of his creatures, to plead their cause with unflinching integrity, and with almost superhuman eloquence demand for them the justice which society has so long denied. These men are the benefactors of their species, to whom the whole human race owe a vast debt of gratitude.

Since the publication of *Oliver Twist, Michael Armstrong*, and many other works of the same class, enquiries have been made by thinking and benevolent individuals, into the destitute condition of the poor in great cities, and manufacturing districts. These works, although revolting in their characters and incidents, brought to light deeds of darkness and scenes of oppression and cruelty, scarcely to be credited in modern times and in Christian communities. The attention of the public was directed towards this miserable class, and its best sympathies enlisted in their behalf. It was called upon to assist in the liberation of these white slaves, chained to the oar for life in the galleys of wealth, and to recognize them as men and brethren.

Then sprang up the ragged schools; the institutions for reclaiming the youthful vagrants of London, and teaching the idle and profligate the sublime morality of sobriety and industry.

Persons who were incapable of contributing money to these truly noble objects, were ready to assist in the capacity of charity and sunday school teachers, and add their mite in the great work of moral reform. In over-peopled countries, like England and France, the evils arising out of extreme poverty, could not be easily remedied; yet the help thus afforded by the rich, contributed greatly in ameliorating the distress of thousands of their suffering fellow creatures. To the same sources we may trace the mitigation of many severe laws. The punishment of death is no longer enforced, but in cases of great depravity. Mercy has stepped in, and wiped the blood from the sword of justice.

Hood's pathetic "Song of the Shirt," produced an almost electric effect upon the public mind. It was a bold, truthful appeal to the best feelings of humanity, and it found a response in every feeling heart. It laid bare the distress of a most deserving and oppressed portion of the female operatives of London, and the good it did, is at this moment in active operation. Witness the hundreds of work-women landed within the last twelve months on these shores, who immediately found liberal employment.

God's blessing upon thee, Thomas Hood. The effect produced by that work of divine charity of thine, will be felt, long after thou and thy heart-searching appeal have vanished into the oblivion of the past. But what matters it to thee, if the song is forgotten by coming generations—it performed its mission of mercy on earth, and has opened for thee the gates of heaven!

Such a work of fiction as The Caxtons refreshes and invigorates the mind by its perusal; and virtue becomes beautiful for its own sake. You love the gentle humanity of the single-hearted philosopher, the charming simplicity of his loving helpmate, and scarcely know which to admire the most, Catherine, in her conjugal or maternal character, the noble, but mistaken pride of the fine old veteran Roland, the real hero of the tale, or the excellent young man, his nephew, who reclaims the fallen son, and is not too perfect to be unnatural.

As many fine moral lessons can be learned from this novel, as from most works written expressly for the instruction and improvement of mankind; and they lose nothing by the beautiful and attractive garb in which they are presented to the reader.

Our blessed Lord, himself, did not disdain the use of allegory, or truth conveyed to the hearer in a symbolical or fanciful form. His admirable parables, each of which told a little history, were the most popular method which could be adopted to instruct the lower classes, who, chiefly uneducated, require the illustration of a subject in order to understand it.

Aesop, in his inimitable fables, pourtrayed through his animals, the various passions and vices of men, admirably adapting them to the characters he meant to satirize, and the abuses he endeavored through this medium to reform. These beautiful fictions have done much to throw disgrace upon roguery, selfishness, cruelty, avarice and injustice, and to exalt patience, fidelity, mercy and generosity, even among Christians, who were blessed with a higher code than that enjoyed by the wise pagan, and they will continue to be read and admired as long as the art of printing exists, to render them immortal.

Every good work of fiction is a step towards the mental improvement of mankind, and to every such writer we say, God speed.

1851

Introduction
to
Mark Hurdlestone, The Gold Worshipper

The story of Mark Hurdlestone, the Gold Worshipper, which I here present to the British public, forms the first of a series, that employed my pen during the long, cold winter nights of 1838-9; when the protracted absence of my husband on the frontier rendered the privations and solitude of my forest home more hard to bear.

In the fall of 1837 a magazine was started by Messrs. Lovell and Gibson in Montreal. In the December of that year Mr. Lovell wrote to me to obtain contributions from my pen, both in prose and verse, for the new-born periodical. With a generosity unusual in this country he requested me to name my own terms.

An offer so unexpected and so liberal from a perfect stranger appeared like a message sent to me from heaven; and, poor as I then was, I felt tempted to contribute what I could gratis. But my infant family of four small children, the eldest not quite six years old, put an effectual check upon my impulsive generosity. I found upon reflection that this was entirely out of my power. Time to me was money—it belonged by right to my family, and was too valuable a commodity to give away. I therefore named five pounds per sheet, as the price required for articles from my pen, which had to be written after the labours of the day were over, and the children were asleep in their beds. The magazine was of large size, with double columns, and in very small type. It required a great deal of writing to fill a sheet.

*　*　*

There is now no lack of books in Canada, of money to purchase them, and persons to read and understand them. The reading class is no longer confined to the independent and wealthy: mechanics and artisans are all readers when they have time to spare; and the cheap American reprints of the best European works enable them to gratify their taste, without drawing very largely upon their purse.

The traffic in books from the United States employs a great many young men, who travel through the country, selling and taking up subscriptions for new works; and the astonishingly low price at which they can be obtained is an incalculable benefit to the colony, however it may interfere with the rights of European publishers.

Of books published in the Colony, we have very few indeed; and those which have been issued from a Canadian press have generally been got out, either by subscription, or at the expense of the author. It is almost impossible for any work published in Canada to remunerate the bookseller, while the United States can produce reprints of the works of the first writers in the world, at a quarter the expense. The same may be said of the different magazines which have been published in the Colony.

Shortly after we came to Canada, a magazine was started in Toronto, called the *Canadian Literary Magazine,* edited by Mr. Kent, a gentleman of considerable talent; and his list of contributors embraced some of the cleverest men in the Colony. This periodical, though a very fair specimen of that species of literature, and under the immediate patronage of the Lieutenant-Governor, Sir John Colborne, only reached its third number, and died for want of support.

Another monthly, bearing the same title, minus the *Literary,* was issued the same year; but being inferior in every respect to its predecessor, it never reached a third number.

A long time elapsed between the disappearance of these unfortunate attempts at a national periodical and the appearance of the Montreal *Literary Garland,* which was published at the most exciting period of Canadian history, on the eve of her memorable rebellion, which proved so fatal to its instigators, and of such incalculable benefit to the Colony.

For twelve years the *Literary Garland* obtained a wide circulation in the Colony, and might still have continued to support its character as a popular monthly periodical, had it not been done to death by *Harper's Magazine* and the *International.*

These American monthlies, got up in the first style, handsomely illustrated, and composed of the best articles, selected from European and American magazines, are sold at such a low rate, that one or the other is to be found in almost every decent house in the province. It was utterly impossible for a colonial magazine to compete with them; for, like the boy mentioned by St. Pierre, they enjoyed the advantage of *stealing the brooms ready made.*

It is greatly to the credit of the country that for so many years she supported a publication like the *Garland*, and much to be regretted that a truly Canadian publication should be put to silence by a host of foreign magazines, which were by no means superior in literary merit. The *Literary Garland* languished during the years 1850 and 1851, and finally expired in the December of the latter.

From the period of its outset, until its close, I was a constant contributor to the *Garland*, in which I earned from twenty to forty pounds per annum, as time or inclination tempted me to contribute to its pages. The flattering manner in which all my articles were received by the Canadian public was highly gratifying to my feelings; and as human nature, with very few modifications, is the same everywhere, it induced in me a hope, that what had won for me respect in the land of my adoption, would not be received unfavourably by my own country; for though my writings must pass through a more severe ordeal, and stand the test of more learned criticism in England, I feel certain, that whatever is worthy of notice will not fail to command a generous acknowledgement from her truthful people. . . .

1853

Part 2
The Novel in the New Dominion

Goldwin Smith
1823-1910

Goldwin Smith, born in Reading, England, was educated at Eton and Oxford. From 1858 to 1866 he served as Regius Professor of Modern History at Oxford, but in 1868 accepted a professorship of English and constitutional history at Cornell University. Three years later he settled in Toronto. A prolific journalist, and an important cultural spokesman in late nineteenth-century Canada, Smith wrote and published the *Bystander* and contributed to *The Week*, the *Canadian Monthly and National Review*, the *Nation* and numerous other journals of his time. His many books include more than two dozen volumes of history, biography, literary criticism and social commentary. "The Lamps of Fiction" was written to honour the centenary of Sir Walter Scott's birth in 1871.

The Lamps of Fiction
Spoken on the Centenary of the Birth of Sir Walter Scott

Ruskin has lighted seven lamps of Architecture, to guide the steps of the architect in the worthy practice of his art. It seems time that some lamps should be lighted to guide the steps of the writer of Fiction. Think what the influence of novelists now is, and how some of them use it! Think of the multitudes who read nothing but novels; and then look into the novels which they read! I have seen a young man's whole library consisting of thirty or forty of those paper-bound volumes, which are the bad tobacco of the mind. In England, I looked over three railway book-stalls in one day. There was hardly a novel by an author of any repute on one of them. They were heaps of nameless garbage, commended by tasteless, flaunting woodcuts, the promise of which was no doubt well kept within. Fed upon such food daily, what will the mind of a nation be? I say that there is no flame at which we can light the Lamp of Fiction purer or brighter than the genius of him in honour to whose memory we are assembled here to-day. Scott does not moralize. Heaven be praised that he does not. He does not set a moral object before him, nor lay down moral rules. But his heart, brave, pure and true, is a law to itself; and by studying what he does, we may find the law for all who follow his calling. If seven lamps have been lighted for architecture, Scott will light as many for fiction.

I. *The Lamp of Reality.*—The novelist must ground his work in faithful study of human nature. There was a popular writer of romances, who, it was said, used to go round to the fashionable watering-places to pick up characters. That was better than nothing. There is another popular writer who, it seems, makes voluminous indices of men and things, and draws on them for his material. This also is better than nothing. For some writers, and writers dear to the circulating libraries too, might, for all that appears in their works, lie in bed all day, and write by night under the excitement of green tea. Creative art, I suppose, they call this, and it is creative with a vengeance. Not so, Scott. The human nature which he paints, he had seen in all its phases, gentle and simple, in burgher and shepherd, Highlander, Lowlander, Borderer, and Islesman; he had come into close contact with it; he had opened it to himself by the talisman of his joyous and winning presence: he had studied it thoroughly with a clear eye and an all-embracing heart. When his scenes are laid in the past, he has honestly studied the history. The history of his novels is perhaps not critically accurate, not up to the mark of our present knowledge, but in the main it is sound and true—sounder and more true than that of many professed historians, and even than that of his own historical works, in which he sometimes yields to prejudice, while in his novels he is lifted above it by his loyalty to his art.

II. *The Lamp of Ideality.*—The materials of the novelist must be real; they must be gathered from the field of humanity by his actual observation. But they must pass through the crucible of the imagination; they must be idealized. The artist is not a photographer, but a painter. He must depict not persons but humanity, otherwise he forfeits the artist's name, and the power of doing the artist's work in our hearts. When we see a novelist bring out a novel with one or two good characters, and then, at the fatal bidding of the booksellers, go on manufacturing his yearly volume, and giving us the same character or the same few characters over and over again, we may be sure that he is without the power of idealization. He has merely photographed what he has seen, and his stock is exhausted. It is wonderful what a quantity of the mere lees of such writers, more and more watered down, the libraries go on complacently circulating, and the reviews go on complacently reviewing. Of course, this power of idealization is the great gift of genius. It is that which distinguishes Homer, Shakespeare, and Walter Scott, from ordinary men. But there is also a moral effort in rising above the easy work of mere description to the height of art. Need it be said that Scott is thoroughly ideal as well as thoroughly real? There are vague traditions that this man and the other was the original of some character in Scott. But who can point out the man of whom a character in Scott is a mere portrait? It would be as hard as to point out a case of servile delineation in Shakespeare. Scott's characters are never monsters or caricatures. They are full of nature; but it is universal nature. Therefore they have their place in the universal heart, and will keep that place for ever. And mark that even in his historical novels he is still ideal. Historical romance is a perilous thing. The fiction is apt to spoil the fact, and the fact the fiction; the history to be perverted and the romance to be shackled: daylight to kill dreamlight; and dreamlight to kill daylight. But Scott takes few liberties with historical facts and characters; he treats them, with the costume and the manners of the period, as the background of the picture. The personages with whom he deals freely, are the Peverils and the Nigels; and these are his lawful property, the offspring of his own imagination, and belong to the ideal.

III. *The Lamp of Impartiality.*—The novelist must look on humanity without partiality or prejudice. His sympathy, like that of the historian, must be unbounded, and untainted by sect or party. He must see everywhere the good that is mixed with evil, the evil that is mixed with good. And this he will not do, unless his heart is right. It is in Scott's historical novels that his impartiality is most severely tried and is most apparent; though it is apparent in all his works. Shakespeare was a pure dramatist; nothing but art found a home in that lofty, smooth, idealistic brow. He stands apart not only from the political and religious passions but from the interests of his time, seeming hardly to have any historical surroundings, but to shine like a planet suspended by itself in the sky. So it is with that female Shakespeare in miniature, Miss Austen. But Scott took the most intense interest in the political struggles of his time. He was a fiery partisan, a Tory in arms against the French Revolution. In his account of the coronation of George IV, a passionate worship of monarchy breaks forth, which, if we did not know his noble nature, we might call slavish. He sacrificed ease, and at last life, to his seignorial aspirations. On one occasion he was even carried beyond the bounds of propriety by his opposition to the Whig chief. The Cavalier was his political ancestor, the Covenanter the ancestor of his political enemy. The idols which the Covenanting iconoclast broke were his. He would have fought against the first revolution under Montrose, and against the second under Dundee. Yet he is perfectly, serenely just to the opposite party. Not only is he just, he is sympathetic. He brings out their worth, their valour, such grandeur of character as they have, with all the power of his art, making no distinction in this respect between friend and foe. If they have a ridiculous side he uses it for the purposes of his art, but genially, playfully, without malice. If there was a laugh left in the Covenanters, they would have laughed at their own portraits as painted by Scott. He shows no hatred of anything but wickedness itself. Such a novelist is a most effective preacher of liberality and charity; he brings our hearts nearer to the Impartial Father of us all.

IV. *The Lamp of Impersonality.*—Personality is lower than partiality. Dante himself is open to the suspicion of partiality: it is said, not without apparent ground, that he puts into hell all the enemies of the political cause, which, in his eyes, was that of Italy and God. A legend tells that Leonardo da Vinci was warned that his divine picture of the Last Supper would fade, because he had introduced his personal enemy as Judas, and thus desecrated art by making it serve personal hatred. The legend must be false, Leonardo had too grand a soul. A wretched woman in England, at the beginning of the last century, Mrs. Manley, systematically employed fiction as a cover for personal libel; but such an abuse of art as this could be practised or countenanced only by the vile. Novelists, however, often debase fiction by obtruding their personal vanities, favouritisms, fanaticisms and antipathies. We had, the other day, a novel, the author of which introduced himself almost by name as a heroic character, with a description of his own personal appearance, residence, and habits as fond fancy painted them to himself. There is a novelist, who is a man of fashion, and who makes the age of the heroes in his successive novels advance with his own, so that at last we shall have irrestible fascination at seven score years and ten. But the commonest and the most mischievous way in which personality breaks out is pamphleteering under the guise of fiction. One novel is a pamphlet against lunatic asylums, another against model prisons, a third against the poor law, a fourth against the government offices, a fifth against trade unions. In these pretended works of imagination facts are coined in support of a crotchet or an antipathy with all the license of fiction; calumny revels without restraint, and no cause is served but that of falsehood and injustice. A writer takes offence at the excessive popularity of athletic sports; instead of bringing out an accurate and conscientious treatise to advocate moderation, he lets fly a novel painting the typical boating man as a seducer of confiding women, the betrayer of his friend, and the murderer of his wife. Religious zealots are very apt to take this method of enlisting imagination, as they think, on the side of truth. We had once a high Anglican novel in which the Papist was eaten alive by rats, and the Rationalist and Republican was slowly seethed in molten lead, the fate of each being, of course, a just judgment of heaven on those who presumed to differ from the author. Thus the voice of morality is confounded with that of tyrannical petulance and self-love. Not only is Scott not personal, but we cannot conceive his being so. We cannot think it possible that he should degrade his art by the indulgence of egotism, or crotchets, or petty piques. Least of all can we think it possible that his high and gallant nature should use art as a cover for striking a foul blow.

V. *The Lamp of Purity.*—I heard Thackeray thank Heaven for the purity of Dickens. I thanked Heaven for the purity of a greater than Dickens—Thackeray himself. We may all thank Heaven for the purity of one still greater than either, Sir Walter Scott. I say still greater morally, as well as in power as an artist, because in Thackeray there is cynicism, though the more genial and healthy element predominates; and cynicism, which is not good in the great writer, becomes very bad in the little reader. We know what most of the novels were before Scott. We know the impurity, half-redeemed, of Fielding, the unredeemed impurity of Smollett, the lecherous leer of Sterne, the coarseness even of Defoe. Parts of Richardson himself could not be read by a woman without a blush. As to French novels, Carlyle says of one of the most famous of the last century that after reading it you ought to wash seven times in Jordan; but after reading the French novels of the present day, in which lewdness is sprinkled with sentimental rosewater, and deodorized, but by no means disinfected, your washings had better be seventy times seven. There is no justification for this; it is mere pandering, under whatever pretence, to evil propensities, it makes the divine art of Fiction "procuress to the Lords of Hell." If our established morality is in any way narrow and unjust, appeal to Philosophy, not to Comus; and remember that the mass of readers are not philosophers. Coleridge pledges himself to find the deepest sermons under the filth of Rabelais; but Coleridge alone finds the sermons while everybody finds the filth. Impure novels have brought and are bringing much misery on the world. Scott's purity is not that of cloistered innocence and inexperience, it is the manly purity of one who had seen the world, mingled with men of the world, known evil as well as good; but who, being a true gentleman, abhorred filth, and teaches us to abhor it too.

VI. *The Lamp of Humanity.*—One day we see the walls placarded with the advertising woodcut of a sensation novel, representing a girl tied to a table and a man cutting off her feet into a tub. Another day we are allured by a picture of a woman sitting at a sewing-machine and a man seizing her behind by the hair, and lifting a club to knock her brains out. A French novelist stimulates your jaded palate by introducing a duel fought with butchers' knives by the light of lanterns. One genius subsists by murder, as another does by bigamy and

57

adultery. Scott would have recoiled from the blood as well as from the ordure, he would have allowed neither to defile his noble page. He knew that there was no pretence for bringing before a reader what is merely horrible; that by doing so you only stimulate passions as low as licentiousness itself—the passions which were stimulated by the gladiatorial shows in degraded Rome, which are stimulated by the bull-fights in degraded Spain, which are stimulated among ourselves by exhibitions the attraction of which really consists in their imperilling human life. He knew that a novelist had no right even to introduce the terrible except for the purpose of exhibiting human heroism, developing character, awakening emotions which when awakened dignify and save from harm. It is want of genius and of knowledge of their craft that drives novelists to outrage humanity with horrors. Miss Austen can interest and even excite you as much with the little domestic adventures of Emma as some of her rivals can with a whole Newgate calendar of guilt and gore.

VII. *The Lamp of Chivalry.*—Of this briefly. Let the writer of fiction give us humanity in all its phases, the comic as well as the tragic, the ridiculous as well as the sublime; but let him not lower the standard of character or the aim of life. Shakespeare does not. We delight in his Falstaffs and his clowns as well as in his Hamlets and Othellos; but he never familiarizes us with what is base and mean. The noble and chivalrous always holds its place as the aim of true humanity in his ideal world. Perhaps Dickens is not entirely free from blame in this respect; perhaps Pickwickianism has in some degree familiarized the generation of Englishmen who have been fed upon it with what is not chivalrous, to say the least, in conduct, as it unquestionably has with slang in conversation. But Scott, like Shakespeare, wherever the thread of his fiction may lead him, always keeps before himself and us the highest ideal which he knew, the ideal of a gentleman. If anyone says these are narrow bounds wherein to confine fiction, I answer there has been room enough within them for the highest tragedy, the deepest pathos, the broadest humour, the widest range of character, the most moving incident that the world has ever enjoyed. There has been room within them for all the kings of pure and healthy fiction,—for Homer, Shakespeare, Cervantes, Molière, Scott. "Farewell, Sir Walter," says Carlyle at the end of his essay, "farewell, Sir Walter, pride of all Scotchmen." Scotland has said farewell to her mortal son. But all humanity welcomes him as Scotland's noblest gift to her, and crowns him, as on this day, one of the heirs of immortality.

1871

William Kirby
1817-1906

After emigrating with his family from England to Ohio at the age of fifteen, William Kirby moved to Canada in 1839 and became a newspaper editor and subsequently a collector of customs at Niagara-on-the-Lake. A fervent patriot devoted to conservative principles of loyalty to Great Britain, Kirby published a narrative poem, *The U.E.: A Tale of Upper Canada* (1859); a collection of lyrics and shorter narrative poems, *Canadian Idylls* (1884); and a local history, *Annals of Niagara* (1896). His major work, however, is *The Golden Dog*, an historical romance of the *ancien régime* of Quebec. The largest collection of Kirby's correspondence is located in the Archives of the Province of Ontario. "Canadian Literature and Copyright" was delivered as an address to the Royal Society of Canada in May, 1883; the essay was serially published in the Quebec *Morning Chronicle* on February 1, 2 and 4, 1884.

[Letter to J. M. Lemoine]

Niagara
March 7, 1877

Dear Sir:

That book of mine has not been issued yet in Ontario nor are there any notices yet that I have seen except in the *Can. Methodist Magazine* and the *Revue Canadienne* of Montreal. I presume you have seen the former as the Magazine contains a notice of your excellent volume of "Quebec Past and Present." I send you the criticism of the *Revue Canadienne* and will send you any other I meet with. Be good enough to return them to me.

I cannot express the pleasure I feel in your hearty approval of *The Chien d'Or* because no one—not even Mr. Parkman—is nearly so well qualified as yourself to pass an opinion that is based on Quebec's history and topography—and all future writers of fact or fiction relating to New France must like me acknowledge the value of your labours therein.

Yet I am sure you must have detected many faults. The book contains lots of typographical [errors]—some of them eyesores to me, but I had not any [revision] sent me before it was stereotyped. Then the story—as Parkman remarks, being a combination of two or three legends, I had to perpetrate an anachronism or two to make the ends of it tie together. But this is talk of the workship which you will know without my referring to it. Anyway, such as it is, I feel proud to have your approval Mr. LeMoine, whatever the world may think of it.

I had a letter today from my friend Benj. Sulte who is preparing a review of it in French. I will send it you when it appears.

I may mention here an anecdote à propos to this matter. In 1865 I think, I was in attendance at Parliament in Quebec, lobbying a bill, in fact, when your excellent "Maple Leaves" came into my hands. I read it with great interest and sitting with Sulte one day in the window of the St. Louis Hotel, I read portions of it to him, remarking that here was the finest subject for a romance that I knew of. We talked much of Chateau Bigot and the Chien d'or. I wanted Sulte as a clever French Canadian to write this story, and finally half in jest, half in earnest, threatened him that if he would not write the story of the Chien d'or I would! That was the beginning of it—the planting of the grain of seed that has grown into the big tree full of leaves, or rather book full of leaves that you see.

With much respect, I remain yours truly,

W. Kirby

[Letter to Lord Dufferin]

Niagara
March 15, 1877

To His Excellency
Earl Dufferin

My Lord

I pray your acceptance of the accompanying volume. A Canadian author feels a natural impulse to pay homage to Her Majesty's representative especially in the person of one who sets out such noble examples in literature as well as statesmanship.

The Chien d'or has the advantage, and disadvantage, of being the first attempt in English to draw from the romantic history of New France the materials for a work of Fiction. Like all first attempts it

remains to be seen whether the time has arrived in our hard practical country for a work of this genre to succeed. I shall be pleased any way if on perusal it meets your Lordship's approval.
I remain

Your Lordship's most obt servant

W. Kirby

[Letter to J. M. LeMoine]

Niagara
January 23, 1879

Dear Sir:

I send you a copy of the 3rd of the series of Canadian Idyls [sic] I have given to Mr. Withrow for the *Can. Methodist Magazine*. The present one will be published in the Feb. 2nd.

I have not seen nor do I wish to see an abusive pamphlet or whatever it is that an empty headed fellow has published charging you with plagiarising—I don't know who—in your late *Chronicles of the St. Lawrence*. Plagiarism indeed! as if historical facts, legends & traditions were not the stuff, the raw material out of which every writer who is worth reading does not exercise his genius in forming them into works of art and things of beauty—if he can! We take things that are brute matter, common property, like unappropriated land and by our work give them value, beauty, life and they become our right and our inheritance. As well dispute Shakespeare a title to his plays because they are a new fusion of old stories refined & recast in his immortal mind. I hope you do not feel annoyed at this braying of asses, literary ones especially.

Wishing you every success in your truly national & interesting works. I remain,

Yours sincerely
W. Kirby

Canadian Literature and Copyright

... Up to about 1842, authorship and book-publishing in Canada were fairly abreast of the times, and held as good a position and prospect relatively as did authorship and book-publishing at that period in the United States. Our publishers were at liberty to publish anything they chose, no law prevented them reprinting British books. The sparse population of a new country, want of capital and a yet undeveloped taste for much reading made progress slow, yet it seemed steady and sure. I venture to say that had it not been for that great stumbling block placed in the way of our rising literature—the passage of the Imperial Copyright Act of 1842—Canadian letters and book-publishing, with all the prestige and power a good literature gives, would have been flourishing to-day among us in a degree worthy of the material progress of our country.

That act extended the copyright of authors publishing in Britain to every part of the empire, and it was the very kernel of the act to restrict the publishing of British copyright works to the United Kingdom.

The object of this enactment was not so much to protect the British author, as to secure the monopoly of printing copyright books to the home publishers.

The effect of the act was momentous. It at once stopped Canadian republication of British copyright works, while it gave no copyright in Britain to colonial authors unless they published there.

It debarred, too, a British author who had taken out copyright in England from entering into arrangements with colonial publishers for the printing of special editions of his works in the colonies.

In Canada, the law worked disastrously for our rising literature, while in the United States book piracy became more than ever the order of the day. The book market of Canada instead of being supplied either by ourselves or by the British publishers, fell almost wholly into the hands of the Americans.

American pirated reprints were after a year or two of dispute allowed to be imported into Canada on payment of an extra duty of 12½ per cent collected for the benefit of the British author, but who has never realized any practical benefit whatever from this duty. He has his copyright, but the Americans sell us his books. We allow American pirated reprints to enter Canada and take full possession of our book trade, while our Canadian publishers are exposed to legal pains and penalties if they reprint a copyright book, even while willing to give a substantial remuneration to the British author, who, if the same remuneration were offered him from the United States, would gladly accept of it.

But the London publishers hold us fast bound by the law, while the Americans bound by no law in their dealings with British copyright supply Canada with the works of British authors reprinted in the United States.

The continent is flooded with cheap editions of reprints of British books. In vain British authors have thundered like Carlyle, bantered like Dickens, ridiculed like Sydney Smith, and down to the very year just past, philosophized over it in vain, like Herbert Spencer. The great American houses grow rich and fat and still more greedy. They not only continue the ignoble piracy of British authors for the supply of their own and our literary market, but they have devised a scheme by which they have finally put an end to all possible competition in Canada, by the purchase from the British author of copyright in our Canadian market and the privilege of using the British author's name in suits for any infringement by Canadian printers of the Imperial Act. British authors, unable to obtain copyright in the United States, do the next best thing for themselves, by *selling Canada* to the American publishers!

Thus between the upper and lower millstone of British copyright publishers and Americans piratical publishers of British books, the business of book publishing in Canada has been ground to powder . . . .

The evil is a great and growing one, and calls urgently for a remedy for the suffering book publishers and authors of our Dominion.

The remedy is simple and obvious. Our Government, as a matter of the soundest policy and common justice to ourselves, should open negotiations with the Imperial Government for the modification of the British Copyright Act, as regards Canada, with the offer of perfect copyright secured to British authors on printing and registering here-with the mutual privilege to Canadians of full copyright in Britain.

A reciprocal arrangement of that kind would, I am confident, be vastly to the benefit of both of us.

British authors would no longer see Canada supplied with American reprints of their works. By printing and registering here they would obtain real copyright in Canada, and be able to free them-selves also in some degree from a sole dependence on the London publishers.

Such a measure would probably result in the opening of the English book trade to Canadian manufactured books of British authors, who choose to take out copyright in Canada. At any rate, it would secure for them the Canadian market, now almost wholly supplied with American reprints, which are sold here without the slightest benefit to the author, except in the case of a sale of the Canadian market.

The American publisher would no longer have it in his power to tie us up, hands and feet, with cords drawn from the English Copyright Act. He would have to reciprocate in copyrights, else he would find no standing place in Canada. He would not then have the power of slaughtering the Canadian book industry, which would be restored to us, or created anew I might say, and Canada instead of being ground between the two millstones would occupy an honorable place between

England and the United States, doing good to both and from both receiving the advantages which are our due . . . .

I am of opinion that nothing short of a *national policy* in literature will suffice to restore to the publishing trade of Canada, and with it, the revival of our magazines and the restoration of Canadian authorship. Our people, as was said, are a reading community. Books they must and will have the newest as well as the best and cheapest. Canada in order to keep wisely the treasures she is winning so industriously—in order to preserve our Dominion from undue foreign influences and foreign ideas—must cultivate her own literature—take pride in her own writers, her own poets, historians, novelists and philosophers.

None but a Canadian ever will or can write the true history of this country. American and English historians, each borrowing from the other exclusively, seem totally blind to the northern lights playing up here. Leeky, the latest and the best intentioned of English writers treating of America, does not seem to have had more than a half glimpse of the part played by the great men who settled Canada, and laid the foundation of our Dominion—none at all of the principles which actuated them, or the kind of men they were.

A remark of Lord Durham was quoted in our Parliament last session, to the effect that "Canada had no history." It showed that even that eminent man had but a superficial knowledge of us, but until we write our history worthily as it deserves, we cannot blame the world for overlooking the fact, that the history of Canada, English and French, is unsurpassed in interest and grandeur on this continent.

Canada no history! Why the country is full of history and heroic achievement!

We find no fault with American writers who never weary of celebrating in prose and verse the arrival in New England, two and a half centuries ago, of a few hundred comfortable though discontented Pilgrims and Puritans, who came leisurely with their families, goods and chattels, and all their wealth, safe under the protection of charters granted by their Sovereign. How much is made of that settlement of New England!

Yet, what was that as a moral and historical event compared with the exile of over a hundred thousand American loyalists just one century ago? Of men who had fought through the seven years of war to prevent the dismemberment of the Empire. Who rather than abandon their loyal and constitutional principles endured the confiscation of every acre of land, of every dollar and dollar's worth of property which they had accumulated by years and generations of honest industry—of everything in short they possessed in the world except their honour and courage—and who, like the exiled Huguenots of a century before them, were scattered abroad to found new dominions or invigorate old ones in various parts of the world.

The settlement of Upper Canada, New Brunswick, and Nova Scotia—the centennial anniversary of which great Canadian event will this very year be celebrated—has a history of the deepest interest. It is one of the finest chapters of humanity. Those U. E. Loyalists have a history, noble as any one in the world.

The richest materials for history in all America are heaped up in those facts and the records of them stored away in our public archives.

If, as has been said, "God sifted a whole nation to send *choice* grain over to America"—that is, the Pilgrims and Puritans—it may no less truly be said, that He sifted America afresh to send his *choicest* grain here in the loyal and patriotic men who settled British America—men whose high, unselfish principles of obedience to the highest law have fixed our national character and given the tone and colour it has to Canadian society.

The life of man is in blood and the life of a people is no less in the principles religious and political that sway them. From these noble progenitors the Canadian people have inherited these sentiments, traditions and principles which distinguish us on this continent.

The full record of our Canadian history has yet to be undertaken. We have many fragmentary and some clever episodes of it, which deserve far more attention than they have received, but nothing as yet quite worthy of the subject.

The late venerable Dr. Ryerson had a just idea of Canadian history. But he commenced to write in the decline of his years and powers. The two large volumes he published only lead us into the vestibule of the temple, which grows and grows the more steadfastly we look at it.

Our numerous clever men and women, for let me do especial honour to so many Canadian ladies who in spite of all discouragements have kept the fire of literature burning among us.

I say our clever men and women are waiting impatiently for the restoration of literary work in Canada by a due and needful encouragement of our publishing industries, and look to our statesmen of all sides for help and counsel and action, by entering into negotiations with the Imperial Government for a modification of the copyright law and such legislation here as will give Canadian authors and publishers a fair field. We want no favour, we simply desire to be placed upon an equal footing with out literary compeers of Great Britain and the United States.

When that is done we shall see what forces are at work among us. Repressed as our literary endeavours have been they have by delay gathered strength and coherence. When their time of flourishing does come we shall see Canada wreathed with noble chaplets of the literature of her own history, poetry, science and philosophy, lacking which she is in this breathing world but "half made up." Without literature a country appears, as Bacon says, "like the statue of Polyphemus without its eye, the part that best shows the sap and spirit of a person.". . .

1883

James De Mille
1833-1880

Born in Saint John, New Brunswick, James De Mille attended Acadia College. Following a tour of Europe, he enrolled at Brown University, Rhode Island, where he received his M.A. in 1854. After his graduation, De Mille opened a bookshop in Saint John, and later taught Classics at Acadia College. From 1864 until his death, he was a professor of English at Dalhousie University. One of the most prolific Canadian writers of his time, De Mille wrote thirty books in fewer than twenty years. In addition to many works of juvenile fiction, his novels include: *The Lady of the Ice* (1870); *The Lily and the Cross* (1874); and the post-humously published *A Strange Manuscript Found In a Copper Cylinder* (1888). His textbook, *Elements of Rhetoric*, was published in 1878.

From
Elements of Rhetoric
Modes of Invention

Invention is of Two Kinds
Invention, or the finding of subject-matter, is of two kinds. The first is where the writer gathers the subject-matter from external sources. This may be called accumulative invention. The second is where the writer supplies the subject-matter by the creative faculty of his own mind. This may be called creative invention.

These kinds of invention are quite distinct, and require separate consideration.

Accumulative Invention
By accumulative invention is meant the finding of subject-matter by study, research, testimony, or observation. The subject-matter of the earlier historians, Herodotus and Thucydides, arose from observation and testimony; those of Gibbon and Macaulay from study and research.

Accumulative invention may also be seen in other narratives, whether poetry or prose, where the writer lacks originality. Roman writers are conspicuous for this. Plautus and Terence adapted Greek plays, or translated them. Virgil did not create the materials for the Æneid, but took them from existing sources, and presented them with but little change.

Accumulative invention is found, first, in narratives made up of facts of actual occurrence, with which the writer has become acquainted in any way; secondly, in all works of the imagination, where the incidents have not been originated by the writer, but drawn from other sources.

Accumulative invention may also be seen in expository subject-matter.

Ist. In writing intended to instruct, where the subject-matter is the result of research, as in Quintilian's Institutes of Oratory.

2d. Where the reasoning is based upon facts of actual occurence, as in Burke's speech on the Nabob of Arcot, or Sheridan's speech on Warren Hastings.

In accumulative invention the subject-matter may be immediately furnished by the memory, so that no preliminary labor may be needed; but it is evident that this labor has already taken place in some way from the existence of those very things with which the memory has been supplied.

In accumulative invention the faculties of the mind chiefly employed are reason and memory.

Creative Invention

By this is meant the finding of subject-matter by means of the inventive powers of the mind. The writer does not gather his material from external sources, but supplies it from within.

In narrative, creative invention is found in all works of the imagination where the things described have been produced by the author's own conception. For example, Dante's Divina Commedia describes a vast succession of scenes, with a multitude of characters, all of which have been created by the powerful genius of the author. In Milton's Paradise Lost we are introduced to supernatural scenes and superhuman characters, with mould and temper transcending anything that has ever existed in real life. Homer intermingles the natural with the supernatural, and blends his own creations with history or legend. Creative invention may also be shown where real facts and the characters of real life are represented, but where the particular characters are actual creations, or are endowed with a life and individuality of their own. This is illustrated in modern novels.

In exposition, creative invention may be seen where the writer sets forth to establish theories, to reason from new combinations of principles, or to reach new conclusions. Here facts may, and, indeed, must form the foundation; but the creative invention of the writer is seen in his power of combination, analysis, synthesis, and generalization, and in his ability to pass from the known to the unknown. This is exemplified in Burke's speech on Conciliation with America, or in Erskine's speech on Hardy.

The faculties of the mind employed in creative invention are chiefly imagination and reason.

The Real and the Ideal.

The chief field of creative invention is fiction, which has three distinct modes of presentation—poetry, prose, and the drama. Among these two classes are to be noted—the real and the ideal.

The Real.—Where the writer represents the scenes and delineates the characters of real life.

The Ideal.—Where the writer describes characters and scenes that are elevated beyond real life. The ideal must rise from the real. The writer takes striking circumstances, as in human life, and builds up an ideal world therefrom.

The same thing may be observed in art. A portrait represents the real, and may be compared with an original conception of the artist—a bust of Julius Cæsar with the Apollo Belvedere. The one is imitation, the other creation, the former is fact, the latter imagination.

Poetic Fiction

The ideal enters largely into poetic fiction. Realistic poetry, as a distinct class, is quite modern, and is found exemplified by Cowper, Crabbe, and Wordsworth. Passages of this sort may, however, be found in all poetry, and not the least in Homer. Dante in conception is intensely ideal, yet, in execution, is intensely real. Like Swedenborg, he combines the most amazing gradeur and subtlety of design with microscopic minuteness of detail.

In the drama the real is chiefly found in comedy, and the ideal in tragedy; the nearest approach to the real being in such historical plays as those of Shakespeare; yet this is only apparent, for the poet idealizes all his characters, and, like the portraits of Vandyke, these living historical personages have the stamp of the artist upon them. The highest examples of the ideal in dramatic writing are the Prometheus Bound, of Æschylus; Shakespeare's Midsummer Night's Dream, Tempest, and Hamlet; Shelley's Prometheus Unbound; and Goethe's Faust.

Prose Fiction.

The modern novel comprises both the real and the ideal. Fielding, Thackeray, and Dickens aim after the real, but in this they are surpassed by Trollope and others, who go so far as to produce what has been called "photographic fiction," from their attention to the pettiest facts of real life, and their exact reproduction of commonplace.

The ideal has many followers, the chief of whom are Richardson, Miss Burney, Sir Walter Scott, Fouqué, George Sand, and Victor Hugo.

The modern novel has attained the largest place in the literature of the imagination, being to us what epic poetry was to the ancient Greeks or the drama to the Elizabethan age. Its sphere is of the broadest possible kind, and its character illimitable, ranging all the way from the lowest to the highest.

In modern prose fiction there are three things to be considered:

1. The plot.
2. The characters
3. The scenery.

1. *The Plot.*—This will be considered elsewhere in connection with the subject of order of thought.

2. *Character.*—According to a recent writer in *Blackwood's Magazine*, this is the dominant force in fiction, and influences not only the plot, but also the scenery. The leading characters should always receive the most careful attention, and stand as studies of human nature. The minor ones serve chiefly to set off the greater. Original creations cannot be expected except from writers of the highest genius; yet common characters may be placed in novel situations, and thereby acquire much interest. Some authors love to delineate a leading character of ideal perfection, to whom is opposed another of commensurate baseness. The former is popularly termed the "hero" or "heroine," and the latter the "villain." Thackeray professed to disbelieve in "heroes;" but even in Vanity Fair he introduces the true and noble-hearted though somewhat stupid Dobbin, and in the Newcomes he has portrayed one of the most striking and best-beloved characters in modern fiction.

3. *Scenery.*—This may be either subjective or objective; the former referring to the display of human emotion, as in the banquet of Macbeth or the ghost-scene of Hamlet, the latter to natural objects. In the one case the description is generally in close connection with the progress of the story—rising out of it and flowing along with it; but in the other this connection is by no means so frequent. And yet in material scenes, no less than in moral, a close relation to the subject should be maintained; and all that which may be called the "scenery" should have its own meaning, which should assist the action.

The Two Kinds of Invention Intermingled.

Although for the sake of convenience these two kinds of invention have been considered separately, yet in literature they are generally intermingled; for the creative sort is never found separated from a basis of real occurrence, except perhaps in such rare instances as Shelley's Promethous Unbound, or Mrs. Browning's Drama of Exile. Thus Homer had the Trojan traditions; the Greek dramatists those of Troy or Thebes. Legends which form the substratum of epic or dramatic poetry are called epopœia, the chief of which are in ancient times the Trojan and the Theban; in modern times the Carlovingian and the Arthurian. The Elizabethan dramatists based their works upon legends, tales, and history; Chaucer upon stories which were current in his day; Spenser upon the Arthurian epopœia; Milton upon that mythology which had grown up outside of the Bible; Scott upon national tradition; and the Idylls of the King rose from the same source as the Faërie Queene.

Of the Two Kinds, the Creative is the Greater

Of the two kinds of invention, the creative is the greater.

It may, indeed, be considered as the highest power which is possessed by the human mind. This creative faculty has been regarded in all ages as the distinguishing mark of the greatest poets, and constitutes the chief difference between them and their lesser brethren. Homer, Dante, Shakespeare, and Milton are the supreme lords of literature. It is in this respect that Virgil is inferior to Homer; Tasso to Dante; Ben Jonson to Shakespeare; Spenser to Milton. For this reason the greatest works of creative invention are regarded as superior to the greatest works of accumulative invention—Homer to Thucydides; Milton to Gibbon; Dickens and Thackeray to Macaulay and Froude; Tennyson to Grote; Longfellow and Bryant to Prescott and Motley. In short, the very best history does not offer so broad a field for the exercise of genius as the very best fiction. In history the materials are accumulated, the multitudinous details are aquired by study, treasured up in the memory and then narrated. In fiction these are all created; the portrayals of characters, their passions,words, acts; the scenery and surroundings. Sometimes beings full of life are brought before us, unlike anything in common experience, speaking words that last forever; and the speaker and the words are all created by the author's own mind.

* * *

Novelists may be divided into two general classes with regard to order of thought.

1. Those who follow the logical order. These writers lay chief stress upon the plot. Characters are of inferior importance; incidents are everything; and these incidents are so arranged as to excite the reader to the utmost. His attention is roused at the ouset by some startling occurence, and then consequences are deduced from this in such a way that his interest is incessantly stimulated until the close is reached. Here it is the series of events succeeding one another in logical order by which the reader is attracted. This is signally illustrated in the "Arabian Nights' Entertainments;" by many French novelists, especially Alexander Dumas and Eugene Sue; and by writers of so-called "sensation novels."

2. The second class is made up of those who attach slight importance to the plot, but regard their characters as of supreme importance. Upon these all the interest of the story is made to depend—their lifelike portrayal, their acts, their words, their thoughts. Dickens and Thackeray belong to this second class. They were both greater in the delineation of character than in the construction of plot. The Pickwick Papers has scarcely any plot at all, but owes its unity to the characters. In Vanity Fair the plot is more visible, but the characters have an interest in themselves quite independent of their fortunes. Balzac may also be mentioned as another conspicuous example of this class.

Some writers unite both. Sir Walter Scott gives an elaborate plot, and his characters are all portrayed with lifelike fidelity. Victor Hugo rivals Dumas in his love of exciting incident, yet his characters are strongly marked; and Jean Valjean is one of the greatest creations of modern genius. George Eliot (Mrs. Lewes) and George Sand (Madame Dudevant) are writers as wide as the poles asunder, yet they have this in common, that they can construct a plot of intense interest, and create characters that live in the memory of the world.

Thus in the modern novel where the logical order is adopted, the story is connected by the framework of the plot; but where the scenic order is used, the story is connected by the characters.

The Fantastic

The fantastic in literature came into being during the Middle Ages. The conversion of the northern nations of Europe destroyed the supremacy of their gods, but did not remove them from the thoughts, fears, and affections of the people. These mythological beings lived anew in the common life of men; driven out from religion, they took up their abode in superstition; and inspired legends, traditions, and the great body of that humble literature known as Folk lore. The richest and the more varied store of such productions of the fancy have been derived from the Teutonic nations. The Celts have contributed largely to the common stock, and much is also due to the Arabians. From the first of these sources we have received sylphs, gnomes, salamanders, sprites, elves, trolls, fairies, witches, goblins, and many others of a similar kind. From the Celts have been drawn all those wonderful beings which form the machinery of the Arthurian legends. From the Arabians we have obtained enchanters, djinns, afrits, peris, and the like. All these, combined and fused together, blended with Christian legends, and out of the union there arose new beings, such as the mediæval devil, with characteristics of horns, tail, and cloven hoof; the mediæval ghost, appearing at midnight and vanishing at cockcrow; the saint, with his power over demons; and all the world of the supernatural.

The result was a new element, which entered into modern literature, and inspired it from the very first. We see its influence in the metrical romance, in Dante, Chaucer, Spenser, and Shakespeare, in Tasso and Ariosto; but its full presence and power can best be seen in works that are based altogether upon this element such as the Thousand and One Nights, and all those fairy tales which have been for ages the delight of young and old, and have exerted no small influence upon literature. This influence shows itself in the effort made by some imaginative writers to form for themselves new scenes and characters which shall rival these time-honored creations of the past. Some of their works do not rise above the level of the common ghost-story; but others are of a far higher order, and may be illustrated in prose by Schiller's Ghost Seer and Bulwer's Strange Story, and in poetry by Goethe's Faust and Coleridge's Ancient Mariner.

The fantastic in literature may be defined as the unrestrained exercise of fancy, where the writer ventures into regions of wild and unbridled speculation, and creates new scenes and new characters, which present a strange compound of the natural and supernatural. Here the beautiful and the sublime are intermingled with the ridiculous, and there result two distinct elements, the first of which may be called the grotesque, and the second the horrible.

I. The grotesque.

The grotesque may be defined as the caricature of the beautiful, or, in other words, as the union of the beautiful with the ridiculous. Thus, in art, a carved face may have well-formed features, but if these are distorted by an exaggerated grimace it becomes grotesque. This is not to be confounded with the ugly, which is simply repulsive; whereas in this case there is no repulsiveness. In literature it is found wherever sentiments and language, pleasing in themselves, are distorted and perverted in a ridiculous fashion. Examples may be found in the Ingoldsby Legends, and in many of the German stories of Zschokke and E.T.A. Hoffmann.

2. The horrible.

While the grotesque represents one side of the fantastic, the other may be found in the horrible. This may be considered as the caricature of the sublime, or the association of the sublime with the ridiculous. The horrible is never far removed from the grotesque; and even where the ridiculous is not at all visible, there is often an undercurrent of grim and ghastly humor. Examples may be found in many of the tales of Edgar A. Poe, especially the Murder in the Rue Morgue and Facts in the Case of M. Valdemar; in De Quincey's Avenger and Murder one of the Fine Arts; in Lewis's Monk; Mrs. Radcliffe's Mysteries of Udolpho; and Mrs. Shelley's Frankenstein.

1878

Graeme Mercer Adam
1839-1912

Born in Midlothian, Scotland, and educated in Edinburgh, Graeme Mercer Adam immigrated to Toronto in 1858. A book-seller, editor and publisher, Adam was also the founder of *The British American Magazine* (1863-4) and *The Canadian Monthly And National Review* (1872-8). Before leaving Canada in 189? to live in the United States, Adam wrote literary criticism, popular history and travel guides and collaborated with A. Ethelwyn Wetherald on *An Algonquin Maiden: A Romance of the Early Days of Upper Canada* (1887). "An Interregnum in Literature" and "Some Books of the Past Year" were published in *The Week* in June, 1884, and January, 1885, respectively.

An Interregnum in Literature

Attention is beginning to be directed to the present-day dearth of original creative work in literature, and to the fact that while our great writers are passing away there are few, especially among the masters of fiction and of song, to fill with acceptance their vacant places. At successive periods we must, of course, naturally look for the ebb and flow of the literary tide, as the world is orphaned by the hushing of its melodious voices, and again sired by the coming of new aspirants for literary honour and historic fame. But while the natural order has sway, and the old yields to the new, the fresh material, it is held, is inferior in quality and lacks the vigour and power characteristic of that which it supplants. Even to the unreflecting reader of contemporary literature this fact is beginning to be realized—that while the area under cultivation is greater than ever, the literary harvests for years have been poor, and the indications for the near coming time are not rich in promise. There is ceaseless literary activity, and this in all departments of human thought; but its results are those of study and research rather than of original creative work. The London *Spectator*, referring recently to the present lull in English literary history, speaks of the attitude of the reading world of the time as "standing by to watch one of those intervals which divide literary periods, and give second-rate men their long-hoped-for chance." The journal goes on to remark that "the lull in the production of first-class fiction, and indeed of good literature generally, is very striking." "Nobody," it affirms, "gives us *enchaining* books,—above all, enchaining fictions." That this is true few who recognize the force of the adjective "enchaining" will gainsay. There is the usual quantum of entertaining, and often clever, novels, ingenious in plot, skilful in dialogue, and wonderfully, often painfully, elaborate in analysis of motive and character. But of books that "enchain," that fasten themselves on all the faculties of the mind, and leave a never-to-be-forgotten, never-escaped-from impress on the memory, there are notably few, and the sum of them will make but a small addition to the permanent literature of British fiction.

What is true of the eminent writers of fiction is also true of the great masters of song. The latter have passed, or are passing, away, and there are few to replace them who either move us by their genius or entrance us with their art. There are always the ninety and nine thousand, of course, who are forever twanging the lyric harp and affect to live apart from the soiling influences of a sordid world. But their harp-twangings are as mechanical as their lives are commonplace, and the divine art is enriched by little that is worthy of their would-be epic life. Even the art of political squibbing, someone reminds us, has disappeared; and our political literature in general, with not a little that claims to be religious, is far from allaying one's moral anxiety. Whatever poetry has done or is doing for the age, it only fitfully refreshes and but feebly inspires the world.

It would be untrue to say that there is little of the poetry of the time that is not marked by high excellence, though not perhaps by genius. There are writers of verse among the modern literary men of England, particularly of the critical school, whose literary faculty enables them with faultless art to construct a sonnet, or give soul and beauty to a lyric, as it enables them to write a literary monograph or a critical dissertation on some notable period of English prose. But the work wrought by minds gifted with that supreme endowment of nature which we call genius is in the present age rare, not alone in song, but in the great undertakings in prose such as have marked the path of English literary history for the past three centuries. In the field of science, and occasionally in that of religious philosophy, we have had writers who if they have not sung in verse have, like Huxley, Tyndall, and Darwin, given us poems in prose. But in the department of literature proper there have been few great achievements; and the writers are not looming up who seem capable of giving to their time any work of signal and sustained excellence. Each age, it is true, has its own literary characteristics, and it is futile to say that we have no modern Shakespeare or Milton, Bacon or Gibbon. In the early decades of the present century we had what some venture to speak of as their equivalents in rank; and, later still, England has produced at least three novelists who, manifestly, were gifted with something more than a good working stock of literary talent. They had the power, in an especial degree, of commanding the reader's attention, and of interesting countless thousands the world over in their creative work. It is further urged that the counterparts of Dickens, Thackeray, and George Eliot are still with us, and that, if it is unsafe as well as invidious to name them, it is because they are our contemporaries and the judgment of the world has not as yet graven their names on the scroll of fame. Moreover, we are reminded that their work is not yet done, and no fair appraisement can be made of their talents or of the place they are likely to hold in literature. But to argue thus is special pleading; and to put forward names as the modern equivalents of the master-minds of the past would be to invite reflection on one's literary judgment. What can be safely done is to point to quantity rather than to quality—to industry and wide-spread dissemination of literary taste and talent, as the characteristic of the age, rather than to the employment of these in any works of great imaginative power and creative genius. The era is a critical rather than a constructive one—an informing, revising, and gathering-up age, rather than a fashioning, quickening and inspiring one. The literary men of the time are, in the main, book-makers. They are compilers, adapters, re-issuers—doing eminent service, it is to be admitted, in making literature attractive to the masses, and apt in chopping up the feed to suit the varied conditions of the mental teeth and digestion. Too often, it is to be regretted however, they put the commerce of literature before their art, and, at the instance of greedy publishers, impair their reputation by continuing to quarry in worked-out veins, or in employing their pens in scattering and ephemeral labour. This literary diffusiveness, in many instances, prevents that concentration of thought and energy necessary to the undertaking of any gigantic enterprise, and drains their work of the strength that might otherwise mark it. Hence come the literary poverty of the time, and the dearth of productions that fire heart and brain and make the period rich in its intellectual possessions.

On this side of the Atlantic the literary interregnum is explained by causes other than those which operate in the Old World. In fiction-writing, our neighbours to the south of us are making an effort to pluck the laurels from English brows; but their authors are heavily handi-capped by the absence of international copyright, and by the competition of the pirated foreign novel. Outraged national justice is thus, in some measure, avenged. But a more serious drawback is that from which we also suffer in Canada, to the detriment both of novel-writing and of every form of intellectual work, viz. the dissipation of time and brain in the reading of newspapers, and the absorption of every faculty of the mind in business. With commercial men, notably, there is no interval for intellectual enjoyment and refreshment; and even the professional classes seem to be losing their poetic sensibilities and becoming indifferent to the claims of culture. In Canada, in addi-tion to this, there is, in the ebbing out of national spirit, a growing intellectual callousness, and a deadening of interest in the things that make for the nation's higher life. Native literature, with nothing to encourage it, is fast losing the power to arrest attention and is perceptibly dying of inanition. In higher education the sympathies of our people are only languidly engaged; and but for denominational pride our universities would be in danger of becoming extinct. Journalism of a certain kind flourishes, but the newspaper, as an engine of culture and a vehicle of independent critical thought, can hardly be said to exist. This may seem a severe indictment of the country's intellectual status, but it is justified by a quarter of a century's observation of facts on the part of the present writer, and by close contact with those who have long striven to make of the desert a watered plain. The commerce of literature has the same depressing story to tell. The testimony of the British and American publishers to the serious falling away, both in volume and character, of the exports to Canada, emphasises the decline of literary interest in the country; and the native wholesale houses confirm the fact by the decay of the better-class book trade. Ask a bookseller, in even one of the larger towns of the Dominion, to compute the number of men who locally devote their leisure to serious reading, and he will count them on his thumbs. Nor is immigration appreciably helping to recruit the dwindling numbers of the cultured class in the community. Want of means and the imperious call to labour for daily bread shut out many from living an intellectual life; and the Government tax on literature, which makes many books an unindulged luxury to the student, is far from smoothing the path of intellectual advancement. The colonial status, and the anomalies of the literary copyright law, which surrender the native book-market to the American publisher, are further serious obstacles to literary progress. To what extent our public men are noting these facts, and are making effort to stay the literary decadence of the country, it is for the patriotic among them to say. If only a few of them will now and then forget the party interests that engross them, and give thought to the things that are more than food and raiment, or the profane equivalents of power and place, the nation may regain what years of political scuffling and absorbing interest in small issues have caused it to lose, and we may see the literary interregnum in Canada, at least, bridged over with honour and with profit. No one wants political intrigue, still less its peculiar morals, transferred to literature; but if literature could have a little of the stimulus which the material concerns of the Dominion have gained from political force, it would be well for our intellectual life and for the dependency we would fain call the nation.

1884

Some Books of the Past Year

...But we pass on to Fiction; and in dealing with the modern novel, what is there, we ask, to say but the trite observation that our novel-writers have gone from the manufacture and pourtrayal of incident, which pleases, to the manufacture and analysis of motive, which keeps us ever on some inquisitorial rack. The good old romantic and imaginative novel of our grandmothers' time seems a creation wholly of the past. What we have in its place is the English melodrama of such books as "Called Back"; the intellectual vivisection methods of the American schools of James and Howells; or, worse still, the loathsome realism and putridity of the school of Zola and France. If we could ever bring ourselves to justify a censorship of the press, it would be on the ground of suppressing the slimy product of the last-named school and its even more foul imitators. In the novels of the past year there have been quantity—that we alway have!—more or less freshness, and considerable variety. It were profitless to lament the fact that we have no new creations of the type of Adam Bede, Esmond, Jane Eyre, Ten Thousand a Year, and Ivanhoe; nevertheless, a dozen fair contemporary novels can be named which have had the rare merit of pleasing, and of fastening themselves on the memory as a good work of fiction

76

only can. Second successes are proverbially rare; and this is true of not a few English writers of fiction who have not fulfilled their early promise. So far as industry goes, and even sustained power, there would seem to be more hope that the laurels would pass to the brow of a woman. Certainly, neither Miss Braddon nor Mrs. Oliphant are out of the running. But it will be fair to wait for later work from comparatively new pens, which have begun well, and in the stories of Vernon Lee, Jessie Fothergill, Mrs. Walford, and Mrs. Humphrey Ward, have achieved more than fair success.

Of American novelists we have left ourselves no space to speak. Not to the present high-priests of American fiction, do we look for much in the way of pleasure-giving effects: from them we shall get only mannerisms, and more, deeper, and unpleasanter psychology, and less of all that is breezy, lofty, wholesome and bright. To Cable, Craddock, and Harris, would we rather turn, and if we may admit a lady, to Blanche Howard, for interest, of a genuine kind, in characters, descriptions, and incidents which amuse and delight, and thus fulfil the first, and we might add, the only mission of imaginative writing.

1885

Sara Jeannette Duncan
1861-1922

Born in Brantford, Canada West, Sara Jeannette Duncan began her career as a novelist in 1890 with the publication of *A Social Departure.* In the following year, she married Everard Charles Cotes, the curator of the Indian Museum of Calcutta, and spent most of her later life in India and England. Although Duncan published eighteen novels, only two directly reflect her Canadian experience: *The Imperialist* (1904) and *Cousin Cinderella* (1908). Before beginning her career as a novelist, Duncan was a successful journalist for newspapers such as the Toronto *Globe*, the Washington *Post* and the Montreal *Star*. Her awareness of changing currents in contemporary fiction is apparent in "Saunterings", her column in the Toronto journal, *The Week*; [The Heroine of Old-Time], [*An Algonquin Maiden*: Romance and Realism] and [New Directions in Fiction] were published there on October 28th, 1886, January 13th, 1887, and August 2nd, 1888, respectively. "Outworn Literary Methods" appeared in *The Week* on June 9th, 1887.

[The Heroine of Old-Time]

Has it occurred to nobody, in his struggles to keep abreast of the tide of new activity that sets in fiction, as in every other department of modern thought, to cast one deploring glance over his shoulder at the lovely form of the heroine of old-time, drifting fast and far into oblivion? It would be strange indeed if we did not regret her, this daughter of the lively imagination of a bygone day. By long familiarity, how dear her features grew! Having heard of her blue eyes, with what zestful anticipation we foreknew the golden hair, the rosebud mouth, the faintly flushed, ethereal cheek, and the pink sea-shell that was privileged to do auricular duty in catching the never-ceasing murmur of adoration that beat about the feet of the blonde maiden! Wotting of her ebon locks, with what subtle prescience we guessed the dark and flashing optics, the alabaster forehead, the lips curved in fine scorn, the regal height, and the very unapproachable demeanour of the brunette! The fact that these startling differences were purely physical that the lines of their psychical construction ran sweetly parallel, never interfered with our joyous interest in them as we breathlessly followed their varying fortunes from an auspicious beginning, through harrowing vicissitudes, to a· blissful close. So that her ringlets were long enough, and her woes deep enough, and her conduct under them marked by a beautiful resignation and the more becoming forms of grief, it never occurred to us to cavil at the object of Algernon's passion, because her capabilities were strictly limited to making love and Oriental landscapes in Berlin wool. Her very feminine attributes were invariably forthcoming; and if the author by any chance forgot to particularise the sweetness of her disposition, the neatness of her *boudoir*—they all had *boudoirs*—or the twining nature of her affections, we unconsciously supplied the deficiency, and thought no less respectfully of Araminta. She was very wooden, this person for whom gallant youths attained remarkable heights of self-sacrifice, and villains intrigued in vain; her virtues and her faults alike might form part of the intricate and expensive interior of a Paris doll; and we loved her perhaps with the unmeaning love of infancy for its toys. She was the painted pivot of the merry-go-round—it could not possibly revolve, with its exciting episodes, without her; yet her humble presence bore no striking relation to the mimic pageant that went on about her. She vanished with the last page, ceased utterly with the sound of her wedding-bells; and we remembered for a little space, not the maiden, but the duels in her honour, the designs upon her fortune, and the poetic justice that overtook her calumniators.

But extinction in time overtook this amiable damsel. Mere complexion began to be considered an insufficient basis upon which to erect a character worthy of public attention in the capacity of a heroine. So we were introduced to the young creature of "parts"—the parts consisting of an immoderate desire to investigate the wisdom of the ancients, as Plato has expressed it, an insatiable appetite for metaphysical conversation, and a lofty contempt for the frivolities of her sex. To keep the balance between these somewhat laudable peculiarities and proper womanly accomplishments, she was usually invested with a powerful and melodious vocal organ, whose minor notes frequently depressed her frivolous associates of the drawing room to tears, and reduced the hitherto invincible heart of the interesting woman-hater of the volume to instant and abject submission. To preserve the unities, charms of feature and philosophical tendencies being somewhat incompatible, she was given a rather wide mouth, and a forehead too high and thoughtful for beauty's strict requirements; while her dark expressive eyes and straight nose sufficed to secure our regard from an aesthetic standpoint. Then came that daring innovator who gave us a countenance all out of line, with freckles on it, a look of restless intellectuality, and a vague charm that was beyond his power to analyse or ours to conceive. The conduct of this young person was usually characterised by the wildest vagaries. She held communings with herself, which she reluctantly imparted to the interesting youth in whom she recognised her mental superior, and therefore her fate; and the sole end of her existence appeared to be to make his as wretched as possible. The plot, of which this ingenuous maid was the centre, usually turned upon a mood of hers—the various chapters, indeed, were chiefly given over to the elucidation of her moods, and their effect upon her unfortunate admirers.

Just about here, in the development of the heroine, do we begin to see that she is not a fixed quantity in the problems of the novelist, but varies with his day and generation. Araminta was the product of an age that demanded no more of feminity than unlimited affection and embroidery. The advent of the blue-stocking suggested the introduction of brains into her composition, though her personality was not seriously affected by them, as the blue-stocking was but a creature of report in the mind of the story-teller, the feminine intelligence not being popularly cultivated beyong the seminary limit. As dissatisfaction with her opportunities infected the modern young lady, her appearance in fiction with a turned-up nose and freckles, solely relying upon her yearnings after the infinite for popular appreciation, followed as a matter of course.

We are not talking, O captious soul—with a dozen notable heroines of the past at your fingers' ends!—of the great people in the world of fiction, but of the democracy of that populous literary sphere. We are discussing those short-lived Ethels and Irenes who have long since gone over, with their devoted Arthurs and Adolphuses, to that great majority whose fortunes are to be traced only at the second-hand book-stalls now; but whose afflictions formed the solace of many an hour in the dusty seclusion of the garret, while the rain pattered on the roof, and the mice adventured over the floor, and the garments of other days swayed to and fro in dishevelled remembrance of their departed possessors. Ah, Genevieve and Rosabel, Vivien and Belinda, how fare ye now whose yellow-bound vicissitudes were treasured so carefully from the fiery fate that awaited them at the hands of stern authorities diametrically opposed to "light reading!" By what black ingratitude are ye reduced, alas! to the pulp of the base material economy of the age on which, perhaps, the fortunes of damsels less worthy and less fair are typographically set forth for the fickle amusement of later generation!

Hardly less complete is the evanishment of Rosabel and Belinda than that of their successors in fiction, and the time-honoured functions they performed. A novel without a heroine used to be as absurd an idea as the play of Hamlet with Hamlet left out. But the heroine of to-day's fiction is the exception, not the rule. The levelling process the age is undergoing has reduced women with their own knowledge and consent to very much the same plane of thought and action as men. It has also raised them to it, paradoxical though the statement be. The woman of to-day is no longer an exceptional being surrounded by exceptional circumstances. She bears a translatable relation to the world; and the novelists who translate it correctly have ceased to mark it by unduly exalting one woman by virtue of her sex to a position of interest in their books which dwarfs all the other characters. It has been found that successful novels can be written without her. The woman of to-day understands herself, and is understood in her present and possible worth. The novel of to-day is a reflection of our present social state. The women who enter into its composition are but intelligent agents in this reflection and show themselves as they are, not as a false ideal would have them.

1886

[An Algonquin Maiden: Romance and Realism]

The publication of a Canadian work of poetry or fiction, or any of the lighter arts of literature, by a Canadian firm, among Canadians, is apt to be received with peculiar demonstrations. Their facial form is that of an elongation of the countenance, a pursing of the lips, a lifting of the eyebrows. This is usually accompanied by the little significant movement of the shoulders which we have borrowed from our French-Canadian relations-in-law expressly for use in this regard. We pick up the unfortunate volume from the bookseller's counter to which its too trustful author has confided it, and we turn its leaves in a manner we reserve for Canadian publications—a manner that expresses curiosity rather than a desire to know, and yet one that is somehow indicative of a foregone conclusion. Our other affairs are of so overwhelmingly important a character that our daily journals have no space for book reviews except at so much per agate line; and have too much to do in "encouraging" the industries to pay much attention to the arts. Commercial, agricultural, and sporting editors abound, but the literary editor is an unknown quantity, to be represented by x^n, who might multiply himself by himself even more frequently than that, as a general thing, without producing any appreciable result. Conversationally we carefully follow the example set us by the newspapers, and ignore the native-born person who has had the audacity to make a votive offering to the literary divinities, and the temerity to print it. If by any chance we refer to him or to his production it is in terms that suggest the dreariness of the void he has attempted to fill, and the futility of his attempt at filling it. As a general thing, however, we relegate them to the list of illustrations which will go to support our position at the next meeting of the Debating Club when Canadian letters form the subject of discussion. There are a great many debating clubs in Canada. It seems the favourite form of our mental activity. They are usually established to promote the humanities among us; and the growth of Canadian literature is a subject much preferred by the members, on account of its pathetic and facetious opportunities, these making an oratorical combination which is known to be irresistible. The conclusion is usually, I believe, that, owing to the obscure operation of some natural law, it is not indigenous to our country—that Canada, like the Congo State and other districts known to us chiefly through the pen of the explorer, must contribute to literature objectively.

It will not be the business of this paper to discover the reason of these extraordinary manifestations, and to set it up for the edification of all present and future debating societies. We will take it for granted that there must be a reason, that such a very distinct and widespread animus against Canadian literary efforts could hardly have taken possession of the compatriot breast without more or less adequate cause. The instinct that so readily guides our hands and eyes to the literary products of the country to the south of us must have sprung from conditions which it is possible to understand. But in view of the fact that such an instinct does control our book-buying operations and our literary appreciation to so great a degree, it is a little surprising that the authors of "An Algonquin Maiden" did not adopt the *ruse* of introducing it to their fellow-countrymen under the disguise of the imprint of Boston or New York. Great caution would doubtless have been necessary to prevent the fact of its home manufacture from prematurely leaking out, a difficulty which would have been enhanced by the reputation in letters which one of the volume's sponsors already possesses. Still, one is convinced that it might have been done; and while it is quite impossible to predict the precise effect of such a course upon the success of the novel, there are few who will deny that its circulation would have been "boomed" to an extent that would have more than counteracted the import tax. It is saddening to think that such an admirable opportunity for duping our hard-headed, political, prohibitionistic, excellent public into commendation of a book of its own has been lost, to say nothing of the tremendous joke of exploding the thing afterwards. Unless "An Algonquin Maiden" changes the situation very materially, however, the opportunity will still exist; and for the benefit of any future Canadian novelist who may not wish his work condemned on that account, I may add that this suggestion is not copyrighted.

How futile is the attempt to make broad highways in any department of literature, and say dictatorially to them that travel in that direction "Walk therein"! True, a general literary movement unfailingly controls the masses, who trot after established leadership with the docility and unanimity of certain quadrupeds; yet the beaten track is as conspicuous for the paths that lead deviously away from it, as for anything else. This is especially true of fiction, the art of which, having for its shifting and variable basis, humanity, is bound to present itself in more diverse forms than any other—constantly to find new ones, constantly to recur to old ones. Yet in fiction, rather more than anywhere else, are autocrats to be found, who announce to their scribbling emulators the only proper and acceptable form of the modern novel, announce it imperiously, and note departures from it with wrath. Hardly more months than one could reckon on one's fingers, and hardly years enough to reckon at all, have gone by since we became familiar with the principles and practice of the realistic school, for instance. We know the true definition of realism to be the everlasting glorification of the commonplace. If the commonplace and the remarkable could, by some reversion of natural laws, change places, we should immediately, we are told, become enamoured of the latter and indifferent to the former to such an extent that societies would have to be formed with the object of bringing the everyday extraordinary under public notice, and exciting public interest in familiar phenomena. Life under these conditions would be one long deification of the commonplace. In the meantime it springs all about us, vital and fragrant, and flowering as some weeds, but neglected—except by the realists—because it is a weed. Gentlemen of the realistic school, one is disposed to consider you very right in so far as you go, but to believe you mistaken in your idea that you go the whole distance and can persuade the whole novel-

82

writing fraternity to take the same path through the burdocks and the briars. Failing this, you evidently believe that you can put to the edge of the sword every wretched romancist who presumes to admire the exotic of the ideal, and to publish his admiration. This also is a mistake, for both of the authors of "An Algonquin Maiden" are alive, and, I believe, in reasonable health; and "An Algonquin Maiden" is a romance, a romance of the most uncompromising description, a romance that might have been written if the realistic school had never been heard of. One need go no further than the title to discover it a romance; "maidens" are unknown to the literary methods of a later date. They have become extinct, and are less euphonically replaced. Even in poetry usage has handed the word over to be, along with his coronet, the exclusive literary property of Lord Tennyson. More than this, the title boldly states, as well as implies, the character of the book. "A Romance," its authors have had the temerity to sub-title it, "of the Early Days of Upper Canada." This must be regarded as nothing less than a challenge to the modern idea of the form of latter-day fiction. One hardly knows whether most to admire the courage that inspired it, or to deprecate the reckless disregard for consequences that sent it forth into a world too apt, as we all know, to be unduly influenced by the opinion of the majority. But we cannot pause too long in this emotional vacillation. The fact is accomplished, published, and in all the bookstores; let us consider the fact.

"An Algonquin Maiden" is the beautiful foster-daughter of an old Indian chief. Her name is Wanda. She probably had another name, but the authors have mercifully left us in ignorance of it. The necessary struggle with the polysyllabic nomenclature of the noble red man has never yet been sufficiently considered among the facts inimical to Canadian immigration. Wanda is a sort of familiar in the household of Colonel Macleod, whose son Edward makes her the object of some-what less than one-half of his divided affections. Edward has a sister Rose, a bright, sprightly, charming little damsel, whose character is said to be an easily recognisable portrait. Rose is in love with one Allan Dunlop, a sturdy young Canadian Reformer, who reciprocates, but somewhat hopelessly, he believes, on account of the political opinions of the gentleman he is anxious to make his parent-in-law, who is a Tory of a type that can only be called cerulean. The remaining character of importance to the working out of the story is Mdlle. Hélène de Berczy, the rival of the Algonquin maiden for the somewhat unstable and irresponsible affections of Mr. Edward Macleod. The story runs naturally and easily through various stages in the affairs of these young people, in which jealousy plays an important emotional part, and the chief incident is an accident to the piquant little Rose, by which she is romantically shut up for some days in the old stone farm house of her Reformer lover, who adds bucolics to politics in his worthy career. True to the traditions of romance, the authors arrange a perfectly satisfactory termination of affairs for everybody concerned.

Odd numbers being incompatible with unalloyed bliss, Miss Wetherald drowns the unfortunate Algonquin maiden, in the chapter before the last, which she styles poetically "The Passing of Wanda"—drowns her in a passage of such sympathetic grace that one becomes more than reconciled to the sad necessity of the act, and convinced that the love-smitten Algonquin maiden herself could ask no happier fate.

One is struck in reading this book by the vast scope for word-painting in the matter of Canadian scenery, that has been lying comparatively waste, so to speak, under the very eyes and pens of former Canadian story-writers. Its opportunities cannot be said to have been totally neglected; but Miss Wetherald, who writes with a strong poetic, as well as romantic, bias, has so enthusiastically availed herself of them as to completely overshadow any former attempt that comes easily to one's memory. The story passes through two summers and a winter of country life in the vicinity of Lake Simcoe, and upon almost every page one may see traces of Miss Wetherald's sympathy with each and all of Nature's moods. This passage seems to come straight from the depths of her impressionable nature, and may be taken as illustrative of much that owns the same source:

> The Canadian winter, with its bright, fierce days and sparkling nights, was upon them, but it held no terrors for the young hearts that met it in a mood as defiantly merry as its own. Only a suffering or a morbid nature sees in winter the synonym of death and decay; fancies that mourning and desolation is the burden of its gaily whistling winds; and regards the bare trees, rid of their dusty garments, and quietly resting, as shivering skeletons, and the dancing snowflakes as the colourless pall that hides from sight all there is of life and loveliness. Nature, when the labours of the year are over, sinks to rest beneath the fleecy coverings, lulled to sleep by the kindly yet frosty arms of the northern tempest. What wild, weird lullabies are sung to her unheeding ears, dulled by the lethargy of sleep. How early falls the darkness, and how late the long night lingers, the better to ensure repose to the sweet mistress of the earth! How bright the starry eyes of heaven keeping watch above her rest!

The dialogue, as a rule, is sprightly rather than strong, the chapter entitled "When Summer Days Were Fair" being an especially gay little bit of writing, and the incident of Lady Sarah Lennox's familiar escapade in Brussels narrated with much happy grace. We are much interested in the Indian annals and legends to which we are introduced by the way; yet the carping critic in us cries out at the idea of putting them in the mouth of an Algonquin chief in such grandiloquent manner as this:

> By its clear light they saw, far in the distance, two strange, enormous things moving towards them. But whether these things were writhing wreaths of thunderclouds descended to earth, or gigantic trees denuded of their foliage and suddenly gifted with the power of motion, or whether they were wild beasts of a size never seen before, they could not tell.

If this is a genuine product of the aboriginal intelligence fifty years ago, one is moved to tears at the thought of its degeneration under the vitiating influences of modern civilisation since.

Mr. Adam's hand is easy to detect in the book. He does not romance. He will be doubtless equally guilty in the eyes of the realistic host with Miss Wetherald in supplying the facts upon which the romance is based; but we do not catch him in *flagrante delicto* anywhere. He does not allude to the Macleod's man-of-all-work as "the ancient servitor," to Edward Macleod as "the young master of Pine Towers," or to Miss de Berczy as "the lovely Hélène," and Miss Wetherald does. Nor does he anywhere stand confessed in such a sentence as:

> Edward rose and beheld in the open doorway Hélène de Berczy; her large glance, darker than a thundercloud, was illumined by a long lightning flash of merciless irony.

As Edward had been kissing the Algonquin maiden, one cannot help feeling that this was precisely what he deserved; yet it is retribution which evokes a certain pity.

To return to Mr. Adam, it is impossible to help wishing that his guiding and restraining hand were evident upon more pages of "An Algonquin Maiden" than it is. Where he assists in the character portraiture, the result is much more satisfactory than Miss Wetherald's unaided creations, delicate and graceful though some of these may be. Allan Dunlop is decidedly the strongest individual in the book, and he owes most of his personality to Mr. Adam. The historical and political parts of the volume, which form by no means too much ballast for Miss Wetherald's more aerial writing, we owe entirely to Mr. Adam; and it will probably be wished in many quarters that we had been given more chapters like that upon "Politics at the Capital," even at the expense of a few of the sort of that upon "A Kiss and its Consequences." Mr. Adam has displayed a tact in this part of the volume which should commend it to all classes in this politically-rent Canada of ours who appreciate anything like a considerate treatment of their prejudices. Well aware that the foibles of both the early pioneers of Reform and the upholders of the Family Compact have descended almost intact unto the second and third generations, and doubtless desirous, above all things, to avoid fanning the flame of Provincial party strife, Mr. Adam alludes to their early disputes in such terms as these:

> Of many of the members of the ruling faction of the time it may not become us now to speak harshly, for most of them were men of education and refinement, and in their time did good service to the State. If, in the exercise of their office, they lacked consideration at times for the less favoured of their fellow-colonists, they had the instincts and bearing of

gentlemen, save, it may be, when, in conclave, occasion drove them to a violent and contemptuous opposition to the will of the people. But men—most of all politicians—naturally defend the privileges which they enjoy, and the exceptional circumstances of the country seemed at the time to give the holders of office a prescriptive right to their position and emoluments.

While the numerous admirers of William Lyon Mackenzie find their ire allayed and their sympathies appealed to by paragraphs like the following:

Chief among these actors, at the time of which we are writing, was he whose printing-presses had just been ruthlessly demolished, and whose founts of type youthful Torydom had gleefully consigned to the deep. The provocation had been a long series of intemperate newspaper criticism of the Government, numerous inflammatory appeals to the people to rise against constituted authority, and much scurrilous abuse of the leading members of the "Family Compact," who wished, as a safeguard against revolution and chaos, to crush the "Patriot" Mackenzie, and drive him from the Province. But, though thorny as was then the path of Reform, and galling the insult and injury done to its martyrs, Mackenzie did not shrink from pursuing the course cut out for himself, and his intense hatred of injustice, and sturdy defiance of those whom he held responsible for the maladministration of affairs, gained him many adherents and sympathizers.

While congratulating Mr Adam upon the diplomacy with which he has compassed a somewhat complex situation, one cannot help observing in the necessity for it another and an unsuspected difficulty which besets authorship in Canada.

1887

Outworn Literary Methods

Once upon a time, quite within the memory of the present generation, there lived and flourished in a well-cultivated quarter of the Literary Field, a colony of highly respectable Subjects. They were remarkable for many things, but chiefly for their integrity and their great age. They could hardly be considered Subjects of current interest, since for reasons of avoirdupois they never ran, but invariably assumed the ordinary gait of dignified pedestrianism. In the matter of pedigree they were irreproachable; most of their ancestors, indeed, had appeared in *The Tatler*, and the preservation of family characteristics was extraordinary. Their conduct in print was as circumspect as these circumstances would lead one to suppose. They never acquired the pernicious habit of foreign travel; but stayed sedately at home in the pamphlets which fate had assigned them. Nor did they permit themselves to be influenced as to their garb by any of the frivolous fashions of the day, but walked abroad with plenty of breadth in their broadcloth and plenty of starch in their ruffles, and commanded the deep respect of all with whom they came in contact. In those days, say the few whose recollection is to be trusted, such as *The Times* or *The Spectator*, less regard was had for the sartorial art in literature, and Subjects of good character and recognised importance were venerated for their sterling merits alone, by a public with a mind above buttons. And we value this opinion more properly when we reflect that it is only through such estimable publications that it is possible to obtain an occasional introduction to any of these worthies that happen to survive. Their descendants, it is needless to say, are to be met everywhere, jaunty fellows, costumed in the latest mode, more knowing by a whole encyclopaedia than their grand-fathers, as is the character of the present generation, taking their cue cunningly instead of giving it dictatorially, clever children of time and circumstance, born often without a conscience, gay, short-lived *flaneurs* of literary society. A democracy in themselves, they are treated democratically, jostled about among the Advertisements, a very common lot, criticised, contradicted, condemned, without scruple. This is true not only of the most degenerate, but of those whose temper the spirit of the age has changed unmistakeably for the better. We did not set out, however, to discuss our own attitude towards brain-creatures that have grown out of the clothes and the manners of their forefathers, but to inspect the cast-off garments and discarded theories of deportment. We shall find them in the attic of every writer's brain, cobwebbed and dusty from their long retirement from public usefulness. Very well he knows that they are there, but he is much too tender a parent to send his offspring forth into a gibing world tricked out in them

For he has discovered that, apart from the peculiar virtue of style most adapted to its treatment, no matter can easily be made acceptable to a public actually spoiled by virtues of style. The themes of civilisation are as old as civilisation. We change, however, within the limits prescribed for us, and we demand change in the treatment of them, lest we become wearied in contemplating the extremely finite nature of our speculations. Originality is little more than dexterity. And this has all been said many times before. . . .

In fiction, that literary department that knows only the limits of human nature, there is the greatest change. All orthodoxy is gone out of it. It does not matter in the least whether there is a heroine or not, and if there is her ultimate fate is of no consequence whatever. To the casual observer little order or method seems to prevail in the set of circumstances taken apparently at random from anybody's experience, and cut off at both ends to suit the capacity of the cover. But in this respect appearances are deceitful. The novel of to-day may be written to show the culminative action of a passion, to work out an ethical problem of every-day occurrence, to give body and form to a sensation of the finest or of the coarsest kind, for almost any reason which can be shown to have a connection with the course of human life, and the development of human character. Motives of this sort are not confined to any given school or its leaders, but affect the mass of modern novel writers very generally, and inspire all whose work rises above the purpose of charming the idle hour of that bored belle in her boudoir, whose taste used to be so exclusively catered to by the small people in fiction. The old rules by which any habitual novel reader could prophesy truly at the third chapter how the story would "come out" are disregarded, the well-worn incidents discarded, the *sine qua nons* audaciously done without. Fiction has become a law unto itself, and its field has broadened with the assumption.

The practical spirit of the age has subtler, farther-reaching influences than we dream of. It requires simplicity in the art of the pen for readier apprehension in a busy time. Even the sciences appear divested of their old formalism and swagger. It demands sensation by the shortest nerve route. It has decided for light upon some practical subjects through plain window panes to the partial exclusion of stained glass embellished with saints and symbols. It asks, in short, that adaptation of method to matter which is so obscure yet so important a factor in all literary work.

1887

[New Directions in Fiction]

Perhaps nothing is more characteristic of the movement in fiction of the last decade than its vigorous trend in the direction of translations. The foreign element in the fiction of the average country town public library used to consist almost exclusively of "Les Miserables" and "Selections" from Balzac, with possibly a translation of "Manon Lescaut" which had slipped in by the inadvertence of the board of directors, or the somewhat limited acquaintance enjoyed by these gentlemen with the French classics. Perhaps it is not much better now, for the country town library is slow of assimilation and its directorate apt to be of the opinion that all foreign literary matter emanates directly from the devil; but there is at least the opportunity to-day for its shelves to be replenished with the very boldest and best of the novelists working under the various independent theories of their age and country. The readers of such libraries may lay themselves under the spell of almost the whole of the imcomparable "Comedie Humaine"; they may know the grace and penetrating charm of Daudet; the throbbing realism of Flaubert; may read between the lines all the subtle philosophy of Georges Sand in the light of her passionate life. A whole new set of ethics in fiction may be revealed to them in the novels of Tolstoi. Tourgenieff they had in English before, and half a dozen other notable Russians are available in French. These two great foreign schools absorb three quarters of the interest of the reading public, but the thought of any number of isolated novelists belonging to other countries reaches our public—of Germany, Italy, Spain, Scandinavia, even of Japan. Popular interest in books of this sort has risen to a height which must astonish the publishers, accustomed as they have been to find a prejudice instead, arising from the unfamiliar names, the unrecognizable social situations, the foreign character ideals of other than Anglo-Saxon fiction makers. The average novel reader likes above all a book in which his imagination will permit him to feel at home, a book in which the people talk as he would like to have talked, and act as he would like to have acted, and a book which makes any number of sacrifices of the probabilities in order to arrive at an orthodox and comfortable conclusion. At least, that is what the average novel reader used to like. And he could not bear the foreign novel because he never could get into relation with it. But his taste appears to be undergoing a change—a conversion to catholicity.

This tendency to the introduction of foreign literature has been made the basis of an argument that deduces intellectual poverty at home. It is not a fair deduction. The last decade in England and America has produced no Balzacs or Tolstois yet recognized, but it must be remembered that Balzac and Tolstoi are of no decade, but each of his century. And we have plenty of native books that compare more than favourably with the minor foreign productions borne in to our shores on the wave that brings the greater ones. It is not necessary either to suppose that because people are reading foreign books they are not also reading home productions. There is no exclusive principle of that sort in literature. The more widely the taste of the people is developed in these matters the keener and readier their appreciation of the things which are at hand. It is certainly pleasanter, and I think juster, to attribute this new and growing interest to the love of travel which has been so increased by the cheap, quick and easy modern means of going abroad, to the object lessons of commerce which throw so strong a light upon domestic and social life other than ours, and to the expanding perception and delight in process which is one of the characteristics of the better literary taste of the age, and which is abundantly gratified in the observation of foreign methods.

Whatever its cause, the result of the admission of these new influences upon the minds of fiction-makers in English must be an interesting one. We have no business rashly to conclude that our novelists were subject to them before, in the original, with all the additional potency of the foreign vehicle for the foreign idea. If the average novelist is much of a linguist, his work, adorned as it often is with the most commonplace of conventional foreignisms, fails to show it. It would be much more reasonable to conclude that he is not usually a university graduate, by the same token and for much the same cause he is not usually versed in the language. The average novel does not represent so much stock in popular interest to its author, upon the dividends of which he can enjoy American conforts at home and European luxuries abroad, pay his taxes and educate his family. A W. D. Howells may enchain the multitude, and go and live sumptuously in Florence on the income from his books, acquiring Italian enough to make him a critic of the poets of that country. A Robert Louis Stevenson may lead it with a torch into regions of psychical darkness unexplored before, and reap the wherewithal to travel to the United States and add all the various dialects of American to his list of lingual acquaintances. But W. D. Howells and Robert Louis Stevenson are not producers of the average novel. A fair type of that class might be taken from among working journalists, professors, lawyers or doctors, men whose efforts, in fiction are put forth chiefly to supplement a main income from another source, and are not at all necessarily indicative of either the desire or the opportunity for lingual accomplishments. The work of an author of this class must be influenced more or less, according to his receptivity, by this new insight into foreign ideals and their treatment. He will miss the subtlest part of the art in the adaptation of the native word to the native uses, but the force of the central idea and the significance of the episodes that cluster about it cannot fail to impress him. The effect of this will not be found in any change of his human and other material, for the average novelist must employ, to be successful, always that which lies close to hand, but in the way in which he regards his material, and the use to which he puts it. And as the great body of society is more affected in its principles and purposes by the average novel than it cares to admit, the effect there will also doubtless reward the observer.

It is not pleasant to note the more frequent occurrence of the novel with theological aims to serve. Before the prejudices awakened by "The New Antigone," in Roman Catholic interests, have quite subsided, comes *Robert Elsmere*, in the interests apparently of a kind of Christianity without Christ. This last book is of a literary stature to attract the attention of two such eminent critics as Mr. Gladstone and Mr. Andrew Lang, who have both reviewed it, although Mr. Lang's article does give one the impression that it was Mr. Gladstone's action in the matter that drew the later reviewer's wondering attention to the novel and led him to believe that it was worth while to record a different opinion. The theological romance always starts with a fair-seeming resemblance to all other romances. If the doctrinal bias of any of its people is disclosed, that of the author is not even hinted at until the reader is well under way, and has allowed himself the luxury of absorption in scenes and events that are new to him. Then by degrees is unfolded the motion of the book, at first almost casually, then with detectible system, finally, with all the passionate sincerity of apostleship. And with conviction upon this point comes to the reader a sense of being treacherously used. He has taken up this romance in the belief, if he has gone to the trouble of believing anything about it, that it shares the prime purpose of all fiction to him, that of amusing the oft depressed human product of civilization. He wouldn't have objected to some large general aims of a lofty character in connection with the amusement, that he should be uplifted by contemplation of heroism or stirred by imaginary contact with generosity. But this interference with his own private and unassailable convictions of dogma, this gratuitous instruction in matters where he firmly believes his education complete, above all this trickery whereby he has been induced to enter an argument, in which there is no personal satisfaction in talking back, he very naturally resents. He leans back in his chair with an air of irritation, and says "Bah!" The interjection explains his state of mind, and it is not a pleasant state of mind to feel one's self liable to as the result of any chance romance that may form one's summer indulgence.

Mr. Lang's preference for taking his theology "neat" is a preference he shares with a good many people. One does not easily think of an essayist more popular in his likes and dislikes than Mr. Andrew Lang. As children object to finding a rhubarb powder in a teaspoonful of raspberry jam, so do we object to finding tenets *perdus* in the seductive pages of our romances. They are not easier to take that way either. As we remember of the other experience, the bitter always stays on our tongues to be swallowed at leisure, while the sweet is quite spoiled by the mixture.

Fiction seems determined to broaden its scope in all directions. Its encroaches upon metaphysical, scientific and economic ground within the last few years have been marked. Imagination alone would form most insufficient capital for the novelist of to-day. And it is quite excusable if in its exultant march forward an ambitious department of literature should take some false steps.

1888

Charles G. D. Roberts
1860-1943

The son of an Anglican minister, Charles George Douglas Roberts was born at Douglas, New Brunswick, and raised in a country parish near the Tantramar Marshes. Following his graduation from the University of New Brunswick, Roberts published his first collection of verse, *Orion and Other Poems*, in 1880. During his career, Roberts was an editor, critic, historian, translator, poet and novelist. Among his best-known novels are: *The Heart of the Ancient Wood* (1900); *Barbara Ladd* (1902); *The Heart That Knows* (1906); and *In The Morning of Time* (1919). Roberts has also been credited with initiating the realistic animal story with works such as *The Kindred of the Wild* (1902) and *Red Fox* (1905).

From
The Kindred of the Wild
The Animal Story

Alike in matter and in method, the animal story, as we have it to-day, may be regarded as a culmination. The animal story, of course, in one form or another, is as old as the beginnings of literature. Perhaps the most engrossing part in the life-drama of primitive man was that played by the beasts which he hunted, and by those which hunted him. They pressed incessantly upon his perceptions. They furnished both material and impulse for his first gropings toward pictorial art. When he acquired the kindred art of telling a story, they supplied his earliest themes; and they suggested the hieroglyphs by means of which, on carved bone or painted rock, he first gave his narrative a form to outlast the spoken breath. We may not unreasonably infer that the first animal story—the remote but authentic ancestor of "Mowgli" and "Lobo" and "Krag"—was a story of some successful hunt, when success meant life to the starving family; or of some desperate escape, when the truth of the narrative was attested, to the hearers squatted trembling about their fire, by the sniffings of the baffled bear or tiger at the rock-barred mouth of the cave. Such first animal stories had at least one merit of prime literary importance. They were convincing. The first critic, however supercilious, would be little likely to cavil at their verisimilitude.

Somewhat later, when men had begun to harass their souls, and their neighbours, with problems of life and conduct, then these same animals, hourly and in every aspect thrust beneath the eyes of their observation, served to point the moral of their tales. The beasts, not being in a position to resent the ignoble office thrust upon them, were compelled to do duty as concrete types of those obvious virtues and vices of which alone the unsophisticated ethical sense was ready to take cognisance. In this way, as soon as composition became a *métier*, was born the fable; and in this way the ingenuity of the first author enabled him to avoid a perilous unpopularity among those whose weaknesses and defects his art held up to the scorn of all the caves.

92

These earliest observers of animal life were compelled by the necessities of the case to observe truly, if not deeply. Pitting their wits against those of their four-foot rivals, they had to know their antagonists, and respect them, in order to overcome them. But it was only the most salient characteristics of each species that concerned the practical observer. It was simple to remember that the tiger was cruel, the fox cunning, the wolf rapacious. And so, as advancing civilisation drew an ever widening line between man and the animals, and men became more and more engrossed in the interests of their own kind, the personalities of the wild creatures which they had once known so well became obscured to them, and the creatures themselves came to be regarded, for the purposes of literature, as types or symbols merely,— except in those cases, equally obstructive to exact observation, where they were revered as temporary tenements of the spirits of departed kinsfolk. The characters in that great beast-epic of the middle ages, "Reynard the Fox," though far more elaborately limned than those which play their succinct roles in the fables of either "AEsop" or "Aesop", are at the same time in their elaboration far more alien to the truths of wild nature. Reynard, Isegrim, Bruin, and Greybeard have little resemblance to the fox, the wolf, the bear, and the badger, as patience, sympathy, and the camera reveal them to us to-day.

The advent of Christianity, strange as it may seem at first glance, did not make for a closer understanding between man and the lower animals. While it was militant, fighting for its life against the forces of paganism, its effort was to set man at odds with the natural world, and fill his eyes with the wonders of the spiritual. Man was the only thing of consequence on earth, and of man, not his body, but his soul. Nature was the ally of the enemy. The way of nature was the way of death. In man alone was the seed of the divine. Of what concern could be the joy or pain of creatures of no soul, to-morrow returning to the dust? To strenuous spirits, their eyes fixed upon the fear of hell for themselves, and the certainty of it for their neighbours, it smacked of sin to take thought of the feelings of such evanescent products of corruption. Hence it came that, in spite of the gentle understanding of such sweet saints as Francis of Assisi, Anthony of Padua, and Colomb of the Bees, the inarticulate kindred for a long time reaped small comfort from the Dispensation of Love.

With the spread of freedom and the broadening out of all intellectual interests which characterise these modern days, the lower kindreds began to regain their old place in the concern of man. The revival of interest in the animals found literary expression (to classify roughly) in two forms, which necessarily overlap each other now and then, viz., the story of adventure and the anecdote of observation. Hunting as a recreation, pursued with zest from pole to tropics by restless seekers after the new, supplied a species of narrative singularly akin to what the first animal stories must have been,—narratives of desperate encounter, strange peril, and hairbreadth escape. Such hunters' stories and travellers' tales are rarely conspicuous for the exactitude of their observation; but that was not the quality at first demanded of them by fireside readers. The attention of the writer was focussed, not upon the peculiarities or the emotions of the beast protagonist in each fierce, brief drama, but upon the thrill of the action, the final triumph of the human actor. The inevitable tendency of these stories of adventure with beasts was to awaken interest in animals, and to excite a desire for exact knowledge of their traits and habits. The interest and the desire evoked the natural historian, the inheritor of the half-forgotten mantle of Pliny. Precise and patient scientists made the animals their care, observing with microscope and measure, comparing bones, assorting families, subdividing subdivisions, till at length all the beasts of significance to man were ticketed neatly, and laid bare, as far as the inmost fibre of their material substance was concerned, to the eye of popular information.

Altogether admirable and necessary as was this development at large, another, of richer or at least more spiritual significance, was going on at home. Folk who loved their animal comrades—their dogs horses, cats, parrots, elephants—were observing, with the wonder and interest of discoverers, the astonishing fashion in which the mere instincts of these so-called irrational creatures were able to simulate the operations of reason. The results of this observation were written down, till "anecdotes of animals" came to form a not inconsiderable body of literature. The drift .of all these data was overwhelmingly toward one conclusion. The mental processes of the animals observed were seen to be far more complex than the observers had supposed. Where instinct was called in to account for the elaborate ingenuity with which a dog would plan and accomplish the outwitting of a rival, or the nice judgment with which an elephant, with no nest-building ancestors behind him to instruct his brain, would choose and adjust the teak-logs which he was set to pile, it began to seem as if that faithful faculty was being overworked. To explain yet other cases, which no accepted theory seemed to fit, coincidence was invoked, till that rare and elusive phenomenon threatened to become as customary as buttercups. But when instinct and coincidence had done all that could be asked of them, there remained a great unaccounted-for body of facts; and men were forced at last to accept the proposition that, within their varying limitations, animals can and do reason. As far, at least, as the mental intelligence is concerned, the gulf dividing the lowest of the human species from the highest of the animals has in these latter days been reduced to a very narrow psychological fissure.

Whether avowedly or not, it is with the psychology of animal life that the representative animal stories of to-day are first of all concerned. Looking deep into the eyes of certain of the four-footed kindred, we have been startled to see therein a something, before unrecognised, that answered to our inner and intellectual, if not spiritual selves. We have suddenly attained a new and clearer vision. We have come face to face with personality, where we were blindly wont to predicate mere instinct and automatism. It is as if one should step carelessly out of one's back door, and marvel to see unrolling before his new-awakened eyes the peaks and seas and misty valleys of an unknown world. Our chief writers of animal stories at the present day may be regarded as explorers of this unknown world, absorbed in charting its topography. They work, indeed, upon a substantial foundation of known facts. They are minutely scrupulous as to their natural history, and assiduous contributors to that science. But above all are they diligent in their search for the motive beneath the action. Their care is to catch the varying, elusive personalities which dwell back of the luminous brain windows of the dog, the horse, the deer, or wrap themselves in reserve behind the inscrutable eyes of all the cats, or sit aloof in the gaze of the hawk and the eagle. The animal story at its highest point of development is a psychological romance constructed on a framework of natural science.

The real psychology of the animals, so far as we are able to grope our way toward it by deduction and induction combined, is a very different thing from the psychology of certain stories of animals which paved the way for the present vogue. Of these, such books as "Beautiful Joe" and "Black Beauty" are deservedly conspicuous examples. It is no detraction from the merit of these books, which have done great service in awakening a sympathetic understanding of the animals and sharpening our sense of kinship with all that breathe, to say that their psychology is human. Their animal characters think and feel as human beings would think and feel under like conditions. This marks the stage which these works occupy in the development of the animal story.

The next stage must be regarded as, in literature, a climax indeed, but not the climax in this genre. I refer to the "Mowgli" stories of Mr. Kipling. In these tales the animals are frankly humanised. Their individualisation is distinctly human, as are also their mental and emotional processes, and their highly elaborate powers of expression. Their notions are complex; whereas the motives of real animals, so far as we have hitherto been able to judge them, seem to be essentially simple, in the sense that the motive dominant at a given moment quite obliterates, for the time, all secondary motives. Their reasoning powers and their constructive imagination are far beyond anything which present knowledge justifies us in ascribing to the inarticulate kindreds. To say this is in no way to depreciate such work, but merely to classify it. There are stories being written now which, for interest and artistic value, are not to be mentioned in the same breath with the "Mowgli" tales, but which nevertheless occupy a more advanced stage in the evolution of this genre.

It seems to me fairly safe to say that this evolution is not likely to go beyond the point to which it has been carried to-day. In such a story, for instance, as that of "Krag, the Kootenay Ram," by Mr. Ernest Seton, the interest centres about the personality, individuality, mentality, of an animal, as well as its purely physical characteristics. The field of animal psychology so admirably opened is an inexhaustible world of wonder. Sympathetic exploration may advance its boundaries to a degree of which we hardly dare to dream; but such expansion cannot be called evolution. There would seem to be no further evolution possible, unless based upon a hypothesis that animals have souls. As souls are apt to elude exact observation, to forecast any such development would seem to be at best merely fanciful.

The animal story, as we now have it, is a potent emancipator. It frees us for a little from the world of shop-worn utilities, and from the mean tenement of self of which we do well to grow weary. It helps us to return to nature, without requiring that we at the same time return to barbarism. It leads us back to the old kinship of earth, without asking us to relinquish by way of toll any part of the wisdom of the ages, any fine essential of the "large result of time." The clear and candid life to which it reinitiates us, far behind though it lies in the long upward march of being, holds for us this quality. It has ever the more significance, it has ever the richer gift of refreshment and renewal, the more humane the heart and spiritual the understanding which we bring to the intimacy of it.

1902

Gilbert Parker
1862-1932

Born at Camden East, Canada West, Horatio Gilbert Parker was educated at the University of Toronto. In 1885 he travelled to Australia where he worked as a journalist, and in 1889 he moved to England where he established a reputation both as a novelist and as a politician. Knighted in 1902, Parker became a baronet in 1915, a member of the Privy Council in 1916. Following the success of his first collection of short stories, *Pierre and His People* (1892), Parker published more than thirty volumes of fiction, including: *The Chief Factor* (1893); *When Valmond Came to Pontiac* (1895); *The Seats of the Mighty* (1896); and *The Right of Way* (1901). "Fiction—Its place in the National Life" was published in *The North American Review* in December, 1907.

Fiction—Its Place in the National Life

The art of fiction, so honored in the world of late years, and somewhat ruthlessly practised, does not, as a definite convention, go further back than the time of Louis XIV of France, and we Anglo-Saxons cannot point to great writers of novels previous to the days of the Guelphs and Defoe, though Boccaccio, in Italy, laid the foundations of the art while yet we had no Boccaccio in England. Painting, beautiful, sensitive, sincere, belongs to the first records of humanity; as witness the drawings upon the walls of the temples of Egypt, five thousand years old, the colors as fresh as the day they were painted. Architecture, too, scarcely less antique, had, four thousand years ago, a massive beauty never reached by mediaeval or modern practice. Music, also, in the mind of man, is almost coincident with the time when, as it is recorded, the morning stars sang together in the first wakefulness of the new-created world.

Yet the novelist is the oldest of them all, existing and potential in the musician, the painter, the architect; for story-telling was the beginning, as it is the end, of all they do, whether the story be of life's material events, the record of emotions only, or the adventures of the spirit. In the infancy of language the sensuous, passionate intellect of man, seeking to record its impressions, its memories and its deeds, had recourse to these other arts, these ciphers or symbols of the expanding soul.

Fiction is not a mushroom trade, a mere side issue of literature, but an art inherently as old as the oldest. Indeed, the story-teller, the first historian of life, is the master of all other artists in essence—as was Ptah the father of the gods—incarnating himself at last through sixty centuries into at least three master craftsmen whom it is the glory of the Anglo-Saxon race to have produced—Scott, Dickens and Thackeray.

The writing of fiction is one of the most curious phases of our own particular era. Everybody tries his or her hand at it. Men of many professions practise it, and ladies use it almost as a birthright. It is the medium of grave sociologists like Mallock, the affectation of historians like the late Mr. Froude, of the scientist-astronomer like M. Flammarion, of the naturalist like the late Mr. Grant Allen, of the scientific student like Mr. Wells, of the millionnaire like Mr. Astor, of the natural mechanician like Jules Verne. It is the secret ambition of more than one Minister and ex-Minister of the Crown, whose despatch-boxes carry plays unbaptized in the dew of public applause, and books intended for a more starry acclamation than Disraeli's. It is the recreation of the duchess beset by *ennui*, who, dowered with a coronet and the strawberry leaves, still reaches out discontented fingers for the bays; it is the umbrageous dissipation of the popular Archdeacon; it is the secret ambition of coming Lord Chief Justices.

It is hardly necessary to say that pamphleteering and covert autobiography, through the medium of character and dialogue, that the emotional sensations of the boudoir transferred to an open highway, paved with press cuttings, are not the art of fiction. Great writers do not grow up in a night. A book may have a fleeting success, and yet be neither a piece of literature nor a presentation of life. It may be a transcript of personal experiences with *cliché* deductions therefrom. It may glorify or decry some passing social fad. It may excite amusement by inserting authentic and piquant facts. It may touch up the idiosyncrasies of well-known people; but that is taking the bread of society journalists out of their mouths.

This leads to another natural inquiry as to the relation of popularity to the practice of any art. Popularity is a dangerous and uncertain guarantee of either the talented, the able or the honest man; and it is no test whatever of genius; but it always has some quality or force behind it. There are novelists almost universally scorned by critics, welcomed gayly by the public, and running through editions of many scores of thousands. We should not cherish the delusion that it is "the people down the area," the waiting-maid and the valet, who read these books. You will find them in the hands of distinguished bankers, lawyers, doctors, and professional and business men of all sorts. If you were to ask one of them why he reads these books, he would say: "I want things to take me out of my business. I don't care whether it is true or not; I want a good story; that is all." He asks, indeed, only that a story-teller tell a good story; and he asks what is the *raison d'être* of the novel.

To the novelist you come for a story, first and before all; and it is the first and last thing he should give you. In the telling of it he may exhaust the knowledge of the universe, he may write what is literature and present the *truth* of life as well; but the story, a simple and elementary thing, is the basis of all. Man's first instinct in his elementary moods is for the story pure and simple, though that story may be the story of a soul, not the exciting accidents of flood and field. Genius tells the story and reaches "the universal heart" as well.

In one respect the art of fiction differs from the other arts: it cannot be taught. The great men by whom so many warring disciples swear did not start with the idea of founding a school of this or of that— of idealism, or symbolism, or romanticism or realism. That spangled glory of turning an influence into a convention and a school belongs to the lesser lights. It is they who form so-called "schools" and "theories," and call them by the names of masters who are dead and cannot resist, or alive and dare not.

In the art of fiction the individual is thrown upon his own innate talent, or genius, as the case may be. He may know and understand how Scott and Victor Hugo and Turgenieff did their work; he may saturate himself with their style and their methods; but unless he has the proper temperament, which schools never give, he cannot pass their style or their method through the crucible of his own mind and spirit and produce a crystal of his own making in the end. The work of genius is always baffling to the ordinary intelligence seeking to probe its secret, and the imitation of it is pitifully bald. The shell is got, but not the kernel; the mannerism, but not the matter; the mask, but not the face divine.

No great and permanent work of fiction can properly or arbitrarily be labelled naturalistic, idealistic, romantic, realistic or symbolistic. Love and fighting are not necessarily romance; nor are soup-kitchens and divorce courts necessarily realism. If realism means minuteness of detail, and to be journalistic, in information, photographic in description and hopeless in finale, then "The Toilers of the Sea," "The Cloister and the Hearth" and "A Tale of Two Cities" are deeply realistic. But if the sweep of wide and powerful imagination, the rush of large ideas, the impact of great conflicting passions, the beauty of sacrifice, the celebration of simple and primitive emotions, the faith in the heart of the writer that good is the final goal of ill, are romanticism, then these tales are also highly romantic. Unhappiness or ugliness and doleful monotony of existence are not necessarily real life, nor are the gay delights of summer love or marriage ceremonies, or successful fightings, or sacrifice and chivalry, necessarily romance.

To my mind, the novelist with the true instinct does not stop to think whether he shall write a book which is realistic or a book which is romantical. If he does, so much the worse for him and for his readers. So soon as he sets out to follow a specific academical purpose, of drawing lines and limits with the calmness of a carpenter, you shall have the work of the carpenter, the special pleader, the feverish partisan of a method. Project human life and character within the precise limits of a system, and you get a cinematograph and a Punch-and-Judy show. Of course I do not say that there are no such things as realism and romanticism, idealism and symbolism; that there have been no great achievements and wide literary and artistic movements such as proceeded from David, Victor Hugo, Flaubert, Wagner, Constable, Turner, Tolstoy and Ibsen; but I do say that their imitators have missed the masters' great glow and pulse and wide motive, and have made into shibboleths and laws what were accidents, not principles, of the great men's methods. That which was incidental they make law; and they carry the law to extremes. For instance, it is much the custom to speak of any novel which deals with the past as romantical, and tales which have a super-abundance of photographic detail, as realistic. They are considered to be especially realistic if they treat of the sordid side of life. Therefore, in some quarters, there is a certain pious canon that nothing shall end well; that life is fatuous and futile; that there is none who is not mulcted by Fate in the long run. Yet the truth lies between these extremes, and I for one cannot but feel that the proportion of happiness and hope is greater than the proportion of despair and misery.

It is well for us not to be deceived by catchwords or phrases or labels. There is only one test for a novel: that it be first and before all a well-constructed story; that it deal sincerely with human life and character; that it be eloquent of feeling, have insight and revelation; that it preserve idiosyncrasy; and, above all, that it be sane and healthy.

As to style, when the man has real character, real power and genius, his style is himself. A book is a personality, though the author be hidden behind what he creates. That is, saturated, as he may have been by a hundred masters—and the more catholic he is the better for himself—out of all his education, out of all he has seen and read, out of the crucible where everything has been fused, is precipitated unconsciously his own style, informed by his own character. His own independence, his own courage of soul, his own way of looking at things, his own intuitions, sensations, temptations, weaknesses, powers, these all go to inform style—these and one thing more, and a reference to that will be made later. Meanwhile, perhaps, it would be interesting to consider the making of a novel.

First, we should set aside any misconception there might be as to great fiction being a transcript of life. Mere transcription is not the work of an artist. Were it so, we should have no need for painters, for photographers would do; no poems, for academical essays and Government Blue-books would do; no great works of fiction, for we have our usual sources of information, if information and presentation are all we want—the divorce court, the police court, the Stock Exchange, the young ladies' seminary, the marriage register, the Houses of Parliament and the peerage. These sources of information are not to be despised, but indeed they are only sources of information. To write fiction you must know facts; but you need not, and you must not, use them baldly. It is only the human significance of the facts which concerns you. It is the inwardness of facts which go to make fiction a history of life, its emotions, its passions, its sins, its reflections, its values. These you cannot photograph nor transcribe. The eye that sees, the instinct which reveals them, are the things that matter.

As to the choice of subject, there seems no reason why the artist should not choose any subject for his work if the finished production itself contributes to the decent satisfaction of the world, presents character, suggests an issue, and, above all, meets the two unchangeable and inevitable demands of art—beauty and truth. Taste is the arbiter of the subject, for true taste is always moral, always decent, always "on the side of the angels."

There are certain things which are only subjects for a technical reformer or précis-writer, for a sanitary inspector and for the physician, not for the novelist. The specialist puts down the facts merely, and they are only convincing if they are bald statements; they must not have literary eloquence; they cease then to be evidence. It is the art of the novelist to appeal to the imagination, to be eloquent; and his vivid and dramatic touch applied, at high pressure and heat, to that which is ugly and unsavory lifts it out of all porportion to its actual place in the life of the community. The motto of the writer of fiction should be, not "to show life as I see it," but "to show life as I know it." The one is the eye, the other is the soul. The first is the work of the photographer, the second the work of the artist.

Further, one is supposed to write of a country and of a people which one knows well. All achievement means knowledge of a kind, and cannot be got without it. The smallest story successfully done necessitates two things: a knowledge of character and a knowledge of the scene. The range may not be wide, but so far as it goes the basis of knowledge must be there.

Suppose that your novel is to be about the sea and the navy—the navy of England of a hundred years ago. To write of the sea adequately, you must know a ship like your hand—the use of every part of it, the duty of every sailor. You must know the tides, winds, weather—the particular waters and the littoral along which your ship moves, with its own peculiarities. Have you sea-fighting in your book? Then you must be able to fight two ships or a dozen with knowledge. You must know the etiquette of fighting as well as its facts. Your knowledge must not be merely imitative, it must be creative. You must not lift a famous or even an obscure sea-fight from history or books of adventure. You must be able on your own account, given certain conditions which you yourself make, to exploit a sea-fight of your own. You must know how to sail in triple line, attack before a wind, or to take attack upon a lee shore; you must know how to conduct a battle when breaking a line, or boarding, or laying athwart a hawse; how to fight in a stream, or in the seaway; how to dispose inside a harbor, or attack a leeward enemy. You must not talk of a sailor eating bread and butter, when, maybe, he only got cheese and oatmeal. You must not give him a pint of beer a day, when he received a gallon. You must not have your captain give a seaman fifty lashes, when, by law, he could only give twelve. You must know thoroughly the history of the time of which you write. All this, not because exactness is the chief thing in a story, but because the feeling of knowledge is security against that which is unreasonable. Manners, customs, dress, speech, mode of living, colloquialisms—all must be known—but not transcribed.

This sort of knowledge is confusingly called by the phrase-makers "local color," that perilous catchword which deludes the public and leads young writers to think that a phonograph and a guide-book are the weapons of fame. But without indulging in local color, it is only right to be accurate if you do indicate a fact. For, even though great critics say, "What does it matter?" when Sir Walter Scott made the sun set over the sea on the coast of Fife, or Victor Hugo in the "Toilers of the Sea" made the tide rise too high at Guernsey, or that master of detail, Kipling, chained the rowers in the galleys to the seats when, on the contrary, they rose up and down with the oar, as they do to-day in

Egypt, the same critics are equally happy when Macaulay walks up the Pass of Killiecrankie to verify the speed of the English army, or Scott gallops across the lea in the Vale of Forth to fix the time for Fitz-James's ride. On the whole, you must *know*, not that you may crowd your work with local color, but that you may give the effect of a true relation. At least you must picture a time and give an atmosphere. You must start with the certainty that you understand. For the world is not kind to those who make mistakes in matters that it knows. If the farmer finds that you make him bring in hay at six o'clock in the morning; the priest, that you compel him to say mass in the evening; the lady, that you describe *chiffon* as *fichu*; the military man, that you have him doff his hat instead of saluting; the naval man, that you put a rose in his buttonhole on the quarter-deck; the politician, that you speak of dissolution when you mean proroguing; the painter, that you speak of foreshortening when you mean perspective; the huntsman, that you send him to a meet in June; the sailor, that you call the scuppers the "bilge"; the citizen of a far country, that you salute his land as "Our Lady of the Snows" when you mean "Our Lady of the Green Parterre"—if all these good folk find you tripping in this way, how much credit do you think you will get for the general excellence of your work from the local critic and the innumerable Columbuses among our genial critics? You may have kept your reader out of bed till the small hours entranced, but if you stumble in one small fact that he knows, then, disregarding all else, he will mercilessly put you in the pillory, before an admiring family, at to-morrow's breakfast-table.

If, as we have assumed, your story be of the sea, then the sea must be the dominant note in it, the prevailing influence, the atmosphere; all that it is, the spirit of it must be yours; something in the look of it, in the feel of it, which possesses the man, which gets into his bone and blood; which possesses the sailor, the seafarer, as the mist, the storm, the mystery, the loneliness and the brooding, varying distance possess the mountaineer in his mountains. Then, as to translating that feeling into words, the whole thing is, What is the sea to you—the artist—to yourself? How do you see it with your naked eye, the eye which God gave you, and not another: as it were, the naïve, unalloyed look of the child, upon the retina of whose sight have not impinged a thousand confusing experiences of life? Turner was showing one of his great pictures to a merchant-prince of London; and, with the candor which only great wealth or great ignorance can beget, the merchant-prince said severely: "Mr. Turner, I shall tell you the truth. I have lived forty years on the Thames, and I never saw it look like that." And Turner replied: "No, but don't you wish to God you could?"

That is the whole question. Turner saw the thing not only with the trained physical eye, but with the eye of the spirit; with the refined directness, sincerity and genuineness of the child, and the great soul of a great man. The merchant-prince saw only a dull river, a highway of commerce, muddy, sluggish and unpoetical. His physical eye was untrained. He had never seen its actual glories of light and color; his soul had never felt its mystery, its piteous passionate story. To him it was common-place, like his own temperament.

The true artist, be he sculptor, painter or writer of fiction, tries to throw over all his characters the feeling of environment, natural, industrial and social, which possesses them, affects them, works upon them. What is it? You go into a city—a strange city. The smell of it has the character of the city; the feeling of the air belongs to it alone; the spirit possessing the people is in the air. What one might call the idiosyncrasy of that city is upon every man in it.

You go into a great manufacturing district, where the clang of the iron is in the footstep of the men; the grim, metallic precision of machinery is in the air—something stern, something severe, yet satisfying; something permanent, concentrated, yet restless; as if the spirit of invention were abroad, and the spirit of activity were laying its hands upon every man. He has soaked in that which is of the air, the idiosyncrasy of climate, the feeling of the soil itself. It is this influence of environment which must be conveyed before all. Almost the same emotional complications universally and throughout all ages occur in every land, every hemisphere; the characters dispose themselves differently in each *mise-en-scène*, express themselves through varying attributes—that is all—each after his kind. The situation is translatable into language of human emotions, derived from the universal Volapuk, the Vulgate of man in the Garden.

Othello the Moor, jealous of his wife, is, except so far as the men and their circumstances vary, little different from Mr. Jones of London, or Mr. Smith of New York, in the same situation. The daughters of Lear, chivying Cordelia from her heritage, are very little distinguishable, save in surroundings and in position, from the squabbling heirs of Chancery Lane. Recognizing these primary and universal elements of human experience, we gather what is true local color and dialect, and what is chiefly photography and superficial habits of speech or manner. A colloquialism, an idiom, a word in a phrase which reveals character, is the only true dialect; the spiritual, the inner atmosphere, is the only real local color.

The practical making of a novel must be permeated by the feeling that first inspired it, the note that should dominate it, with character not only individual but national, and above all with a universal humanity. The story should be constructed as a house is built, with knowledge and feeling as to which portion shall give the principal effect, with fine sense of proportion as to the parts. Consider how important a thing is the first page, the first scene in a book. Out of a whole life, or a number of lives, you must choose one incident, one scene, which shall act as a pivot for the whole story. You must strike the note which shall recur throughout the book like the *motif* in an opera, the Greek *Anamnesis*. No word should be written, no incident set down, which shall not appear later on, in effect, as inevitable to the end of the story as the beat of the pulse is to life. A story runs in a circle; it comes with philosophic certainty, and by natural throwing back, from its last effect to its first cause. A character is a law set in motion, its author cannot make it deny itself; it lives in the book according to the law of its being. It is, therefore, likely to lead the author rather than to follow him. There is no inspiration in the development of a character —that is a matter of pure logic. There is no inspiration in construction —that is a matter of strong brain, good reasoning power and architectural skill.

But we will suppose that you know your *mise-en-scène* as you know your pocket; that you feel your atmosphere, that you have your material heaped up before you, that you have your story in your mind; then comes the one thing needful beyond all others. That one thing needful is the inspiration of an idea—a central idea—the only true inspiration in a book.

A distinguished critic in a letter to me not long ago said: "I put down this book with joy; it contents me; there is in it one whole idea." A book can always be resolved into a phrase. The thing that gives vitality to skill, observation and experience is a thing you cannot touch. You cannot lay your finger on it and say, "I have it." It is the true artistic temperament; it is what may be called the flair of imagination. And to that temperament alone is given the rare idea which possesses, absorbs; which, by its own intensity, sweeps the author along to his achievement.

There is no true artist in fiction, painting and music but knows when his work has failed. Often he knows it and cannot help it. In 1891, as I stood with Sir Frederick Leighton in his studio before his half-finished picture "Solitude," he said to me: "Somehow it won't do. Look," said he, "there are a dozen studies I have made of this picture. I went into the country time after time to make sketches for it; but, after all, it hasn't come off. I have only six weeks before the Academy, and it mayn't come off at all." The next week, however, he went down again into the country, and brought back a new study. Now, at last, he had the idea right—the figure, the pose, the atmosphere, the feeling, the meaning; and now you shall find "Solitude" hung upon the walls of a thousand homes. There is no true artist but knows when his work has not come off. And this is the only revenge "we poor artist *vauriens*" can have upon our critics: they may praise us for our occasional virtues, or condemn us in Cambyses' vein; but we ourselves are the only people who do really know what is wrong. No great work was ever done unless there was a great central idea mastering the mind and heart of the artist, lifting him, driving him on, giving him dynamic power.

Mattnew Arnold called poetry a criticism of life. In that office it does not work alone. For a hundred and fifty years, fiction has played a part in the criticism of life, which is as definite, if not as profound, as that played by poetry. Imagination is the very root of progress in a nation's life—the power to visualize things unseen from a knowledge of things seen. No nation makes progress which has not a deep intellectual life, in which poetry and the arts, offspring of the imagination, are not renewing the blood, invigorating the pulse of the people, giving a spiritual impulse to the actions of men and governments, quickening the life of the family. Point to a country decadent materially, and you will find a nation with no living literature, art or scientific development —for science must not be dissociated from the spiritual and moral life of the people. Profoundly analytical and critical and dissolvent as it is, its highest office is to construct and create, harmonize, develop and apply the product of imagination to the practical issues and labors of usual life. Imagination is the very soul of all development—the prefiguring of the possible, the inspiration to do, which comes from spiritual discovery. Fiction, as a product of the imagination, should become a greater factor; it should play a higher and higher part, in the moral welfare of the nation. It is now a reflex of the life of the people, not so much by transcription of human experience, as in giving the central, moral and intellectual attitude towards all the grave questions which make the real history of a nation. In the field of fiction you will find the real position of the great sociological problems, not because they are deliberately dealt with, but because you discover in them the point of view taken involuntarily and unconsciously by the writer himself, who, whatever his class, is the product of his time. Dickens's and George Meredith's early novels are as much a history of the religious, moral and social conditions of England in that splendid period of its development, the early Victorian Era, as the works of John Henry Newman, Carlyle, Ruskin, Arnold, Tennyson and Kingsley specifically are a representation of the condition of certain departments of national thought and national life. And it is singular that the wonderful renaissance in religion of that day synchronized with progress in every other department of national existence. It was a time which brought forth Huxley, Darwin, Tyndall and great captains of a scientific industry which revolutionized the whole material life of the nation. It was all of a piece; all rose from the same Pierian spring; all was born of a great intellectual and moral and spiritual revival. The word "moral" is not here used in the sense of "morals" as represented by obedience to the Ten Commandments, but in the sense of a sane and wholesome right-mindedness which represents a people's character, gives it its position of influence in the world. It is natural to forbear making any comparisons between this time and that, further than to venture the opinion that we have progressed in the things that matter, while progressing also in purely material things. Yet perhaps we are also living in a narrow margin of safety, and there is all too apparent a tendency among a very large portion of the Anglo-Saxon world towards superficiality, towards a growing distaste to face the serious facts of life; and the immense popularity of fiction is one of the signs. There is less history, biography, popular science and travel read to-day—in England, certainly—than a generation ago, and this is incontestably true of poetry. Accumulated wealth, the vast conveniences of daily life and the tremendous multiplication of pleasures, have made us more restless, less reflective than we were, and our solid reading and thinking have declined. Newspapers and fiction are the chief intellectual pleasure of the great mass of the people, and particularly of young people—which is more serious. Fiction has taken an unduly prominent place in the life of the people; its influence is disproportionate to its value in the national life. For it is not books like "The Cloister and the Hearth," "Henry Esmond," "David Copperfield" or "The Heart of Midlothian", representing the best that the mind may profit from, which are eagerly and widely read, but the thousand inferior books which have in them neither literature, nor life, nor real imagination. It is to be hoped that the tide will turn; that simple biography and travel and popular history—with good fiction, good poetry and good drama—will more largely seize the minds of young men and young women.

The popularity of historical fiction was to be welcomed and approved. We have great reason to be grateful to Conan Doyle, Stanley Weyman and the American Winston Churchill for giving us, as did Kingsley, Charles Reade and Thackeray, tales of other days, inspired by the facts and circumstances of the time, a mirror of the life; for imagining and reconstructing the past, as does a great anatomist from the handful of bones given him the animal of whom they were the relics.

It is good to think that we have masters of fiction yet alive who hold the flag high, whose standards are the standards of their own forebears in the art. In England we have George Meredith and Thomas Hardy and Mrs. Humphry Ward; in America there are Mark Twain and W.D. Howells, captains of pure literature of which any nation should be proud—pure literature, whether in relation to the quality of the writing, or in the choice of subject and its treatment. They have done their part; and none more nobly, and in a more distinguished way, than Mr. Howells, who has been a great craftsman, a true and faithful observer of life, and a writer with as urbane and beautiful a style as lives. The world owes him much, his nation owes him more; and there are hundreds of thousands of people in "the States" whose tastes have been cultivated directly and indirectly by his books of fiction, through which there moves a personality of infinite charm.

Fiction in the United States has represented the birth of an intellectual life among the masses. There was once an aristocracy of intellect and culture in the United States, but now the democracy have reached out eagerly and definitely for "culture" as represented by good books in every department of thought; and fiction, as found chiefly in historical novels (some of them bad, others, like "Pembroke" and "Richard Carvell," good) has played a great part in stimulating the people at large to reading, outside the mammoth daily and weekly papers. The editors of the great magazines have been able to keep the standard of fiction high; and to-day, if a book popular on both sides of

106

the water sells a thousand in England, it sells ten thousand in America. And what is the end of it all, of all this writing of fiction? Is it no more than an aristocratic recreation? Is it only an amusement provided by a mummer? It is, it should be, a recreation of the noblest design; but I believe it is more still than that. All the good books, good paintings, good statuary, good buildings, if they are to be permanent, if they are to influence mankind, must make for beauty and for peace.

What is it that makes the oldest monuments of the world, those of Egypt, so powerful in their influence on the world? Look upon the temples of Karnac and of Thebes, upon the solitary Colossi seated in the Libyan plain, upon the stupendous repose of the giant figures cut out of the mount of granite at Abou Simbel. They seize and hold the mind and the heart of the spectator with so compelling a fascination that, in this modern civilization, you have a great illusion: six thousand years are displaced, and you live with Osiris and Amen-Ra and Seti and Rameses once again. What is it that you feel when you stand before the couchant Sphinx out there by the Pyramids of Egypt? It is not age alone: it is power; it is art; it is soul.

You stand beside a statue with a broken nose, a battered face. Think what it is to see this ruined profile, which, in real life, would make us turn away in pity and disgust, and then conceive the persistent, communicable power, the intrepid, unconquerable beauty, in your statue, which makes you sit longing, wondering; you yourself transported from this opulent Twentieth Century and the grossness of modern living into that beatitude of mind which is a severe simplicity, an exquisite calm, a tender sternness; a glory in stone which is as varying as the color on a girl's face in the springtime of her youth.

Art, even the art of fiction, must have beauty—the beauty of order, of discipline, of temperament, of imagination, of mystery—all these which are greater than exact facts, or details, which express the soul of things rather than the concrete image. And in the thing that is great there is no eccentricity, nothing that is morbid; it is all normal; but the normal form and power are infused with life, composed of genius. That which is eccentric is unnatural. Sanity, a supreme and perfect sanity, this is the great quality of art. To see things with right-mindedness; to judge coolly, and, having judged, then with the splendor of the imagination to fashion the thing which the brain conceived, and the hand performs—that is art, even the art of fiction.

This is one of the reasons why great books are read on and on. They are an artistic and intellectual investment and heritage. They are a human document offered in exchange for the nation's bonds. They have a place in the nation's life; they have permanency; they belong.

It is the joy of art and of the artist that no loving care is wasted; that the root you water and the plant you nourish, with careful affection and desire for its well-being and that of the world, gives shade and pleasure and content somewhere—to some human being; that, while the intrinsic excellence, the perfect detail, the good art and philosophy may often be passed over by the multitude, the sound humanity of the book does its work, it clothes people of the imagination with the illusion of reality and truth.

For us who write songs, tales or histories, nature and beauty repay us by so much as we let them come near to our souls. The nearer we let them come, the more generously are we repaid. The moral glow in the ambitions of him who strives, however inadequately, to express himself, to translate spiritual power and vision into practical being, strengthens the life of the nation, plays its part in the progress of humanity, though the man himself, at last, be buried deep under the discarded manuscript of his life's dreams. But indeed all arts, sciences, mechanisms, labors, businesses, industries and offices should lead to the one end—the enlightenment of race, the deepening of pure patriotism, the sense of common responsibility for the welfare of that particular family in the races of the world to which those who employ our human crafts belong. Character is what we should be making in all the arts, as in all the industries and labors of life. What better epitaph can you wish, statesman, merchant, scientist, farmer, mechanician, hewer of wood, drawer of water and writer of fiction, than these last words of Thomas Hardy's exquisite "Woodlanders":

"He was a good man and he done good things!"

1907

Charles Gordon
1860-1937

The son of a Presbyterian clergyman, Charles Gordon spent his early years in Glengarry County, Canada West. After studying at the University of Toronto and at the University of Edinburgh, he became a minister of the Presbyterian Church in 1890. Gordon's first novel, *Black Rock*, appeared in serial form in 1898 under the pseudonym Ralph Connor. The success of this work anticipated the popularity of two dozen later novels, including: *The Sky Pilot* (1899); *The Man From Glengarry* (1901); *Glengarry School Days* (1902); *The Foreigner* (1909); and *Torches Through the Bush* (1934). *Postscript to Adventure. The Autobiography of Ralph Connor* was published posthumously in 1938.

From
Postscript to Adventure. *The Autobiography of Ralph*
Connor
The Coming of Ralph Connor

Black Rock is an example of that rather rare thing in writing, a successful novel with a purpose. *Black Rock* is really a phenomenon in a way, indeed in several ways. I am too far on in life now, I hope, and moreover I have seen too much of the real things in life to lay myself open to the charge of egotism if I speak frankly about Ralph Connor and his books. When I sent those first three articles to Jim Macdonald I had no more thought of a book in my mind than I have now of flying to the North Pole. Slightly less in fact, for I should dearly like to encircle the pole in an airplane.

My sole purpose was to awaken my church in Eastern Canada to the splendor of the mighty religious adventure being attempted by the missionary pioneers in the Canada beyond the Great Lakes by writing a brief sketch of the things which as clerk of the biggest presbytery in the world I had come to know by personal experience.

When Jim Macdonald received my sketch he found no name attached as author and under the urge of the "printer's devil" he wired me in a frenzy, "What name shall I sign?" Now the choosing of a nom de plume is no easy matter. Desperately I scanned every horizon in my mind for a name, but all in vain. Nothing would come to me. In this crisis my eyes, roving over my desk, lit upon the heading on the note paper I was using as secretary of the British Canadian Northwest Mission, which was abbreviated into the form "Brit.Can.Nor.West Mission." The two contractions in juxtaposition caught my eye. I ran my pencil round them and had Can.Nor. So I wired Macdonald, "Sign article Cannor." The telegraph operator had never heard of such a being as "Cannor," but the Irish cognomen "Connor" was perfectly familiar to him. Hence the wire reached the editor "Sign article Connor." But this left my editor friend still in a quandary. Everyone would know it was a pseudonym. I can see him with his great hands tearing his shock of red hair as he vainly tried to fit all the Irish names he knew to Connor—"Mike," "Pat" "Terence"! At length straight out of the blue came "Ralph" and thus was born into the world of letters "Ralph Connor"—not an uneuphonious name. I have from the first quite liked it.

The name for the sketch with three chapters was found, but as yet there was no book and no thought of *Black Rock*. After reading the three chapters Macdonald wrote asking for three more. With my characters clearly conscious in my mind and with abundance of material lying at hand this was no difficult task. I sent to my editor three more chapters and followed with a third three. Thereupon Macdonald wrote me saying, "We will make a book." Having decided upon "a book," the next consideration was to find a publisher. With his nine chapters Macdonald went to New York. But America at the moment had slight interest in making books—she was busy making war with Spain. Besides, *Black Rock* would never go in America. It was "too religious," "too temperance." But Jim Macdonald thought he knew better. He determined that he would publish the book in Canada and publish it himself.

This was a daring venture. Few novels had ever been published in Canada, but he decided to risk the thing. But how large an edition? Macdonald was advised by leading Canadian booksellers to risk an edition of 800 copies. But the extraordinary interest which had been aroused in Canada by the nine chapters already published made Macdonald reckless. He determined "to go the whole hog," as he wrote me and publish an edition of 1,000 copies. Before the day of publication the element of risk had vanished. The first edition, I am glad to think, was published in Canada and reached the hitherto unapproached figure of 5,000 copies.

By this time, too, an American publisher had been discovered. In the publishing house of the Fleming H. Revell Company of Chicago there was an enterprising young clerk who was developing a nose for books, George H. Doran by name, a Canadian by birth and a bookman by the gift of God. He had followed the chapters in the *Westminster Magazine* and came to Macdonald with an offer for *Black Rock* which, though it was too late now to copyright in the United States, he was eager to publish. Macdonald accepted his offer and thus I came first into touch with George H. Doran who became eventually one of the three greatest publishers in America and one of the best and closest friends I have made during my life. Though he is no longer a publisher I am glad to say he is still one of my intimate friends. Before a year had passed, Jim Macdonald and George Doran's faith in me had been more than justified. *Black Rock* had gone some hundreds of thousands while with *The Sky Pilot*, which followed during the succeeding year, and *The Man from Glengarry*, two years later, the total issue was estimated by my publishers as over five million copies.

I have often tried to analyze the reaction upon my mind of this unique experience. But I have always failed. The comments and criticisms in the magazines and newspapers in both Britain and America were amazingly enthusiastic. I have attempted to explain this reception by a variety of reasons: *Black Rock* and *Sky Pilot* gave an authentic picture of life in the great and wonderful new country in Western Canada, rich in color and alive with movement, the stamping ground of the buffalo and his hunters, the land of the trapper, the Mounted Police and that virile race of men and women, the first pioneers who turned the wild wilderness into civilization. Then, the pictures were from personal experience. I knew the country. I had ridden the ranges. I had pushed through the mountain passes. I had swum my bronco across its rivers. I had met the men—Hi Kendal and Bronco Bill and the rest were friends of mine.

Another cause of the phenomenal editions of these Ralph Connor books, and a very influential cause, was the fact that though in fiction form they possess a definitely religious motif. Religion is here set forth in its true light as a synonym of all that is virile, straight, honorable and withal tender and gentle in true men and women. And it was this religious motif that startled that vast host of religious folk who up to this time had regarded novel-reading as a doubtful indulgence for Christian people. I have received hundreds of letters expressing gratitude for a novel that presented a quality of religious life that "red-blooded" men could read and enjoy.

Of all men, the most surprised at this reception of his books was Ralph Connor himself. He had not the slightest ambition to be a writer. He made little effort after polished literary style. Things just came to him and he put them down. Let me give a quite remarkable instance of that fact. While I was writing *Sky Pilot* it happened that one Sunday morning I was addressing a congregation of children and young people on the general topic, "The good that pain can do for us," a difficult enough problem to deal with. As I was standing before that gathering of youngsters there flashed upon my mind a picture of a canyon I knew well in the foothill country and then and there without preparation I told them the story of "how the canyon got its flowers":

"At first there were no canyons, but only the broad, open prairie. One day the Master of the Prairie, walking out over his great lawns, where were only grasses, asked the Prairie, 'Where are your flowers?' and the Prairie said, 'Master, I have no seeds.' Then he spoke to the birds, and they carried seeds of every kind of flower and strewed them far and wide, and soon the Prairie bloomed with crocuses and roses and buffalo beans and the yellow crowfoot and the wild sunflowers and the red lilies all the summer long. Then the Master came and was well pleased; but he missed the flowers he loved best of all, and he said to the Prairie: 'Where are the clematis and the columbine, the sweet violets and windflowers, and all the ferns and flowering shrubs?' And again he spoke to the birds, and again they carried all the seeds and strewed them far and wide. But, again, when the Master came, he could not find the flowers he loved best of all, and he said: 'Where are those, my sweetest flowers?' and the Prairie cried sorrowfully: 'Oh, Master, I cannot keep the flowers, for the winds sweep fiercely, and the sun beats upon my breast, and they wither up and fly away.' Then the Master spoke to the Lightning, and with one swift blow the Lightning cleft the Prairie to the heart. And the Prairie rocked and groaned in agony, and for many a day moaned bitterly over its black, jagged, gaping wound. But the Little Swan poured its waters through the cleft, and carried down deep black mold, and once more the birds carried seeds and strewed them in the canyon. And after a long time the rough rocks were decked out with soft mosses and trailing vines, and all the nooks were hung were clematis and columbine, and great elms lifted their huge tops high up into the sunlight, and down about their feet clustered the low cedars and balsams, and everywhere the violets and windflower and maidenhair grew and bloomed, till the canyon became the Master's place for rest and peace and joy."

I am not ashamed of that canyon picture. One Sunday night after I had preached to a great congregation in Pittsburgh on the theme, "The Problem of Pain" the minister of the church, after the genial American custom, invited any who desired to come forward and shake hands with the preacher. A thousand people and more passed before me shaking my hand. I remember only one, a girl, pitifully deformed, who paused before me and holding my hand in both of hers lifted a face pale, and bearing the marks of pain, but radiant and said in a low voice, "Oh, thank you for Gwen!" Then with a quick rush of tears in her eyes, "the flowers are beginning to grow in my canyon too." Of the many hundreds I have received I cherish the canyon letters most. They bring me the love and gratitude of those whose canyons of pain have been brightened with the flowers that bloom only in the canyon.

The Glengarry books, too, received an extraordinary welcome. George Doran has often said to me that it was *The Man from Glengarry* that won for him his place among American bookmen. His first American edition ran to ninety-eight thousand copies, later editions to many hundreds of thousands. One thing is true of the books. They grew out of Glengarry soil, out of Glengarry humanity. Let me tell you a story which I had from a young Glengarry lad whom I met in Winnipeg some years after the publication of the books.

"Those old Glengarry boys," he said, "believe them as they do the Bible. One old patriarch who in all his life had never read a novel until *The Man from Glengarry* and *Glengarry School Days* said to me, 'I know every man of them fellas except wan and him I cannot place.'

" 'But, Mr. McKenzie, you don't think that Ralph Connor is writing about actual people,' I said.

" 'And what else would he be doing?'

" 'Well, Ralph Connor is a novelist. He just makes up those things, you know.'

" 'Makes up them things, is it?' The old gentleman became indignant. 'And do you mean to tell me that a meenister of the gospel would be writing lies?' My old friend had not grasped the distinction between a novelist and a liar."

No one ever paid me a finer compliment than Mr. McKenzie.

The material of *The Man from Glengarry*, its color, action, its historic background, its human quality, all account to a certain degree for its extraordinary vogue. But not altogether. The best of the book I drew from the same source as that from which I drew my life. That Highland preacher with his mystic fire, his indomitable courage, his passionate loyalty to Scotland and all that belonged to it, its glens and lochs and purple heather hills, its weird ghost stories, its pibrochs and its Calvinistic theology, had much to do with the making of *The Man from Glengarry*. But the soul of the book, whatever of intellectual quality it has, its response to the appeal of beauty whether of the woods and wild flowers or of the things of the spirit, and all that is best in it Ralph Connor had from the Lady of the Manse. From her, too, he inherited a photographic quality of mind. Let me illustrate.

At the age of ten I left Glengarry with my family. Fifty years later I was driving with a school friend, Johnnie Robertson, north from the eighteenth concession.

"Johnnie, I know this road," I said. "It takes a turn to the left through a swamp about half a mile from here."

"Well," said Johnnie, "the turn is there sure enough but the swamp is gone."

"Yes, and half a mile farther you come to the Brick Church and across the road to the east is Malcolm Fisher's house and beside it old Widdie Matheson's and to the north the little wooden Congregational Church."

"They're there still."

"And going east from the crossroads on the right were the Munroes and beyond them the Sinclairs and across from them Donald Alec used to live and next to him was Dickson's brick yard and beyond him the McNaughtons and the Fergusons."

"Every one right! Man, it's amazing!" exclaimed Johnnie.

And so I went on giving him a perfect photographic reproduction of the whole countryside. That quality, too, helped make vivid the Glengarry books.

Indeed so many persons, places and things entered into the making of those books that Ralph Connor's part seems almost incidental. However, he got hold of the string and "as he pulled the story grow."

1938

Lucy Maud Montgomery
1874-1942

Born at Clifton Corner, Prince Edward Island, Lucy Maud Montgomery was educated at Prince of Wales College in Charlottetown and at Dalhousie University. After working as a journalist and as a school teacher, she became famous as a novelist when her first book, *Anne of Green Gables* (1908), was an immediate best-seller. After her marriage in 1911 to Reverend Ewan Macdonald, Montgomery moved to Ontario where she died in 1942. In addition to seven sequels to *Anne of Green Gables*, Montgomery's novels include: *The Story Girl* (1911); *Emily of New Moon* (1923), and *The Blue Castle* (1926). Her correspondence to her close friend Ephraim Weber in the years between 1905 and 1909 was published in 1960 as *The Green Gables Letters*. "I Dwell Among My Own People" was first published in 1925.

[Letter to Ephraim Weber]

Cavendish, P.E.I.,
Thursday Evening,
Sept. 10, 1908.

My dear Mr. Weber:—

I know my correspondents all think I'm dead. I'm not—but I'm so tired and worn out, after a summer of steady grind, that I might almost as well be, as far as real *living* is concerned. To tell the truth, I feel horribly "played out."

You see, Anne seems to have hit the public taste. She has gone through four editions in three months. As a result, the publishers have been urging me to have the second volume ready for them by October—in fact insisting upon it. I have been writing "like mad" all through the hottest summer we have ever had. I finished the book last week and am now typewriting it, which means from three to four hours' pounding every day—excessively wearisome work; I expect it will take me a month to get it done—if I last so long.

Thank you for your kind remarks on Anne. I suppose she's all right but I'm so horribly tired of her that I can't see a single merit in her or the book and can't really convince myself that people are sincere when they praise her. You did not make the criticism I expected you to make and which a couple of the reviews did make—that the ending was too conventional. It was; and if I had known I was to be asked to write a second Anne book I wouldn't have "ended" it at all but just "stopped." However, I didn't know and so finished it up as best I could.

There has been some spice in my life so far this summer reading the reviews. So far I have received *sixty*, two were harsh, one contemptuous, two mixed praise and blame and the remaining fifty-five were kind and flattering beyond my highest expectations. So I feel satisfied as far as that goes. I wish you could see the reviews; but as you can't I'll copy the main points herewith. Don't think me extremely *vain* for doing so. I know you are interested in your fellow-writer's adventures.

114

I enclose the Toronto *Globe* review of which I have a spare copy and you may keep it.

Phila. *Inquirer.* "A wholesome and stimulating book."

Montreal *Herald.* "A book which will appeal to the whole English speaking world—one of the most attractive figures Canadian fiction has produced."

Boston *Transcript.* "Anne is one of the most delightful girls that has appeared for many a day. She is positively irresistible."

St. John *Globe.* "A truly delightful little girl."

Pittsburg *Chronicle.* "Those who enjoy originality, quaintness, and character portrayal of a high order will make a grievous mistake if they ignore *Anne of Green Gables!* The heroine is one of the cleverest creations in recent fiction."

Boston *Herald.* "It could only have been written by a woman of deep and wide sympathy with child nature. A delightful story."

Detroit *Saturday Night.* "Here's to your good fortune, Anne. You will brighten many a career and darken nary a one."

Montreal *Star.* "The most fascinating book of the season."

Record Herald, Chicago. "Here is a literary bouquet full of life and naturalness and quiet humour and pathos."

Milwaukee, *Free Press.* "Anne has the elusive charm of personality. Every word she utters partakes of it and every one of her quaint expressive ways. She is full of flavour. A better book for girls there could hardly be for it possesses a freshness and vivacity very rare indeed among books for girls, or indeed among any books for children."

N.Y. *American.* "An idyllic story, one of the most delightful books we have read for many a day."

Phila. *North American.* "One of the most delightful characters in juvenile fiction—with graceful touches of fancy and in an original and captivating vein of humour."

Brooklyn *Times.* "Anne is very funny but she is not convincing."

N.Y. *Times.* "A mawkish, tiresome impossible heroine, combining the sentimentality of an Alfred Austin with the vocabulary of a Bernard Shaw. Anne is a bore."

N.Y.*World.* "The people in this book are delightfully studied and it is a pleasure to know them."

The Outlook. "One of the best books for girls we have seen this long time, with plenty of character and originality."

Buffalo *News.* "A story after the true lover's heart—full of absorbing interest from first to last."

Boston *Budget.* "A very engaging miss. She is too precocious a youngster for real life but very diverting as a book heroine. The story is fresh and entertaining and the author is to be congratulated on her maiden effort."

Chicago *Inter-Ocean.* "The most notable thing about the book is the accurate and sympathetic observation of nature."

Well, I fancy you're tired of this—so I'll let you off. One intended criticism in an otherwise favourable review tickled me immensely. "This is a very charming story but the author has missed an opportunity in her setting. Although this is Prince Edward Island which is virgin ground for a story writer, there is *nothing in the book distinctive of the place*. The scene might as well be laid in any New England village."

The italics are mine. I suppose the critic imagines that I am some American who laid the scene of her story in P.E. Island by way of getting something new in geography but who has no real knowledge of the weird and uncanny lives led by the inhabitants thereof! Another review said, "What most impresses an American is how these people of Canada *resemble ourselves.*"

What did that poor man suppose we were like down here???...

1908

I Dwell Among My Own People

There are two questions which I am repeatedly asked. They have always exasperated me and always will. I feel that, before long, I will throw something—something hard and heavy for choice—at the next person who asks me either of them. These questions are: "Is so-and-so in your book a real person?" and "Why don't you try your hand at a problem novel?"

So-and-so—he, she or it—is never a "real person"—if by that is meant any unfortunate existing person whom I have put bodily into a story. I know many people who have repeatedly asserted that they are acquainted with "the originals" of my characters—there are not lacking those who have said it to my face. Now, for my own part, during all the years I have studied human nature, as I saw it around me, I have never met one human being who could, as a whole, be put into a story without injuring it. Any artist knows that to paint exactly from life is to give a false impression of the subject. Study from life we must, copying suitable heads and arms, appropriating bits of character, personal or mental idiosyncracies, but the ideal must be behind it all. A writer must create, not copy her characters, or they will never be life-like.

I never "try my hand" at a problem novel for four reasons. The first is that a problem novel never yet solved any problem. The second is that most folks have problems enough in their own lives and want something different when they seek a little rest and relaxation in a book; and the third and fourth reasons are—I don't want to.

116

The people I know best and love best, having lived among them and been one of them all my life, are not very deeply concerned with what are known as "present-day problems." Their problems are simple and belong to yesterday and to-morrow as well as to-day. They live in a land where nature is neither grudging nor lavish; where faithful work is rewarded by competence and nobody is very rich and nobody very poor; where everybody knows about everybody else, so there are few mysteries; where there is always someone to keep tab on you and so prevent you from running amuck with the Decalogue; where the wonderful loveliness of circling sea and misty river and green, fairy-haunted woods is all around you; where the Shorter Catechism is not out of date; where there are still to be found real grandmothers and genuine old maid aunts; where the sane, simple, wholesome pleasures of life have not lost their tang; where you are born into a certain political party and live and die in it; where it is still thought a great feather in a family's cap if it has a minister among its boys; where it is safer to commit murder than to be caught without three kinds of cake when company comes to tea; where loyalty and upright dealing and kindness of heart and a sense of responsibility and a glint of humour and a little decent reserve—great solvents of any and all problems if given a fair trial—still flower freely on the fine old country stock—such are my people—with the flower and romance of the Celt, the canny common sense of the Lowlander, the thrift of the English, the wit of the Irish, all beginning to be blended into something that is proud to call itself Canadian.

I love the little island province where I was born—I love the rich red of its wandering roads—I love the emerald of its uplands and meadows—I love the radiance of its encircling sea—I love its elusive subtle charm of beauty with a hint of austerity—I love its life and its people. And so I write about them because I want my readers to know and love them too.

1925

Stephen Leacock
1869-1944

Born in Hampshire, England, Stephen Leacock immigrated with his family to a farm near Lake Simcoe in 1875. He was educated at Upper Canada College, the University of Toronto and the University of Chicago. After earning his doctorate, Leacock accepted an appointment to the Department of Economics and Political Science at McGill University in 1903. He remained at McGill until his retirement in 1936 and published volumes of political science, literary criticism, history and autobiography. Following the publication of *Literary Lapses* in 1910, however, Leacock's reputation as a teacher and scholar was overshadowed by his renown as a humorist. Inspired perhaps by Leacock's clever parodies in *Nonsense Novels* (1911) and *Winsome Winnie and Other New Nonsense Novelists* (1920), critics have often identified novelistic elements in *Sunshine Sketches of a Little Town* (1912) and *Arcadian Adventures with the Idle Rich* (1914). *How To Write* (1943) reflects Leacock's awareness and understanding of the changing literary tastes of his generation.

From
How To Write
[Realism and Romance]

. . .In the old-fashioned novel writing the writer was seldom content to stand entirely outside of his picture. Quite apart from any narration by a character in the first person, he had a way of stepping in and out of the story himself, and inviting his reader to observe *this* and to notice *that*, and adjuring him not to think so and so or to conclude something else; or, if the story seemed to be getting dull, to cheer the reader up with the assurance of lots more things coming. The author of the period especially loved to address the person whom he called "my fair reader." This was a sort of come-along compliment to the dumpy, sentimental ladies of forty-five who were more apt to be reading a three-decker novel than would a fly-away girl of fifteen. The "fair reader" in that case was at least flattering; but not so applicable to a grimy old miner reading a paper novel in a log cabin. But to the Victorians it was all one. These superficial tricks of writing, in reality matters that lie upon the surface and are no deeper than passing fashion, now-a-days put us off the older books. Unless appreciated when young an effort is required to "get into them."

Much deeper than fashion and below the surface in the very life of fiction is the varying method of relation that corresponds to what we may call *tone*—for want of a better word. If *tune* may be used . . . for the run of the words and sentences, then *tone* may serve to indicate the difference of the author's voice in the relation; whether he throws into it the sentiment of what he relates or relates it only as it happens—the difference between romance and realism, between sentiment and statement, fantasy or photograph. French writers and French critics have analyzed and discussed this aspect of fiction far more than we have in English, and have been far more self-conscious in regard to it. Students of writing should get a clear idea of what is meant here by

118

romantic, a thing very different from the wider and more usual meaning of romantic. The two are cognate but not the same. When we talk of romantic scenery we mean scenery which suggests and suits strange stories, scenery where lovers might have walked and wooed—a glade in a green wood, a forsaken garden, a broken mill, a ruined castle—as distinct from a city street beside a stock exchange. Wherever love may sigh (in suitable sighing places), or danger lurk, or gallantry defy it—wherever golden fortune breaks the closed circuit of daily life—there is romance. To its portrayal the world has devoted the softest of its music, the most appealing of its poetry, most stirring of its dramas and the thousand and one tales of its imagination.

When we speak of romantic writing, we recall the heroes and the heroines of Walter Scott or the figures (wax and otherwise) of Tennyson's *Idylls of the King*. To what extent such people as Tennyson's "Blameless King Arthur" are possible, what difference there is (if any) between King Arthur and a stuffed shirt, is another matter. To the proper kind of reader of their day, if they were not true to life they were at least much better than life. Ordinary life, as compared with them, was as a ham sandwich to a banquet.

But it is also possible to write stories about people who live not in castles, but on Main Street and fall in love with people as commonplace as themselves. Stories in fact can be told all the way from cowboys and cabbages up to kings. Everybody understands in a general way the difference between romantic and realistic stories, tales of life as it might be and narratives of life as it is.

But a further difference comes up when we refer not to the subject and characters of a story, but the way of writing it. It would be possible, in this sense, to write romantically of very poor and simple people, as Dickens often did, or to write realistically of kings and castles as many writers try to do now. In this sense romantic writing means a way of telling a story in which the author's own feeling and sentiments blend with and colour the narrative. The realistic way of telling a story is to state the facts and not to weep or laugh over them, not to express approval or disapproval, but to leave that to the reader. Take a simple example:

The poor old man thus found himself out in the bitter cold with no home to go to etc. etc.

Observe the word *poor;* that's the author's opinion about the old man, expressing his sympathy for him. A realist wouldn't call him that, unless he meant the word in the other sense as *penniless*, to express a fact. But observe also the word *bitter;* that is all right here even for a realist because it refers presumably to the thermometer. But if we wrote *the cruel cold*, that would be romantic writing. In other words the ideal of the realist writer is to make a purely impersonal picture (a photograph) a purely impersonal narrative (a record).

119

The difference between the two methods and the conscious cultivation of either has been much more emphasized in France than in England. Indeed this field of art became for a time a sort of battleground of rival schools. The writer whose name is chiefly connected with realistic style is Guy de Maupassant who practised it with a perfection of technique seldom attained. Students of the art of writing may turn to the story *La Parure (The Necklace)* as a perfect specimen of his work.

In Britain and in America the fiction of the nineteenth century was overwhelmingly romantic in method, though rather by instinct than by art. But in the twentieth century the tendency has been more the other way, though the two methods of treatment have always blended and intermingled. Dickens, for example, was overwhelmingly romantic; the very life of his stories is the colour of sentiment, of approval or disapproval that runs through them. He joins his readers in roars of laughter or sobs of tears at his characters. He would put in such epithets as the "noble Mrs. Gamp," the "magnanimous Mr. Pecksniff"—which have nothing to do with the story but just comment on the character, and that a satirical one. Yet Dickens at times wrote pages of realism—clear, direct and wonderful in its appeal. Turn to the account of Mr. Dorrit's sudden mental seizure at his own grand banquet, when his mind carries him again to the Marshalsea prison and his horrified guests see him rise and call to his daughter in perplexity, "Amy, is Joe on the lock?" There is no "poor Dorrit" in this, no Dickens so to speak, no comment and none needed, just a picture, a record, tragic and overwhelming in the plain truth of its narration.

Now as a matter of fact it is not possible to separate realistic writing completely from romantic. The very facts that the writer selects imply a preference over other facts. The writer thinks them more interesting. If Guy de Maupassant hadn't thought the idea of *La Parure* pathetic he wouldn't have written it. After all heroism will out, tears will flow and have done so ever since the Roman poet said "the world is full of weeping" (*sunt lachrymae rerum*)—and even before. The stock in trade of the romanticists is part of human nature itself. We come to it by instinct. Our "boys' stories," as Mr. Chesterton once said in a wonderful phrase, "still drive their dark trade in heroes."

But the valid basis of realism is its protest against the exaggerated sentiment, the "sob-stuff," the mock heroism and the stock heroism into which treatment can so easily degenerate. The Victorian age loved tears, even when it did not propose to wipe them away. Barefooted street boys, emaciated chimney-sweeps, girls stitching a shirt as a prelude to throwing themselves into the Thames, fathers who refuse to come home from a saloon even when sung to—all this drew ready tears. Tears are indeed of the very fountain of life. But there is danger in them. We may be led to substitute weeping for action, and sympathy for relief. One is apt to suspect that the Victorians felt as if their flood of generous tears had washed them free from obligations.

In our more realistic age we are impatient of impotent weeping. We are apt to say, "Stop crying about it and see what can be done." Hence we change the *Song of the Shirt* to the plain talk of a minimum wage statute, and try at least, to drag father out of the saloon with a prohibition law. "Tears, idle tears, and yet I know not why," said the Victorian. He seemed to sit and gulp, and like himself for it. We want to know why, and if we fail today we mean to succeed tomorrow, even if it is a long tomorrow in coming. Yet it is hard to judge. There are dangers both ways. It may be that tears water the flowers of life and feed the roots of action. Some of the Victorian sobs and songs—like the *Song of the Shirt* itself—helped to make the world's history. The new use now beginning to be made of this very term realistic shows where the new danger may lie. A *realistic* point of view, to our newspapers at any rate, now means one that depends on fact and force, and not upon agreement or obligation by honour. A realist is becoming the new name for the man who used to be called an "unprincipled scoundrel."

As with the sobs of grief so with the ecstasies of love. The romanticist and the realist try to capture them, each in his own way. The Victorian age loved love as it loved tears. Hence, its impossible heroines who became a stock-in-trade of nineteenth century fiction. The heroine had to combine an ideal beauty, an impeccable virtue, a modesty and an innocence that ran idiocy hard.

There was no attempt to make the heroines true to life. They were supposed to be better than life. As the reader liked them that way then no harm was done and everybody was pleased. To all her other graces the heroine added a power of language rarely found outside of a legislative assembly. This was her weapon with which she could compel even the blackest villain to "unhand her." . . .

But if the romantic heroine is unsatisfactory, what about the realist one? If we are to portray the heroine just as she is, what is left of her? You cannot depict love inside a frame of fact. It needs a mist to dissolve in. You cannot tell a love story just as it is—because it isn't. There is something else there, something higher than our common selves and perhaps truer. When a young man sees in his girl an angel, and a young girl sees in her lover a hero, perhaps they are seeing what is really there—the self we each might have but which we grasp only in our higher moments and too late. Hence you cannot in the art of narration bind love within the fetters of fact. It slips through as easily as radio through a prison wall. A "realistic" love story is either grubby, or false, or both. It is probable that the distorted image of a Kate Nickleby is nearer to what a young man sees when in love, than any picture that can be drawn by loveless observation.

With that one comes back round the circle of discussion that revolves round realism and romance. . . .

121

[Historical Novels]

... Historical fiction began in earnest for Britain and America with the novels of Sir Walter Scott. ... The success and acclaim were immediate. ... It is said that when *Waverley* appeared people stopped one another, book in hand, on the streets of Edinburgh, to ask "Have you read it?" Yet *Waverley* was in a sense scarcely historic to the people who first read it. Its second title, *'Tis Sixty Years Since*, shows it merely in the retrospect of a vanishing horizon, that verge of the present retreating into the past, that is history to the young and yesterday to the old, yet near to both. Scott reached back to the Middle Ages and the Crusades—the real thing—with *Ivanhoe* and the *Talisman*, then for the most part confined himself to the romance of Scotland.

With Scott began the weaving of the unending web of historic fiction, which at times slackened, waxed or waned but has never stopped. Washington Irving followed with the picture past of *Father Knickerbocker* in New York and *Rip Van Winkle* in the hills of the Hudson, seen, as it were, through tobacco smoke. Fenimore Cooper in Indian feathers crawled through the underbrush, not snapping a single twig and all Europe crawled, breathless or breathing hard, behind him. Charles Dickens wrote of today. To him the past was as rotten as it was to Mark Twain. Once—it was after reading Carlyle's *French Revolution*—he reached back towards the past in his *Tale of Two Cities*, and made a better French Revolution than the real one. But after all the Revolution was still a thing of yesterday. In *Barnaby Rudge* Dickens reached a little back to the Lord George Gordon Riots of 1781. But this is not history writing, since in unchanging England Mr. Willett's Maypole Inn and all that went with love and locksmiths, was still there when Dickens wrote. Dickens, indeed stuck to today (his day) and moved along with it. When the railway train came in he saw at once the "romance" of it and used it to kill one of his villains under its headlights.

But other writers moved backwards. Thackeray revived colonial America. Harrison Ainsworth contrived a bloody mixture of towers and dungeons, blocks and axes which would be terrifying if it weren't tedious. One of his sentences is four feet long. Then came Bulwer-Lytton, most historical of all, and all the world walked the colonnaded porticoes and tessellated pavements of ancient Rome, groped their way with Lydia, the blind girl, and sought shelter in vain from the black destruction that overwhelmed Pompeii.

The current never stopped. Boys walked the Saxon forest and sailed the Spanish Main with Charles Kingsley. Such a writer as the late Mr. Henty turned history stories to mass production, adapting every epoch of the world for reading under a school desk during classes. In *Ben Hur* General Wallace, a Civil War veteran, whirled in furious

122

chariots around the Roman arena and in *Quo Vadis?* Henryk Sienkiewicz asked the world again the agelong question, "Whither goest thou?" and lifted the curtain on the inspired days of Christianity in Rome. The turn of the century for a time witnessed feudalism in a flood. Then came the adjunct of the moving picture with its marvellous power of instantaneous presentation to the eye of scenes hitherto produced word by word to the ear. Whether it obliterates or stimulates imagination no one yet knows.

The moving picture should have killed the historical novel. It didn't. It only made it longer—and made success more rapid, wider and more evanescent—the best seller withers like the grass on the prairies; the old books remain like the mountains on the horizon; not as being better but as made when the world was young. But the historical novel, influenced by the moving picture as the induced currents flow in parallel wires, changed its scope. It has stepped out, so to speak; no longer wants to be decorous and ponderous and dignified but must have its characters up-to-date, so real, as we said above, that they are unreal, so much alive that they seem galvanized rather than living, and with just enough nastiness in it to attract clean-minded people. . . .

1943

Part 3
The Rise of Realism

William Arthur Deacon
1890-1977

William Arthur Deacon, born in Pembroke, Ontario, was educated at the University of Toronto, and at the University of Manitoba where he received a law degree in 1918. Two years later he was appointed literary editor of *Saturday Night,* and in 1928 he became literary editor of the *Toronto Globe and Mail,* a position he held until his retirement in 1960. Among the first Canadian journalists who concentrated on literary criticism, Deacon wrote articles and reviews for numerous Canadian and foreign journals and published several books including two collections of his essays, *Pens and Pirates* (1923) and *Poteen* (1926). "The Canadian Novel Turns the Corner" was published in *The Canadian Magazine* in October, 1936.

The Canadian Novel Turns the Corner

Best sellers from other English-language countries still wash over us in wave on wave, generally soon receding and forgotten. The "universally" known names of authors—meaning more or less familiar to readers in English-language countries—are still English and American.

But the Canadian is puzzled over the faint, persistent calls to look into the books of his countrymen. Is this patriotic cry a racket? If these were as good as foreign rivals, would they not be as widely bought?

Shakespeare's fame is comparatively modern. Living, he was successful enough to earn his cheese and beer with leisure in old age; and then he was half forgotten.

In 1837, young Waldo Emerson made a plea at Harvard for American literary independence; and for his heresies was not asked to speak again at his alma mater for more than twenty years. He had told his people that their brains were as good as English brains, and that they could have a strong native literature if only they had confidence in themselves.

Canada, having now completed her long ascent of political autonomy by the Statute of Westminster, is still far from conscious of her economic strength. Centuries of colonialism have induced self-inferiority as a habit of mind. So, while nations sure of themselves, like Britain and the United States, consume 80% of their own books (since readers normally enjoy familiar scenes and idioms and points of view), Canada goes on importing something like 98% of books read here— apart from such compulsory reading as school texts, which are Canadian printed but often predominantly foreign in content.

Yet, with all the handicaps of a small local market and the well organized invasion of volumes from two countries, the course of Canadian literature has been steadily upward. As it must go.

For I am a critic who believes that literature is not a thing apart, independent of everything except its creators. I believe rather that it is one of the natural and necessary forms in which the general life expresses itself; and that, to an unrealized degree, the writers are recorders—specialists as craftsmen, but using ideas and emotions growing out of the common soil, like hay or daisies. Canada's progress forces the sprouting, exactly as her national timidity interferes with the quantity and quality of the yield.

After generations of colonial poets, with their eyes directed elsewhere, Charles Mair in 1868 first showed consciousness of the beauty of his native landscape. It was the impetus of Confederation that threw up Roberts, Carman, Scott and Lampman. These poets dominated Canadian literature till 1926, in which year all of them were represented by more or less valedictory volumes that appeared side by side with mature work by Pratt and MacDonald of the new generation.

In 1927, exactly fifty years after the publication of Kirby's "The Golden Dog" had set the fashion in costume novels around the fall of Quebec, Canadian fiction first diverted attention from poetry. Mazo de la Roche won the *Atlantic Monthly* prize with "Jalna"; Frederick Philip Grove published his most popular book, "A Search for America"; and Laura Goodman Salverson was represented by her most finished performance, "The Lord of the Silver Dragon". To this group must be added Morley Callaghan's first novel, "Strange Fugitive", which came in 1928.

Canada may thank her stars that there is no school of Canadian fiction, as there was of Canadian poetry from 1880 to 1926, and as the Group of Seven went far to stylize Canadian painting. Whatever political difficulties are created by internal differences, art is the richer for cultural diversity. The technique and mood of Louis Hemon's "Maria Chapdelaine" cannot be applied with success to Service's "The Trail of '98". Therefore I rejoice that the Canadian novel turned the corner in 1927 without the possibility of a common denominator.

Grove, of Swedish-Scottish stock, spent most of his life in Manitoba as farm laborer and school teacher. Callaghan is an Irish Catholic, born and still living in Toronto. Mrs. Salverson, of Icelandic descent, was born in Gimli and lives in Port Arthur. Miss de la Roche, born in Toronto, is living by preference in England. Her childhood was spent near Clarkson, where she still maintains a house; she later lived with an uncle who kept a hotel at Newmarket; and I am informed that she began earning her living as a dressmaker. Equally and healthily varied are the pictures of life made by this still dominant quartette, and diverse their paths.

Mrs. Salverson, a romantic, in thrall to the sagas of her race, excels in the action story and recently has given us "The Dove", a capital adventure tale of Viking prisoners in Algiers in the period of the Barbary slave-raiders. With all the elements of popularity, this book reached few Canadians because of the miserably crowded type used in its production; it should be reprinted in legible characters. Yet Mrs. Salverson is Canadian, too, and the coming publishing season contains one surprise in the kind of book she will contribute. It is sure to attract immediate attention.

Miss de la Roche's sense of humor has become encased in the Whiteoaks family, not merely to exploit an initial success but obviously because she likes the tribe of expatriate English on the old Ontario strand. This interminable continuation of a single chronicle has the practical disadvantage that most people soon get enough of one thing, though "Young Rennie" was the best-selling novel in the United States for five successive weeks last summer. It and "Finch's Fortune" are able extensions of her narrative, but neither can touch "Whiteoaks of Jalna" as a story in itself.

Protest as Canadians may and do that Canadian farm life is misrepresented in her series, Miss de la Roche (who readily admits the family is not typical) remains the Canadian novelist whose books have had the widest world circulation through translations into many languages. Their vitality is indicated by the protracted run of the play in a London theatre last spring. The sexual preoccupation of her characters has become an unfortunate habit; and the movie version's scene of a butler dusting the banisters in the farmhouse in the early morning is the index of how far her fertile imagination, rather than observation, has directed her plots.

Mr. Grove, who received the Lorne Pierce Gold Medal at the age of sixty-seven, has settled comfortably on a farm near Lake Erie, whence he issues an odd novel at leisure. Keeping to the Manitoba farm setting he knows so well, in 1930 he achieved a tragic masterpiece called "The Yoke of Life", beyond which he can hardly be expected to pass. This story of a boy, who lacked opportunities commensurate with his ambition and abilities, shows both powerful concentration, with the whole action directed to a single, inevitable end, and a masterfully controlled artistic balance between parts that suggests architectural harmony, coupled with the solidity of good masonry. It is one of the defects of the commercial machinery, on which our literature depends, that so strong and finely finished a piece of work should be allowed to go out of print merely because it did not win immediate popularity. The next step must be devising practical means for keeping in circulation in cheap form Canadian books of outstanding artistic merit. The first to be rescued from oblivion should be "The Yoke of Life."

Most spectacular advance among these four leaders has naturally been made by the youngest of them, Morley Callaghan. As I had the privilege of predicting seven years ago, when he was starting his career, his economy of effective language, together with inherent strength and great sincerity, early marked him as a coming writer of power. During the interval, more by self-realization than by improvement in technique, he has come to occupy the foremost place among Canadian novelists.

Callaghan has discovered that he does not belong to the hard-boiled school of contemporary American writers, with whom he was first identified. Instead, he is deeply moved to pity for humble people in trouble. His initial show of callousness has been dropped in favor of a beautiful sympathy, which is moving readers in increasing numbers. Another token of his maturity is retreat from a too-simple view of life and reading of character. Inner conflicts of emotion and finer shadings of motive and circumstance mark the widening and deepening of his outlook. I hope and believe this process is not yet complete, and that the coming decade will carry him to interpretative breadths as well as artistic heights beyond anything yet done in Canadian fiction. There is an integrity in this man to warrant such faith, as well as command of craftsmanship of the highest order.

Still young Callaghan has given earnest of his genius in two novels of the first rank—"Such is My Beloved" (1933) and "They Shall Inherit the Earth" (1934). It is noteworthy that both were banned by the Toronto Public Library as the Winnipeg Public Library banned Grove's first novel, "Settlers of the Marsh". It should also be remarked that Callaghan, who is regarded in the United States as one of the best living short story writers, has not been equally accepted at home. The fact that he is unique among Canadian novelists in depicting city life may have affected the disparity in appreciation. Americans are much more conscious of both the complexities and miseries of the urban scene. Anyway, Callaghan continues to plod upward, writing necessarily for the better class American periodicals, but keeping his roots nourished from his native pavements.

"Such is My Beloved" is the tragedy of a Toronto priest, who took too literal a view of Christ's injunctions for a worldly world. Trying to help two unfortunate girls, he won the enmity of wealthy parishioners and his ecclesiastical superiors, who accomplished his ruin. The tender handling of this little drama is persuasive. One feels with and for all these persons rejected by respectable society. "They Shall Inherit the Earth" is a larger and more complex story, primarily of the estrangement of father and son; but it contains also, in the lowly romance of Anna Prychoda, a singularly sweet love episode. Followers of Mr. Callaghan's novels are acquiring a fresh familiarity with the geography of downtown Toronto. One looks at Bowles cafeteria, opposite the City Hall, with remembrance that a Callaghan character had lunch there on a certain occasion; and this immediacy of interest is new in Canadian fiction.

Two other recent Canadian novels stand out, the one for its quick popularity from readily grasped sentiment, the other by reason of an exquisite sensitiveness. I refer to Patrick Slater's "Yellow Briar" and Alexander Knox's "Bride of Quietness".

The humor and pathos of "Yellow Briar", both laid on thick, were yet genuine. Weak in plot, this story of an Irish immigrant boy in the Mono Mills district eighty years ago poses as autobiography and the illusion is strengthened by the author's use of actual incidents and persons, who were still residing there within living memory. The appeal is directly to the heart, and the whole conception rose out of the author's love of this countryside and passionate admiration for the pioneers who settled it. The result is a jolly and fragrant book that became a favorite over night. It has the sweet flavor of a good winter apple, resulting from an unashamed use of sentiment. We hope shortly to hear again from John Mitchell, who does not always masquerade as the late Mr. Slater.

Knox, who spent his boyhood in Pembroke and is now an actor in London, gave us in "Bride of Quietness" an idyll of the Oiseau Rock on the Upper Ottawa, and is the first novelist to use the elaborate palette of colors afforded by the Laurentian country. Amid these scenic splendors, an adolescent experiences the innocence of first love. This, too, is a new kind of book to come from a Canadian; and while its candor shocked some readers, its delicacy should have prevented any revulsion. "Bride of Quietness" was not banned—merely discreetly ignored.

Quite as cheering and significant as the headliners is the constant flow of good, if less ambitious, novels. As a group these show more seriousness than the products of previous decades. Which is another way of saying that whereas earlier story writers in Canada seemed to be under some compulsion to preach a way of life, the new novelists are mainly concerned with demonstrating life as it is, through selective interpretations. It is a great gain that the consciously moral (hence often priggish) attitude has yielded place to conscientious fidelity of portraiture.

We therefore find Francis Pollock, an Ontario bee-keeper, writing an unspectacular but veracious account of the life of a bee-keeper. This is minus glamor, but interesting as a human document under the apt title of "Bitter Honey". Mr. Pollock's forthcoming novel, "Collision" is said to deal with a Bohemian circle in Toronto. Similarly, Bernard J. Farmer, in "Go West, Young Man", honestly dramatized the rough adventures of an English engineer in Canada without the old whinings that once marked such recitals. In "The Homesteader", Ethel Chapman deals with the farmers of Northern Saskatchewan in a matter-of-fact though optimistic manner. This is also true of Jessie L. Beattie's "Hill-Top", about parental cruelty to a child on a farm in the vicinity of Blair and Doon. J. E. Middleton, long known as a whimsical essayist, has more or less astonished his friends by the competence of the novels he has recently issued. In "The Clever Ones", he treats the Communist menace with his customary humor and charity.

So we might proceed through a list encouragingly long. For example, Allen Roy Evans, of Vancouver, has made splendid use of original material in "Reindeer Trek", telling of the long drive of Canada's new herd from Alaska to the mouth of the Mackenzie. And this fall season has already opened with an excursion into the novel by that versatile genius, Bertram Brooker, whose "Think of the Earth" is not only photographically accurate as a picture of a Manitoba town, but breaks new and difficult ground as a study of a mystic on the borders of religious mania. Raymond Knister's novel, "My Star Predominant", which won the *Graphic* prize and was published post-humously, was so much a life of Keats as hardly to rank as fiction; yet its quality renews regret that this able craftsman was drowned without fulfilling his promise in his chosen field of the novel.

Desisting from enumeration, but not for lack of material, we should ask at the conclusion of such a summary what traits are emerging with the increase in quantity and improvement in quality of the Canadian novel. Except for Mabel Dunham's "Conestoga" series on a Mennonite family at Kitchener, from the pioneers to their present descendants, there has been no attempt at the century type of story covering three generations, which has marked the last decade in English and American fiction, and has now reached the state of standard pattern, or "formula" in writers' jargon.

If this were a clear case of concentration on the individual at the expense of social continuity, it would be most significant; but it may mean nothing beyond the general restriction in design that has always limited literary efforts in Canada. It may be no more than a reflection of Canadian publishers' unwillingness to risk the expense of manufacturing a narrative of many hundred pages. But we also find, save for Gilbert Knox's satiric novels of Ottawa, a complete dearth of the community type of story, in which the social framework is dominant and individuals suppressed to their relative statures. Perhaps this tendency to isolate the human unit for study accounts for the lack of urban fiction, where the community life surrounds and moulds the individual and that novelists prefer, instead, to plant him on a farm or take him almost solitary into the woods. The preponderance of village fiction suggests that the easiest method has been taken of playing up the individual while employing a manageable background and ready-made types for relief.

Allowing for sparcity of data, it seems clear from the novels of the past seven years that Canadians have little consciousness of race and almost none of nationality. Apart from Harold Baldwin's "Pelicans in the Sky" (a Saskatchewan novel published in London and unknown to most Canadians, even by name), we never discover a character in a Canadian novel gloating over distinctively Canadian things as English characters are always doing with pride in their island. The Canadian novelist seems to think in regional terms only and to be, in general, quite indifferent to historic cause-and-effect relations, whether political or social or economic or otherwise.

Did we have any reason for believing this trend to flow from deep conviction that life only matters as it surges through the individual soul, it would be quite possible to argue for that view. As the case stands, there is enforced by regional thinking so wide a diversity of scene and types that one marvels at the still unexplored territories and sorts of people. Our literary artists are certainly still free from any joint preconception about life in general and their country in particular.

This is good insofar as it leaves creative writers free to apply whatever treatment the case requires, without conforming to any ideas currently subscribed to. But I suspect that Canadian novelists, as a group, are merely ignorant of and indifferent to those dynamic mass-movements that are making this the century of change. Secure, remote, in a placid place, the Canadian novelist carries on sedately as though Victoria were still on the throne. One may be far from desiring stimulated output of Wellsian yarns and yet question the validity of any national fiction that is so blandly unaware of the convulsions that are shaping the world, from science to ceramics.

In this, of course, they truly echo the vocal element in the land that produced them; they reflect faithfully a national policy of *laissez faire* and drift; but the time has surely come for Canadian creative writers to pierce below appearances to realities and show some consciousness of contemporary forces already in play. Where is the Canadian novelist who has ever offered intellectual leadership in any field, or spoken out on any public issue after the manner of A.P. Herbert, J.B. Priestley, John Galsworthy or Phyllis Bentley? It is hard to conceive one of the Canadian men or women named in this article rising to fiery utterance as H.M. Tomlinson did in "Snows of Helicon".

Glad as I am to hear the last of the evangelical note in Canadian fiction, and realizing fully the artistic dangers inherent in stories with a purpose, I am yet uneasy over an apparent and probably real blindness to great forces that even now are making for sweeping changes throughout the world. Our novelists, however, are in this respect reflecting Canadian apathy, unconsciously but with considerable accuracy. They are certainly pursuing their profession with new courage and heightened capacities. Some are achieving fame outside our borders and all are entitled to more support and appreciation than they get within them. If a lack is indicated—and, if a lack, it is serious— Canadians at large must assume blame for the tendency to create an escape literature as far as current mass 'forces are concerned. On the reverse side of the case, a big factor is that the Canadian temperament, rustic and ruminative, takes kindly to the mental isolation of such pronounced individualism as farmers automatically acquire. Recent developments in psychology hint that expansion of consciousness in the individual is the only safe key to group reforms that can be of real benefit. Canadians and their novelists, appearing to lag behind more effervescent countries, may possibly be on the more direct road to lasting progress out of present unrest.

1936

Frederick Philip Grove
1879-1948

Frederick Philip Grove (Felix Paul Greve) was born in Radomno on the German-Polish border in 1879 and grew up in the city of Hamburg. After attending university in Bonn and Munich, he moved in 1902 to Berlin where he published poems and novels in German and worked as an editor and professional translator. In 1909 he immigrated to Canada, and three years later he became a school-teacher in Manitoba. After moving to Ontario in 1929, Grove worked for a year as editor for the Graphic Press in Ottawa and then settled on a farm near Simcoe, Ontario, where he lived until his death. Grove's first Canadian book, *Over Prairie Trails* (1922), a collection of realistic landscape sketches, was followed by collections of essays, short stories and eight novels, including: *Settlers of the Marsh* (1925); *A Search for America* (1927); *Fruits of the Earth* (1933); and *The Master of the Mill* (1944). "The Novel" and "Realism in Literature" were included in Grove's first collection of essays, *It Needs to Be Said* (1929).

132

The Novel

The question which I propose to treat of in what follows may seem to be in no need of an answer. Nearly everybody believes that he knows that answer. Yet, how many have ever given any real thought to just what the novel is?

Now, first of all, it is one of the forms of literary art. The aim of art—to define man's emotional reaction to life or to the outer world, to all that is not I—is one and indivisible; the methods which artists employ to achieve that aim are as manifold as human temperaments. According to the method employed, there are many forms of art.

One of them uses words or language for its tool; it we call literature.

True literature is that in the given utterances of a given age and country which, by virtue of its excellence and general validity, will endure; which will remain as the document of its time and origin throughout the ages.

Within the realm of literature we have the province of narrative art.

This branch of literature has, during the last two or three centuries, assumed an importance which is phenomenal and unheard-of in the history of the last two or three thousand years. The reason is, of course, that, with the development of printing, the circle of readers has enormously widened; the circle of listeners and spectators has almost proportionately contracted. Even true plays are more commonly read these days than seen. Naturally, then, prose narration, conceived and written to be read, not memorized and recited to an audience, is the form most commonly chosen by the artist of to-day as the one most directly adapted to his purpose which is, of course, to waken an emotional reaction and response, in the largest possible number, to a given set of conditions, data, circumstances, events, and characters.

If, then, we take the vast mass of works of more or less permanent value which have accumulated under this heading of narrative prose, we find that we can roughly classify them in three groups which, for our present purpose, have a special significance. In ascending order of importance (without prejudice to their artistic value), we might call them The Tale, The Short Story, and The Novel. All three try to achieve the aim common to all art by depicting a section of human life.

In order to define the novel, I cannot do better than briefly delineate the border lines between the three groups.

Edgar Allan Poe wrote Tales. He took his subject matter, as it has been well said, from the border-provinces of human life—in contradistinction to its main stream. Poe presents things which happen "on the margin of life".

From this follows one important deduction: the tale is not *socially significant*.

133

Its incidents may have the interest of anecdotes, the charm of dreams, the novelty of a surprise; its characters may be interesting as pathological cases or as physiological accidents, like a man with either a diseased liver or with a hump-back on his shoulders or six fingers on his hands. But no conclusion can be drawn from either incidents or characters as to the state of society in which they are set.

The tale is not necessarily a short narrative: the Russian Dostoievski, the Pole Joseph Conrad have written tales of five hundred pages each.

But the secret of its appeal and at the same time its limitation lies in this that it consists of accidental or incidental things. It deals with the unusual, in character as well as in event. It satisfies our occasional appetite for the adventurous, the mysterious, or the horrible.

In juvenile literature, we have, characteristically, the Fairy Tale. In literature written for adults, we have Hoffmann, De Quincey, Poe, Chesterton, Conrad, the greater part of Hamsun's work, and many others. In its vile and decrepit degeneration, it has flooded the market with Conan Doyle and his congeners, satisfying at last no human need any longer except the itch of a vulgar curiosity.

The feature, to repeat, which marks it off from Short Story and Novel is the unusual quality in character and incident; to put it briefly, its "marginal" quality.

Both Short Story and Novel, on the other hand, deal with *socially significant* things from the main stream of life. In them, both characters and happenings must be more or less typical for a given society. They must be the normal, natural growth of given conditions actually existing in our midst. In reading them, we must be living the lives depicted as if they were our own.

The exceptional, the unusual thing in character or incident has no place in either except in so far as it may be exceptional or unusual merely in degree, being the quintessence of the typical. In this respect, in fact, it is imperative, if the short story or the novel is to be of value, that the unusual element enter largely into its composition. But of that I shall speak a little further on. In life, a pure type is rarely met with; you and I, and our next-door neighbour are mixed types; but in art the pure type has demonstrated its vitality;* that is all we can say unless we wish to reason from a-priori premises.

Next, then, what, summarized in a very few words, is the difference between short story and novel? Is it a mere difference in length? No; for there are true novels in existence which are shorter than certain true short stories. Let us see.

In studying anatomy, the medical student is sometimes puzzled by the difference in behaviour of certain parts of the animal body according as these parts and their reactions are studied within the body or excised—*in situ* I believe the medical phrase has it, or *in vitro*.

*George Meredith, *The Egoist*

134

The short story presents characters or incidents, or more commonly both, "excised" from the social body or *in vitro*.

A character with which it deals it takes for granted; it defines it and shows it in reaction to one single crisis, choosing, of course, most commonly the chief emotional crisis in the life of that character. The conditions under which the incident or the crisis takes place, it merely outlines, without relating them to the wider social background in which they lie embedded.

The Russians Gorki and Tchechov, the German Keller, the Frenchman Maupassant—at least at his best—the Englishmen Quiller-Couch, Hardy, Walpole, Hope, Galsworthy have written true short stories in which some phase of the human life of their times is epitomized.

Like the short story, the novel presents an emotional crisis in the life of its hero or heroine.

But the emotional crisis is not barely "sprung" on the reader; it is led up to from its antecedents in circumstance and character; its unavoidable necessity is shown.

The characters of the men and women involved in it are not, as in the short story, merely depicted and taken for granted; they are explained and developed from their initial impulses, their origins—and unfolded by their reactions to circumstance—successes and failures, human contacts.

From a series of novels written at various periods of a given century, it would be possible to write the history of the manners and morals of that century, within the social strata with which they deal. For, if a given work be a true novel, it will root the crisis and the characters involved in it in the social conditions of the period which it depicts.

Knut Hamsun's *Growth of the Soil*; Tolstoi's *War and Peace, Anna Karenina, Resurrection*; Mann's *Buddenbrooks*; Balzac's *Les Illusions Perdues*; Thomas Hardy's *Tess of the D'Urbervilles* and *Jude the Obscure*; George Meredith's *Richard Feverel, The Egoist, Harry Richmond*—all these are true novels, to mention only a few. As for American authors, from this or the other side of the border, I am at a loss to name one which I should care to class with any one of these.

Let me summarize.

The novel, as a work of art using the form of prose narration, presents an emotional crisis in the life of its hero, developing that crisis from the data of ordinary, every-day life, and at the same time unfolding the potentialities dormant within the hero's character which must be such that we feel, "There, but for the grace of God, go I."

Is there any domain of life which is excluded from treatment in the novel? To my mind, there is none. If the novel is to be read, it must interest, of course. Personally, I have certain aversions. Thus marriage, to me, is a beginning, not an end: the problem of sex is broached, not solved at the altar. For that reason I abominate the common love-story—the story of prenuptial love—almost as violently as I abhor the

135

gramophone, the telephone, or the radio. In life, both young men and young maids are peculiarly uninteresting at a time when they see each other as they are not. Apart from that, judging as a reader, anything is grist that comes to my mill.

Perhaps, from what I have said, and considering that I dabble in this field myself, you will say that my idea of the novel is rather ambitious. It is. It is as ambitious as my idea of the tragedy.

Having briefly defined the subject matter of the novel, it remains for me to say a few words about its treatment of that subject matter. And nothing will help me so much to make clear what I mean as a brief reference to the tragedy; for the simple reason that I can refer to a writer of tragedies whom I may presume to be universally known.

Shakespeare, in a series of tragedies, has treated various socially significant aspects and relations of human life. For instance, the relation between a father and his grown-up children, in *King Lear*; or between a boy and a girl who fall in love, in *Romeo and Juliet*; or between a jealous man and his wife, in *Othello*; or between an over-ambitious man and the world in which he lives, in *Macbeth*.

Having once grasped his problem, having isolated it, as it were, he proceeded to build it out into almost titanic proportions. Every father is a King Lear. The eternal conflict between parents and children results always in some sort of a tragedy. If the children are vitally stronger, the tragedy is that of the parents; if the parents are vitally stronger, the tragedy is that of the children. Ordinarily, in every-day life, these are small tragedies, shot with comedy and a good deal of neutral life which is neither. In order to make the relation as he saw it a fit subject for his art, Shakespeare raised the conflict to a plane where we think we see demons and demi-gods pitched against each other in some twilight of subversion. The slights inflicted on their parents by ordinary, every-day children seem to be enormities committed by Goneril and Regan.

Only thus could they have that unlimited appeal which, in the audience, demolishes individuality and fuses a thousand divergent minds into a mass whose feelings sway jointly and willingly according to the dictate of the poet.

Shakespeare was one; novelists are many and of many ranks. But unless the novelist does something of that nature, he will never really take hold of his readers' hearts and minds. Out of any given conflict he must distil its very essence, he must concentrate, must saturate his solution of it; he must raise it to a plane above the pettiness of cavil and rebellion on the part of his readers. Life, in order to become a fit subject for art, must be reborn in the spirit. It must show connections more clearly; it must lay bare significances more ruthlessly and conclusively than the most tragic reality ever does.

It is this fact—that the case, in a novel, is necessarily overstated— together with the second fact that the novel condenses and omits and thereby rearranges the whole aspect of life, making the picture fundamentally truer than any mere reality can be, because we never see reality as a whole (for only a work of art has a beginning and an end)—which makes unsympathetic or unsusceptible people say, "That is not how things proceed in real life!" The point is that, were it, the novel would no more be art than a newspaper report or the minutes of a proceeding in chancery. A novel must be a whole; it must have beginning and end; and something of an infinitude between the two.

I come to the last point in this bird's-eye view. There are hundreds of thousands of so-called novels in existence. Out of this enormous mass every reader will probably pick a different set for his library. His choice will be determined largely by chance. Yet every reader reads many more novels than he would care to pick for the companions of his life. So do I.

What is the test by the help of which I accept or reject?

As a young man I did my accepting and rejecting instinctively, that goes without saying. But as the years piled up, I came to formulate my judgments in a more or less precise way. I did that exactly as the centuries do it, by looking back and analysing those books which "had stayed with me". I came to look for three things in a book. Finding none of them, I rejected it; finding one or two, I said the book was not without its merits; finding three, I knew that I had indeed made a "find".

These three things I have come to call Power, Depth, Beauty.

Beauty, to me, is that which makes me go back to a thing. After a possible lesson contained in a book has been assimilated; after its characters have been understood; after the incidental curiosity interest has been satisfied—there remains, about that which is artistically well-done, a challenge and a provocation which leaves a desire to be again thus challenged and fascinated; in fact, this challenge and fascination is heightened, not lessened, by a second experience. A good book tempts to look back rather than forward. . . . I need hardly add that this quality has nothing whatever to do with the presentation of so-called beautiful things. An ugly thing may be described, a revolting scene may be presented in such a way as to give the treatment this element of beauty in the highest degree.

Depth I might define as significance. If the author of the book succeeds in forcing me to supply the background of human nature; if he compels me to fill in the thousand and one things which must necessarily remain unsaid; if he conveys to me the feeling that what he gives is given as a significant sample only of the enormous mass of things which he might have given but did not give; and if, at the same time, he makes me divine at least their trend; if, in reading, I am conscious not only of what is explicitly "denoted"—by the words as well as by the scenes presented—but also of the much larger number of things which are "connoted" only—in other words, if I am conscious, not so much of the author's leadership, as of the enormously stimulated activity of my own mind—then I say the book has depth. I am speaking, here, of course, of fiction only; for it may be quite different in the literature of

137

science; but with this restriction I would say that no author has depth who speaks his whole mind. He who, having made a survey of what he has to say, says one third of it and scatters the rest between the lines gives a depth and a relief to his utterance which is the most inspiriting thing which I can imagine. It is depth in a book which rouses the reader to the exertion of his own powers. A book which does not so rouse me I lay aside as paying me the poorest compliment an author can pay me, namely that of presuming that he must do my thinking for me.

Power in a book is the ability to make the reader see. By seeing I do not mean the mere process of reproducing in my mental vision the aspect of a thing—or its sound, smell, or taste, or even its emotional content. I may have looked at a thing a thousand times and yet never have seen it. To see it, in its true significance, in its relation to other things, in a true and yet novel bearing, as a part of that web of things and events which we call the totality of human life—that is the function of the artistic temperament. If to this artistic temperament there is joined the ability to make others see, then we have what I call artistic power. Whenever I read a new book, I ask myself what new thing, unknown to me, I have learned to see by reading this book. There are a thousand different methods to achieve this power; what does the method matter so long as the aim is achieved? Power is the ability of making you see, so that you stop and marvel because you never saw before. It consists in the moving up of the thing to be seen, so close that you cannot get away from it; that you must look and cannot turn your back. That you see, not only it, but through it human life, recognizing with a sudden thrill its whole, abounding significance.

Measured by this triple standard, I have, in my own little library, perhaps thirty novels, of which perhaps ten are in English—novels which I value as being of the very first order of excellence.

If we, you and I, as far as we are readers, accepted only what measures up to such a standard; and if we rejected ruthlessly what falls short, then we should soon have less books to bewilder us; but, since it is only human nature in our many authors to give us more or less what we demand, we should perhaps have a Canadian literature worthy to exalt our name among the nations.

1929

Realism in Literature

. . . There is a common acceptation of the word realism—in literature—against which I must define my attitude, if for no other reason than to avoid a possible misunderstanding of what is to follow.

In this vulgar and, to my mind, erroneous sense of the word, realism means frankness in matters of sex.

Now, sexual matters are, of course, among the weary "facts of life". All "facts of life" are, in my opinion, legitimate subjects of artistic presentation. In a literature addressed to grown-up minds—and does anything that even remotely deserves the name address itself to any other?—I cannot see a single valid objection to the choice of sexual relations for its subject matter. Yes, more, I cannot but ascribe, in a large measure, the very insipidity of the vastly greater part of the American literature of the last few decades to the prudery with which this fundamental fact, sex, has been either ignored or banned. Love affairs and even married life have been treated, where they formed the topic, as if the actors involved in them had no bodies but only etherealized, that is, thinly diluted souls. The sex instinct which is at work in us and claims a large fraction of the energies of the normal man and woman, exalting some of their activities, interfering with others, has been treated as if it were a shameful thing; and the consequence is that there is no field of human activities in which ignorance and stupid prejudice prevail to such an appalling and disastrous extent. For we have reached the point where that very ignorance becomes, in life, the source of tragedy and of unnecessary tragedy. Among enlightened people there are those who assert that one half of what a man or woman may get out of life depends on his sex relationships. I myself would put it at a third or perhaps a quarter. Yet we leave all sex matters to the hit-or-miss methods of chance. In this large domain of life we allow our young people to blunder their way into some sort of understanding and some sort of personal reaction; and on the whole, of course, with disastrous results.

So, where the topic calls for it, I advocate frankness in matters of sex; clean, searching, unimpassioned, and unprejudiced discussions of their bearings and their importance. Sex is real; as real as mountain tops and barren sea; as forests in a storm or fields in the first tender green of spring. Whatever exists is the legitimate subject matter of the literary artist, be he romantic or realist.

But—and this is the important point—realism in this mistaken sense is a matter of the choice of subject, not of literary procedures realism in my sense is a matter of literary procedure, not of the choice of subject. . . .

What, then, is realism?

I open a small popular dictionary, Annandale's, and find this definition, "the endeavour to reproduce nature or to describe real life just as it appears to the artist".

Does this eliminate the artist from his work? For realism is sometimes called the "objective method". If realism consisted in nothing but the unimpassioned, untinged, or objective reproduction of that which is, we might perhaps preferably look at life itself instead of at a work of realistic art? But before a work of literature can be a work of realism, it must be a work of art and conform to the canon of art; and in art the artist is an indispensable medium through which we see things.

As a record of fact the camera and the gramophone are without doubt vastly more reliable than the human eye; the photographic plate or the phonographic record vastly more retentive than the human memory. The essential point, however, is that neither interposes that interpretative stratum which, in a work of art, is furnished by the artist's soul; neither, in other words, mirrors and evokes an emotional reaction. Camera and gramophone see and hear things from the outside, as it were. The artist fuses and reproduces them from out of his soul. In order for anything whatever to become a fit subject matter for art, it must be reborn in the soul of the artist. Thus the artist necessarily tinges the picture which he gives; if only by the fact that, in the face of a vast continuity of happening, he gives his work a beginning and an end; by this mere fact he has begun to interpret emotionally what he presents.

It is quite true that in the vast crowd of writers there are those who at least aim to be mere reporters of fact; who chase after accuracy in the little things which they can observe; who fill note-book after note-book with minute bits of actual truths: the very method of science, but stopping short of classification. Let us suppose for a moment that they succeed in catching, within their word pictures, a surface likeness to reality; and that, out of such material, they try to make a book—a novel which is to live. At the very best, namely if he who attempts this method is, in addition to being a reporter, a great artist, he will, by this synthetic method, succeed in piecing together the outer garment of an inner body; that inner body still remains to be inferred; and the artistic activity in the true sense is once more analysis. The synthesis is at best an inverted analysis; and in the analysis—which is interpretation—the artist is inextricably involved as a spiritual entity.

"The endeavour to reproduce nature or to describe real life just as it appears to the artist." I have no fault to find with that definition.

Eliminate the artist? As God is omnipresent in the world, thus the artist is omnipresent in his work—or anyone could be an artist, just as anyone could be a reporter; though even there, degrees of excellence remain.

However, the realist, being concerned with the presentation, not of himself, but of that other thing, human life; and having learned, besides, that he alone is nothing; that the work of art can spring only from an intimate almost mystical fusing of the two things which are needed—a thing presented and a soul presenting—will never step forward into the lime-light as a person. The moment he exlaims, "*Ecce homo!*" or "*Ecce Pulchrum!*" he ceases to be a realist who speaks through things and human figures whom he marshals about on his stage; he becomes the pedant who points his moral, be it with an ever so magic wand.

140

By the very fact that he cannot reproduce except what was potentially in him, he is, in the totality of his creation, present to the spectator or reader. By the very fact that he cannot convincingly represent a character or a happening which finds no echo in himself, he delimits his work by his own personality. Here we lay our finger on greatness. For who, in that vast world which goes by the name of Shakespeare, can point to an opinion expressed or to a feeling evoked and say, Here speaks the poet, not the character whom he created? And who, by contrast, when he thinks of Marlowe, is not instantly aware of his personal predilections, his superhuman reaches into chaos, and the failure of his hand to grasp what it reached for? Shakespeare, by that criterion, was a realist while Marlowe was a romantic. Greatness, did I say? Yes, greatness; for the drama and the epic call for realism; romanticism is the method of the lyric; and in the drama and the epic, therefore, lyricism can appear only within a hybrid.

The realist, then, while necessarily, by the mere conception of his work as a work of art, omnipresent within it, must, as it were, remain invisible as a bodily or mental or emotional concrescence.

But he must do vastly more. It is one of the fundamental tenets of my own theory of art that what makes a work of literature or any other craft a work of art is the fact that it mirrors a more or less universal human reaction to what is not I. This human reaction, individual to every artist, yet universally valid, is a matter of emotion. Emotion is a matter of interpretation. Interpretation is a matter of making conscious and articulate what was, previous to the act of interpretation, unconscious and inarticulate. The artist—or the realist; for to me, personally, within at least the realm of drama or epic, the two terms are synonymous—must mirror, in his presentation, an emotional response to the outside world and to life which is, as nearly as such things can be, a universal response or at least capable of becoming such. Or, as I have latterly come to express it, a work of literature or of any other craft is a work of art to that exact extent to which it disengages the generally tragic reaction of the human soul to the fundamental conditions of man's life on earth.

True realism always develops a conflict in such a manner that we see all sides, understand all sides, sympathize with all sides taken separately, and yet cannot tell how that conflict can be avoided which, as it unfolds itself, crushes our sensibilities. That is the tragic necessity which we find in all great works of literary art and which exalts us as it crushes us; that is the "fate" of the Greek tragedy; it is the inexorable quality of life itself. Give it, and you have given an image of life; give it, and you have given art; and you have given it by the true method of all dramatic and narrative art, namely realism. All other things are inessentials of procedure.

If, then, I were asked to furnish a short formula by which to express what I mean by realism, I might say: there are three criteria by which I distinguish realistic art from what, for want of a better term, I will call romantic art. Firstly, in realistic art the creative spirit as such will never appear in the first person; whatever it has to say it will say indirectly, through the medium of action and character; it will submerge itself in the world of appearances. Secondly, it will, in the indispensable and unavoidable interpretation which all artistic activity implies—an emotional interpretation—aim at giving an as nearly universally valid reaction to the outside world as is possible to its own human limitations. Thirdly, it will place itself and thereby the reader in the heart of things in such a way that they look on at what is happening from the inside, as if they were themselves a world-consciousness which has its ramifications in all human beings that appear on the stage of the work of literature. As God is a spirit, and, of that spirit, part is in us, thus the author of a book should be, and therefore should make the reader, a spirit transfusing all things and embracing them in its sympathies. . . .

1929

Morley Callaghan
1903-

Born in Toronto, Morley Callaghan was educated at the University of Toronto and studied law at Osgoode Hall. In 1926 he published his first short story in the Parisian literary journal, *This Quarter*. Following the appearance of a novel, *Strange Fugitive* (1928), and a collection of stories, *A Native Argosy* (1929), Callaghan spent several months in Paris where he associated with many of the expatriate writers of England and America; his recollections of that time are recorded in *That Summer in Paris: Memoirs of Tangled Friendships with Hemingway, Fitzgerald and Others* (1963). After returning to Toronto, Callaghan continued a career as a writer that has extended over fifty years. In addition to many short stories, his best-known work includes novels such as: *Such Is My Beloved* (1934); *More Joy In Heaven* (1937); *The Loved and the Lost* (1951); *The Many Coloured Coat* (1960); *A Fine and Private Place* (1975); and *Close to the Sun Again* (1977). "The Plight of Canadian Fiction" was published in the *University of Toronto Quarterly* in 1938.

From
That Summer in Paris
[Metaphor and Cezanne's Apples]

...I was getting along. In the mornings there was the hotel beat, and loafing from hotel to hotel, in the hope of encountering a visitor who might make a good interview, my thoughts were usually on writing. Visitors to the hotels might be strange characters I could use in stories. Why did I dislike so much contemporary writing? I would wonder. The popular writers of the day like Hergesheimer, Edith Wharton, James Branch Cabell, Galsworthy, Hugh Walpole, H. G. Wells—except for *Tono Bungay*—I had rejected fiercely. Show-off writers; writers intent on proving to their readers that they could be clever and had some education, I would think. Such vanities should be beneath them if they were really concerned in revealing the object as it was. Those lines, *A primrose by a river's brim a yellow primrose was to him, and it was nothing more*, often troubled me, aroused my anger. What the hell else did Wordsworth want it to be? An orange? A sunset? I would ask myself, Why does one thing have to remind you of something else? Going from hotel to hotel on my job I would brood over it.

I remember deciding that the root of the trouble with writing was that poets and storywriters used language to evade, to skip away from the object, because they could never bear to face the thing freshly and see it freshly for what it was in itself. A kind of double talk; one thing always seen in terms of another thing. Criticism? A dreary metaphor. The whole academic method! Of course there were lines like *Life's but a walking shadow*.... Just the same, I'd be damned if the glory of literature was in the metaphor. Besides, it was not a time for the decorative Renaissance flight into simile. Tell the truth cleanly. Weren't the consequences of fraudulent pretending plain to anyone who would look around? Hadn't the great slogans of the first World War become ridiculous to me before I had left high school? Wilsonian idealism! Always the flight of fancy. And Prohibition. Another fantasy. It was hilarious, a beautiful example of the all-prevailing fraudulent morality; and at college it had become a social obligation to go to a bootlegger's, and a man came to have a sneaking respect for those who openly broke the law—not for the policeman standing on a corner.

And the philosophy of St. Thomas Aquinas which I got in my college classroom? All the big words, the metaphysics, were to be treated with grudging suspicion. Nothing could be taken for granted. Nothing could be taken on authority. A craving for authority had led to Prohibition and stupid censorship in Boston. Orthodoxy was for fat comfortable inert people who agreed to pretend, agreed to accept the general fraud, the escape into metaphor. All around me seemed to be

143

some kind of a wild energy that could be tapped and controlled. In the dance halls I heard the jazz sounds coming from Chicago. That town, Chicago! The bootleggers, the shootings, the open disrespect for all that had been thought of as socially acceptable. And Sherwood Anderson and Carl Sandburg had lived in Chicago.

Yet Chicago didn't beckon to me. Nor did Greenwich Village. Edna Millay, Eugene O'Neill, Floyd Dell, Max Bodenheim. I knew all the names. But the Village seemed to me to be a place full of characters. I was against all writers who wanted to become "characters." The whole contemporary world was full of characters. Women rode on the wings of airplanes, men sat on flagpoles, there were stunt men of all kinds, jazz musicians, young ladies going gallantly to hell on bathtub gin. But there was also the way Jack Dempsey fought. His brutal mauling style seemed to be telling me something: do the thing you want to do in your own way. Be excellent at it. Seek you own excellence. Having no use for pure aesthetes or aloof intellectuals, I went on playing ball, and enjoyed the skill required of a pitcher working on a hitter. I tell this to show the kind of thinking, the thoughts about writing, of a young reporter doing the hotel beat. In the hotels I sat talking far too long with opera singers or visiting senators.

In the hotel one day I remember encountering a British author, a nice middle-aged gray-haired man. And in no time I was telling him firmly that writing had to do with the right relationship between the words and the thing or person being described: the words should be as transparent as glass, and every time a writer used a brilliant phrase to prove himself witty or clever he merely took the mind of the reader away from the object and directed it to himself; he became simply a performer. Why didn't he go on the stage? The elderly British writer, regarding me thoughtfully, asked me how old I was. "An interesting view of style. Look here," and he took a page out of his notebook and wrote on it his name and the address of an English publisher. If I ever wrote anything I was to send this note along with it to the English publisher.

I remember one time at twilight, sitting at the typewriter in the sunroom of my parents' home. I could smell the lilacs. A night bird cried. A woman's voice came from a neighbor's yard. I wanted to get it down so directly that it wouldn't feel or look like literature. I remembered too being with a girl one night, and on the way home, walking alone, I felt the world had been brought close to me; there seemed to be magic in the sound of my own footsteps, even in the noise of the streetcars—all mingled with the girl's kiss, the memory of the little run I had noticed in her stocking, the way she said good-bye to me. None of it had to be written up. There it was, beautiful in itself. A "literary guy" would spoil it. . . .

Everybody in Paris seemed to paint, and in store windows in strange little streets you would see reproductions of Matisse, Derain, Rouault, Chirico, Modigliani, Picasso, Utrillo, and in the Quarter the surrealists

Picabia and Miro were famous names. At that time there was still a common language of painting; the language hadn't got broken up. The painters hadn't quite entered their tower of Babel.

Some writers like to sit for long hours at their desks. Not me. At that time the *New Yorker* had written asking if I had any stories. I began to work on some. And I was also working on the novel that was to be called *It's Never Over*. But the Paris streets were my workshop. While loafing along the streets ideas for the stories would grow in my head. Little street scenes would seem to distract me, would indeed get my full attention: the intent expression on the faces of men hurrying to the street urinals; workingmen quarreling under the eyes of a gendarme, each seeking the triumph of provoking the other to strike the first blow and get arrested. Or some little street whore would make me wonder, "Why are so many of these girls of the same short solid build as the whores Lautrec loved to paint?" A writer is always working. I can remember watching the ease and style with which Lacoste and Cochet handled Big Bill Tilden in the Davis Cup tennis matches and telling myself it had something to do with style in writing. When I got back to the apartment I would sit by the window overlooking the prison wall and write rapidly, most of the work having been done in my head before I came home. Often it rained. It was the time for reading. Very late at night was also a good time. From the window I could watch the bicycle patrol, the three tough French cops no one wanted to tangle with, come peddling slowly down the street.

Even when reading a writer is busily at work watching how an effect is achieved on the page. But whether I was reading D.H. Lawrence or Tolstoi or Virginia Woolf I would notice that when I hit certain scenes I would be so carried away I would cease to be aware of style or method. What then made good writing good? That was always the question. Freshness? Verbal felicity? No, there always seemed to be some other quality. There had been at the time a quarrel about the methods of Arnold Bennett and Virginia Woolf; Bennett's or Zola's camera eye and Virginia Woolf's interior flow of impressions. But it seemed to me, reading so late at night in my room overlooking the prison wall, that there could be no quarrel at all. The temperament, the character, the very identity of the writer was in his kind of eye. Virginia Woolf had a sensibility so fragile it must have been always close to the breaking point; she couldn't have written any other way. And Lawrence? Again the writer's own character gave his work its identity. He must have been an Anglo-Saxon puritan with an inborn uneasiness about female flesh; he must have hated this uneasiness, and hungered for the expression of ecstasy; therefore the natural poetry of sex. But then I would wonder why Lady Chatterley's correct copulations didn't move me as much as one surrender by Anna Karenina, or one of poor Emma Bovary's fugitive rolls in the hay.

At the cafés, of course, one could always get an argument on these questions. But I knew what I was seeking in my Paris street walks, and

145

in the typing hours—with Loretto waiting to retype a chapter. It was this: strip the language, and make the style, the method, all the psychological ramifications, the ambience of the relationships, all the one thing, so the reader couldn't make separations. Cézanne's apples. The appleness of apples. Yet just apples.

Wandering around Paris I would find myself thinking of the way Matisse looked at the world around him and find myself growing enchanted. A pumpkin, a fence, a girl, a pineapple on a tablecloth—the thing seen freshly in a pattern that was a gay celebration of things as they were. Why couldn't all people have the eyes and the heart that would give them this happy acceptance of reality? The word made flesh. The terrible vanity of the artist who wanted the word without the flesh. I can see now that I was busily rejecting even then that arrogance of the spirit, that fantasy running through modern letters and thought that man was alien in this universe. From Pascal to Henry Miller they are the children of St. Paul.

1963

The Plight of Canadian Fiction

Speaking at the Toronto Book Fair, I pointed out that a young Canadian writer who had an authentic talent for creative prose, and wanted to develop it honestly, had little or no chance in this country; immediately people protested that Ralph Connor had made a million dollars, and that anyway it was sour grapes for a writer to make faces at people for not reading his work.

All I can say is that I felt perfectly free to make this criticism because ever since I started to write I had earned my living in the United States and expected to go on doing so. At the time I was thinking of those young prose writers in this country who were trying desperately to get started, and who, being Canadians, seemed to think they ought to get published in their own country. I was simply trying to tell them that if they were very good and had a distinctive talent and wrote honestly the chances were that they would not get published at all in this country unless they were first of all published some place else.

It has been said that it takes an honest fiction writer who loves his work about ten years to force himself upon the public. Some very great writers meet with no acclaim until years after their death: but sooner or later they get it. Yet even with this nice consoling thought in the back of his head a young writer knows that he has to find somebody to publish him; he won't grow and ripen, book after book, in the darkness of his own attic. He has to have some kind of an audience.

There are two ways for a man to get his fiction published: he may sit down and study the fiction market offered by the big magazines, and if he is intelligent and not impatient and has the gift at all he may succeed in giving the editors the thing they want. He meets the market. Success may come to such a writer very quickly. In no time at all he may have an enormous income, because there are vast profits to be made from writing for the big slick magazines.

What such a writer has to do is be very careful to see that he is always saying the thing that people want to have said: he must never demand that a reader turn his head sharply to the left or the right: he must forever curb his instinct to say to the reader, "Look at it my way. You never looked at it before like this. But look at it." If he should make this mistake, and the editor should let it get by him, the consequences are apt to be pretty terrible for everybody concerned. The reader may have been made to feel uncomfortable. Worse still, he may actually have been made unhappy. He may write to the editor, or simply stop reading that particular writer and advise his friends to do so. The circulation of the magazine will drop if the same thing happens two or three times. If this dubious and revolutionary activity continues, the editor himself becomes the unhappiest man of all; he is out of the job. And properly so. He has failed as a comforter. . . .

But what about the writer who wants to have his own growth and look at reality with his own eyes and record adult experience in a fresh form he moulds for himself?

Not that it is enough, Lord knows, just to be honest: you can be honest and terribly dull and have no creative imagination: but in the trade, I understand, the agents and editors make this general distinction between honest writers and writers who are just entertainers.

The greatest joy that comes to a writer comes when he goes on year after year doing the thing he loves in his own way, never yielding, and maybe taking a bad beating now and then, and suddenly finds that he has won for himself an audience and that people have learned to look at it in his way. With this triumph may come his death as an artist. The general acceptance and adulation may well ruin him. He may devote the rest of his life to trying to keep his audience without ever offending them. He may become a comforter just like the slick creator of drugstore literature we were talking about a minute ago. But he had that one hour of triumph.

However, the Canadian writer need never fear that such a triumph in Canada may mean the death of his spirit. Such a triumph is impossible here. The kind of writer I am talking about now can have no beginning in this country, no growth here, no "being" as a Canadian writer. Why? Because he has no place here to publish his wares.

But what about our great national magazines, what about the book fair, what about the customs duties that protect Canadian publishers and writers from the influx of literature from the United States?

147

Our national magazines are comparable to the national magazines in the United States, magazines like *Colliers, The Woman's Home Companion, etc.* —what are called the big "slicks." They want a certain kind of fiction running to a formula and comforting to millions of people. From time to time they will publish what they call a "quality" story, but hardly ever by a newcomer.

In the United States the hope of the beginning writer who has some ambition and love of his work is the "quality" group of magazines—*Harper's, Scribner's,* the *Atlantic, Esquire, The New Yorker.* He hopes that he will write in these magazines till he becomes very famous, and then the national circulation magazines will want to print him.

But in Canada there are simply no magazines of this kind. The country doesn't seem to be able to afford them. There are a few papers like *The Canadian Forum,* but they cannot afford to pay for contributions. Obviously then, the Canadian story-tellers, the Canadian Chekhovs, Maupassants, Andersons, Katherine Mansfields, if there are ever to be any, are not going to bob up in these parts: they are going to put their heads above water in the United States, and then maybe later on be read at home.

If the new Canadian writer has written a novel he has a little better chance than the short-story writer. There are Canadian publishers, though they operate under very special conditions as far as Canadian fiction is concerned, and certainly in a country that is no publisher's paradise. In the whole of Canada there are about eleven million people. The French language is spoken by some four million of the population, which leaves the Canadian publisher seven million customers to work on, seven million distributed across the continent, and this doesn't offer the publisher a field for his activities as large as the population of the city of New York.

I say that the Canadian publisher operates under special conditions because he can remain in business as a distributor of fiction and never publish a work of fiction by a Canadian writer. Why should he take such a chance on work he knows will be unprofitable, he may ask. Hasn't the most ambitious of the Canadian publishers pointed out that his profits on Canadian literature amount to one per cent? So the publisher imports the fiction lists of the English and American publishers—and everybody is quite satisfied.

This is a special condition, I say, because Canada, culturally, is sandwiched in between two countries that speak the same language, which makes it a good deal different than if the people of France, say, were asked to read only the fiction of Germany and England. . . .

But these dreadfully melancholy musings lead inevitably to one terrifying thought. If an honest sincere Canadian writer can't live off the avails of his creative work in this country, if there is no place for him to print his work here, and if he finds that, even when he writes books that sell, the mother publishing house is apt to be in the United

States, is, then, the Canadian literature we hear so much about at various times of the year really necessary?

This is a bad question to ask. It leads you to wondering just what Canadian literature really is. And then you take a look at the map and you wonder if a recording of the life of Vancouver on the Pacific in creative prose is closer culturally or regionally to a recording of the life and landscape of a lake city away on the other side of the continent like Toronto, than it is, say, to a novel about Seattle. Or then again, some impious fellow, with an evil sneer on his face, may duck his head in and ask why a Toronto school of literature should be more important than a Buffalo or Detroit school of literature. While it is readily conceded that groups in both cities are of equal importance and that it is possible for a regional literature to come from the districts they represent, it should be plain to any writer that he will have to make his way in the big outside world no matter what kind of a local reputation he has.

Maybe I'm wrong about this: I haven't spent much time on it and don't intend to. But with all the lip-service being rendered these days on the hustings to Canadian literature, with all the energy being let loose in the way of banquets, speeches, the hearty advice and *obiter dicta* of big brothers, men who offer themselves as spirit guides and the wistful souls who long to be presidents of some literary society or other, it is very important that the provincialism of these people shouldn't be allowed to take on the air of patriotic dignity or great cultural nobility. Let these affairs provide a round of social activities for those restless people who need them, but for heaven's sake let not the few writers in the country be touched by them. I admit that it's probably very terrifying to the three or four fiction writers in the country when the hundred and fifty cheer-leaders rush at them, glassy-eyed, to organize them and comfort them and put them on the right track. Yet it should be possible to take it all in the spirit of good clean fun. No writer worth his salt should be harmed. Maybe it will even be possible for him to get a word in and explain that there is no spiritual gratification to be found simply in the sale of any book, no matter what kind of tripe, in Canada, any more than there is in the sale of a package of tea; and that anyway the trouble with Canada is not that Canadians don't buy books as well as the people of other countries—in terms of comparative populations Canadians do buy books; the trouble is that there is not much sense of adventure in reading in our people: they go for the books that have a big sale in other countries. Maybe this is inevitable. Maybe Canadians never will have a separate taste or awareness distinct from the provincial cities of North America. Maybe it isn't even desirable that they should have, especially when their writers have to sink or swim and be broken or made outside the country.

In the meantime then, to repeat, writers of fiction need not expect to be nursed along in their own country. But should they be unhappy about this? I don't think so. Fewer Canadian writers will get published, but the ones who do will have to be good enough to compete with their

149

brethren from across the line. The going may be pretty rough for young writers till they are ready to spread their wings, but if they have the itch they will go on. Of course it may be a little maddening to them at times if they are present when the local medicine men are feasting and having a big cultural pow-wow; but if they get into the banquet on a rain check they can always bring everybody down to earth by getting up and asking humbly how many writers of adult fiction have appeared in the country in the last ten years.

1938

Bertram Brooker
1888-1955

Born in Croydon, England, Bertram Brooker came to Canada in 1905 and became a journalist for the *Winnipeg Free Press*. After moving to Toronto in 1921 he worked as an advertising executive but made his reputation as a painter and as a writer. *The Tangled Miracle*, a mystery story published under the pseudonym Huxley Hearne, appeared in 1936. In the same year, his novel *Think of the Earth*, won the first Governor-General's Award for fiction. Brooker's third novel, *The Robber* was published in 1949. "The Future of the Novel in Canada" first appeared in the *Association of Canadian Bookmen's Literary Bulletin* in 1938.

The Future of the Novel in Canada

When Miss Phyllis Bentley, the well-known English novelist, paid a visit to Canada last year, she made a statement at two of her public appearances, which was received by a few of the writers who heard her—myself among them—with rather mixed feelings. Miss Bentley said, in effect, that if we wished to produce a number of outstanding novels in Canada, we must have many more people writing many more novels.

The mental and physical task of conceiving and writing a novel is one which few writers will undertake unless they have a fair amount of confidence in their ability to carry it out. And this degree of confidence, which comes not merely from doing a lot of writing, but from seeing a lot of one's writing published somewhere, is naturally rare in Canada, because of the obvious restrictions of our market.

Consider further the case of a man or woman who has succeeded in getting a first novel published. What encouragement has such a person to go on and write the second novel, which is almost bound to be better than the first, and then the third, which is almost certain to be better than the second? Unless the writer can find a publisher and a market, either in the United States or in England, as well as in Canada, the encouragement is almost nil. He never, by any chance, makes any money out of a first novel—not as much as he would make by writing for some obscure paper at a cent a word or less. Money, however, is rarely the incentive which starts people writing novels. But they do look for some sort of recognition, and until lately the recognition of Canadian novelists by the press and the public has discouraged publishers from risking the publication of Canadian fiction. There has been little or no demand for it.

The situation has changed in very recent years. You can count those years on the fingers of one hand. More than one book publisher today can be found in Canada who is receptive to native material, and even enthusiastic about it. And one reason for the change is that the authors themselves have organized themselves into bodies which fulfil a dual purpose—mutual encouragement, and the popularization of Canadian Books in the eyes of the public. There are now press clubs, writers' clubs, arts and letters clubs, branches of the Canadian Authors' Association, and branches of the Association of the Canadian Bookmen, in the principal cities of Canada, and through their efforts the public of Canada is at last becoming conscious of the fact that there are a few worthwhile writers in this dominion.

To some it might appear to be unduly aggressive on the part of authors and publishers to band themselves together and organize such an event, for example, as the National Book Fair, for the avowed purpose of selling their wares to the Canadian public. The answer to that is that if the aim were entirely mercenary few authors would have anything to do with such organizations, and the public, scenting a purely commercial atmosphere, would not respond as they have done to the various means which have veen invented to awaken their interest in Canadian books.

The truth is that the increased sales accruing to any one author in Canada as the result of all these efforts combined, hardly ever amount to enough to buy a second-hand typewriter. The time spent by an author in the organization work, at meetings, and in the preparation and delivery of addresses, is almost entirely a labour of love, and springs far more from the desire to acquaint the public with the work of some colleague he admires, whose books, he considers, should merit a reception equal to that of writers of similar calibre in Europe and the United States.

And if, at times, these functions take on the air of a mutual admiration society, I hope what I have said will cause you to feel that a little appreciation and encouragement—which, at present, many writers can expect only from discriminating fellow writers—are necessary to offset the almost complete lack of monetary return in a market as small as ours.

The more I think about it, the more I am impressed with Miss Bentley's notion that the future of the novel in Canada depends on greater productiveness—on the encouragement of more people to write—and on the encouragement of novelists who have published one book, to go on and write a second and a third. I don't see how writers in Canada can expect a more receptive attitude from publishers than they have been getting in the last five years. If the situation is to be improved at all the change must come, it seems to me, in the attitude of the public. And there are at least two ways in which the book-buyer can help.

I have often wondered why it is that people generally do not seem to share the glow of satisfaction I get myself when I discover that somebody in Canada has written a book or painted a picture that is without question superior to the work of someone with a puffed-up reputation in another country. It is an old story, this business about the prophet being without honour in his own country. It is perhaps far too late to try to say anything new about it; and yet I would venture this. It seems to me that the law, if it is a law, does not apply at all equally to the many fields of endeavour in which men engage. This may be a warped point of view, but I will give it for what it is worth. In sport, in medicine, in music, and even in painting, there are many people who do not lack honour in Canada. In literature, on the contrary, there are few writers of reputation, except those who have gained it elsewhere and whose books come in to Canada on a par, so to speak, with importations of foreign writers. . . .

Here is something which can and should be urged on the book-buying public of Canada:—that they might develop at least a little more curiosity about the work of their fellow-countrymen in the field of literature. It would be futile to urge a greater appreciation, but curiosity is another matter, and it is precisely that which these A.C.B. Book Fairs and other functions are attempting to arouse. One is tempted to place a good deal of stress on the possibility of a wider market because the materials at hand in Canada out of which good fiction can be made, are peculiarly rich, as rich as they are in many other directions, and it seems a pity to let such a wealth of raw material lie undeveloped.

To begin at the beginning, we have a very glamorous and historical background here, unrivalled perhaps by any other country in the world, when material for historical fiction is considered. It is true that many European countries have their heroic figures and their costume periods, their great wars and revolutions, their extravagant courts and their vicious slums; but there is scarcely a country anywhere which has packed so much colourful adventure over so vast a geographical range in such a short space of time as Canada. It is hardly necessary to enlarge on the combination in Canada of so many elements which should fire the imagination of the novelist. The old world and the new world met and fought out their struggles here, against a scenic background of lakes and rivers, prairies and mountians, providing in themselves these terrific odds and handicaps out of which epics are made.

The building of a new and mixed society in this enormous country offers tremendous scope to the novelist, and although several fine novels have been hewn out of the available material—one thinks immediately of *Maria Chapdelaine* of the novels of Frederick Philip Grove, of Jane Rolyat's *Lily of Fort Garry*, of Marius Barbeau's *Temlahan*, and many others—nevertheless, as they say in mining, the surface has hardly been scratched.

For the novelist who draws his inspiration from the contemporary scene, the outlook is not quite so colourful, nor as easy to manipulate. The Canadian people to-day seem to pride themselves on being as little distinctive and eccentric as possible. Our women like to look as though they had just stepped out of a fashion show in Paris or New York, and as far as our men are concerned, the ubiquitous grey hat and blue overcoat have become almost a national costume. We delight in being thought reasonable, conservative, unhysterical, and the result is that on the whole we appear rather middling.

We lack character—not in the sense of moral stability, which is generally regarded as very high in Canada—but in the sense of strong individuality, divergence of temperament, in a word, eccentricities—either national or personal—which, of course, are valuable to the novelist in making his characters interesting, amusing or tragic, as the case may be.

And if we look into the future the promise of any better material in this regard is not hopeful. All over the world a levelling process is going on which threatens a rather grey, equalized, regimented scene for the future novelist. . . .

In conclusion I should like to ask what effect, if any, the current experimentation elsewhere with new writing techniques will have on our future novel writers. So far, our novelists have shown little tendency to experiment, and with such a strong national disposition to stay in the middle of the road, it is almost certain that within the next few years, unless a miracle happens, we shall have mostly sound, solid, conventionally-built novels.

We have a very exciting country, but a very unexcited people. We pay the penalty in a certain humdrummery which pervades our whole life and literature; but, on the other hand, we reap what most Canadians consider to be the richer rewards of solidity, quietude and comfort.

1938

Philip Child
1898-1978

Born in Hamilton, Ontario, Philip Child was educated at the University of Toronto, Harvard and Cambridge. He returned to the University of Toronto in 1936 after teaching at the University of British Columbia and at Harvard University and became Chancellors' Professor of English at Trinity College in 1942. In addition to two volumes of poetry, Child published five novels: *The Village of Souls* (1933); *God's Sparrows* (1937); *Day of Wrath* (1945); *Mr Ames Against Time* (1949); and the pseudonymously published *Blow Wind, Come Wrack* (1945). "Fiction" appeared in *Canadian Literature Today*, a transcript of a series of broadcasts sponsored by the Canadian Broadcasting Corporation in 1938.

Fiction

Among many definitions of literature is the following: "Literature is the expression of a nation's mind in writing."* If twenty years ago, we had judged Canadian fiction by such a standard we should have had to question whether Canada had achieved a national fiction at all. For we had not then become a nation, and our fiction was English or American fiction, even though it happened to be written in Canada by Canadians. It was inspired only superficially, if at all, by the spirit of a country still engaged in finding itself. Our fiction was such as would fit readily into the pattern of taste of British or American readers. Indeed it had to be. Canada was a sparsely populated, pioneer country. Where was the Canadian public which could give a Canadian novelist his bread and butter?

Of course there had been excellent novelists in Canada: Haliburton, Kirby, Sir Gilbert Parker, to name a few chronologically. But taking Canadian fiction by and large, it lacked intensity of feeling. It was written in fashions of sentiment or adventure formed in other countries; it was derivative; it represented a migration of culture from elsewhere and did not, as it were, live off the land. It was thin—it lacked an eye for the Canadian character, for those qualities which distinguish us as a people from, say, our American neighbours. With such rare exceptions as Sir Charles G.D. Roberts's animal stories, it had given to the world of letters no innovations in subject or technique. Canadian novelists were expected to choose romantic and exotic themes which

*Channing, *Remarks on American Literature*

154

would appeal to readers elsewhere. They were constrained to romanticize old Quebec. Costume romances far inferior to Kirby's *Golden Dog* appeared, rich in history perhaps, but stuffed with characters who were lay figures, not living, breathing Canadians of the past. Or they had to sentimentalize in conventional vein the struggle on the frontier, accentuating the virility of pioneer life and veiling its tragedy. Somehow the less spectacular and, after all, more characteristic elements of Canadian life were not explored. Where was that typical Canadian, *homo Canadensis*, voter, democrat, business man or farmer, fisherman or workman, that man of British or foreign stock, subtly altered by his Canadian environment? He remained undiscovered. Canadians were indifferent to him, while to the American and British publics he lacked exotic glamour.

What of the present situation in Canadian fiction? Well, it is still true that a Canadian novelist or short-story writer must look to the United States or Britain for his living. But as our country emerges from pioneer youth into adulthood as a member of the British Commonwealth of Nations we are becoming increasingly aware of our writers. Intelligent citizens realize that we must undertake the intellectual and artistic responsibilities of a maturing nation as well as the social and political. A small but growing body of Canadian readers is ready to send forth novelists, so to speak, in search of Canada, in the belief that writers have their part to play in the spiritual task of forming a nation. The novelist have responded, sporadically it is true, but with a new note of sincerity.

The most encouraging portent in recent fiction is the trend towards realism, and by realism I do not mean a morbid concern with the sordid and tragic aspects of life, though these, too, should not be veiled, but simply the attempt of the sincere novelist to distil in literature something distinctively and characteristically Canadian. Time, unfortunately, permits only the arbitrary selection of a few examples for discussion.

The prairies, where the struggle for existence has been perhaps nearer the elemental than elsewhere, has proved the natural home of realism. Robert Stead, Arthur Stringer, Laura Goodman Salverson, and Martha Ostenso have formed an assured niche for themselves as Canadian writers who paint the true western life with fidelity and vigour. The last two novelists are Canadians of foreign descent and perhaps that fact has helped to give them a more objective insight into our country and its people than is the case with such of our writers as simply take their roots for granted. Laura Salverson's first novel, *The Viking Heart*, tells the story of a band of Icelandic settlers who, though friendless in a strange country with nothing to help them but the courage of the Viking heart, rise from obscure poverty to—not affluence, mark you; the author has avoided the vulgar materialism of the ordinary "success story"—but to a position of influence where they too, they the erstwhile "foreigners," can make their inherited contribution to the new Canada. She has a fine eye for the Canadian landscape, a vivid appreciation of character, and a feeling for the enduring spiritual elements in our changing country.

Bertram Brooker, in his novel *Think of the Earth*, has written a most unusual book for a Canadian. It is the story of a mystic and an introvert, troubled by the mystery of human life and by the age-old problem of evil, who is

Wandering between two worlds, one dead,
The other powerless to be born.

He is a reader of the mystics, of Blake and Dostoyevsky and Pascal, and his search in life is for something far different from the worldy goal of success in its various forms; his search is essentially the philosopher's search for some certitude of the mind, some Ultima Thule of the spirit, where mankind's sense of guilt will be resolved in a higher vision. The author subjects him to the acid test of reality in a somewhat crude Manitoba town of thirty years ago. This novel aims high; for of all the realms of human thought philosophy is the most difficult to reduce to the medium of fiction. Realistic in the ordinary sense it is not, and yet currents of thought and culture which are universal are sifted through the prism of a Canadian environment. In a field where even Dostoyevsky, the great philosophic novelist, sometimes failed, one should not look for a triumphant masterpiece. Nevertheless a novelist so daring as to present to the limited audience of Canadians interested in such a genre, a not unsuccessful philosophic novel, richly deserved his success in winning last year's Tweedsmuir award.

Of painters of the Ontario scene I have time to discuss only two—Mazo de la Roche and Morley Callaghan. Both of them in their different ways are powerful writers; neither of them, alas, can be said to picture the average Ontarian, that forgotten, or perhaps undiscovered, man of Canadian fiction.

Miss de la Roche has brought honour to Canadian letters and she deserves her fame, not only for the charm of her characterization, but also for her sensitive, beautifully lucid style. The characters of the *Jalna* series are a transplanted English family of means; they are sporting folk, arrogant, self-sufficient, and humorous. It is, I think, unfair to cavil at her, as some do, for not writing of typical Canadians; indeed in an earlier novel, *Possession*, she did write of them, and with realism too. Nevertheless I, for my part, hope she will apply her admirable talent to yet another group of Canadians; and I hope that the unaccountable muse who directs the imagination will allow them to be—say, city folk. I, for one, should like to see what Miss de la Roche would do with city live.

City life is the usual theme of Morley Callaghan. I shall not say that he depicts average city life; it is neither his intention nor his forte to charm the reader with life's sunny hours. The humour, the amusements, the cheerful tolerance of Canadian men and women are not often the subjects of his pen, though in his last book he has broadened his canvas somewhat. He is in deadly earnest. His is a world of shabby streets and mean lodging houses, of wounded spirits baffled by the complexities of civilization, of undernourished lovers reaching pathetically for beauty—and there is beauty, tragic beauty, in Mr. Callaghan's books! He will never be popular with the careless thousands; he paints too gloomy a picture. But he is an honest writer, and a writer of quality; we ought to do justice to an intensity of feeling not common in Canadian letters. Moreover, he is just the kind of Jeremiah-figure we need, unless we want to hide ourselves, ostrich fashion, in the wrong kind of optimism—the kind that comes from the smugness of mere indolent thinking.

I have reserved to the last an extremely significant Canadian writer—Frederick Philip Grove. *Settlers of the Marsh* and *Our Daily Bread* are full of local colour, of the sweep and lure of the prairie, of the enticing promise of its fertile vastness and of the remorseless withdrawal of that promise sometimes, so that the final harvest is frustration. He is a writer of breadth and cultivation; and most valuable of all to Canadian fiction, he has freed himself from the strangling tradition that certain subjects—for instance any treatment of sex that is not conventional—shall be taboo to Canadian writers even though Canadians can and do read of them in other literatures. Upon this subject let Mr. Grove speak for himself. "Is there any domain of life," he asks, "which is excluded from treatment in the novel? To my mind, there is none. If the novel is to be read, it must interest, of course. Personally, I have certain aversions. Thus marriage, to me, is a beginning, not an end: the problem of sex is broached, not solved at the altar. For that reason I abominate the common love story—the story of prenuptial love. . . . In life, both young men and young maids are peculiarly uninteresting at a time when they can see each other as they are not. Apart from that, judging as a reader, anything is grist that comes to my mill." From this passage you will see what an honest realist he is. He is not a morbid sensationalist with, as the French say, a nostalgia for the mud, but he is unflinchingly sincere. His appeal as a novelist is not to those who read in order to forget themselves rather than to find themselves more richly in the ordered significance of a work of art.

There are other Canadian novelists as worthy of discussion as those I have mentioned. I might, for instance, have spoken of the late Grey Owl, a distinctive Canadian writer if there ever was one, though hardly a novelist. No geographical section of Canada is without its representative writer sincerely endeavouring to paint life in that region as he sees it. Purposely I have confined myself to those novelists who seem best to illustrate a turn in the affairs of Canadian letters that augurs well for the future. For the great novels of all lands have been written by realists and Canadians, too, must be realists if we are to develop a really national literature.

We Canadians are a very conservative people. The danger is that our conservatism should harden into stolidity. In literature as in all the provinces of our life we are the inheritors of a great tradition which developed in another climate and which we received already fashioned. This we wish to preserve, but we wish, surely, to preserve it to our use and not as something rigid and confining and incapable of development to suit our own needs. Should we not be more than tolerant, should we not be alert to encourage originality in our literature, knowing, as we do, how heavily the economic scales are of necessity weighed against it in Canada? In conclusion may I quote a fine saying of Goethe's concerning the use and development of tradition? "What we have inherited from our forefathers we must earn over again for ourselves if we would truly possess it."*

*Was du ererbt von deinen Vätern hast,
Erwirb es, um es zu besitzen.

1938

Part 4
Regionalism and Nationalism

Desmond Pacey
1917-1975

William Cyril Desmond Pacey was born in Dunedin, New Zealand, and educated at the University of Toronto and at Cambridge University. In 1944 he became head of the English department at the University of New Brunswick where he later became dean of graduate studies and vice-president. One of the most influential and prolific critics of Canadian literature in the middle decades of this century, his work includes a pioneering critical survey of Canadian literature, *Creative Writing in Canada* (1952); a series of biographical and critical studies of Canadian poets, *Ten Canadian Poets* (1958); and numerous articles on Canadian literature, several of which are collected in *Essays in Canadian Criticism: 1938-1968* (1969). His work on F.P. Grove includes: a collection of previously unpublished stories, *Tales from the Margin* (1971); a critical study, *Frederick Philip Grove* (1945); and *The Letters of Frederick Philip Grove* (1976). "The Novel in Canada" was published in *Queen's Quarterly* in 1945.

The Novel in Canada

The recent popular success of three Canadian novels has served to arouse a high degree of enthusiasm for the prospects of that branch of our literature. Bruce Hutchison's *Hollow Men*, Gwethalyn Graham's *Earth and High Heaven*, and Hugh MacLennan's *Two Solitudes* have all been chosen by one or other of the large American book-distributing clubs, have maintained high places for a considerable period on the list of best-sellers in the United States, and have been favourably reviewed in leading American magazines. Such a threefold Canadian triumph is, I believe, without precedent, though it is sobering to remind ourselves that novels by Gilbert Parker and Ralph Connor were best-sellers a few decades ago.

My purpose in this article is not to deplore the fact that this enthusiasm has been created, nor to engage in a "debunking" of the three novels named, but rather, by pointing to the difficulties and deficiencies which have characterized the history of Canadian fiction in the past, to restore our critical perspective and to suggest that our enthusiasm should be tempered with caution.

That our fiction has lagged behind our poetry is well known. It is true that we have yet produced no preëminently great poet, but in pioneers like Sangster and Mair, in the Lampman-Scott and Roberts-Carman groups, and in contemporaries such as Pratt, Birney, Livesay and Smith, we have a gallery of poetical figures to whom we can point without embarrassment. In the novel, however, there are no comparable names which would evoke general assent. Of novelists of the last century, there would probably be general approval for the claims of Haliburton, though *Sam Slick* is rather a series of humourous sketches than a novel proper; and William Kirby would probably also be chosen, though his fame rests upon a single novel, *The Golden Dog*. But who today—apart from professional students of our literary history—remembers Richardson, author of the once famous *Wacousta*, or Mrs. Leprohon, prolific producer of historical romances a century ago? In this century, because our memories are fresher, there are many more names which we might suggest for inclusion, but of them all, how many do we seriously believe to be candidates for fame? Personally, I believe that the novels of Frederick Philip Grove, because of their honest if rather laboured portrayal of the Canadian scene, will be so remembered. Morley Callaghan has written several distinguished novels, but seems, unfortunately, to have deserted the craft in mid-career. Mazo de la Roche, a writer of great gifts, has devoted her career to the romantic portrayal of one thoroughly unrepresentative family. Many others have written one or more novels of promise or distinction, but I think it is fair to say that none of them has yet produced a sufficiently large body of first-rate work to secure a permanent place in our literary history.

What have been the chief deficiencies in Canadian fiction? First of all, too few of our novels have dealt in an adult manner with life as it is lived here and now. In its most obvious aspect, this tendency has taken the form of writing historical romances rather than novels of contemporary life. Almost all Canadian novels written in the nineteenth century—both in English and French—were historical romances, with Richardson, Mrs. Leprohon, Kirby, and Gilbert Parker as their chief architects. In this century, the tradition of historical romance has been carried on by such novelists as Frederick Niven, Laura Goodman Salverson, T.H. Raddall, and Franklin Davey McDowell. Now it would be foolish to argue that historical novels are valueless, still more so to suggest that in themselves they are pernicious. As Henry James has said, we must grant the novelist his material; what we have a right to criticize is his method of treatment, what he makes of his material. Historical novels can be great novels, as the works of Scott, Thackeray and Tolstoi abundantly prove. Human nature is at least relatively constant, and its strengths and weaknesses can be illuminated as clearly by a distinguished treatment of the life of the seventeenth century as of the twentieth. Moreover, historical romances frequently give us a more vivid sense of the past than historical textbooks. But all is not well in the literary atmosphere of a nation which sees something like eighty per cent of its novelists turning from the present to the past for their subject-matter. It suggests a weakness either in the writers themselves or in the society in which they live.

For though it is possible to write great historical novels, the temptations and difficulties of the form are severe. The temptation in writing historical novels is to desert the ordinary, the representative, and to try for factitious glamour and false excitement; and this temptation few of our authors have successfully resisted. The difficulties of the form are many: the securing of adequate historical detail and the blending of fact and fiction, to mention but two of the most obvious. All the difficulties stem from this crucial fact, that the writer has deliberately cut himself off from the richest source of fictional material—direct observation of the life about him.

But even when our novelists do direct their attention to the Canadian present, many of them approach their material in as unrealistic a spirit as the purveyor of the most factitious historical romances. Perhaps next in bulk among our novels are the edifying books, and of the toally false impression of Canadian life which they give it is unnecessary to speak. The same is true of our books for juveniles, by people like L.M. Montgomery and Norman Duncan, though here the lack of realism is perhaps more excusable. Most serious is the fact that even our relatively important novelists tend to approach our life in a similar spirit. In spite of the flexible style which Mazo de la Roche has at her command, and her sensitivity to the beauties of nature, the behaviour of animals, and the souls of children, the dominant note of her work, from the early *Possession* to the latest

161

volume in the Jalna series, is a shallow romanticism. Even Morley Callaghan, whose best novels (*Such is My Beloved*, for example) I greatly admire, is often guilty of sentimentalism.

What is needed, then, is not merely more novels which treat the contemporary Canadian scene, but more which treat it in a realistic and critical spirit. We need to see the festering sores in our social body, as well as its areas of healthy tissue. Our novelists of the past, with a few honourable exceptions, have been cautious souls, afraid to incur the wrath of the public, and producing either sugar-coated tracts or novels of escape.

In order that this criticism of our national life may be informed as well as passionate, our novelists must subject themselves to intellectual discipline. Our fiction hitherto has been almost devoid of ideas. From how many of our novels would it be possible to extract a coherent and profound philosophy of life? From the novels of Frederick Philip Grove, as I have suggested, such a philosophy may be extracted, though even in his case there is considerable confusion and obscurity; but I am at a loss to suggest any other Canadian novelist of the past or present to whose work such an analysis might be profitably directed. All the great novels of the world, however, have been sustained by a firm philosophical or sociological foundation. We have yet far to go before we can regard our fictional output with any degree of complacency.

A critical awareness of the contemporary scene, and a sustaining philosophy, then, are two wants which our novelists have yet adequately to supply. We miss in them also an adequate awareness of the technical advances made in the art of fiction during the last fifty years. Technically, all our novels cling to the safe paths of the nineteenth century. For all the evidence one finds of it in Canadian fiction, the work of Henry James, James Joyce, André Gide, Marcel Proust, Franz Kafka and other such creative exponents of the novel form, might never have been accomplished. This is strange, especially in view of the influence which the modernist movement has exercised upon recent Canadian poetry. Although we do not want mere imitativeness, the experimental work in other countries cannot be ignored with impunity by our own writers. The Canadian novel is not some delicate exotic flower which will magically bloom only in isolation: it must strike its roots in the great creative achievements of the past, and entwine its branches with the most flourishing growths of the present.

But it is easy to point to the defects of Canadian fiction. A more difficult task is to explain why this branch of our literature has lagged behind our poetical achievement. I propose to offer a tentative answer to this question, conscious of its incompleteness but hopeful that its formulation may encourage further analysis.

When I put this question recently to a practising writer who has had a measure of success in both media, his answer was that it is easier to write a poem than a novel. The reply was made casually, almost flippantly, but I believe it is of some significance. There is a sense in which it is preposterous to discuss the relative difficulty of works of art. In terms of the creative imagination required, it is just as difficult to write a perfect lyric of ten lines as a novel of ten thousand. But there are other senses, surely, in which such a discussion is not preposterous. In terms of the physical effort required, for example, the novel is obviously a more formidable task.

The fact is that our poetical achievement has been made largely in the form of the short lyric, and it seems to me that there are many ways in which a novel is more difficult to write than a lyric. First of all, a novel demands much more of the writer's time. To give one concrete example: Frederick Philip Grove began to write *A Search for America* in 1893; in its original form it ran to half-a-million words; he revised it seven times; it was finally published over thirty years later, in 1927. I do not think that the most conscientious reviser among our lyric poets could offer a parallel. Now this may seem like a trivial or even irrelevant point, but if it is true, as critics have maintained, that most if not all Canadian writers must have another trade or profession and do their writing in their spare time, then it becomes important. The leisuretime artist, if faced with the alternative of writing novels or lyric poems, can hardly be blamed if he chooses the latter. This would be particularly likely if the writer could expect only a meagre financial return from his novel—and this, though the large sales of the three novels mentioned above may herald a change, has undoubtedly been the prevalent expectation.

The novel also, generally speaking, demands a greater degree of social understanding than the lyric. Most lyrics, certainly most Canadian lyrics, exploit either the landscape, or the poet's personal emotions, or a fusion of the two. I hope it will not be construed as a slight upon lyric poetry if I say that these subjects are relatively accessible and even relatively simple. Most novels, on the other hand, involve a critical examination of a social structure: it is no accident that the English novel began to flourish in the eighteenth century, when a mature society became conscious of itself. It follows that in a country where the landscape is inspiring and society somewhat immature the lyric is much more likely than the novel to be produced. In Canada we have landscapes of exceptional beauty: hence, in poetry, Lampman and his fellows, and in painting, the Group of Seven. Our society, on the other hand, is only just emerging from the pioneer, colonial stage, lacking both the eager experimentation of the United States and the rich traditional features of Old World cultures. In such circumstances it is no wonder that our potential novelists either do not write at all or choose the more glamorous portions of our early history for treatment.

And even should the novelist be sufficiently sensitive to respond to the drama which lurks beneath the rather drab surface of Canadian society, the task which then confronts him is one of unusual difficulty. Let us suppose that he decides to emulate Fielding, and do for contemporary Canada what Fielding did for eighteenth-century

England. First of all, the mere size of the country proves an obstacle. It is given to few men to know this country from coast to coast, especially to know it in the full sense of being intimately acquainted with its various cultural areas. Fielding could divide England into London and the rest—Town and Country—and not fall far short of inclusiveness; it would be a rather inadequate picture of Canada which divided it into Montreal (or Toronto, or Vancouver, or Winnipeg) and the rest. Other contrasts may be suggested: Fielding could rely upon a clearly defined and generally accepted class structure, whereas here such divisions, though they undoubtedly exist, are subtle and tenuous to a degree. England had, and has, one cultural tradition; Canada, two major ones and many minor.

It amounts to this: Canadian society, for all its immaturity—or perhaps because of it—is a peculiarly difficult society to reduce to order. To make generalizations which will apply to all sections of it is almost impossible. It is for this reason that we are not likely to have for some time anything approaching a national novel; the best we can hope for are solid regional studies. But it might be argued that the very diversity and complexity of our society should have proved a challenge to our novelists, both to attempt the herculean task for creating a national novel and the no less important task of interpreting the various regions to one another. Here we encounter two other factors which, I believe, have inhibited the development of Canadian fiction.

For the production of great fiction there is required not merely a developed society but a society which has become conscious of itself. The novels of Fielding and Thackeray, of Turgenev and Tolstoi, of Balzac and Flaubert, were produced when currents of social criticism were flowing strongly in their respective countries. In Canada, however, until recently, the habit of social analysis has been but weakly developed. As a nation, we have been rather apathetic toward broad political and social questions. Although this country has frequently been the scene of agitated social controversies, such controversies have tended to centre rather about immediate *ad hoc* issues—railways, tariffs, conscription, for example—than about more fundamental issues of political and social philosophy. Whether in foreign or domestic policy, our tendency has been to delay action until delay proved no longer possible, and then to improvise a policy on the basis of immediate circumstances rather than on the basis of a clearly reasoned philosophy of government. If this is so, it is not surprising that we have as yet produced no great sociological novels.

Another inhibiting factor is that we have not yet developed a strong national consciousness (though here again there are recent signs of change). This lack is a barrier to the production not only of national novels, but of strong regional ones. A regional consciousness in itself is not sufficient to evoke regional art. Where a merely regional consciousness exists the tendency is towards an inverted, and therefore non-productive, provincialism: the inhabitants of a given region may be assumed to know the nature of their own life, and not to need its representation in art. It is when a strong regional consciousness is supplemented by an equally strong consciousness of the world beyond the region that the need is felt to interpret this region to others. The great novel, however, will demand not only a profound knowledge and understanding of our national society; it will demand also the assimilation of ideas which transcend the barriers of space and time. We do not demand of lyric poetry that it deal in profound ideas: if we did, our Lampmans and Carmans would fall woefully short; but the novel, because of its greater scope and scale, will omit them at its peril. Responsiveness to international currents of thought, however, is not one of our strong points as a nation. We tend to be suspicious of ideas, to accept them only reluctantly when they have been tried and accepted (and occasionally, in turn, discarded) elsewhere. It is true that we expect the novelist to be in advance of the national average in matters of this kind, but he is one of us, and inevitably shares to some extent our weaknesses.

These, then, seem to me the major reasons why our novels have not matched, in either quantity or quality, our poems: the relative drabness of our society when compared with the beauty of our landscape, the amorphous quality of that society, the weakness of our habits of social analysis, our lack of a strong national consciousness, and our distrust of ideas. It is in the light of these considerations that, as Canadians, we should regard the three novels mentioned at the beginning of this article. There is ground for encouragement, even for temperate enthusiasm, in their appearance, but it does not consist in the fact that they have achieved popularity in the United States. On the other hand, to suggest that because they have attained best-seller status they are therefore poor books seems to me pure snobbishness. The encouraging thing is that in these three books, especially in those by Mr. MacLennan and Miss Graham, and in other recent novels such as Grove's *Master of the Mill*, Sinclair Ross's *As for Me and My House*, and Mrs. Baird's *Waste Heritage*, we have genuine if still striving efforts to wrestle in fiction with the complexities of contemporary Canadian society. None of these novels are great; they are all open to serious criticism in terms of both philosophy and technique; but cumulatively they mark a definite advance. Their joint appearance argues hopefully not only for the maturing of our novels, but also for the maturing of our nation. The end is not yet.

1945

165

Edward McCourt
1907-1972

Edward McCourt was born in Ireland, and his family immigrated to Canada in 1909. He graduated from the University of Alberta in 1932 and entered Oxford University as a Rhodes Scholar. Following his return to Canada in 1937, he taught at colleges and universities in Ontario and New Brunswick before joining the Department of English at the University of Saskatchewan. His published works include: novels; travel books; short stories; and a study of prairie literature, *The Canadian West in Fiction* (1949). Among his best known novels are: *Music at the Close* (1947); *Home is the Stranger* (1950); and *The Wooden Sword* (1956). "The Canadian Historical Novel" appeared in the *Dalhousie Review* in 1946.

The Canadian Historical Novel

When Michael Drayton, writing in the year 1606, hailed the New World as "Earth's only Paradise" where

> the Golden Age
> Still Nature's laws doth give,

he was, no doubt, availing himself of the license permitted to one who is both poet and prophet. But if, by means of a Wellsian time-machine, Drayton had been able to project himself into the future far enough and long enough to read the story of Canada as her novelists have told it, he would have found that his sole error lay in locating earth's Paradise specifically in Virginia rather than some seven hundred miles farther north. There, if our novelists are to be believed, heroes conceived in the tradition of Rider Haggard and Stanley Weyman shaped the destinies of our nation in a setting which is a pleasing mosaic of Ruritania, Arcady and the Bonnie Braes of Atholl.

The Canadian historical novel was not always thus. John Richardson, whose *Wacousta*, published in 1832, is the earliest true example of the *genre* written by a Canadian, acknowledged that the historical novelist is bound within certain limits to tell the truth as he sees it. It is to be admitted that outside these limits Richardson moves at times in dimensions since explored only by Walt Disney and Superman: thus the villain, Wacousta, climbs a flag-pole while holding a well developed young lady in his arms, climbs down again and carries off his prize in the teeth of an entire British infantry regiment. The dialogue, too, is as grotesque as much of the action, the characters talking like the young ladies and gentlemen of the novel of sensibility at its worst, rather than like the products of a military and frontier environment. The heroine, having observed a beaver (in reality a disguised Indian) swimming towards a rowboat in a remarkably purposeful manner, calls the attention of her companion to the phenomenon in the following terms:

> My heart misgives me sadly, for I like not the motions of this animal, which are strange and unusually bold. But this is not all; a beaver or a rat might ruffle the mere surface of the water, yet this leaves behind it a deep and gurgling furrow, as if the element had been ploughed to its very bottom. Observe how the lake is agitated and discoloured wherever it has passed. Moreover, I dislike this sudden bustle on board the schooner, knowing, as I do, there is not an officer present to order the movements now visibly going forward. The men are evidently getting up the anchor, and see how her sails are loosened, apparently courting the breeze, as if she would fly to avoid some threatened danger. Would to heaven this council scene were over,—for I do, as much as yourself, dearest Clara, distrust these cruel Indians.

And Lieutenant Murphy, a popular and gallant Irish officer being mortally wounded by a sniper, announces his impending death in words appropriately weighty:

> His aim has been too true. The ball of the villain has found a lodgement in my breast. God bless ye all, my boys; may your fates be more lucky than mine.

But there are times when Richardson appears to be looking at life steadily, if not whole. There is, in *Wacousta*, no attempt to glorify the Noble Savage, no attempt to represent the war between the French and the English as anything other than a cruel, internecine strife in which the stakes were gold and not glory. Richardson may have been deficient in imagination and in technical skill, but his ideal of the historical novel was a worthy one.

His realism found, however, little favour with his successors, most of whom succumbed to the spell of Longfellow. Longfellow's influence on the Maritimes tourist trade has long been gratefully acknowledged. indeed it would seem only fitting that the New England bard be adopted as the patron saint of Nova Scotia, since he has created for that province a legend which has enabled the Land of Evangeline to compete on at least equal terms with Mount Vernon and the Alamo. But it is less generally recognised that Longfellow's influence on the Canadian historical novel has been equally profound. The Land of Evangeline as he conceived it (his imagination being happily unhampered by any first-hand acquaintance with his subject), has become a type setting for Canadian novels dealing not only with the expulsion of the Acadians, but with almost every phase of the Ancient Regime.

What may we rightfully ask of our historical novelists? John Buchan has defined the historical novel with admirable succinctness as "simply a novel which attempts to reconstruct the life and recapture the spirit of an age other than that of the writer." G. M. Trevelyan requires of the historical novelist "an historical mind apt to study the records of a period, and a power of creative imagination able to reproduce the perceptions so acquired in a picture that has all the colours of life." The task of the conscientious historical novelist is thus a twofold one; to study to the fullest extent of his means and ability the records of the period with which he proposes to deal; and to exercise his imagination in the creation of life within the authentic setting established by his research.

But even the most cursory examination of the Canadian historical novel suggests that it is scarcely the work of historical minds "apt to study the records of a period." The Ancient Regime as depicted by our novelists has little in common with Parkman's reconstruction of the same period. To the novelist, the Ancient Regime is indeed the New World's Golden Age. Over it the mellow blight of Longfellow has fallen; and in the cloak-and-sword romances of Thomas Guthrie Marquis, Sir Gilbert Parker, Frances Harrison and a score of others, gaily dressed puppets perform their antics against a backdrop as charming and unreal as a Forest of Arden in Sadler's Wells.

Even Willa Cather, one of America's greatest novelists, has not been proof against the spell. Her exquisite idyll, *Shadows on the Rock*, is far superior in prose style and imaginative power to any other novel dealing with the Ancient Regime. But asceticism and hardship and death are softened and beautified in the gentle light of Miss Cather's imagination as it plays over the picture of a day long past. In *Shadows on the Rock* the ancient citadel of Quebec is conceived not in the harsh light of reality, but in some rare and lovely dream.

It is in the numerous retellings of the story of the Acadian expulsion that Longfellow's influence is most apparent. Sir Charles G.D. Roberts, Marshall Saunders, and more recently Evelyn Eaton, have repeated with only minor variations the Longfellow pattern,—

There, in the midst of its farms, reposed the Acadian village. . .
There in the tranquil evenings of summer, when brightly the sunset
Lighted the village street and gilded the vanes on the chimneys,
Matrons and maidens sat, in snow white caps and in kirtles
Scarlet and blue and green, with distaffs spinning the golden
Flax for the gossiping looms, whose noisy shuttles within doors
Mingled their sound with the whir of the wheels and the song of the
    of the maidens. . . .
Thus dwelt together in love these simple Acadian farmers,
Dwelt in the love of God and of man. Alike were they free from
Fear, that reigns with the tyrant, and envy, the vice of republics:
Neither locks had they to their doors nor bars to their windows,
But their dwellings were open as day and the hearts of their owners;
There the richest was poor and the poorest lived in abundance.

One feels that Mr. Thomas Raddall could tell the story of the expulsion if he chose. His incidental account of the Acadians, in *Roger Sudden*, carries conviction. But even Mr. Raddall, certainly the most promising historical novelist to appear in Canada in recent years, seems to be in some danger of self-betrayal. His first novel, *His Majesty's Yankees*, was a fine and stirring achievement; his latest, *Roger Sudden*, shows a very considerable falling away. This story of the founding of Halifax and the capture of Louisburg exhibits Mr. Raddall's characteristic attention to background and regard for the historical record. But in his personal exploits, both amatory and political, Roger Sudden is painfully reminiscent of the heroes of Ouida. This is a pity, because Mr. Raddall is a man of exceptional gifts.

There are, in addition to Raddall, perhaps half-a-dozen novelists who have dealt with various phases of the Ancient Regime as honestly as their talents have permitted. William Kirby, whose ponderous account of corruption in high places, *The Golden Dog*, was published in 1877, at least escaped the influence of Longfellow, although the shade of Dumas *père* seems to have been ever present at his elbow. A more recent novelist, Franklin Davey McDowell, has told the story of the early Jesuit missions to Huronia. The background in *The Champlain Road* is admirably conceived, but McDowell has seen fit to introduce into his novel a preposterous love idyll more appropriate to Graustark than Huronia. The martyrdom of the priests is well described, but suffers by the inevitable comparison with Mr. E.J. Pratt's magnificent realisation of the same incident in *Brébeuf and His Brethren*.

It is to be regretted that professor Philip Child has not returned to the field which he explored in his first novel, *The Village of Souls*. A reconstruction of Canadian frontier life during the middle decades of the seventeenth century, it is one of the few imaginative works dealing with the period that bear the stamp of honest and intelligent craftsmanship.

Sir Walter Raleigh's definition of romance as "the magic of distance" may explain why our novelists have shown such a strong prediliction for the Ancient Regime, to the comparative neglect of later periods. But it seems strange none the less that so few Canadian writers have found subject matter in the migrations of the United Empire Loyalists. Thomas Raddall, in *His Majesty's Yankees*, has given an excellent account of the conflicting allegiances of the Maritimers during the Revolution, but only Kenneth Roberts, an American novelist, has made successful use of the Loyalist movement in its larger aspects. One may disagree with the point of view which Roberts expresses, but it must be acknowledged that *Oliver Wiswell* is the work of a skilled craftsman.

The War of 1812 has been touched upon by Grace Campbell in her slight but charming novel, *The Higher Hill*. Unfortunately, the intensely idyllic strain which persists throughout the book creates an atmosphere of unreality at variance with the sombre historical background. Ralph Connor in *The Runner*, and John Elson in *The Scarlet Sash*, have also dealt with the War of 1812, but both writers have shown more concern with the construction of conventional plots than the creation of human beings within the historical framework. The Rebellion of 1837 forms the background of a typical novel by Sir Gilbert Parker, *The Pomp of the Lavilettes*. In *The Pomp of the Lavilettes* Parker exploits his favourite plot situation—the intrusion into a French-Canadian village (the perfect replica of Grand-Pre) of a disturbing stranger from the outside world, who in the end dies gracefully and well as the only means of resolving the difficulties which his presence has created. The characters are types rather than individuals—The Curé, the Notary, the Bad Girl Who is Good at Heart, the Fascinating Stranger, and so on. Considered as a pastoral idyll, *The Pomp of the Lavilettes*, like *The Right of Way* and *When Valmond Came to Pontiac*, has some merits; but of all our novelists, Parker has been the most cavalier in his treatment of the historical record.

Oddly enough, the opening of the West forms the background of relatively few Canadian novels. Agnes Laut's *Lords of the North*, an exciting account of the struggle between the Hudson's Bay Company and the Nor-Westers, is probably the best of an indifferent group. This comparative neglect of the story of the West is all the more surprising in view of the wealth of material available in the records of the early explorers, missionaries and fur-traders—men like Thompson, Fraser, Father Lacombe, Robertson, and John MacDougall. The material thus provided is at least as rich as that from which Willa Cather fashioned her superb romance of missionary enterprise in the South-West—*Death Comes For the Archbishop*. But so far nearly all our novelists have ignored it.

There is one notable exception. Frederick Niven, a Scottish novelist who settled in British Columbia in 1920, undertook to tell, in the guise of fiction, the story of the Canadian West. Thirty years ago Niven was considered one of the most promising novelists of his generation. His *Justice of the Peace*, a magnificent re-creation of the Glasgow of Niven's boyhood, had earned the enthusiastic praise of such discerning critics as Rebecca West, W.L. George, Hugh Walpole and William McFee. But in spite of his genuine talents—which included the ability to create living people—Niven failed almost completely in the task which he set himself. The first novel of his trilogy, *The Flying Years*, covers the development of Alberta from 1870 to 1920; *Mine Inheritance* goes back half a century or more to the time of the first Red River settlements; *The Transplanted*, unfinished at the time of Niven's death, deals with the opening up of British Columbia. In all three Niven displays the most meticulous regard for the historical record, and there are traces of the earlier excellent prose style; but the trilogy is lacking the breath of life. The plots are slow-moving and laboured; the settings authentic enough, but without vividness; nor, what is much more serious, does the author create a single memorable character. Niven

170

loved the Canadian West, but the new environment, unlike the old, was not a part of him. Perhaps it is true that before a writer can capture the spirit of a region and interpret it to the world his roots must have struck deep.

The significance of the historical novel has often been questioned. Miss Gwethelyn Graham, no doubt pardonably exalted by the popularity of *Earth and High Heaven*, has even gone so far as to call upon young Canadian authors to "write about our national problems of today and get rid of the impulse to turn out historical novels about grandma chopping down the virgin forest in her crinoline." But G.M. Trevelyan, certainly one of the most brilliant of living historians, views the contribution of the historical novelist, as exemplified in the work of Sir Walter Scott, with profound respect. Scott, he says, "did more than any professional historian to make mankind advance towards a true conception of history, for it was he who first perceived that the history of mankind is not simple but complex, that history never repeats itself, but ever creates new forms according to time and place. The great antiquarian and novelist showed historians that history must be living, many coloured and romantic if it is to be a true mirror of the past."

In recent years many American novelists, including Willa Cather, Howard Fast, Hervey Allen and Neil Swanson, have proved themselves not unworthy disciples of Scott in the sense that they have shared his ideals if not his achievement. They have brought to the writing of the historical novel a high degree of competence and a strong sense of responsibility. In their pages the men of Plymouth and Valley Forge and Gettysburg and the embattled frontiers live as recognisable human beings—men who fought the enemies of the flesh and the spirit, not always wisely, not always successfully, not always with a clear sense of the issue at stake, but always with an unquenchable faith in their own strength. And because they are recognisable human beings rather than romantic puppets they have provided for many an individual distracted by a world gone mad, not escape but reassurance.

But in Canada the function of the historical novel has always been escapist, and except in one or two instances continues to be so. And so long as Canadian novelists continue in the traditional mode, established by Longfellow and his immediate successors, so long will the Canadian historical novel be no more than an idle tale written to while away an idle hour.

1946

171

From
The Canadian West in Fiction
Spokesman of a Race

The writer who seeks to inform his readers of the peculiar quality of a region such as the prairie provinces should be a pictorial artist able to describe accurately the physical features of a characteristic prairie landscape; he should be a poet with power to feel and to re-create imaginatively the particular atmosphere which invests the prairie scene; and lastly, he should be a psychologist with sufficient knowledge of human nature to be able to understand and describe the influence of the region upon the people who live within its confines. True regional literature is above all distinctive in that it illustrates the effect of particular, rather than general, physical, economic and racial features upon the lives of ordinary men and women. It should and usually does do many other things besides, but if it does not illustrate the influence of a limited and peculiar environment it is not true regional literature.

Among our Western Canadian writers there have been several—among whom Frederick Niven is outstanding—who have described adequately the physical characteristics of the prairie landscape; one or two, including W. O. Mitchell and Sinclair Ross, who have suggested with unusual sensitivity the peculiar atmosphere of the prairie region; but so far no one has indicated with more than partial success the subtle modifications of character which inevitably result from the influence upon ordinary men and women of a highly distinctive environment. The greatest single weakness of our Western writers is their inability to understand people in relation to their surroundings. Without such understanding the great novel of the prairies cannot be written.

Among Western writers Frederick Philip Grove seems to have seen more clearly than any other the responsibility of the writer who would give artistic expression to a distinctive regional spirit. He at least never minimized the magnitude of the task nor the probability of failure. In his autobiography, *In Search of Myself*, he recalls a self-evaluation made in 1912 when he paused for a moment at middle age to ponder what he might do in the future:

> Meanwhile there was, in this casting-up of accounts, one thing which stood on the asset side, against much which I must necessarily put down in the list of liabilities. The one asset consisted in this: that I could truthfully call my knowledge of the pioneering section of the west of the North American continent unique. At a glance I could survey the prairie country from Kansas to Saskatchewan or Alberta; and at a thought I could evaluate, in my own way of course, the implications of pioneer life. I, the cosmopolitan, had fitted myself to be the spokesman of a race—not necessarily a race in the ethnographic sense; in fact, not at all in that

sense; rather in the sense of a stratum of society which cross-sectioned all races, consisting of those who, in no matter what climate, at no matter what time, feel the impulse of starting anew, from the ground up, to fashion a new world which might serve as the breeding place of a civilization to come. These people, the pioneers, reaffirmed me in my conception of what often takes the form of a tragic experience; the age-old conflict between human desire and the stubborn resistance of nature. Order must arise out of chaos; the wilderness must be tamed. No matter where I looked, then as today, I failed to see that the task of recording that struggle with nature had ever adequately been done, not even by Hamsun, who, for the sake of a pleasant ending, gave, to Isaak, Geissler. To record that struggle seemed to be my task. Perhaps, very likely even, I was foredoomed to failure in my endeavour; in fact, I seemed to see even then that I was bound to fail; but the attempt had to be made.

The premonition of failure here suggested was not the consequence of ordinary lack of confidence. Grove never underestimated his own powers. Indeed it is a serious weakness in him that he never seems to have been aware of the uncertainties of technique which mar much of his work and which humble self-appraisal might have done something to remedy. Rather, he felt that the petty necessity of earning his bread and butter prevented him from achieving the detachment which the great artist must have if he is to preserve his spiritual integrity:

> In the last analysis it all came down to an economic problem. In order to see things once more from the outside, I must regain my distance; in order to regain my distance I must, economically and otherwise, get away from my present milieu.

But Grove was never permitted to escape from his "present milieu." It was his fate to be harassed all his life by the grimmest kind of economic necessity. None the less, the attempt to record adequately the "age-old conflict between human desire and the stubborn resistance of nature" was made. That attempt, as Grove had anticipated, failed. But the causes of failure lie not so much in the physical circumstances surrounding the act of creation, as Grove himself seems inclined to believe, as in his incomplete understanding of men and women. . . .

It is never enough that the novelist understand fully the technique of his art, or that he have the power to describe exciting incidents in vivid terms, or that he have a philosophical view of life which he expounds with eloquence; he must, above all else, know people intimately and be able to bring them to life in his pages. It is not possible to quarrel seriously with Virginia Woolf's assertion that all novels "deal with character, and that it is to express character, not to preach doctrines, sing songs, or celebrate the glories of the British Empire, that the form of the novel, so clumsy, verbose and undramatic, so rich, elastic and alive, has been evolved." But Grove's people are only occasionally human beings; the main figures are shadowy symbols around whom gather swarms of puppets—the Elliotts and the

Spauldings, and the neighbours who are seldom anything more than names, and occasionally grotesques like Mr. Pennycup and Mr. Suddaby and John Elliott, Junior, who live awhile in the memory because their remoteness from reality startles us into looking at them twice. . . .

But although Grove is not a great novelist there are some things in his writing which are memorable. The tragedy of his artistic life is that so much of his work was done in a medium for which he had little talent. His best bits of writing are descriptive and philosophical rather than narrative. In a milieu less harassing it is possible that he might have been a distinguished essayist. He has a keen eye and the power to record accurately what he sees. There are, too, some fine passages of philosophic meditation in the novels, such as the reflection, in *Our Daily Bread*, on the farmer's way of life; and in the same book, the sombre moving soliloquy on death expressed in the form of the thoughts which pass through John Elliott's mind as he sits by the bedside of his dying son-in-law, which do much to make the banal dialogue and inadequately realized characterization tolerable. But it is not possible to read Grove's two collections of descriptive pieces, *Over Prairie Trails* and *The Turn of the Year*, without feeling that his best work lies in just such things as these. In them he is able to combine an accurate eye for description and the philosophic strain so strong in him without impeding the development of plot or characterization. The pity of it is that Grove, either because of economic pressure or a mistaken estimate of his own powers, felt impelled to work in a medium which was not suited to his peculiar talents.

Not that we would willingly give up any of the novels of the Canadian West which Grove wrote. Imperfect though they are they reflect a maturity of intellect lacking in most of our fiction. Grove is not a great novelist, for the power to create living people was denied him; but he brought a cultured and philosophic mind to the contemplation of the Western scene, and an eye for specific detail which will make his work a valuable source of information to the rural historian of the future. His statement of purpose in writing *Fruits of the Earth*—"to infuse a dramatic interest into agricultural operations and the attendant rural life thereof"—holds true of all his Western novels. He failed to infuse adequately the dramatic interest, but his record of "agricultural operations and the attendant rural life thereof" is one of the most accurate in Canadian fiction.

1949

Gwethalyn Graham
1913-1965

Born in Toronto, Gwethalyn Graham was educated at Havergal College, Toronto; Pensionnet des Allières, Lausanne, Switzerland; and Smith College, Massachusetts. She received the Governor General's Award for each of her two novels, *Swiss Sonata* (1938) and *Earth and High Heaven* (1944). Two years before her death, Graham joined with Solange Chaput-Rolland in the publication of *Dear Enemies* (1963), an exchange of letters on the subject of bicultural relations in Canada. "Why Books Cost Too Much" appeared in *Maclean's Magazine* in 1946.

Why Books Cost Too Much

Going the rounds among Canadian writers there is a story that in a recent poll taken to find out what Canadians do with their leisure time, the majority of the people questioned said, "Reading." It was a gratifying result, if a little surprising, because somehow or other one is not accustomed to thinking of Canadians as a nation of bookworms. Nor are they, as it turned out. On being asked *what* they were reading, only 10% of them said, "Books."

To anyone familiar with the book situation in this country, even 10% seems fairly high. Most books cost so much in Canada that relatively few people can afford to buy them, and public library facilities are provided for only half the total population. In rural areas only one country-dwelling Canadian out of every 20 can borrow books. The other 19 just have to go without.

This nation-wide book shortage is obviously bad for our educational and cultural life. More than that, since the scarcity of good Canadian books is part of the general scarcity, it weakens our sense of national identity and contributes to our lack of identity in the eyes of other nations.

Most of us still find it easier to define an American or an Englishman than to define a Canadian, largely because we have read far more books about Americans and Englishmen than about ourselves. As someone said long ago, nations may exist by their exports but they live in the eyes of the world by their arts. One good novel can give the outside world a clearer idea of what Canadians, for example, are like, than 10,000 tons of aluminum or a million bushels of wheat. So far, however, we have concentrated on the aluminum and the wheat, with the result that, as everyone who has ever travelled outside Canada has found to his dismay, almost no one knows anything about us.

We exist; we are a geographic, economic and political fact, but that is about all.

The most important single factor in this situation in my view is books—the high cost of books in Canada compared to the cost of books in other countries, the scarcity of public libraries in Canada as compared to other countries, and the limited quantity and quality of Canadian books.

This brings us straight to the organization of the Canadian book trade. The moment you begin to realize how our book trade works, you come up against a staggering anomaly. The book trade, that most important single factor on the three levels of education, culture and national identity, operates largely on the principle that Canada is still a colony.

First of all, most Canadian book publishing houses publishing in the English language are neither Canadian—since they are branches of English or American firms—nor are they primarily publishers. They are primarily jobbers; what publishing they do is on the side. Except for schoolbooks and some college textbooks, the great majority of books sold in Canada are published in the United States or England. They are imported into this country by the Canadian jobbers, who not only handle the books of their own parent firms in England or the United States but also act as agents for a dozen or two other British and American publishers. This is an economic necessity in a country of such distances and with such a small population, for no Canadian publisher could afford the overhead and sales costs involved in handling just one list of books. . . .

With almost no exceptions, authors published in the United States get only half royalties or less on Canadian sales. Authors published in Britain suffer an average cut of 20% in royalties on Canadian sales. Since the normal royalty on a $3 book is 30 to 45 cents, such a cut means a lot to an author.

American and British publishers try to justify the reduced royalty on Canadian sales on the ground that the price to the Canadian jobber is lower than it is to the American and British bookseller and they have to make up the difference some way or other.

In case you are wondering just how American and British publishers come to be disposing of *Canadian* rights, the answer is that under all standard American and British contracts Canadian rights are automatically thrown in with American and British rights. The question of who gets Canada, the American or British publisher, is determined only by who gets there first to sign a contract for that particular book.

In other words, so far as book contracts are concerned, both the United States *and* Great Britain regard us as a colony. It is obvious that this system is not only insulting to Canadians in general but peculiarly insulting to Canadian publishers. What it means is that those Canadian publishers who would really like to publish instead of spending most of

176

their lives jobbing other people's books rarely get a chance to do anything else. By the time they have even heard of a book it is already under contract to some American or British publisher who has already grabbed off Canadian publishing rights.

The obvious solution to this particular problem is for American and British authors to insist on separate Canadian contracts. The chief point in mentioning it here is to make it clear that if the Canadian public and the Canadian author are at the mercy of the Canadian publishers, in at least one very important sense the Canadian publishers are at the mercy of the British and American publishers.

Why authors have put up with reduced royalties and the "Canada clause" in their contracts for so long is hard to understand—except that, again owing at least partly to that lack of a national literature, nobody takes Canada seriously from a cultural standpoint. And owing at least partly to the jobbing system which results in increased prices, decreased sales and reduced royalties, few authors take Canada very seriously from the economic standpoint. And finally, most non-Canadian authors don't even know that there *are* any publishers in Canada.

As for the Canadian author, unless he gets a separate Canadian contract (as some of them do), the best that he can hope for is the same terms as the American and British author—a 50% cut in royalties on Canadian sales if his contract is with a U.S. publisher, or a 20% cut if he has a British contract. The fact that Canada happens to be his own country just makes it that much harder to take. The worst he may get can be very bad indeed. . . .

Besides his inevitable contract troubles, another occupational hazard facing the Canadian author is that most Canadian publishers don't know how to sell books. Jobbing the books of well-known American and British authors is not "selling" at all. It is simply a matter of unloading them, particularly when you are handling the lines of from 10 to 20 first-class American and British houses; and it is both a great deal easier and a great deal safer than setting up and printing at home. The result is fear, fear of unsold stock, and the incredible combination of inefficiency and just plain indifference displayed by some Canadian publishers to the exasperation of booksellers and authors alike.

For example, there is the case of a young Canadian author whose first book went through two editions in England and one in the United States. For a first novel this is not bad at all. The total Canadian sale, however, in spite of an exceedingly good press in all three countries, was some 800 copies.

What happened was the usual story; as the English publisher had Canadian rights, he notified his Canadian agents and suggested a separate printing of 2,000 copies for Canada. What he got back was an order for 50 copies. There was nothing he could do about it, so 50 it was. The next order was for 100 copies, the third for 150, and finally the

Canadian "publisher" took his courage in both hands and ordered 250. It was the largest single order he ever placed. After that he lost his nerve again and went back to lots of 50 and 75. This is sheer murder from the author's standpoint. The lifetime of the average first novel is almost never more than three months. Since the interval between each order varied from three to six weeks, for 90% of the lifetime of that particular novel the Canadian publisher was out of stock.

Another somewhat more spectacular example is the case of a book which was serialized in the U.S., bought by an American book club, bought by Hollywood—all months before publication—for which the initial Canadian order was 1,500 copies. That particular book ultimately sold about 25,000 copies in Canada, but it was a long, slow and painful process during which the booksellers across the country were continually putting in orders for 200 copies and receiving 25. Incidentally, on asking *why* the advance order was for only 1,500 copies, the author was told by the Canadian publisher that even 1,500 was a bit risky, because a lot of people would read it in serial form, and, worse still, a lot of copies would be coming into Canada under the book club arrangement.

But perhaps the greatest single handicap against the successful production and distribution of good books in Canada is a psychological handicap. Publishing is neither art nor business but a mixture of both. For that reason it is probably the most fascinating business there is. But unlike jobbing, it is not safe. It is one gamble after another. Furthermore, outside of the reprint houses, it is not even big business. The profits are not very large and the greater percentage always has to be turned back into the firm. The basis of good publishing lies not in "best sellers" but in what is called "a balanced list." A balanced list, by and large, is made up of a lot of different kinds of books—of "reliable" books, that is literary classics, some history and biography, some textbooks and some technical books, for all of which there is a modest but more or less steady demand. Then comes a best seller or two if possible, or, at any rate, a backlog of established authors—and finally the young unknowns.

It is the ability to pick the right young unknowns and then to stand by them both psychologically and financially which, among other factors, will ultimately determine whether a publisher is a good publisher and whether or not he stays in business. It is the unknowns who become the backlog of the future and who then, in their turn, pay for a fresh crop of books by people nobody ever heard of. Before the war an English or American publisher who sold 2,000 copies of a first book was very well pleased with himself. He had recovered costs and hadn't made a penny.

Most first novels don't sell anything like 2,000 copies. If the reviews were favorable however, and—far more important—if the publisher himself thought the author had talent, he would back the author's next book, and the book after that, possibly losing money on every one of them. That is what you expect, if you are a publisher, because if you are a publisher you know that authors of the stature of Galsworthy, Sinclair Lewis, Mary Webb, Steinbeck, Arnold Bennett and Virginia Woolf have often been colossal failures from a financial standpoint, for not one book but five, and sometimes six.

All this is the precise opposite of jobbing. It isn't safe at all, and it requires just that initiative which becomes paralyzed in years of jobbing. It requires that combination of imagination, generosity and patience which no jobber ever needs. The jobber's psychology is probably the chief explanation for the fact that Canadian book publishers as a group have yet to revolt against the present system—even though it is far more profitable to set up and print a separate Canadian edition once a sale of 3,000 copies has been reached.

The Canadian market is small; there is that hurdle of 3,000 copies to get over—Canadian costs, particularly binding, are higher at the moment than American or British costs, though a decrease in the present shortages of materials and the great increase in volume which would result from the setting up of a genuine publishing business in this country would inevitably bring those costs down. With certain notable exceptions, most of the Canadian firms seem to be well-satisfied with things as they are.

As for authors, they are queer people doing an extraordinarily difficult job—two facts which have been recognized by every good publisher down through history. The result of that recognition is the phenomenon known as "the author-publisher relationship." The publisher frequently has to act as a combined nursemaid, father confessor, editor and banker, and there is no relationship quite like it in any other form of business. Nevertheless this relationship between publishers and authors has probably been responsible for as much of the best writing ever done in this world as any other single factor.

If you want to know how difficult writing is, get rid of that idea that you just wait for "inspiration" and then start what amounts to taking dictation. Instead, imagine yourself sitting down at your desk right now, with a pen or typewriter and 500 sheets of blank paper, faced with the prospect of going on sitting at your desk for the next year, or the next two years, or the next three years, until you end up with a complete book. A doctor has his patients to work with; a lawyer, his clients; a truck driver, his truck; a housewife, her house and family—but the author has only himself, a desk, a pen, and an empty room.

One of the results of having nothing but himself to work with is that the author, like all artists, tends to be balanced precariously between a state of mind where he believes that he has something so worth saying that it is not silly to go on sitting at his desk for two years, and a state of mind where the whole project seems absurd. And when he no longer believes in himself he is through. He just gives up and goes

179

back to practicing law, or editing, or teaching, or selling shoes, or to whatever it was that he was doing before. . . unless he has a good publisher.

If he has a good publisher, and he has talent, then the chances are he doesn't give up because his publisher won't let him, and gradually something called "a national literature" is created. For the function of a good publisher is just as much a matter of faith as it is a matter of the amount of money he makes. Back of more great, near-great, or simply successful authors than anyone ever dreams of was some publisher who refused to quit in the face of book after book which lost money, and who refused to allow the author of those books to quit either.

You don't become a good publisher by being afraid to set up and print books yourself or by being afraid to order more than 50 copies; you don't become a good publisher by playing safe, nor by that attitude of mind which, at the moment, is characteristic of the majority (though not all) of Canadian publishers. You don't become a good publisher by somehow or other leading your authors to believe that in asking for a decent contract they are getting too big for their boots; that they represent a dead loss; that anything they are paid in the way of royalties is a sort of handout; that asking questions, even legitimate questions, is at best rather bad taste, and at worst, impertinence. Nor by these means do you play your part—which is almost as indispensable as the part the authors play—in creating a national literature. You just go on jobbing and leave the creation of literature to someone else.

Yet, in the last analysis, the Canadian book publishers are as much the product of the system as the Canadian public and the Canadian authors are the victims of it. The Canadian publishers did not invent the system; they inherited it. It is a hang-over from our colonial days; it is hopelessly out-of-date, and while it may suit some Canadian publishers, there are others who dislike it as violently as anyone.

On the one hand, then, you have some Canadian publishers; on the other, you have the British and American publishers filling orders for 50 copies and knowing that even those 50 copies may be overpriced. You have the Canadian author, who is penalized in all directions simply because he is a Canadian. Finally, you have the Canadian public, unable to buy or borrow enough books and often unable to buy or borrow any at all, because they cost so much.

This is the book situation in Canada, and there would be nothing strange about it if the year was 1847. But the year is 1947, and we are no longer a colony.

1947

Thomas Raddall
1903-

Thomas Raddall was born in Hythe, England, and immigrated to Halifax with his family in 1913. Since the appearance of his first collection of stories, *The Pied Piper of Dipper Creek* (1939), he has published five historical novels, several collections of short stories, and three novels with contemporary settings including *The Nymph and the Lamp* (1950). "The Literary Art" was published in the *Dalhousie Review* in 1954.

The Literary Art

These are times when everyone is concerned about the quality of the literature, or perhaps I should say the quality of the reading matter, chiefly in the form of fiction, now being put before the public. The advent of the so-called pocket book especially has produced a flood of fiction to be had for twenty-five cents or fifty cents a copy at any drugstore or wayside refreshment stand. Its appeal is set forth usually in a picture on the cover, and some of our moralists are more concerned, it seems to me, with the picture on the cover than they are with the printed matter inside.

I suppose I should blush when I mention this because some of my own novels, after the regular publication in cloth covers, have appeared in the drug stores in paper covers; and one of my fellows in a Canadian learned society last year complained that the picture on one he had seen showed a good deal more of the Nymph than of the Lamp. I informed him that I had not been consulted about the picture, indeed I was not consulted about the pocket book arrangements at all, that being a matter reserved by my regular publisher in his contract with me. But when the first and worst of these pictures came to my notice I wrote an indignant letter. My publisher's reply was illuminating. "I was shocked myself," he said, "but it was too late to do anything about it. The pocket book people have distributed about two hundred thousand of their edition all over the United States and Canada. However you may comfort yourself with this reflection, that a lot of unsuspecting people are going to find themselves reading a good book under false pretences."

However that may be, the fact remains that we are witnessing the sale of enormous quantities of fiction, in cloth and paper covers, with or without pictures, which do describe the human being as a creature devoted to sex and bloodshed. What is the explanation? Some of it undoubtedly reflects the convulsions of our time, which tore the cover off what we had believed to be a civilized world and left us gazing with a dreadful fascination at what we saw beneath.

But it seems to me that in the long view this printed obsession reflects something else, an extreme swing of reading taste away from the stuffy prudery of the nineteenth century and the early part of the present one. Most of the Victorian and Edwardian novelists portrayed men and women as creatures with no more blood than fish, as creatures without sex, or at any rate distinguished one from the other chiefly by their mannerisms and their clothes. The picture was false, of course, and the best of them knew it. Thackeray for one complained of the restraints put upon his pen by the false modesty of the age in which he lived. And he, who wrote so much about a previous age, must have known that the Victorian attitude was a reaction from the literary license of the eighteenth century, just as, before that again, the excessive sobriety of the Puritans was a reaction from the bawdy days of the cavaliers.

Apparently these things go in cycles, and it seems likely that the present output of grossness in print will bring about a reaction eventually that may go all the way back to the namby-pamby before the pendulum swings again. One extreme is as bad as the other, and I say a plague on both. We shall do well to consider the truth of the late Lord Tweedsmuir when he said, "Frankness in literature is an admirable thing if, as at various times in our history, it keeps step with social habit; but when it strives to advance beyond, it becomes a disagreeable pose."

The social habit nowadays is very frank indeed, and I think that what we have to consider is not a deliberate assault upon the morals of the public so much as a disagreeable pose on the part of so many writers in our time. As such it will pass, and we need not alarm ourselves unduly about it. Good taste is not to be created by laws and censorships. It can come only from a clean palate in the public itself; and that is a matter best cultivated in the home and the school, where current writing can be tested against the best writing of the past, and where it may be shown that good fiction, without recourse to the macabre or the obscene, can be exciting and full of the color and "stingo" of life.

With a clean public palate the blood-and-sex poseur will cease to exists, for he will cease to be read, which is the same thing; and the writer of sincere purpose and commonsense will continue to keep his pen between those fraudulent extremes, trying to give life its full value, an existence not without its crimes and follies but also with its noble themes of love and courage and self-sacrifice. Evil there is, and it must be set forth, but so must be the finer aspect of mankind; and each in its true proportion to the whole, no more, no less.

In a famous *mot* Stendhal remarked, "A novel is a mirror walking along the road." That is not quite enough. Mirrors cannot feel, and the writer must. Otherwise Stendhal is right. And the mirror walking along the road must keep a steady gait. It cannot linger by the pig-sty any more than it can come to a full stop before the wayside shrine. It can only reflect what is there and pass along.

How is this actually done? There is no magic formula as we well know. But this much is clear, and it is the foundation. The best creative writing, the stories that have survived the mills of time, were the work of writers who regarded their profession not merely as a trade (and most worth-while authors have written for their living) but as the satisfaction of an instinct, a craving if you like, to capture with ink and paper the spirit, good or evil, of mankind. And this inner drive, this personal daemon, qualified the task. It gave them in fact a two-fold law; to write with absolute honesty and to make it *readable*. For all good writing is just that. Joseph Conrad, one of the most honest writers in English literature, put it in this way: "My task which I am trying to achieve is, by the power of the written word, to make you hear, to make you feel, it is before all to make you see. That and no more—and it is everything."

To do this it seems to me the writer must set himself apart—not physically, for he must mingle closely with humanity in order to feel its warmth and learn its heart and mind—but apart in thought, apart from his own prejudice as well as the prejudice of others, seeing mankind with the eyes of a curious stranger. Perhaps this sounds a little cold, as if mankind were just a fly beneath the lens, but I do not mean it in that way. The observer may be moved to tears or laughter. He may convey loathing or compassion or exaltation at what he sees and feels. But there he must stop. It is not for him to lecture or to preach. That is best done by the teacher and cleric, whose business it is, and who are better qualified. Some very good writers have indulged in pet social or political theories or in hammering home with obvious blows whatever moral might be in their tale; but their book lived in spite of these intrusions not because of them, and it is proof of their general excellence that the book survived at all.

Of course books may be aimed at particular groups, and that is a legitimate object; but it is not the legitimate object of literature, whose appeal must be universal. As a rule, the moment a writer begins to intrude upon the reader with his own views of politics, morals, religion or anything else that does not belong absolutely to the story he set out to tell, in that moment he begins to lose "readability", and when a writer ceases to be readable his whole object has been lost. In the words of Somerset Maugham, "The novel, I cannot repeat too often, is not to be looked upon as a medium of instruction or edification, but as a source of intelligent entertainment." Or as he expresses it in another place, "I think it is an abuse to use the novel as a pulpit or a platform. Fiction is an art, and the purpose of art is not to instruct but to please."

Now, to please does not mean to pander to whatever public taste may be current. It does mean to set forth what is in the writer's or the painter's or the sculptor's mind so that it has the form, the color and substance of the thing he saw, in the way he saw it, and because it satisfied him in that way. His obligation is always to the truth. In whatever degree he falls short of that he fails in art or his craft or whatever you wish to call it. . . .

If you are a Canadian writer beginning the long struggle for recognition there is always a devil who repeats that savage quip of old George Bernard Shaw to a delegation from the Canadian Author's Association years ago—"Who ever heard of a Canadian author?" And he goes on to crush you with, "My poor fool, who are you to offer your miserable wares in the marketplace where people come to buy Maugham and Hemingway?" And there is his fellow devil who comes along nowadays, smites you over the head with the full weight of the Massey Report, and cries, "Canadians don't buy Canadian books. It's a proven fact. And if they won't, who will?"

There is the devil who turns up after you have toiled for some years and whispers, "Look here, why not take the cash and let the credit go? After all money's the only measure of success. And you've got yourself to think about. You don't want to drag out your old age in poverty or on the charity of your friends like almost every Canadian writer in the past, do you? Now be sensible. Here's the formula. It's quite simple. Katherine Windsor and Mickey Spillane have done it, why not you?"

There is the devil who takes your book in his long artful fingers and says, "It's alright in its way but after all this is regional stuff. It's merely provincial. Why don't you aim at the Great Canadian Novel?"

There is the devil (sometimes a he-devil, sometimes a she-devil) who says, "Now with regard to your characters, the men are alright. Some of them are magnificent. But it's plain to be seen that you don't know a thing about women." And there is the devil who comes right along behind and says, "Nonsense! I like your women. Anyone can see that you've made an intimate study of women all your life. But your men!"

There is the devil who says, "Now look here you've written something very good about sailors (or prairie farmers or unhappy suburban wives or Julius Caesar's bodyguard) and obviously that is your natural line. You should stick to it. For you there should be no other people in the world. Get right down in that groove, my friend, and stay there."

There is the devil who looks down his nose and says, "I hear your last book didn't sell very well. But then I always said you hadn't got the touch for that sort of thing." Or he comes to you and says, "So your new book is a success. I'm sorry I can't congratulate you. It's so obvious that you've thrown away your principles."

And so on. Devils and devils. And some of them such charming devils, too. They take such an interest in your work.

Do you remember Monsieur de Vauversin, the strolling player whom Stevenson found on his Inland Voyage? I have always liked poor

Vauversin, and what he said to R.L.S. has meant something to me in the quest that begins when one first takes up the pen and can end only with one's life. For it fits my own notion of workmanship and it has a value in that blind journey towards the mysterious realms of art which all of us experience. You will remember that Vauversin had known better days in the theatre but that he and his lady were reduced to playing in wayside barns, before audiences of indifferent yokels. At the close of one such performance he gave the voyagers his profession of faith.

"I must go about the country gathering coppers and singing nonsense. Do you think I regret my life? Do you think I would rather be a fat burgess, like a calf? Not I! I have had moments when I have been applauded on the boards. I think nothing of that. But I have known in my own mind sometimes, when I heard not a clap from the whole house, that I had found a true intonation or an exact and speaking gesture; and then, messieurs, I have known what pleasure was, what it was to do a thing well, what it was to be an artist."

That has always seemed to me a pretty good philosophy for a writer, too, especially a Canadian; for the Canadian writer as a matter of necessity has to look abroad for most of his income and his fame. He may not have to go about the world singing nonsense for coppers. There may be times indeed when like Vauversin he will be applauded as an artist, and on the boards of Paris itself. But like Vauversin he should think nothing of that. What matters first and last is within himself, a passionate care for his craft. If he lacks that he has nothing. If he has that, nothing else matters, whether he sells his work at home or abroad, for coppers or a fortune, and no matter what diabolical whispers he may hear behind the leaves. I hope that some of you here will turn your ambitions to the pen and take up the task of refuting the late Mr. Shaw.

1954

Hugh MacLennan
1907-

Hugh MacLennan was born at Glace Bay, Cape Breton Island, and studied at Dalhousie and Oxford Universities before earning his Ph.D. from Princeton University in 1935. Following the completion of this degree, he began teaching at Lower Canada College, and in 1951 he joined the Department of English at McGill University. MacLennan's first novel, *Barometer Rising* (1941), has been followed by: *Two Solitudes* (1945); *The Precipice* (1948); *Each Man's Son* (1951); *The Watch That Ends The Night* (1959); and *Return of the Sphinx* (1967). Many of the interests evident in these novels have also been examined in collections of MacLennan's essays such as *Cross Country* (1949), *Scotchman's Return and Other Essays* (1960), and *The Other Side of Hugh MacLennan* (1978). "Where Is My Potted Palm?" was first published as "My First Book" in the *Canadian Author and Bookman* in 1952. "The Future of the Novel as an Art Form" was presented as an address at the Golden Jubilee of the University of Saskatchewan in October, 1959.

Where Is My Potted Palm?

Sixty years ago a volume of essays, called *My First Book*, was published in London. In it twenty-two authors famous in the sunset of Victoria's age tell the separate stories of how they got into print. Accompanying each narrative are illustrations of the author's houses, drawing-rooms, and studies. Their homes were expensive, the drawing-rooms were period pieces, and few moderns can look at the *décor* of the studies without laughing. Seldom have I read a book which better corroborates the theory that authors reflect the times in which they live.

It was a fascinating epoch, the last two decades of Victoria's reign, and one of the most difficult to respect in British history. It was the time of "let's pretend" and the "white man's burden", of middle-class respectability and middle-class sentimentality. Most of the writers in this book did their work in dens and snuggeries cluttered with aspidistras and potted palms. Some of them wrote with quills. Some of them hid behind stained-glass windows. Marie Corelli kept a lute and a harp in her drawing-room and Hall Caine wrote at a small desk surmounted by a huge bust of Shakespeare. This was the heyday of the romantic novel. Many of the novelists who then were famous died with the belief that they were sages as well.

Now I have been asked to talk about my first book, and I recall this volume with misgivings. Where are Hall Caine and Walter Besant now? Who reads Marie Corelli, or Israel Zangwill, or that deep-bosomed, strong-jawed lady who wrote under the pen name of John Strange Winter? True, Stevenson occupies a modest place toward the end of the book. Conan Doyle and Kipling are there. But so, also, is a writer called M.E. Braddon and another called F.W. Robinson and still another called George R. Sims. These were all famous men in their day, and the public thought them interesting enough to want to know how they wrote their first books. Today, so far as their novels are concerned, they might never have existed, and the period they celebrated, the period most of them believed was more brilliant, interesting, and elegant than any other, is seldom mentioned unless by someone who wants to ridicule it.

What of our own period? No novelist writing at the present time can seriously maintain that it is a great one. Middle-class sentimentality has been replaced, in our fiction, by a peculiar middle-class *chic* which finds homosexuality more interesting than normal relationships, which is interested in women only if they are bitches, which believes ostensibly in liberal politics, yet views the materialistic society produced by the triumph of liberalism with a fascinated revulsion. The late Victorians, who fancied themselves romantic, were as hard as nails, and selfish too. Our period, which thinks itself realistic, has adopted in the fiction its critics praise the realism of an alcoholic or a potential suicide. No wonder the book-buying public is turning aside from the novel to buy non-fiction at the rate of seven to one.

At a time like this I find it hard to think back and remember how different was the public attitude then to the art of the novel. I also find it a little absurd to write about my own first effort as though it any longer mattered to anyone. Except in matters of technique, I am quite unable to see my own objectively. Obviously the subjects and characters I have written about must have seemed interesting to me; otherwise I would not have spent years working with them. For a brief time they have seemed interesting to a few thousand people, or the books would never have been bought. But most fiction, even the kind considered successful, has the life span of one season's leaves. A novel must be execptionally good to live as long as the average cat. It must approach greatness to last for a generation. If it survives beyond that time it possesses some quality so indefinable that neither the author nor the contemporary critic recognizes it when the book is new. At least this has been true ever since the beginning of the nineteenth century, when the taste of cultured men abandoned the classics and failed to discover any norm of excellence to put in their place.

So in talking about *Barometer Rising* all I can speak of is the general attitude I had toward fiction at that time.

When I first thought of writing this novel Canada was virtually an uncharacterized country. It seemed to me then that if our literature was to be anything but purely regional, it must be directed to at least two audiences. One was the Canadian public, which took the Canadian scene for granted but had never defined its particular essence. The other was the international public, which had never thought about Canada at all, and knew nothing whatever about us.

As drama depends on the familiar, and as the social and psychological novel depends on the capacity of the public to recognize allusions, to distinguish the abnormal attitude from the normal, to grasp instantly when a character is prompted to act by the pressures of his environment and when by his own idiosyncracies, it seemed to me that for some years to come the Canadian novelist would have to pay a great deal of attention to the background in which he set his stories. He must describe, and if necessary define, the social values which dominate the Canadian scene, and do so in such a way as to make them appear interesting and important to foreigners. Whether he liked it or not, he must for a time be something of a geographer, an historian, and a sociologist, to weave a certain amount of geography, history, and sociology into his novels. Unless he did this, his stories would be set in a vacuum. He could not, as British and American writers do, take his background values for granted, for the simple reason that the reading public had no notion what they were. He must therefore do more than write dramas, he must also design and equip the stage on which they were to be played.

Whether my judgment of the situation in 1939 was right or not I do not know. Some critics have since deplored this intrusion of sociological material into my early books, and have done so with confidence because (as a few of them have pointed out) writers like E.M. Forster and Sherwood Anderson made it a special point of their art to leave it to the audience to deduce such background influences. In justification I can only say that Forster and Anderson were writing of backgrounds that had been amply defined and described by hundreds of other writers who had come before them. Unless the Canadian writer could discover native material, as Mazo de la Roche did, which slipped naturally into a pattern that seemed familiar to foreign readers, he would be neither read nor understood at that particular stage in our development. Gratien Gélinas's *Tit-Coq* was considered a masterpiece in Canada. In New York the critics almost without exception condemned it because they were unable to recognize the marvellous aptness of the allusions or to appreciate the subtle accuracy with which Gélinas presented the French-Canadian scene.

At any rate, it was my conviction when I planned *Barometer Rising* that I must write consciously for two audiences—the native one and the foreign one—and that I must pay especial attention to the background. In *Barometer Rising* the background is the most essential part of the book. The plot is melodramatic and some readers have said it is improbable, but the catastrophe which struck Halifax (more improbable than any novelist's plot) was at least an historical event.

The book is more a *tour de force* than a novel; when I wrote it I regarded it as an experiment. It amazes me to hear from time to time that it is still in demand, though the amazement is not untempered with pleasure.

The point of view from which I wrote *Barometer Rising* is now largely a thing of the past. I don't believe Canadian novelists need worry so much any longer about the problem of unfamiliarity. Before 1939 Canada was apathetic about herself, neither a colony nor a nation, and in the literary world she was little better than a dumping-ground for foreign books. Now she has become one of the most self-conscious nations in the world. That self-consciousness is, of course, a symptom of growth out of adolescence into maturity. For the novelist it is a much better state of mind than the precocious decadence which has infested so much fiction in Britain and the United States since the war. It is not *naïveté* which is destroying the prestige of the novel; it is the belief, abetted by avant-gardists who have little perspective in philosophy and history, and no knowledge of science, that technique is more interesting than content and that a novelist who contemplates his own navel with self-pitying elegance is a true reflection of an epoch which is not only the most terrifying since the fall of the Roman Empire but which is utterly new as well, since science has abrogated so many human patterns which historians of the past have regarded as laws.

Having said this much about my state of mind when I first got into print, I trust some future publisher who wants to include me in a volume called *My First Book* will not feel it necessary to print a picture of the room in which I work. It contains a bed, an office desk, a typewriter, a lot of untidy papers, and a very large waste-basket. But no modern equivalent of a lute, an aspidistra, or a potted palm.

1952

The Future of the Novel as an Art Form

Somerset Maugham's *Cakes And Ale* contains a passage every professional novelist should recall when tempted to make pronouncements about what is valuable and what is not valuable in literature. Ashenden, the narrator of *Cakes And Ale*, himself a novelist very like Mr. Maugham in character and taste, remarks in one passage: "I read *The Craft Of Fiction* by Mr. Percy Lubbock, from which I learned that the only way to write novels was like Henry James. After that I read *Aspects Of The Novel* by Mr. E.M. Forster, from which I learned that the only way to write novels was like Mr. E.M. Forster. Then I read *The Structure Of The Novel* by Mr. Edwin Muir, from which I learned nothing at all."

As most of us have read at least something about the art of fiction written by Somerset Maugham himself, it would be indelicate to point out that if he has described Mr. Forster's attitude correctly, he and Mr. Forster have at least one attribute in common.

The moral is that no writer should be trusted when he makes value-judgments about other men's literary styles and attitudes. For that matter nobody can be. What is criticism, after all, but the finding of reasons to justify your personal likes and dislikes? Often these reasons are valid, but if an author's vision is totally alien to your own, it takes a superhuman objectivity to be fair to him. On the other hand if the author is congenial to you in temperament, you are very likely to overrate him. In *The Green Hills of Africa*, Ernest Hemingway makes the laconic statement that all American literature begins with *Huckleberry Finn*. Most of us were under the impression that Melville,

Hawthorne, Irving, Emerson, Dana and Whitman were senior to Mark Twain, but for Hemingway the statement is probably true. For him American literature really does begin with *Huckleberry Finn* and for him that settles the matter.

In talking about the novel I am like any other writer: I cannot be superior to my own tastes, experience and problems. If I like another writer and have been helped by him, I am grateful and think he is important. But all I mean by this is that he is important to me.

The reverse is equally true. In my early days I was under the spell of some brilliant friends who believed that if anyone refused to recognize that *Ulysses* was the master-novel of the twentieth century, he was unfit to make a literary judgment in a kindergarten. I got so much fun out of thinking myself a member of the *avant-garde*, it was so delightful to spend long hours in smoke-filled rooms ridiculing every author admired by the bourgeoisie, that for two years I cramped my style by trying to write like James Joyce. But I never honestly liked *Ulysses* well enough to read all of it, and when I got older I noted a peculiar thing: only a handful of the very people who claimed to admire *Ulysses* extravagantly had ever read it through consecutively from cover to cover. As far as I could tell, what most of them read was the first three chapters and what all of them read was the last chapter about Mrs. Bloom falling asleep.

The reason why *Ulysses* has been such a stumbling block to critics of all sorts, it seems to me, is the discrepancy between Joyce's aims and quality as a writer and his actual achievement in this and later works. In *Ulysses* he sought to write an absolutely new kind of novel and in this he surely succeeded. Inevitably the *avant-garde* loved him for his example. But the question for practising writers is not whether the method of *Ulysses* is original, but whether it is useful.

Last summer in the Alexander Graham Bell Museum in Nova Scotia I found myself thinking of James Joyce. He and Bell, utterly dissimilar in character, had at least one thing in common: their early work was more successful than their later work. The young Joyce wrote two beautiful, lucid books; the young Bell invented the telephone. But the older Bell, turning his interest to aeronautics, lost himself in a maze of complexities. He left behind him a series of the most intricate kites, and they display a mind of astounding ingenuity. The work was not useless because it explored many wrong theories of flight to dead ends, but the principles of flight as we know them are beautifully simple and now Bell's kites are in a museum, built in memory of the inventor of the telephone. The analogy between the older Bell and the older Joyce seems pretty clear to me. The novel may be mysterious, but its mystery is not that of a jigsaw puzzle or a private language.

It has been said of the police that they never overlook the importance of the obvious, and I think literary judgments would be clearer if literary men respected this element in the policeman's mind.

A novel, to say something extremely obvious, is a communication in story form. Hence it follows that if a book does not communicate and does not tell a story, it is not a novel.

A novel's chief value lies in its capacity to entertain and in its characters. If it lacks interesting, vital and important characters, not all the style and grace in the world will prevent the public from rejecting it.

A novel is neither a play, a poem nor a social dissertation. It may contain peotry, drama and social revelation, but if it does not contain these ingredients legitimately within the story, it bores the public and fails. No writer can survive if he fails to realize that the most fatal sin he can commit is to bore his readers.

The novel is, of all literary forms invented, the most sensitive and subtle, and until recently it was also the most accurate. (I do not say the most memorable, valuable, intense or important.) As these claims may not be self-evident, I suppose I should offer some evidence to support them.

The novel is more sensitive than the play because its form can contain many more nerve-ends and open up many more varieties of experience within a single book. A successful play seldom has room for more than one plot, and a successful poem, at least since the demise of the epic, becomes tedious if it is long. But a novel can run to more than a thousand pages, contain a dozen interconnected plots, a continuing rain of accurate detail, and yet, if the story-line is firmly directed, hold the reader from beginning to end.

The novel's subtlety is dependent partly on this rain of detail and partly on its length. It has room for analysis. Shakespeare can *reveal* psychological depths better than any writer who lived, but if he had tried to weigh and analyse motive with the precision of a Dostoievsky, he would have emptied his theatre. Nor can any playwright permit himself the series of delayed-action climaxes which makes the novel, in a master's hand, so true to life. Though Shakespeare can give us the young Juliet, he cannot give us the mature Juliet within the same play because his form forbids him that luxury. But look at Tolstoy's Natasha! In the beginning of *War and Peace* she is a child; in the middle a marvellous, wayward girl falling in love. But at the end she is a mother feeding her latest baby without a thought of romance in her head. Then we realize with a start of wonder that Natasha's driving force, all along, has been exactly the same as Juliet's. It was simply the mother-instinct.

It is this true-to-life aspect of good fiction, this freedom from the tyranny of the theatrical climax, which is responsible for yet another of the novel's values: its power to become an active agent within a society. The novel can make social situations live; it can clothe political and economic forces with flesh and blood. T. S. Eliot is probably a better artist than George Orwell and Arthur Koestler, but *The Wasteland* is a poet's lament, not the kind of social revelation which causes thousands of people to change their attitudes on public questions of moment. Novels like *Darkness At Noon* and *1984* are masterpieces of the novelist's art, but they are more than this: they have been, and still are, social forces.

One of the words used by people of novels they like is "satisfying". Though it has become a cliché of the advertisers, the word is still useful. Novels we feel to be satisfying do certain things for their readers.

First, the satisfying novel must entertain them; it must so grip them that when they enter the book they cannot be easy until they have finished it. Then it must make the reader a part of the world of the novelist's creation, and this it does by creating fictional characters more real than the reader's personal friends. In order to make characters like these, the novelist must also create the backgrounds and locales in which the characters move, and make them consistent and vivid. A satisfying novel must also hold all of its characters, all of its descriptions, dialogues, ideas, arguments, scenes and actions, within a whole which is harmonious, within a whole where the surprises are seen in retrospect to have been inevitable. And in the supremely satisfying novels, as in all good works of art, there is finally a mystery.

For all these reasons *War And Peace* is still the greatest novel ever written. It begins clumsily and is slow to get off the ground, it is probably too long and in places it is certainly too diffuse, but these defects vanish when the reader has absorbed its total impact. For *War And Peace* is a whole, coherent world. It includes peasant and emperor, saint and murderer, families and lonely individuals, politicians, generals, soldiers and business men, children and old men. It has more than a dozen different life-stories interwoven either with each other or within the texture of the novel itself. And all these incidents, lives and stories are comprehended within the author's vision of history and religion.

No other literary forms can produce a miracle like *War and Peace*. Other miracles they can and have produced, but not this particular one. On the basis of *War and Peace* alone, I could rest my case that the novel is the most sensitive and subtle literary form ever invented, and to these claims add yet another. It is also the most mature.

Now I must change the key. The novel, which has bestrode the literary field for more than a century, which has ruled almost without a rival, is now in jeopardy and is coming into disrepute.

Around the year 1950 people with their fingers on the pulse of the literary market began to note a new phenomenon. The public was turning away from the novel in droves. Non-fiction, never a serious competitor before, was outselling fiction in cloth covers at the rate of close to five to one. So uncertain was the future of any novel that publishers were loath to introduce new writers, and many established novelists were forced to turn to other work in order to earn a living. Why and how did this happen? The question is still being pondered by writers and publishers; it is even being pondered by critics.

To some extent this change in the market was caused by new methods of selling literature, of which the development of the paperback book was an important one. Many readers were unwilling to pay four dollars for a novel, the subject of which they did not know in advance would interest them, and preferred to wait a few years and buy the same book for fifty cents. But there is more to the novel's decline than this. There is the sure fact that what are called satisfying novels have become rarities, and to some extent the novelists cannot help this. Anyone who writes fiction today knows ruefully that the public is harder to satisfy than it ever was. But the important question is why it is harder to satisfy. Why has a situation come about in which people can legitimately ask whether this marvellous literary form may be in danger of extinction?

Institutions—and the novel can almost be called one—pass away for two reasons. One is internal decay, the other is the triumph of its competitors. Because it is easier to identify the nature of the competition than to examine the symptoms of decay, I shall talk about that aspect first.

The chief competitor of modern fiction—of this there can be no doubt at all—is the great fiction already written. There have been so many excellent novels, they have dealt with such a vast variety of themes, they have created such an army of memorable characters that the modern writer would be inhuman if he did not quail before the prospect of competing with the great dead. There is nothing new in this situation, as any musician can testify. The chief reason why it has been so hard to produce a musical masterpiece since 1830 is that Scarlatti, Bach, Handel, Vivaldi, Haydn, Mozart and Beethoven still overshadow everyone else in the field.

The second competitor of fiction is one I have already referred to: it is non-fiction. Ever since Lytton Strachey proved it possible to write a biography in novel form, utilizing all the tricks of the novelist's trade, non-fiction writers have steadily been transforming their art, and already they have defeated the novelist's art in the field of accuracy. I believe that future ages will recognize that the chief contribution made to literary form in this century has not been made by T.S. Eliot and James Joyce, but by writers of non-fiction. Biographies of real people used to be as dull as obituaries; now they are fascinating. Accounts of historical and current events used to be handled in the prose of scholars and reporters; now they are handled with consummate art and a wealth of artifice. The factual, and historically accurate, account of the sinking of the *Titanic* has been reproduced in this modern non-fiction style with far more excitement, drama and surprise than in any of the numerous novels written around the same subject. People say of Walter Lord's *A Night to Remember* that it reads like a novel. So it does. It was intended to.

For all I know, this really is the age of non-fiction. What novelist, after all, could invent a character like Hitler and make him credible?

Could even Tolstoy create a Winston Churchill? Could Jules Verne tell a story as astounding as the Russian moon shot? Could any modern Goethe produce a modern Faust with a career as horrifying as that of Nazi Germany?

But this is really beside the point. It takes more than exciting material to make a book interesting; it takes art and craft. The most thrilling story on earth can be made as dull as a board report if it is told by a German professor in the professor's own style. Readers who leave fiction for non-fiction delude themselves when they say that they do so only because they prefer truth to imagination, or because they wish to be informed about history, science and life. Undoubtedly they do wish to be informed about history, science and life, but historians, scientists and sociologists have been publishing for years without the general public storming the university libraries. The real reason why scientific books like Rachel Carson's *The Sea Around Us* become best sellers is that they are entertaining.

The third competitor to the modern novel is television, but its competition, once you examine it, is seen to be more indirect than direct. Non-fiction competes fairly on its own merits, but television does not and cannot. Its success as a competitor of the novel depends neither on its style nor its content, but on its capacity, unwittingly, to employ the services of a mighty ally of which the average televiewer is usually unconsicous. On the side of television in its battle for public support is a law of life.

The average organism, be it man, bird, beast or fish, tends to satisfy what it believes, or instinctively feels, are its basic needs with the minimum of effort. If squirrels live near apartment houses containing kindly old ladies who throw them food, the squirrels do not hoard. Of course, if the old ladies stop feeding them, as they did in my district during an abnormally long cold spell when an opened window chilled the house for hours, the squirrels die of starvation. But while food is there, they do not think of this.

The basic need of the average person between dinner and bedtime is usually to be able to sit in a chair in his living-room without being so bored that he can't stand himself. In the past, the period between dinner and bed was the great time for novel reading. Generally what was read was worthless, but it bred the reading habit and sometimes what was read was good.

Television has changed all this because of the law of life to which I have referred: watching television takes less effort than buying and reading a book. It is also easier than to get dressed and go out to the movies. It even seems cheaper, though I doubt if many familes spent more money on the movies in the past than they spend now on buying and maintaining a TV set. Television has shaken the economic basis of Hollywood to the bedrock simply because it enables millions to avoid palpable boredom with no effort at all. You can already see its results in some of the students now entering college, who can hardly remember a time when a TV set was not in the family living-room. They associate reading with school and homework, and they don't like it.

But television cannot compete, it cannot even afford to compete, with any form of literature for the serious time of people who have acquired the reading habit and do like it. Most of its fare is, and must be kept, what the lawyers call free and harmless. It can permit the truth to come out in a debate or in the report of a political convention; it can show a ball game happening just as it does. But it cannot permit too much truth to come out in its plays and stories. Hollywood producers always understood that it is fatal to the box-office to offend vested interests, fraternal organizations, or occupations to which large numbers of the public belong. One of Hollywood's perennial problems has been to create a really plausible villain. He cannot be permitted to belong to any known church, to any minority racial group in the United States, to any lodge or labour union that is named. He cannot be a citizen of any foreign country which buys Hollywood products unless it is clearly pointed out that he is regarded by his fellow countrymen with the horror we reserve for an absolute pariah. It is safest for the villain simply to be a villain, with no further explanation offered. And surely one is naïve if one is surprised by this. The bigger the organization, the greater its cowardice. The larger the economic base of an enterprise depending for its profit on the public, the more readily does it succumb to the bullying of pressure groups.

The television industry is not only up against this age-old problem; it is up against still another. It must carry the commercial on the back of every programme commercially sponsored. From the standpoint of the sponsor, the commercial is what the show exists for, and if the show is so intense that its interruption by the commercial annoys the audience, only the most public-spirited of sponsors will underwrite it. A sponsor can hardly be blamed if he takes a poor view of an entertainment which competes successfully with his product.

Whether or not television can reduce the reading habit to the point where publishing becomes unprofitable and dies, only time will tell. My own guess is that it will not, for book publishing never was a big industry and I don't think it can become one. Its smallness enables it to be fairly independent, and if it offends a bully, the bully can't do anything important to get his own back. Its market was always much smaller than book-lovers assumed, and it still is. A Gallup Poll recently published showed that only eighteen adult Americans out of a hundred read even one book a year, and the poll made no mention of the quality of that one book. At a calculated guess, I would estimate the serious book-reading public in the English-speaking world at a little above three million people. This is only a guess and possibly the figure is exaggerated: there is no known way of determining who is a serious reader and who is not. But let it stand. Three million people is about three fifths of the population of Shakespeare's England, and in Shakespeare's time only a tiny percentage of Englishmen could even read their own names. Three million is a potential audience large enough to keep the novel alive and kicking. Even half a million might suffice. For this reason I believe that the novel's future depends mainly on itself. Relatively it cannot hope to reign over its competitors as it did in Victoria's time, but those who are committed to it have some solid reasons for believing that it should be able to survive as long as people want to read anything.

Non-fiction, after all, cannot entirely supplant the need for good novels because it cannot be so intimate. The non-fiction writer can describe a Churchill, a Hitler, a Wellington, a Florence Nightingale, he can infer their motives and feelings, analyse what he believes to have been their characters and relate with accuracy and excitement the record of their actions and lives. But he cannot *become* them because he has not created them out of himself. Non-fiction cannot hope to give us a Hamlet, an Othello, a Natasha, an Alyosha Karamazov, a David Copperfield. Because its subjects are usually men and women of mark it can seldom if ever deal successfully with the humble. If you want Sam Weller or the old fisherman of Hemingway's book—for that matter if you want yourself—you still must go to some form of fiction.

For these reasons I do not believe that the competition of non-fiction can supplant the need for good novels, though it has already, and properly persuaded serious readers that they waste their time if they read fiction which presents characters externally, or offers characters which are uninteresting or stereotypes.

That is why so many novelists are in trouble today; that is why it has never been so hard to write a serious novel the public will accept. Not only is it more difficult than ever to make a fictional character credible; it is harder still to make him seem interesting and important. So far as the public for novels is concerned, its threshold of boredom is the lowest it has ever been. Yet a lot of us write, and occasionally we succeed. But we would be stupid indeed if we pretended that our form is not in the position of having to prove its necessity, and even more stupid if we refused to ask ourselves why.

The novel is losing readers because only rarely today does it satisfy the only public it should consider. That public is not a coterie of highbrow *afficionados* of literature nor again is it the mass-man of the television audience. It is the serious reader who knows himself to be an individual and is also a responsible citizen competent to earn a living, raise a family and even to vote. He may be a business man or a worker, he may be a farmer, a fisherman or a schoolteacher, he may be a lawyer, a doctor or a student. More often than not—far more often than not—the profession of the serious reader today, when the reader applies for a passport, is classified as housewife. All of these readers with their various backgrounds have one thing in common: their awareness, often subconscious, of their own uniqueness as human individuals. None of them belong to the amorphous crowd, and most of them are people of goodwill.

Therefore they are ill at ease in this atomic, consumer world which changes so fast; they are ill at ease and are not afraid to admit it. Externally the world is changing so fast that the military power mustered by the United States in 1945, contrasted with that of now, stands out half-way between that of now and the force presented by Henry V at Agincourt. Internally this brave world is newer still, for our knowledge of what Dr. Penfield calls the microcosm of the brain, itself as marvellously complex as the microcosm of the firmament, has altered, among those who know anything about it at all, most of the materialistic concepts of life on which our outward shows of government, economics and practical philosophy are based. Psychology as a science is so new it can hardly be called a science, yet already it has been able to shake our traditional concept of our own inner selves.

And of course (the average organism satisfies its basic needs with the minimum of effort) this new science was barely out of the cradle before it was prostituted, with the result that thought-controllers and psychological engineers, highly paid by politicians and people with goods to sell, have invaded the territory once entered with reverence by poets and prophets.

What wonder, then, if novelists who learned their craft in the Twenties, and acquired their vision of life still earlier, are now out of their depth? In the Thirties some of the most respected men in modern fiction used the Marxist philosophy as a frame for their stories; a few years later most of them realized that deeper causes than any dreamed of by Marx were responsible for the horrors of the twentieth century. Even worse is the plight of some younger writers who have emerged since the war. Facing a situation that frightens them, they either try to escape it or to exorcize it. If they do the latter, they concentrate on peripheral characters, invariably unpleasant, whose very existence is a slap in the face to the conformist society of the advertisers which they loathe. If they escape it, they usually follow one of two courses. They bury a commonplace tale about commonplace people under a mountain of self-conscious symbolism inherited from Eliot and Joyce, or they create a world for two in which an ordinary boy and an ordinary girl spend the first half of the book trying to get into bed with each other and the last half trying to get out. Nobody can blame sensible people for turning away from these clichés. Up to a point some of the novels have been true and honest—I think, for example, of *The Catcher In The Rye*—but compared with the great fiction of the past they have been astonishingly, even alarmingly, limited in their outlook and maturity.

Yet even in the last decade there have been some strong novels published, though few have been written by Americans, and a number of them have even been successful in the market. Invariably they have been books dealing with real people in situations in which the cards were not stacked arbitrarily against them. Some were even books which accepted as a living force an entity dismissed with derision in the Twenties and Thirties. That entity is the mystery the Stoics called the World Soul and Christians and Jews call God. Some novels have even presented decent people as interesting and competent.

I have been a writer too long to dismiss the importance of fashion in literature and criticism. Fashions change like the fashions in women's clothes. But there is one thing about writing I know is true.

No writer can indefinitely get away with it if he despises the public, nor can any writer hold the public if he consistently distorts truth.

The former crime has been committed again and again by the conscious highbrows, the latter by some famous writers who have never been able to shake themselves free of an outworn fashion.

The novel in the Twenties and Thirties often seemed cynical because men of goodwill were in revolt against clichés inherited from the Victorians. One of these was that war is glorious and another was that true love should be disembodied. The realism of this period was like a gale of fresh air, and it produced a vital literature.

But the fashion outlived its usefulness, and cynicism became a habit. Cynicism, after all, is the last resort of the clever, for no cynic is likely to look a fool. But this does not mean that cynicism is more intelligent than faith. It is certainly not intelligent to deny evidence, and there is as much evidence to suggest that the Giver of life did not intend life to be a dirty trick as in Einstein's conclusion that God does not play at dice. A man in despair may cry that as flies to wanton boys, so are we to the gods. But in the end it was Hitler, not Churchill, who went to destruction. Honour is not always defeated by dishonour, and virtue wins in more important fields than in the pages of the slick paper magazines. Decency may, on occasion, even triumph in the state of Mississippi.

I believe that the serious public has bitterly resented this automatic cynicism of so much of the recent literature it has been told to admire. Since the last war the novel, especially in the United States, has failed worst of all in dealing with the very subject in which it should excel. That subject is love. The fact that the human body was kept out of love by the Victorians seems an inadequate reason for keeping the human soul out of it today. Yet it is a fact that in novel after novel the act of love is treated like the description of a problem in mechanical engineering. My heart sinks when I read through a long narrative dealing with the lives of lawyers or business men and come to the inevitable breaks, like the breaks for the television commercial, in which the hero goes to bed with the wife of his best friend and neither gets any fun out of it. I know perfectly well that this sort of thing causes a good many thousands of morons and deprived people to buy books they otherwise would not buy, but I still believe it is a passing fashion. Inside another decade most Americans should be aware of what a naked woman looks like, and they may even prefer the reality to the literary shadow. The novel today is in much the same position as the English theatre at the time of Addison, when playwrights automatically reproduced the stale intrigues of the Restoration dramatists, when the sole purpose of an alderman or a business man on the stage was to provide a wife whom a man of fashion might seduce. What was yesterday's realism is today's cliché and for a simple combination of reasons: men are imitative and life keeps changing.

If the future of the novel lies anywhere, it is in the very fact that modern life is unable to be static. If it were static, I don't suppose we could look forward to any more literature of quality than the Romans got after Aurelius. But where change exists there is life, and where life exists among the educated, there is need of precisely the kind of communication the novel can make to a man reading in solitude.

For the novel, which has developed technically to the point where it can contain almost any symphony of ideas and feelings a writer wishes to pour into it, is still an available form. I am Scotch and by nature inclined to anticipate doom, but I honestly know of no other form of entertainment which can offer the novel's peculiar combination of intellectual satisfaction and emotional catharsis. There will be fewer novels in the future than in the past, and fewer still the public will accept as important. To write a great novel will become increasingly harder as the serious public grows increasingly more demanding. But it can be done, and because it can be done, it probably will be done. For though the novel may not any longer be the most accurate and popular form of literary art, it still has no rival that can be as subtle, wise, intimate, sensitive and mature.

1959

Ernest Buckler
1908-

Ernest Buckler was born in Dalhousie West, Nova Scotia, and educated at Dalhousie University and the University of Toronto. In addition to his best-known work, *The Mountain and the Valley* (1952), he has written another novel, *The Cruelest Month* (1963); a memoir, *OxBells and Fireflies* (1968); a travel book, *Nova Scotia: Window on the Sea* (1970); and numerous articles, radio scripts and short stories including those collected in *The Rebellion of Young David and Other Stories* (1975). "My First Novel" was read by the author for CBC radio in 1953.

My First Novel

What I happen to be is a farmer who writes, not a writer who farms. That's why my novel had to be composed almost entirely on second wind. It's physically impossible for me to assemble two consecutive thoughts in the morning. Even if that were *not* the time for milking, or mowing, or what not. Mornings, my colons are really sluggish. If a leaky pig's trough didn't have to be stuffed with birch bark—or it wasn't the day for the brindle heifer's romance or something such—I tried to do a little work on the book in the afternoons. But my life as a writer really began after supper. Then, after a short pause for braiding up my nerves with a little reading, I slugged it out with the muse for exactly three hours. Perhaps, though, my most *productive* periods were those in bed, when the darn thing kept me awake.

I know it's sticking your neck out to say this novel was one you *had* to write. Too many people are free to reply that they find no such compulsion to read it. But—despite that risk—mine was.

It certainly wasn't done for pleasure. If there is any purgatory more undiluted than attempting to trap the quicksilver of life with the laggard spring of words, I don't know it. You so often feel like those fatuous ancients who thought to enclose the bird with a wall. For life is so infinitely tangential. It flees touch like a ball of mercury flees the finger. And you find not its smallest feature in clear-outline, but always in solution. And so dauntingly various. *War and Peace* is alleged to have said everything about everything. But it doesn't. Even if Tolstoy had included the yacht race he so flayed himself for omitting, it wouldn't have. The greatest novel ever written is a mere phrase, a word, a letter, if you like, in the infinite language of human relations.

How, then, can you precipitate even the tiniest crystal from this solution? Must you suspend some sort of string in it, as physicists do to precipitate salt crystals? And, if so, what string?

One writer's idea of how it's done is no better than another's. All are mere personal whim. But I think that the string you use is your characters. Know them thoroughly at the beginning, put them into the solution, and somehow the novel will accrete around them. I tried to get my characters straight right at the start—to know exactly where they were going to wind up—And then I let them more or less work their own passage. Although it wasn't quite as clinical as that sounds. Nothing was worked out altogether cold-bloodedly or singly. I think in those projects which you find really compelling, characters, theme, development, and, above all, the sort of—shall we say, "climate" of the thing?—come to you all together. In embryo, at least. The rest is largely nurture and photograpy.

I didn't fret too much about action. For myself, as soon as complications in a book start popping, I always feel like muttering to the characters: "Oh, for heaven's sake, stop scurrying around advancing the plot! Sit still a minute till we get a squint at your insides." For I think that insides are far more important . . . *and* interesting—than outsides. That action—despite the wired-upper-lip and prose-clipped-with-mat-scissors school—is far less important than its motivation. Nor did I ever wait on inspiration. I think that inspiration, by and large, is one great big myth. What really happens: you work and work toward an idea, and some sort of mold of the thing desired forms in your mind. Then—while you're chopping, or hoeing, or whatever—the subconscious gets going: fitting images against this mold, and when one of them—phrase, incident, or whatever—slips into it, that tiny click you hear, that's what's mistaken for inspiration.

What I always *did* wait too long for, though, was a feeling of rightness about even the first draft. I had an incurable distaste for using, even temporarily, the stand-in phrase, the tentative line! And that can be crippling. Because nothing unlooses a chain of ideas like one, any one, already put down. An approximate idea can introduce you to just the one you want, as it is so often through your half-friends that you meet your whole ones. And it is so often curiously true that the only way you seem to arrive at the right spot is by the wrong path. Truth should be the *only* destination; but you should remember that the paths to it are expendable.

If there was anything else I learned, it was this: when you accomplish a bit that reads as if, brother, *that* must have been something hard to get expressed, don't stick your thumbs in your galluses and gloat. Spend another hour, or day, on it—until it sounds as if, hell, anyone could do that. You rarely achieve that happy effect, of course; because after rewriting so long, you can no longer tell if you're pruning fat or nerve. But it's a good target to aim at.

By the way, this novel—though it did try to show the texture of life in a village not altogether unlike the one I do know—and love—best, was not literally *autobiographical*. Except as all writing is—between the lines—autobiographical.

The six years the novel took, I spent in almost complete isolation. I've often been asked how much I minded being so out of contact with other writers. Well, it's wildly lonely, of course—especially when you have some little success you'd like to celebrate, with the only others who *can* know just what it means to you. But I had my mailbox. And the Godsent Diana Lockhart's travelling Bookmobile. Which brought me Elizabeth Bowen—who, incidentally, is the woman I love—E.M. Forster, Henry James, Dylan Thomas, Hemingway, Faulkner, Proust. In batches of twenty, sometimes.

And I think that isolation, however shriving personally, may be a good thing for a writer's work. My thoughts, anyway, are like mice. When the mind is quiet, they seem to pop out of their holes and scutter about much more freely than when I'm in company. I think, too, that when writers congregate in clutches, or coveys, or whatever the word is in that connection, they talk too much. They dissipate with their tongues what they should be funnelling through their pens. And when this talk is about work in progress, it takes the edge off the performance itself. Writer's shop talk isn't half as rewarding as people's, anyway. To cite the first instance that comes to mind: I once said to a country friend of mine—91 years old, and just starting to get the old age pension—I said, "What are you going to do with all that money?" He said, "I'm going to spend every damn cent of it on *women!*" He meant it too. Now where would you pick up anything like that in an atelier?

Another danger, I think, is that when writers associate too much with each other, a sort of inbreeding starts to develop. You half-hear them saying: Now we'll form a hermetically sealed little group, and the password will be Yoknapatawpha, or Anna Livia Plurabelle, or something, eh? And so on. Which is disastrous. And eventually they may come to write almost entirely about writing. Which is ruinous. At best, writing is only shadow. Writing about writing, then, is a dim second carbon indeed. On the other hand, you mustn't, except *while* you're writing, have lived entirely to yourself. Pure ivory tower stuff may be as miraculous and delicate as the silk a spider spins out of *his* own viscera—but it's equally thin. So thin that you could use it too for bombsights. But only for the most microscopic of targets.

Now comes the hard part. It's very difficult to mention the success of your own novel, without striking a note either of insufferable conceit or nauseating modesty. But simply as fact—mine has done all right. In the States, anyway. Promotion there, and critical response, were all anyone could ask for. And sales there, though not exactly astronomical, have been very good indeed. Critical reception in Canada has also been most heartening. But I'm afraid I can detect no brush-fire of popular enthusiasm. Again, this is fact, now winging: All the yachts you could build with your Canadian royalties you could sail in your bathtub.

And, of course, for every person here who welcomes the novel's frankness, there's another, who recoils from any mention of life's (which is to say, his own) basic impulse, as if it were a Lazarus Bell. Just the same, I think that Canadian writing is definitely breaking away from this crocheting of little tea-cosies of genteel prose for the excruciatingly prim—and is turning out stuff of real flesh, blood, bone, *and* spirit. Witness Bill Mitchell.

And it's also heartening to note that all this flapdoodle about the Canadian writer's first obligation being to write like a Canadian (however that is) is dying down. If you're a Canadian, and write as honestly as you can about what you know—here or anywhere else—and the result doesn't *sound* Canadian—well, no conscious attitude you strike will ever make it sound so. If you're a Canadian and want to write a distinctively Canadian novel, I'd say: just trust your natural processes, Mac, just trust your natural processes. Don't *try* to write *like* anything—except yourself. Again, witness Bill Mitchell.

So your first novel is finally done, such as it is. You look at the first bound copy, and you feel a mite like a lady who once said to me about the beautiful job a mortician had done on her late aunt: "I tell you, Ern," she said, "if I hadn'ta knowed her, I wouldn'ta knowed it was her!" The book's shape is so compact. If a novel were to bear any physical likeness to its genesis, it would look more like one of those tortuous deltas of the nervous system. You pick it up. The print has a kind of almost strident assurance. As if it were quite satisfied with itself, whereas you were never absolutely sure you were satisfied with any of it. And it looks so immaculately clean. You'd half-expected that the hours of indecision about that particular passage, writing in and then rubbing out in your brain, would somehow turn up as a smudge on the physical page. You'd half-expected that the countless half-entertained ideas you'd later discarded would show up as shadow. Where are all the ramifications that each period cut short? You'd half-expected to see them, trailing like fibrous bookmarks from each end. And where is the big white gap—which should represent that whole evening you sat there, but not one word came. On the credit side, the irreducible clumsiness of this passage seems somehow to have righted itself. But, alas, what's happened to the resonance of that one, which detonates now like a damp fuse? But there the book is. At least something tangible. (And, by the way, there'll be nothing like it to winnow your true friends from your false, one way or another.) Why, then, don't you feel the glee you'd always envisioned for this point? But you don't. You feel, instead, as hollow as a conch. As if you'd dipped yourself completely dry, and no more ideas would ever seep back in.

But eventually—after what George Moore called "the agony of being without a theme"—they do. And then you transfer your ambitions—much chastened, though—to the next book. And the first one takes on a little the character of some past indiscretion you'd half prefer to forget.

Yes, you do tackle another. Knowing quite well that you're facing all over again another endless see-saw of those two almost equally agonizing days: the one when you feel that—if you could somehow circumvent that curious little block—it's just on the tip of your tongue to be Shakespeare. And the other, when you feel that the whole bloody works has been one big self-delusion: that what you were really cut out to be was an egg-candler.

Why do you do it, then? The answer, I guess, *is*: that if writing is hell, not writing is worse.

1953

203

Ethel Wilson
1890-1980

Born in Port Elizabeth, South Africa, Ethel Davis Bryant spent her early childhood in England. Following the death of her parents in 1898, she came to Canada to live with relatives in Vancouver. After completing her education in England and Vancouver, she worked as an elementary school teacher until her marriage to Dr. Wallace Wilson in 1920. Wilson published her first short story in 1937 and has since written several novels and collections of stories, including: *Hetty Dorval* (1947); *The Innocent Traveller* (1949); *The Equations of Love* (1952); *Swamp Angel* (1954); and *Love and Salt Water* (1956). "The Bridge or the Stokehold" was published in *Canadian Literature* in 1968.

The Bridge or The Stokehold?
Views of the Novelist's Art

Our subject is Canadian Literature, and you will be justified in saying, "She did not talk about Canadian Literature." And I shall be justified in saying, "Oh, yes, I did, really. I talked about an approach to making it."

These remarks should, I believe, have a bearing on Canadian novels. It would be easier to talk about Samuel Hearne's journeys, or Donald Creighton's life of Sir John A. Macdonald, or Miss Neatby's fine formidable book on education, or Margaret Ormsby's *History of British Columbia*, or Charles Camsell's *Son of the North*, or Roderick Haig-Brown's books about waters, and fly-fishing, or R.M. Patterson's *Dangerous River*, or Wallison's *Place Names of British Columbia*, or James Gillis's naively solemn and funny *Cape Breton Giant*, and others, with pleasure and detachment.

But in the matter of Canadian novels I have to choose between two positions—detachment and involvement. They are separate and different. Detachment is the easier position (that is, to some extent, your position), but I have to choose involvement.

Turning to my private addiction, writing, I am not consciously aware in my personal act of writing (how could one be?) of "the Canadian novel" or "the English novel" or "the American novel", as the critic or the critical reader must be aware, and as I am aware when I transfer to the position of the critical reader. When I think of the universal yet private and, I hope, critical approach as a working writer to this novel itself, the happier I am—free, and devoid of personal or national self-consciousness, which is the way I like it. Self-consciousness is a triple curse. But in retrospect I see my Canadianness, for example, in that my locale in a sustained piece of writing (that is, in a book) has to be British Columbia. There are other places in the world that I know and love, but none that I know, and feel, and love in the same way. But I did not choose it. It chose. It is very strong.

If one moves over from the place of the person engaged in this particular act of writing to the place of the person on the bridge looking at the view and interested in "the" Canadian—or any other—novel, I assure you that your view from the bridge (which I also enjoy enormously when I am there) differs from the view in the stokehold where the stoking goes on. I should like to talk, a little, from the stokehold. Let us consider one childishly simple yet eternally complex question—from what place do people in a work of fiction (the "characters") arise, swarming like moths from the dark into the area of light, illuminated by that novel? The question is at once universal and particular, whether one is a West Indian or a Canadian.

Character and plot are a kind of chicken and the egg, depending on the writer. Happily, the material and structure and population of a novel lie within a writer's ambience and choice, unlike history where the question of technique and approach would always baffle some of us; but this private piece of work, when finished, may take a place in a national literature as a Canadian novel, if the natural infusion is strong enough, and if it is good enough, or bad enough. It is a sort of distillation of the writer. I shall try to present, briefly, considerations of origins of "characters" that seem valid to myself. The first examples comes from two great writers outside our time and place, and none the less valid for a Canadian writer.

In the second introduction to the novel *Victory*, Joseph Conrad states with simplicity the natural way in which he first comes to know his characters (which then take shape in a world which is both his inner world and an outside world), and it is a way that I understand and believe in. A novelist is, no doubt, a born watcher. He may not be as planned and deliberate as a bird watcher, yet he cannot help watching. The great writer Conrad, a small man of sombre mien, walks along the quayside or sits down at a café table, and he watches. That watching, passive as it is, is also an actively functioning part of anyone who in some degree becomes a novelist. Conrad observes a man, a woman (never to be seen by him, perhaps), and that man, that woman, is his. There may not be a studied imitation, but there is a sort of active principle at work, a union. He sees a look and perhaps only a look—yet what is more powerful than a look?—or the abstraction in a look, even; and the woman who looks will live and breathe and feel and speak and take her part in some future story (in *Victory*, it may be) and become a person who affects him, and us, deeply. Her actions will be implicit in that look and will somehow derive from the same source, whatever that same source may be. Even her death will derive from it. That look lights a slow fire in the writer Conrad who—observe—is a Pole but writes as an Englishman.

Further, much further, went Marcel Proust. Towards midnight Proust, a very sick man, muffled up, arrives at the house of old friends whom he has not seen for a long time—M. and Mme. de Caillavet who have a young daughter Simone. I quote from Maurois' *Life of Proust*:

> "Madame, what I ask of you now is that I should be permitted to see Mlle Simone tonight."
>
> "But Marcel, she has been in bed for ages!"
>
> "I implore you, Madame. . ."
>
> Simone was brought downstairs. . . What was it he hoped to find in her? The impressions that he needed in order to paint the portrait of Mlle. de Saint-Loup, the daughter of the woman whom the Narrator had once loved.

You and I can see those large dark eyes mournfully exploring the face and demeanour of the young girl. We see him returning in haste to his room. But Proust sometimes blended many persons. In his own notes he says: "(Félice—a certain Marie—another old servant from the Illiers days—Françoise)."

Proust is not wholly in fashion now, although book succeeds book about this enigmatic man. Perhaps too much has been said. His reputed colossal faults do not concern me at all. His achievements do, very deeply. What has he to do with Canadian Literature? He has to do with our universal master and servant Time, and with people moving in Time.

A novelist may be exposed to the temptation of portraying some tantalizing intimately known person. If the novelist yields to this temptation and turns his person loose into his book, he may produce a better book than he could otherwise have done, but at the high cost of peace of mind. Not so, naturally, if the work is planned as a commemoration of love, or an explanatory or affectionate commentary. There is a temptation which I can only describe as excruciating; for truth is far far stranger than fiction or may be much more interesting, and who knows the temptations? I do.

My own experience, which is not great but varied enough for reference, indicates to me the curiously wide spread or narrow concentration of influence in the origins of stories and characters. A novel of mine, or its main character, grew directly from a few words dropped almost at random in a previous book. The words were, ". . . formed other connections." What connections? I had never seen and did not know the girl in question. She did not exist in my knowledge any more than a fly in the next room, but I considered certain aspects and likelihoods, and wrote a book called *Lilly's Story*. On the way, characters multiplied, their outlines at first dim, later clear. I cannot imagine willingly employing even a marginal character without knowing his outside appearance so well that he could be identified in the street by myself and for my own purposes.

Speaking still of people in a book, there comes the influence of light, which may change everything. There was, lately, a freighter which, surprisingly, came to anchor very close to shore and just below our study windows. It caused me intense and daily pleasure. On a grey evening, the ship was a lovely ghost. On a fine morning the freighter was dazzling white where the sunshine fell and the silver gulls flew over. The light faded, and the ship became a dirty tub. The ship was the same ship; the light was different; its effect was perhaps false. Upon us all, light falls, and we seem to the beholder to change; and upon the impending work of the novelist, light falls, and changes a scene and the people in a room. In the book *Victory*, a false light falls upon the man Heyst and its effect is lethal.

Somewhere, I think, the person in a story must touch not only the constructive imagination, but also the earth (that is to say, the writer's own experience) in the course of the struggle, and receive life and strength from that earth.

There is a skilful writer who seldom presents visual characters. They present themselves through the medium of conversation. Yet a character occasionally rises into view, like the body of a seal showing through a breaking wave. Here is Bullivant: "Bullivant relaxed his bearing and turned towards Horace almost with a smile, being adept at suggesting a facial movement without executing it." That is not much; but we see plainly that below the wave, where the writer's mind exists, there is Bullivant and his unsmiled smile.

It seems to me that the problem of the stoker (or the craftsman, or the artist) are universal, for people who are writers are first writers, and then they are Canadian writers, Polish, French, Russian, English writers. I understand so well what the Canadian novelist Mordecai Richler said when he was asked, "Are you a Jewish writer or a Canadian writer?"

He answered, "Neither. I am a writer." Yet he is a Canadian writer, and so am I.

1960

Part 5
The Contemporary Novel

George Woodcock
1912-

Born in Winnipeg, George Woodcock received his early education in England and began his career as a writer in association with figures such as Roy Fuller, Herbert Read and George Orwell. Aligned with the anarchist movement in England during the 1940's, he edited anarchist journals such as *Freedom*. Woodcock returned to Canada in 1949 establishing a reputation as a writer of poetry, biography, literary criticism, radio and television drama and political commentary. In 1959, he became founding editor of the influential journal, *Canadian Literature*. In addition to many reviews, articles and essays, Woodcock has published more than sixty books and monographs and is one of Canada's foremost men of letters.

Don Quixote's Dilemma, or, the Future of Fiction

"To make and end to the matter, I imagine all I say to be true," declares Don Quixote during an argument over the real nature of the

Lady Dulcinea. "And in my imagination I draw her as I would have her be, both as to her beauty and her rank. . . Let anyone say what he likes, for though the ignorant may reproach me for it, men of judgement will not condemn me." Thus, in the first novel of modern times, the hero proclaims the validity of a world of subjective invention. At the same time, obliquely, the novelist defends the pretensions of the literary artist who, resembling Don Quixote, creates his own realms beyond the dimensions of actuality.

Yet, as the misadventures of Don Quixote are designed to demonstrate, the claims of temporal living are not negated by the ideal constructions of the mind; we must satisfy both, and the Knight of the Sorrowful Countenance is defeated ultimately because he refuses to reconcile what happens in the solitude of the mind with the physical facts of a world where no man is alone. His fate might serve as a parable of the dilemma that perennially faces those who have followed his creater, Cervantes, in developing the art of the novel.

Every art, it is true, succeeds only in so far as its works can exist in a dynamic suspension between the ideal and the actual, between the world of imaginary forms and the concrete existence whence emerge the images through which these forms become manifest. Towards both worlds all artists must, Janus-like, make recognition. But the ambivalence that results from these dual claims is particularly evident in the case of the novel because of its specifically human preoccupations, because of its almost exclusive concern with the nature of man and with those complex relationships with his fellow beings, with his environment and with death that constitute the human predicament.

In this necessary immersion in concrete living lies the novelist's Quixotic dilemma. If they are to be ultimately convincing, the fictional microcosms he constructs must manifest the originality and self-consistency that give them aesthetic validity; no more than any other art can fiction escape the imperatives of form. At the same time, the elements that constitute such autonomous worlds must bear a viable relationship to the ephemeral experiences from which they are ultimately derived. Every novel has first and last to justify itself as a statement concerning the lives of men.

Yet though of all arts the mirror of human existence, the novel is a magic mirror that changes the image it throws back in accordance with its own truths, and hence a mirror of infinite recessional possibilities. What we see in the glass of each individual work will be determined in the degree of its luminosity by the thoroughness with which the novelist is, on the one hand, an observer, noting, divining and analysing human behaviour, and, on the other hand, a creator, inventing and nurturing the imaginary beings through whom the matter of his observations can be taken into the timeless world of art. In this way he follows, concurrently, the procedure of science and the procedure of art; neither can be avoided, for the naturalistic myth of a novel based only on observation and analysis had proved in practice as chimerical as the symbolist myth of a "pure novel" conceived as an act of the detached fancy.

This problem of making the novel a sensitive instrument for recording human behaviour and at the same time transfiguring the record into an aesthetically meaningful statement has haunted the novelist in varying manners ever since the days of Cervantes, but it has assumed a progressively greater intensity among writers during the present century.

This development has been coupled with a growth of technical sophistication and psychological complexity in the writing process, but not necessarily with any change in the quality of the formal solutions which novelists have achieved according to the aesthetic preoccupations of their own periods. Madam de la Fayette, writing in the seventeenth century, and Marcel Proust, writing at the beginning of the twentieth, differ deeply in their approaches to human character, in their protrayals of aristocratic society, in their conceptions of time and of love; Proust's methods not only display greater ingenuity and artifice than those of Madam de la Fayette but also an analytical compulsion bred largely of two centuries of scientific speculation. Yet it would be difficult to demonstrate a progress in quality from *La Princesse de Clèves* to *À la recherche du temps perdu*. Each succeeds in terms of the writer's aims; each shows the artist going beyond a mere representation of the life of his age towards the creation of a self-consistent vision capable of survival in the ageless equality of great art. The very uniqueness of the two novelists' achievements precludes a qualitative comparison.

Yet between these two novelists who typify as well as transcend their respective generations, one is aware of a radical difference in attitude towards the novelist's function. Madam de la Fayette lived in an age when the rules of art, like social manners, were clearly defined. In an accepted, classical style she wrote of people whose lives, like those of Greek heroes, became tense and tragic in proportion as their feelings led them to abandon the current norms of behaviour; her attitude towards the situations of passionate rebellion she portrayed was inspired by the moral outlook of a society that thought itself stable as well as just. Like most of her contemporaries, she was neither disturbed by the vast social and psychological uncertainties nor afflicted by the itch for originality that have been constant elements in literature since the Romantics appeared less than two centuries ago. So little self-conscious, indeed, were the novelists of her time about their roles as artists that, if one could call one of them back to be questioned about his or her reason for writing, there would certainly be talk of instruction and entertainment—goals that are anathema to the serious modern novelist—but probably very little would be said about the aesthetics of the craft. Certainly a seventeenth century fiction writer would find it hard to think of a novelist's technical concerns being sufficiently

211

interesting to become themselves a leading subject of fiction—as they have been among us for half a century and more—and he would be astonished and almost certainly shocked to witness the emergence of the writer rather than the person of quality as hero.

It is this phenomenon—present in the work of the most significant of recent novelists, from James and Mann to Joyce, and from the juvenile Gide in the first quarter of the century to the writers of the *nouvelle vague* in the third quarter—that most dramatically typifies the preoccupations of experimentalist writers in the twentieth century (and almost by definition any significant writer of that period has been experimental). With relatively few exceptions—Benjamin Constant being perhaps the most important—the novelists who wrote before the 1880s set out to portray their characters objectively even when they wrote in the first person, to invent personages following pursuits and often coming from classes different from their own, whom they watched in the role of outside observers and commentators. Even Flaubert sustained a theoretical objectivity, though more than any of his contemporaries he neutralized the theory in his practice; the recognition implied in his famous remark, "La Bovary, c'est moi!", was a revolutionary one. Today the novelist as commentator, with his Olympian omniscience and patronizing asides, has retreated to the verges of popular fiction, and contemporary writers have tended to live out imaginatively and subjectively, rather than observing and describing, the inner as well as the outer experiences of their characters.

In this development cultural and social changes have played their parts. The great and still uncompleted cycle of political upheaval that began with the French Revolution; the rise of individualism that accompanied the economic shifts of the nineteenth century; the alienation of the artist from bourgeois society so that his links are mainly with other sections of his own declassé half-world; the encouragement given to introspective enquiry by the development of psychology as an applied science; and the general temptation for the sensitive and the intelligent to construct private worlds of retreat from the age's monstrous and recurrent crises: all these phenomena have encouraged the modern novelist in his tendency to operate with an ever closer and more solipsistic circle of observation.

It is, in fact, a tendency that is inherent in the nature of the novel itself, and it might well have emerged, though perhaps less boldly and rapidly, even without the external stimuli I have noted. Inevitably, as the earler novelists cultivated to exhaustion the overt aspects of human behaviour, their successors began to search for fresh impulses in the more private regions of the mind. There is a limit to variations on the picaresque, and Fielding and Smollett, having emptied the vein uncovered by Cervantes, had inevitably to give place to Jane Austen, and Jane Austen to Henry James and other, less predictable successors. This trend, present even during the eighteenth century among the analytically-minded French fiction writers (e.g. Choderlos de Laclos and even Crébillon fils), was encouraged from within the world of literature (now beginning to emerge as a detached and self-consistent *social* entity) when the Romantics shifted the emphasis from man in society to man in solitude, from the rational to the irrational, from moral criticism to a celebration of the emotional life. After Stendhal's magnificent panoramas, at the breaking point between classical and romantic, of the surface of the human conscience and consciousness, the nineteenth century novelist went on into those shadowy depths of the personality which Dickens and Balzac dimly perceived as fascinating caverns filled with nightmares, but which for Dostoevsky and his successors—and for Flaubert in a different way—became the imaginative writer's self-renewing reservoirs of inspiration and material, later to be given a quasi-scientific validation in Jung's theory of the collective unconscious.

Inevitably, at some stage in this process of turning away from the outer towards the inner man, novelists came to realize that, when he was occupied in observing and analyzing the actions of other people, no matter how well he might know them, a writer could glean only approximate insights, dependent for their reliability on his own intuitive sensibility. Only in his own mind could he proceed with assurance in his quest of the hidden depths of human motivation, those depths of the half-conscious mind where one so often finds the keys to understanding other minds. It is true that in a sense novelists in all times have drawn upon themselves—often without realizing it—in creating their characters, but it was the writers of the post-Romantic age of frank introspection who realized the nature of this process and used it with deliberation, moving from the classic novelist's ostensible concern with Man-as-the-Other and towards the contemporary novelist's overt concern with Man-as-Oneself. More and more, the writer of our own age has become his own subject, not outwardly observed, but inwardly experienced, and for the autonomy of such a writer's position Gide has spoken clearly.

> Everything derived from him. He is the only one to vouch for the truth of what he reveals, and the only judge. All the heaven and hell of his characters are in him. It is not himself that he depicts, but he could have become what he depicts if he had not become everything himself. It was in order to be able to write *Hamlet* that Shakespeare did not let himself become Othello.

The realization that characters in fiction, even when they are not recognizable derivations from the author's externalized personality, are still emanations of those possibilities which together form his creative persona, has dominated and inspired the important fiction of our time. It led the contemporary novelist into increasingly narrow and personal worlds of perception. It undermined the social and political pretensions even of writers like Malraux and Sartre, Orwell and

213

Camus, since all of them were forced to dwell on the predicament of the lonely self as sole experiential reality in a universe surrendered to absurdity. And, by bringing the novelist closer than ever before to the source of his material, by robbing him even of Flaubert's illusion of detachment, it made the task of artistic transmutation so complex that modern writers bring their aesthetic and even their technical problems explicitly into the very centres of their novels, like Gide in *Les Faux-Monnayeurs* and Proust in *À la recherche du temps perdu*, both of which are largely novels about the way in which one writes novels, novels about the author as character. At no time has the novelist been more absorbed than during our century in himself and his task or more conscious of his absorption. Even the school of French novelists, led by Robbe-Grillet and Michel Butor, who sought to liberate themselves under the banner of *Choseisme* from the tyranny of the introspective mind by building their fiction around perceptions of things, merely proved how strong was the urge towards introspection, since the one factor that united the perceived emanations of the material world was the disembodied membrane of the perceiving mind.

Such a shift in perspective among novelists inevitably changed not merely the content but the very form of the novel. The narrower focussing of attention on the inner self led to a loss of range and of tonal variety; it would be difficult to imagine panoramic social tapestries like *La Comédie Humaine* or *War and Peace* being fabricated in our century, which instead has given us Proust's enormous subjective meditation on Time and Memory and the absurdist tragedies of a world where history loses meaning in the episodic pattern of crises of personal choice. History, for the twentieth-century novelist, has largely been an abstraction dwindling into meaninglessness beside the eternal moments of individual experience. (The process was largely delayed in Russia by political Calvinism and in Canada by the retarding influence of colonialism which preserved a cultural ambiance in which as late a writer as Hugh MacLennan could attempt with some success the role of Balzac le Petit for an emerging nation, a feat impossible for the past half-century in any western European country.) At the same time this concentration on individual rather than social experience led the novel to become more intimate in its re-creation of feeling, more penetrating in its pursuit of the submerged motive, more ruthless in its lifting of masks. The growing thoroughness with which, decade after decade in the first half of our proudly experimentalist century, explored the inner landscapes of the mind, led in the end to a change in our conceptions of the roles of personality, action and theme in the novel so radical that in the mid-twentieth century—the 1950s and 1960s—one of the favorite subjects of critical discourse was "The Crisis of the Novel", or, more baldly put, "The Death of Fiction".

Did the changes of outlook evolved during the experimentalist decades make it impossible for the novel as it developed during the classic age of mass-audience fiction—the more or less realist narrative

214

with symbolic overtones—to survive in any recognizable form? Were such traditional elements of the novel as plot and character rendered obsolete by the opening of action into the gratuitous and by the breaking down of the fictional personage through such devices as stream-of-consciouness and subsequent exercises in solipsism? Will the novel not in fact be replaced during the present century—as the romance was replaced in its time—by some new form of fiction better adapted to contemporary ideas of the function of imaginative writing?

Such speculations no longer have the point they seemed to have twenty years ago, and this is partly because we have moved into a clearly post-Modern age, while critics in the 1950s were still partly bemused by the curiously millenarian feeling of the 1920s and the 1930s which led even sensible critics of those decades to see world literature moving in a vast mutation that would lead to qualitatively as well as quantitatively greater flows of imaginative creativity. The great works of modernism, in writing, painting and music, were seen as promises, whereas in fact they were achievements. Now, in the mid-1970s, having seen Modernism foundering in self-parody with neo-Dada and neo-Surrealism and—ultimate absurdity—neo-Art-Nouveau, we can recognize that while at the time of its publication a work like *Finnegan's Wake* appeared to initiate a new and revolutionary voyage in fiction, in fact it was the termination of a quite different voyage of literary exploration that began with Don Quixote's grapplings with reality.

As we now begin to understand, that voyage has been circular, its starting point also its destination, for what the Modernist novelist achieved through following Don Quixote's quintessential subjectivism was entanglement in Don Quixote's dilemma. The fact that fiction of any serious kind rapidly lost its audience after the death of Conrad was due not entirely to the debasement of popular tastes through such rival media as film, radio and television; it was due also to the failure of the Modernists to reconcile the solitudes of the mind, and the abstractions which writers construct in such solitudes, with the facts of a world where no man is alone. An art that becomes solipsistic is by definition an art that has become sterile, a mirror without a looker.

In fact, fiction is not now dead, though critics twenty years ago imagined it would be so. In the form that seemed most moribund a generation ago it is, in Canada at least, flourishing as never before. I refer to the short story, and suggest there are two quite distinct reasons for its revival. The first is that it has proved a most sensitive instrument for expressing the regional, ethnic and generational particularities of Canadian life; the second is that it is the only kind of fiction that operates successfully outside durational time and so allows the flash of recognition between two solitudes which only lyric poetry among the other genres can achieve.

So far as longer fiction is concerned, a return to the realistic novel as the great Victorians and nineteenth century Russians practiced it has been impossible, partly because the achievements of Tolstoy, Dickens and their major contemporaries are terminal in the sense of a complete fulfilment of the task they attempted, and partly because, since the thirties, reportage has taken over much of the function of the traditional novel, just as the camera took over the function of *trompe l'œil* painting. The novelist has had to find another way than that of the socio-historical epic to cope with the fact that man is a member of a congregation of tribes as well as an individual. He has found it by wandering on the verges of those dubious sciences in which imagination and reason productively mingle, the misty frontiers of psychoanalysis and anthropology, where Jung and Frazer preside as vast presences, half-priest and half-poet, to offer the uniting images and myths. The parable, the fable, the myth-born picaresque of search and initiation: these are the significant modern forms, anticipated by works of earlier decades like Orwell's *Animal Farm* and Morley Callaghan's fabulist novels of the Thirties, and Herbert Read's unjustly neglected single work of fiction, *The Green Child*, which set Jung himself dreaming. The mythopoeic insights that Frye took from Frazer have been perhaps less appropriate to the poetry to which Frye mainly applied them than to fiction, for myth is after all a truth of fiction rather than a truth of poetry.

Among Canadian books I find the significant pioneer work, pointing to a solution of the Quixotic dilemma, in books like Howard O'Hagan's *Tay John* and Sheila Watson's *The Double Hook*, neither of which was popular at the time of publication or has become so since, yet both of which tend towards a reconciliation through myth of subjective and collective truths. And for the same reason among the youngest writers I find most relevance and promise in those like Margaret Atwood, Gwen MacEwen and Robert Kroetsch who have developed the mythic insights that O'Hagan and Watson applied to fiction illuminating the Canadian ambiance.

I suggest that in this direction lies the possibility of a genuine broadening of the popular appeal and also of the social relevance of the novel. Works that search back into collective myth and memory awake responses on many levels, as was demonstrated by the extraordinary number of different publics to whom the fantasy novels of Tolkien appealed. But the writer who in recent years—it seems to me—has most promisingly developed this new type of novel is Ursula Le Guin. Ursula Le Guin is a Pacific Coast American who knows the myths which western Canada shares with the northwestern states of America, since her father was the anthropologist Köhler who did extensive studies of Indian societies from Alaska down to Oregon. Because she deals in fantasy and because space-and-time journeying is one of her areas of speculation, Le Guin's books tend to seep away from serious attention through the science fiction shelves. But her scope is in fact far wider than that of science fiction as generally understood. Her *Earthsea* trilogy, for example, deals ostensibly with magic, but in doing so

216

advances into regions of myth and collective psychology that make it far richer and more complexly interesting than the ordinary Morrisian magical romance, while *The Left Hand of Darkness*, which is perhaps the best of her books yet published, applies a futuristic approach that twists back, as do some of her later fantasies, to show us our own socio-political dilemmas and our own problems of personality development in a kind of luminous mirror writing—all in an English as limpid and as evocative of visual images as the best of nineteenth century travel writing.

Utopias formed a minor and marginal fictional genre in the past, largely because they narrowed the possibilities of interpretation and speculation down to the dimensions of the rather rigid and authoritarian minds of their creators. What most dismally characterized books like *Utopia* itself was the sense that in the world they portrayed time had stopped, and change—once it had been achieved according to the creator's whim—had frozen into a static pattern in which no room was left for innovation or imagination. Now—in the works of Le Guin and others who are developing beyond the technological fantasy characteristic of orthodox science fiction—appears a kind of opened-out and speculative utopianism, with its roots as deeply in past cultures as in present sciences, which accepts human continuity, however distantly attenuated, and plays with its possibilities in a way to stimulate our imaginative involvement in a future that must be vastly different from the human present if there is to be any future at all. So, out of the very breakdown of the society which at its height had Balzac and Stendhal, Tolstoy and Dickens, for its bards and portrayers, there has emerged the need for a new kind of collective literature, oriented towards future possible rather than present imperfect; such a need can only be met by a conception of the novel that finds its role not in the plausible reconstruction of actuality but in the authentication of integrated and autonomous social visions based on myth and symbol and millenial thought. This is the direction in which I believe fiction is moving with every great emphasis, rapidly abandoning the writer himself as its obsessively constructing theme, and swinging out once again from the point where Don Quixote maintains the reality of subjective truth and goes forth to encounter the windmills, which in fact he subdues by surviving them in the only world he acknowledges, that of the imaginative recreation of actuality. The contemporary fiction writer's destination is somewhat different; the imaginative realization of possibility.

1976

Robertson Davies
1913-

Born in Thamesville, Ontario, Robertson Davies was educated at Queen's University and Oxford University. After working with the Old Vic Repertory Company in London, Davies returned to Canada to become literary editor of *Saturday Night* (1940-1942) and editor of the *Peterborough Examiner* (1942-1960). He now teaches at the University of Toronto and is Master of Massey College. The author of more than a dozen plays, Davies has also published six novels including the trilogy comprising: *Fifth Business* (1970); *The Manticore* (1972); and *World of Wonders* (1975). A collection of comments on the art of reading was published in 1960 as *A Voice from the Attic*, and a second collection of essays, *One Half of Robertson Davies* appeared in 1977.

From
A Voice From the Attic
Experiment and the Antinovel

Comparatively few writers, however, are truly experimental in a large sense. They are still leaning heavily on the revolution in material brought about by Freud and his followers, and the revolution in manner which stems chiefly from James Joyce. Small variations on these basic themes content them. There is always plenty of room for experiment, and one realm which has not been explored seriously in our time is the verse narrative.

This is the more astonishing when we reflect upon how many of the good modern novelists are also poets. Some of them—the names of Frederic Prokosch and Lawrence Durrell come to mind—have drawn on their poetic powers to enlarge their narrative scope. But what has been done in this realm which can be called daring? What, for instance, attempts to follow where Browning led in *The Ring and the Book*—one of the most remarkable psychological novels in English, and one of the most neglected great poems? The public taste which once rose so eagerly to the verse romances of Sir Walter Scott, and which gave Byron's *The Corsair* a sale of 10,000 copies on the day of its publication, is not dead; it is asleep, and rouses easily, as the success of Benet's *John Brown's Body* in 1927 plainly showed. Are the breadth of theme or the depth of penetration demanded by verse narrative uncongenial to the poets of our time? Do they lack the gusto and variety and sustained energy which such composition demands? If experiment in form is wanted, here is a realm in which it can be tried, and the possibilities of adventure are boundless.

Another sort of literature which has been little explored and which promises rich experiment is the film scenario. Tennessee Williams's *Baby Doll* has appeared in this form, and so has Dylan Thomas's *The Doctor and the Devils*; both are excellent reading. Is it always necessary that an actual filming should be in prospect for a writer to take this form and use it? Has it not qualities of its own which make it interesting, without reference to actual realization on the screen? In making this suggestion, I certainly do not wish for a Closet Cinema to partner in dowdiness the Victorian Closet Drama, but rather a new attack on narrative which would jettison some of the machinery of the novel. Miss Ivy Compton-Burnett has perfected for her own use a type of novel which is virtually dialogue, with connective tissue little more extended than stage directions. The scenario offers the chance of an equally incisive medium, employed on a broader scale.

A widely discussed experimenter of our time is Samuel Beckett, whose recognition has been slow in coming. The material he chooses is not of the kind which attracts the great mass of readers and keeps at bay many of the timid among the clerisy. The interior monologue of an old man on his deathbed (*Malone Dies*) or the anxieties of a decrepit fat woman who is married to a blind curmudgeon whose ambition is to kill a child (*All That Fall*) do not, on the face of it, engage our fancy. But when we have read them, they linger in the mind, not merely because they are extraordinary and rather nasty, but because they have taken us behind the scenes of life and have shown us some aspects of it in a thoroughly unaccustomed light.

Consider his novel *Molloy*. It has been extravagantly praised. M. Jean Blanzat, writing in *Le Figaro Littéraire*, says it is one of the most profound investigations ever written of the disaster of man's destruction. From the first page we are engulfed in confusion and mystery, from which we pluck scraps of communication which after a time assemble into a ghost of narrative. Molloy is an old man, filthy, ragged, and diseased, who is wandering about the outskirts of a city, searching for his mother. He lacks most of the emotions which hold mankind together, and such relationships as he has with people, including his mother, are either violent or indecent. He is suffering from a failure of his legs which at last reduces him to dragging his body through the dirt with his hands. He encounters a man who kills him.

After this point the story becomes the inner monologue of Jacques Moran, a detective who is given orders—why and by whom we are not told—to track down Molloy. Moran is a cruel man who tortures his son with purgatives, and puts on a fantastic dress which includes a huge straw hat with an elastic under the chin, for his chase. He too has trouble with his legs—the "torso-man" whose limbs are failing is a favorite character of Beckett's—and one of his knees makes walking almost impossible. Moran's degradation and sense of loss and failure grow as he pursues his victim. At last he meets a man and kills him without knowing who he is. The man was Molloy.

No place to go for a laugh, you might say, echoing the schoolboy's comment on the works of Matthew Arnold. But baffling and occasionally maddening as *Molloy* is, a laugh is precisely what you do get, from time to time. In this welter of lunatic despair—despair gone far beyond such emotions as sadness or regret—there are humorous flashes worthy of Joyce himself. The atmosphere is nihilist, but not boring or depressing. On the contrary, it leaves me, for one, with a sense of exhilaration and clearer vision which convinces me that *Molloy* and Beckett's other books and plays are true works of art of an unusual kind. But they are not for Nice Nelly; the exhilaration and the fresh vision are bought at the cost of a steep descent into squalor, and abandonment or reversal of all the ordinary values.

This is not caprice; it is the turning inside out of the Classical novel. An English critic, Miss Christine Brooke-Rose, calls Beckett's works antinovels and antiplays; she likens them to *Don Quixote*, *Tristram Shandy*, *Les Faux monnayeurs*, and *The Skin of Our Teeth*. The comparison, and especially with *Tristram Shandy*, I find enlightening and helpful. In that extraordinary and delightful work the life of the hero has not passed beyond infancy when, at the end of the eighth volume, the conclusion is reached; as a life of Tristram Shandy it is nothing, but considered from any other point of view it is rich fare. In the works of Beckett every positive becomes a negative, and everything subsides to pointlessness and oblivion; he that is down need fear no fall, he that is low, no pride. That it should be stimulating is superficially strange, but I mean later to return to this point.

Dangers in the Avant-Garde

It is by no means easy to distinguish between a valid and a durable literary attitude, such as that exhibited by Beckett, and the quickly fading enthusiasms of the *avant-garde*. Within the past few years we have seen the rise and fall of the Angry Young Men in Britain, and the sun is setting on the Beat Generation of the United States. In both these instances the enthusiasm and the name came from outside the group concerned, and the writers comprising these two coteries were unified less by common aims and sympathies than forced together by foolish adulation and foolish attack. In the March 1958 issue of the *London Magazine* its editor, John Lehmann, confessed to embarrassment at having to tell French inquirers that Kingsley Amis was of Britain's *avant-garde*; Mr. Lehmann did not think Mr. Amis sufficiently ahead of the crowd. Mr. Amis's opinion on the matter was not recorded, which was a pity. He, as much as any writer today, has been the victim of a label and an association which he did not seek, but did not resist with sufficient force. In consequence, his books which have followed *Lucky Jim* (1954) have been scrutinized for new evidence of Angry Young Manhood, and the decline observable in *That Uncertain Feeling* (1955) and even more marked in *I Like It Here* (1958) is due at least in part to this pressure to keep up an attitude. Mr. Amis never was very angry; on the contrary, he was good-natured. But he has been trapped in an attitude. In *I Like It Here* his fancy is exhausted, and he is brought down to the level of bladder and toilet fun, and does not scorn to employ even so jejune a device as a confusion of "word" with "turd." Any tiresome duty or work he classifies as "bum"—a word of titillating obscenity in some areas of English society; there are whole bum sequences in this unhappy book, and he extends his exquisite device by such variants as "buttocks" and "nates." He puts the crown on this drollery by a daring use of "shit." The anti-intellectualism which was amusing in *Lucky Jim* has dropped to the point where he describes that exquisite poem *The Dream of the Rood* as "a piece of orang-utan's toilet requisite." To be wittily scatalogical is one thing; this sort of writing, which might be called *l'ésprit de la chaise-percée*, is quite another. But is Amis wholly to blame? He was labeled as soon as he raised his head, and he cannot wash the label off. And now Mr. Lehmann thinks seriously of drumming him out of the *avant-garde*. How much better if the critical press gang had never dragged him into it!

Technical experiment as well as attitude can mark the *avant-garde* writer, and can trap him just as surely. Great interest is fittingly aroused by Alain Robbe-Grillet's desire for a prose cleansed of "the myth of depth of meaning in objects"; as displayed in his own novels, *Le Voyeur* and *La Jalousie*, this results in a kind of antihumanism. He is in revolt against an anthropomorphic attitude toward objects which demonstrably have no human feeling; he would, for instance, deplore any reference to a *pitiless* storm, or a *smiling* sun. He will not admit that it is valid writing to say that a village *crouches* in its place; it is situated there, and nothing more. All of which is reasonable enough, and good writers have always taken pains to avoid cheap effects which arise when this style of description is abused. But matter is vastly more important than manner in writing, and it will be interesting to see if M. Robbe-Grillet can maintain this sort of abstinence for long. Matter dictates manner; to work the other way about is to do violence to the writer's inspiration, for it subordinates his creative to his critical faculty. Every writer is critical of his work after he has written it, but he is on unsteady ground when he puts himself to work to demonstrate a critical theory. He may do it once or twice, but it will be strange if he bases his career on it.

These matters of labels, of theories, of the strength or weakness of the *avant-garde* are properly the concern of critics, rather than the clerisy in general. Reading for pleasure, they are concerned with effects, not causes. Are they, therefore, unconcerned about the development of literature? By no means, but they will not follow that development far unless it produces some pleasure for them. Pleasure is not mere tickling of the senses, a good laugh or a good cry; standards of which even the self-conscious and specifically literary reader may not be fully aware have to be satisfied if any book or group of books is going to enjoy a success on a generous scale. The reader must be satisfied; a fine style, a lively plot, interesting characters are of little avail if the book does not persuade the reader that the writer has been honest with him, and such honesty demands a sincere revelation of the writer's mind and heart.

1960

From
One Half of Robertson Davies
[A Moralist's Novels]

The novels of mine which have been most warmly received are the three last to appear; they are called *Fifth Business*, *The Manticore*, and *World of Wonders*. They are usually referred to as a trilogy, and I am quite in agreement with that, but honesty demands that I say that I never meant to write a trilogy. I wrote one book about three men, and it was well liked, especially by a large and generous group of readers in the United States. But I still had things to say about another of the men who was essential to the story, so I wrote a second book. It was never my intention to follow it with a third, but at last I did so, because the matter of the third book was still troubling me, and there was only one way to get it out of my mind. But there was no planned trilogy, I assure you.

Why did people like it? I think it is because I have discovered, over the course of the years, what I am. I have already told you that as a boy I was without the fervour that inspired my rivals in the public-speaking contests. I have confessed without a blush that I am no poet. But I seem to have emerged as a moralist; my novels are a moralist's novels.

It sounds dreadful, does it not? But if we are faithful to that careful use of words that I was talking about earlier, we quickly set aside the notion that a moralist is a sad creature who points to the right as the rest of mankind rush blindly to the left. A moralist is one who looks at human conduct with as clear an eye as he can manage, and says what he sees, drawing, now and then, a few tentative conclusions. He is not necessarily someone who beats the drum for a particular code of conduct, someone who rebukes what he believes to be sin, someone who looks down on people who are driven by passion, craving, or fear. But if passion, craving, or fear are what ail them, he will not pretend that it is otherwise. He is compassionate but he strives not to be deluded.

Of course he will be driven now and then to come to a few conclusions, but he will be cautious about giving them a too general application. He will observe that quite often people reap what they have sown. If he is honest he will admit that it is sometimes very difficult to know what they have sown, or to be certain about what the harvest is.

That is the principal theme of my trilogy. I began it because for many years I had been troubled by a question: to what extent is a man responsible for the outcome of his actions, and how early in life does the responsibility begin? I concluded, not without long debate, that it began with life itself, and that a child was as responsible as anyone else if it chose a course of action knowingly. In *Fifth Business*, in the first few lines, a boy makes a choice: he wants to hurt his companion, so he throws a snowball at him, and in the snowball is a stone. The snowball hits somebody else—a woman who is brought to bed prematurely of a child whose struggle for life is long and heroic. The consequences of the snowball with the stone in it continue for sixty years, and do much to shape the lives of three men, and in a lesser way to influence the lives of many people whom they encounter. One man becomes a speculative scholar with a touch of the saint about him: one man lives a sensual, self-serving life and dies, at the age of seventy, because he is suddenly faced with the reality—or one of the realities—of what he is: the third man lives heroically, in the sense that his life is a struggle against severe odds, and achieves a queer kind of fame. Any of the three is a man whom we might like, or detest, if we met him casually. All three are, in various ways, liars. All three do some good in the world and some evil. But it is in the inner life that one is almost a saint, one a failure, and one a hero.

Because I do not think it part of a novelist's task to bamboozle and puzzle his readers, the novels are written in a fashion that makes them seem to be simpler than in fact they are. I strive to write as clearly as I can. Because of this limpid quality in the prose some readers think they have understood what in fact they have missed. Teachers ask young people to read the books who are not really ready for them, and the results are sometimes amusing. A couple of weeks ago a very nice young man of seventeen came to see me because he had to write an essay about this trilogy, and when he appeared he was equipped with a list of questions. He fired the first one at me as soon as he sat down. 'What do you consider the chief structural weakness in your trilogy?' he said. I looked him in the eye and said: 'I don't think it has any structural weakness; I think it's just great.' He was not prepared for that; his teacher was training him for criticism, and of the monstrous vanity of the artist he knew nothing. But he was a nice boy and he said: 'Well, you see, there's no unifying theme that runs through all three books.' 'Is that so?' said I, and suggested that the theme of the single action that bore results for sixty years might meet his need. He had not noticed that, but he was very severe with me about my unhappy proneness to coincidence, which was, he said, not like life. But, I countered, 'This is a novel; if you want life, you can find it on the street, and an incoherent mess it will be; a novel is a work of art, not *cinema vérité*. And I am an artist, not a child with a Kodak and a tape-recorder.' We parted on very good terms, and I was so bold as to suggest that his teacher might not be doing him a favour by making him take novels apart with a critical apparatus of the approximate delicacy of a wrecking-iron.

1977

Mordecai Richler
1931-

Mordecai Richler was born in Montreal and attended Sir George Williams University. For many years he lived in England where he worked as a free-lance journalist and wrote scripts for radio and television. He returned to Canada in 1972 and now lives in Montreal. Since the publication of his first novel, *The Acrobats* (1954), Richler has written short stories, essays and several novels, including: *Son of a Smaller Hero* (1955); *The Apprenticeship of Duddy Kravitz* (1959); and *St. Urbain's Horseman* (1971). "Why I Write" was first published in *Works in Progress* (The Literary Guild of America) in 1971.

Why I Write

As I write, October 1970, I have just finished a novel of intimidating length, a fiction begun five years ago, on the other side of the moon, so I am, understandably enough, concerned by the state of the novel in general. Is it dead? Dead *again*. Like God or MGM. Father McLuhan says so (writing, 'The Age of Writing has passed') and Dylan Thomas's daughter recently pronounced stingingly from Rome, "Nobody reads novels any more."

I'm soon going to be forty. Too old to learn how to teach. Or play the guitar. Stuck, like the blacksmith, with the only craft I know. But brooding about the novel, and its present unmodishness, it's not the established practitioner I'm grieving for, it's the novice, that otherwise effervescent young man stricken with the wasting disease whose earliest symptom is the first novel. These are far from halcyon days for the fledgling novelist.

Look at it this way. Most publishers, confronted with a rectal polyp, hold on to hope, tempting the surgeon with a bigger advance. They know the score. What's truly terminal. Offered a first novel or worse news—*infamy*—a short story collection, they call for the ledgers which commemorate last season's calamities. The bright new talents nobody wanted to read. Now more to be remaindered than remembered, as *Time* once observed.

I know. Carting off my cumbersome manuscript to be xeroxed, it was my first novel that was uppermost in my mind, *The Acrobats*, published in 1954, when I was twenty-three years old. At the time, I was living in Montreal, and my British publisher, André Deutsch, urged me to visit his Canadian distributor before sailing for England. So I caught the overnight Greyhound bus to Toronto, arriving at 7 a.m. in a city where I knew nobody and walking the sweltering summer streets until 9.30, when offices would open.

The Canadian distributor, bracingly realistic, did not detain me overlong with *recherché* chitchat about style, content or influences. "Have you written a thick book or a thin book?" he demanded.

A thin one, I allowed.

"Thick books sell better than thin ones here."

A slow learner, I published five more before I at last surfaced with a thick one, *St. Urbain's Horseman*, which was all of 180,000 words. And retrieving my seven xeroxed copies, I couldn't help but reflect that the £80 I forked out for them was only slightly less than the British advance against royalties I was paid for my first novel sixteen years ago. The American publisher, G.P. Putnam's Sons, was more generous; they sent me 750 dollars. But I was disheartened when I received their catalogue. Putnam's was, at the time, trying a new experiment in book selling. If you didn't enjoy one of their books, your bookseller would return you the money, no questions asked. Only two books listed in the autumn catalogue conspicuously failed to carry this guarantee, mine, and another young writer's.

The *Acrobats* ultimately sold some 2,000 copies in England and less than a 1,000 in the U.S., but it was—as I pointed out to my aunt, on a visit to Montreal—translated into five foreign languages.

"There must," she said, smoothing out her skirt, "be a shortage of books."

My uncle, also a critic, was astonished when he computed my earnings against the time I had invested. I would have earned more mowing his lawn, and, furthermore, it would have been healthier for me.

The novel, the novel.

Write a study of the Pre-Columbian butterfly, compose an account of colonial administration in Tongo, and Nigel Dennis, that most perspicacious and witty of British reviewers, might perversely enshrine it in a 1,000 word essay in the *Sunday Telegraph*. Or Malcolm Muggeridge might take it as the text for a lengthy sermon, excoriating once more that generation of younger vipers who will continue to enjoy, enjoy, after he has passed on to his much-advertised rest. But novels, coming in batches of twenty weekly, seldom rate a notice of their own in England. Sixteen are instant losers. Or, looked at another way, payola from the literary editor. Badly-paid reviewer's perks. The reviewer is not even expected to read them, but it is understood he can flog them for half-price to a buyer from Fleet Street. Of the four that remain, comprising the typical novel column, one is made especially for skewering in the last deadly paragraph, and two are destined for the scales of critical balance. On the one hand, somewhat promising, on the other, ho-hum. Only one makes the lead. But it must lead in four of the five influential newspapers, say, the *Sunday Times*, *Observer*, *Times* and *Guardian*, if anybody's to take notice. Some even buying.

"Basically," a concerned New York editor told me, "the trouble is we are trying to market something nobody wants. Or needs."

The novel has had its day, we are assured, and in the Age of Aquarius, film, man, film's the stuff that will do more than fiction can to justify God's way to man. Given any rainy afternoon who wants to read Doris Lessing fully-clothed for forty bob when, for only ten, you can actually see Jane Fonda starkers, shaking it for you and art, and leaving you with sufficient change for a half-bottle of gin?

To be fair, everything has (and continues) to be tried. Novels like decks of playing cards. Shuffle, and read it anyway it comes up. Novels like jokes or mutual funds. You cut your potential time-investment loss by inviting everybody in the office to pound out a chapter. *Naked Came the Stranger. I Knew Daisy Smutten.* Or instead-of-sex. Why weary yourself, performing badly perhaps when, if only you lose yourself in *The Adventurers*, you can have better-hung Dax come for you? And, sooner or later, somebody's bound to turn to the cassette. No need to bruise your thumbs turning pages. You slip the thing into a machine and listen to Racquel Welch read it. "The latest Amis as read by. . . ."

On a recent visit to Canadian university campuses, I found myself a creature to be pitied, still writing novels when anybody could tell you that's no longer "where it's at." But I've tried the logical alternative, screen writing, and though I still write for the films from time to time, it's not really for me.

The trouble is, like most novelists, I am conditioned to working for years on material I discuss with nobody. To adjust from that to script writing is too much like what Truman Capote once described as group sports. Even so, five years in a room with a novel-in-progress can be more than gruelling. If getting up to it some mornings is a pleasure, it is, just as often, a punishment. A self-inflicted punishment. There have been false starts, wrong turns, and weeks with nothing to show except sharpened pencils and bookshelves rearranged. I have rewritten chapters ten times that in the end simply didn't belong and had to be cut. Ironically, even unforgivably, it usually seems to be those passages over which I have laboured most arduously, nurtured in the hot-house, as it were, that never really spring to life, and the pages that came too quickly, with utterly suspect ease, that read most felicitously.

Riding into my second year on *St. Urbain's Horseman*, disheartened by proliferating school bills, diminished savings, and only fitful progress, I finally got stuck so badly that there was nothing for it but to shove the manuscript aside. I started in on another novel, a year's heat, which yielded *Cocksure*. Anthony Burgess clapped hands in *Life*, *Time* approved, *Newsweek* cheered, and the British notices were almost uniformly fulsome. Encouraged and somewhat solvent again, I resolved to resume work on *Horseman*. After twelve years in London, I was to return to Montreal for a year with my wife and five children, to report for duty as writer-in-residence at Sir George Williams University, my *alma mater*. Or, put plainly, in return for taking a "creative writing" seminar one afternoon a week, I could get on with my novel, comparatively free of financial worry.

Ostensibly, conditions were ideal, winds couldn't be more favourable, and so I started in for the ninth time on page one of *St. Urbain's Horseman*. I didn't get much further before, my stomach crawling with fear, I began to feel I'd lost something somewhere.

I got stuck. Morning after morning, I'd switch to an article or a book review, already long overdue. Or compose self-pitying letters to friends. Or dawdle until eleven a.m., when it was too late to make a decent start on anything, and I was at last free to quit my room and stroll downtown. St. Catherine Street. Montreal's Main Stem, as the doyen of our gossip columnists has it. Pretending to browse for books by lesser novelists, I could surreptitiously check out the shops on stacks of the paperback edition of *Cocksure*.

Or take in a movie maybe.

Ego dividends. I could pick a movie that I had been asked to write myself, but declined. Whatever the movie, it was quite likely I would know the director or the script writer, maybe even one of the stars.

So there you have it. Cat's out of the bag. In London, I skitter on the periphery of festooned circles, know plenty of inside stories. Bombshells. Like which cabinet minister is an insatiable pederast. What best-selling novel was really stitched together by a cunning editor. Which wrinkled Hollywood glamour queen is predisposed toward gang shags with hirsute Neapolitan waiters from the Mirabelle. Yes, yes, I'll own up to it. I am, after eighteen years as a writer, not utterly unconnected or unknown, as witness the entry in the indispensable *Oxford Companion to Canadian Literature.*

> Richler, Mordecai (1931—) Born in Montreal, he was educated at Sir George Williams College and spent two years abroad. Returning to Canada in 1952, he joined the staff of the Canadian Broadcasting Corporation. He now lives in England, where he writes film scripts, novels, and short stories. The key to Richler's novels is. . .

227

After eighteen years and six novels there is nothing I cherish so much as the first and most vulnerable book, *The Acrobats*, not only because it marked the first time my name appeared in a Canadian newspaper, a prescient Toronto columnist writing from London, "You've not heard of Mordecai Richler yet, but, look out, she's a name to watch for"; but also because it was one book I could write as a totally private act, with the deep, inner assurance that nobody would be such a damn fool as to publish it. That any editor would boot it back to me, a condescending rejection note enclosed, enabling me to quit Paris for Montreal, an honourable failure, and get down to the serious business of looking for a job. A real job.

I did in fact return to Montreal, broke, while my manuscript made the rounds. My father, who hadn't seen me for two years, took me out for a drive.

"I hear you wrote a novel in Europe," he said.

"Yes."

"What's it called?"

"*The Acrobats.*"

"What in the hell do you know about the circus?"

I explained the title was a symbolic one.

"Is it about Jews or ordinary people?" my father asked.

To my astonishment, André Deutsch offered to publish the novel. Now, when somebody asked me what I did, I could reply, without seeming fraudulent to myself, that I was indeed a writer. If, returned to Hampstead once more, I still tended to doubt it in the early morning hours, now *The Acrobats*, in shop windows here and there, was the proof I needed. My novel on display side by side with real ones. There is no publication as agonizing or charged with elation as the first.

Gradually, you assume that what you write will be published. After the first book, composing a novel is no longer self-indulgent, a conceit. It becomes, among other things, a living. Though to this day reviews can still sting or delight, it's sales that buy you the time to get on with the next. Mind you, there are a number of critics whose esteem I prize, whose opprobrium can sear, but, for the most part, I, in common with other writers, have learned to read reviews like a market report. This one will help move the novel, that one not.

Writing a novel, as George Orwell has observed, is a horrible, exhausting struggle. "One would never undertake such a thing if one were not driven by some demon whom one can neither resist nor understand." Something else. Each novel is a failure, or there would be no compulsion to begin afresh. Critics don't help. Speaking as someone who fills that office on occasion, I must say that the critic's essential relationship is with the reader, not the writer. It is his duty to celebrate good books, eviscerate bad ones, lying ones.

When I first published, in 1954, it was commonly assumed that to commit a film script was to sell out (Daniel Fuchs, Christopher Isherwood, Irwin Shaw), and that the good and dedicated life was in academe. Now, the inverse seems to be the Canadian and, I daresay, American case. The creative young yearn to be in films, journeymen retire to the universities: *seems* to be the case, because, happily, there are exceptions.

All of us tend to romanticize the world we nearly chose. In my case, academe, where instead of having to bring home the meat, I would only be obliged to stamp it, rejecting this shoulder of beef as Hank James derivative, or that side of pork as sub-Jimmy Joyce. I saw myself no longer a perplexed free-lancer with an unpredictable income, balancing this magazine assignment, that film job, against the time it would buy me. No sir. Sipping Tio Pepe in the faculty club, snug in my leather winged-back armchair and the company of other disinterested scholars, I would not, given the assurance of a monthly cheque, chat about anything so coarse as money.

—Why don't you, um, write a novel yourself this summer, Professor Richler?

—Well, Dr. Lemming, like you, I have too much respect for the tradition to sully it with my own feeble scribblings.

—Quite.

—Just so.

Alas, academe, like girls, whisky, and literature, promised better than it paid. I now realize, after having ridden the academic gravy train for a season, that vaudeville hasn't disappeared or been killed by TV, but merely retired to small circuits, among them, the universities. Take the Canadian poets, for instance. Applying for Canada Council grants today, they no longer catalogue their publications (the obsolete accomplishments of linear man) but, instead, like TV actors on the make, they list their personal appearances, the campuses where they read aloud. Wowsy at Simon Fraser U., hotsy at Carleton. Working wrinkles out of the act in the stix, with a headliner coming up in the veritable Palace of the Canadian campus circuit, the University of Toronto.

If stand-up comics now employ batteries of gag writers because national TV exposure means they can only use their material once, then professors, playing to a new house every season, can peddle the same oneliners year after year, improving only on timing and delivery. For promos, they publish. Bringing out journals necessary to no known audience, but essential to their advancement.

Put plainly, these days everybody's in show business, all trades are riddled with impurities. And so, after a most enjoyable (and salaried) year in academie—a reverse sabbatical, if you like—I returned to the uncertain world of the free-lance writer, where nobody, as James Thurber once wrote, sits at anybody's feet unless he's been knocked there. I returned with my family to London, no deeper into *St. Urbain's Horseman* than when I had left.

Why do you write?

Doctors are seldom asked why they practise, shoemakers how come they cobble, or baseball players why they don't drive a coal truck instead, but again and again writers, like housebreakers, are asked why they do it.

Orwell, as might be expected, supplies the most honest answer in his essay, "Why I Write."

"1. Sheer egoism. Desire to seem clever, to be talked about, to be remembered after death, to get your own back on grownups who snubbed you in childhood, etc. etc." To this I would add egoism informed by imagination, style, and a desire to be known, yes, *but only on your own conditions.*

Nobody is more embittered than the neglected writer and, obviously, allowed a certain recognition, I am a happier and more generous man than I would otherwise be. But nothing I have done to win this recognition appals me, has gone against my nature. I fervently believe that all a writer should send into the marketplace to be judged is his own work; the rest should remain private. I deplore the writer as a personality, however large and undoubted the talent, as is the case with Norman Mailer. I also do not believe in special licence for so-called artistic temperament. After all, my problems, as I grudgingly come within spitting distance of middle age, are the same as anybody else's. Easier maybe. I can bend my anxieties to subversive uses. Making stories of them. When I'm not writing, I'm a husband and a father of five. Worried about pollution. The population explosion. My sons' report cards.

"2. Aesthetic enthusiasm. Perception of beauty in the external world, or, on the other hand, in words and their right arrangement." The agonies involved in creating a novel, the unsatisfying draft, the scenes you never get right, are redeemed by those rare and memorable days when, seemingly without reason, everything falls right. Bonus days. Blessed days when, drawing on resources unsuspected, you pluck ideas and prose out of your skull that you never dreamt yourself capable of.

Such, such are the real joys.

Unfortunately, I don't feel that I've ever been able to sustain such flights for a novel's length. So the passages that flow are balanced with those which were forced in the hothouse. Of all the novels I've written, it is *The Apprenticeship of Duddy Kravitz* and *Cocksure* which come closest to my intentions and, therefore, give me the most pleasure. I should add that I'm still lumbered with the characters and ideas, the social concerns I first attempted in *The Acrobats.* Every serious writer has, I think, one theme, many variations to play on it.

Like any serious writer, I want to write one novel that will last, something that will make me remembered after death, and so I'm compelled to keep trying.

"3. Historical impulse. Desire to see things as they are. . . ."

No matter how long I continue to live abroad, I do feel forever rooted in Montreal's St. Urbain Street. That was my time, my place, and I have elected myself to get it right.

"4. Political purpose—using the word 'political' in the widest possible sense. Desire to push the world in a certain direction, to alter other people's idea of the kind of society that they should strive after."

Not an overlarge consideration in my work, though I would say that any serious writer is a moralist and only incidently an entertainer.

After a year on the academic payroll, I returned to London in August 1969, abysmally depressed, because after four years *St. Urbain's Horseman* was no nearer to completion and, once more, my savings were running down. I retired to my room each morning, ostensibly to work, but actually to prepare highly impressive schedules. Starting next Monday, without fail, I would write three pages a day. Meanwhile, I would train for this ordeal by taking a nap every afternoon, followed by trips to the movies I simply had to see, thereby steeling myself against future fatigue and distractions. Next Monday, however, nothing came. Instead, taking the sports pages of the *International Herald-Tribune* as my text, I calculated, based on present standings and won-lost ratios, where each team in both major baseball leagues would end the season. Monday, falling on the eighth of the month, was a bad date, anyway. Neither here nor there. I would seriously begin work, I decided, on the 15th of the month, writing *six* pages daily. After all, if Simenon could write a novel in a week, surely. . . . When I failed to write even a paragraph on the 15th, I was not upset. Finally, I grasped the real nature of my problem. Wrong typewriter. Wrong colour ribbon. Wrong texture paper. I traded in my machine for one with a new type face, bought six blue ribbons, and three boxes of heavy bond paper, but still nothing came. Absolutely nothing.

Then, suddenly, in September, I began to put in long hours in my room, writing with ease, one day's work more gratifying than the next, and within a year the novel was done, all 550 typewritten pages.

The first person to read the manuscript, my wife, was, like all writers' wives, in an invidious position. I depend on my wife's taste and honesty. It is she, unenviably, who must tell me if I've gone wrong. If she disapproved, however diplomatically, there would be angry words, some things I would have to say about her own deficiencies, say her choice of clothes, her cooking, and the mess she was making of raising our children. I would also point out that it was gratuitously cruel of her to laugh aloud in bed, reading *Portnoy's Complaint*, when I was having such a struggle with my own novel. All the same, I would not submit the manuscript. If she found it wanting, I would put it aside for six months to be considered afresh. Another year, another draft. And yet—and yet—even if she proclaimed the manuscript a masterpiece, radiating delight, I would immediately discount her praise, thinking she's only my wife, loyal and loving, and therefore dangerously prejudiced. Maybe a liar. Certainly beyond the critical pale.

After my wife had pronounced, foolishly saying *St. Urbain's Horseman* was the best novel I'd written by far (making me resentful, because this obviously meant she hadn't enjoyed my earlier work as much as she should have done) I submitted the manuscript to my editors. Another hurdle, another intricate relationship. I deal with editors who are commonly taken to be among the most prescient in publishing—Robert Gottlieb at Knopf and, in England, Tony Godwin at Weidenfeld & Nicolson—but once I had sent them my manuscript, and they had obviously not dropped everything to read it overnight, wakening me with fulsome cables, long distance calls, champagne and caviar, I began to arm myself with fancied resentments and the case that could be made against their much-advertised (but as I had reason to suspect) over-rated acumen. As each morning's mail failed to yield a letter, and the telephone didn't ring, I lay seething on the living room sofa, ticking off, in my mind's eye, all the lesser novelists on their lists, those they flattered with larger ads, bigger first prints, more generous advances, more expensive lunches, than they had ever allowed me. In fact I had all but decided it was time to move on to other, more appreciative publishers when, only a week after I had submitted the manuscript, both editors wrote me enthusiastic letters. Enthusiastic letters, that is, until you have scrutinized them for the ninth time, reading between the lines, and grasp that the compliments are forced, the praise false, and that the sour truth hidden beneath the clichés is that they don't really like the novel. Or even if they did, their taste is demonstrably fallible, and corrupted by the fact that they are personal friends, especially fond of my wife.

Put plainly, nothing helps.

1970

Hugh Hood
1928-

Hugh Hood, born in Toronto, received his Ph.D. from the University of Toronto, and in 1961 joined the Department of English at the University of Montreal. His first collection of short stories, *Flying a Red Kite*, appeared in 1962. Subsequent publications include several volumes of short stories and essays and novels such as: *White Figure, White Ground* (1964); *A Game of Touch* (1970); *The Swing in the Garden* (1975); and *Reservoir Ravine* (1979). The last two works are part of a projected twelve-volume series of novels under the collective title The

New Age/Le Nouveau siècle. "Sober Colouring. The Ontology of Super-Realism" appeared in *Canadian Literature* in 1971.

Sober Colouring:
The Ontology of Super-Realism

Super-realism, yes, because that is how I think of my fiction, quite deliberately and consciously, very likely unconsciously too. When I started to write novels and stories about the year 1956, I had no clear idea of what I was doing. I had had a literary education, and knew something about critical theory and method as applied to the work of other writers, the classics especially, and some moderns. I got a Ph.D. in English in late 1955. After that I did more or less what I wanted. I began to write independently, feeling liberated from the need to defer to what other people might think. I was glad to get out of the graduate school.

I had no theory of my own writing, and belonged to no school, so I wrote most of a novel which was never published, and a dozen stories, in 1956 and 1957, instinctively, making all the important artistic decisions as I went along, with no theoretical bias for one kind of writing as against all the others. Instinctively, then, I turned out to be a moral realist, not a naturalist nor a surrealist nor a magic realist nor in any way an experimental or advance guard writer. That was in effect where I began.

All my early writing dealt with the affairs of credible characters in more or less credible situations. As I look back, I see that this instinctive moral realism was tempered by an inclination to show these credible characters, in perfectly ordinary situations, nevertheless doing violent and unpredictable, and even melodramatic, things. A brother and sister go to visit their mother's grave and are unable to find it in a cemetery of nightmarish proportions; a man kills his newly-baptized girl friend thinking that she will go straight to Heaven; a young priest molests a child sexually; a young boy goes mad under great strain. A yachtsman runs his boat on a rock and sinks it, drowning his wife and her lover, who are trapped below deck. I would never choose actions like these nowadays, not because of their violence but because of their improbability. I still write about intense feeling which leads to impulsive and sometimes violent acts, but I am better able to locate these feelings in credible occasions.

In those days, and for several years afterwards, I tried to control these melodramatic tendencies—murder, suicide, hanging about in cemeteries, drowning in burst boats—by a strong sense of the physical form of stories. I arranged my pieces according to complex numerologies. A novel might have seven main sections, one for each day of a specific week in a given year, so that the reader could tell exactly what time it was when something happened. Or the book might be divided in three main parts, each with a specific number of subdivisions. I once wrote the rough draft of a book in two main sections and when I had finished each half of the manuscript was precisely a hundred and forty-four pages long: twelve twelves doubled. This play with numbers is a recurrent feature of my work. *Around the Mountain* follows the calendar very precisely, with one story for each month from one Christmas to the next. I have always had a fondness for the cycle of the Christian liturgical year. My first, unpublished, novel was called *God Rest You Merry*, and covered the seven days from Christmas Night to New Year's Eve, in a most elaborate arrangement.

I still do this. My new novel, which will appear in the fall of 1972, *You Can't Get There From Here*, is in three parts. The first and third sections have ten chapters each; the middle part has twenty, which gives us: 10/20/10. The Christian numerological symbolism implied is very extensive. It makes a kind of scaffolding for the imagination.

I had then, and still have, an acute sense of the possibilities of close formal organization of the sentence, syntactically and grammatically, and in its phonemic sequences. I paid much attention to the difficulties of writing long sentences because I knew that simple-minded naturalists wrote short sentences, using lots of 'ands'. I did not want to be a simple-minded naturalist. I hoped to write syntactically various and graceful prose. I took care to vary the number of sentences in succeeding paragraphs. I rarely used the one-sentence paragraph; when I did so I felt mighty daring. I kept a careful eye upon the clause-structure of each sentence. I wouldn't use the ellipsis mark (. . .) because Arthur Mizener wrote to me that he considered it a weak, cop-out sort of punctuation.

I sometimes use the ellipsis now . . . and feel guilty.

My interest in the sound of sentences, in the use of colour words and of the names of places, in practical stylistics, showed me that prose fiction might have an abstract element, a purely formal element, even though it continued to be strictly, morally, realistic. It might be possible to think of prose fiction the way one thinks of abstract elements in representational painting, or of highly formal music. I now began to see affinities between the art I was willy-nilly practising and the other arts, first poetry, then painting and music. I have always been passionately attached to music and painting—I have gone so far as to marry a painter on mixed grounds—and have written many stories about the arts: film-making, painting, music less often because it is on the surface such a non-narrative art. I find that it is hard to speak about music.

I have also written some stories about a kind of experience close to that of the artist: metaphysical thought. My stories "A Season of Calm Weather" (with its consciously Wordsworthian title) and "The

Hole" are about metaphysicians. The second of the two tries to show a philosopher's intelligence actually at work, a hard thing to do. Like musical thought, metaphysical thought seems to take place in a non-verbal region of consciousness, if there is such a thing, and it is therefore hard to write about, but to me an irresistible challenge.

My novels *White Figure, White Ground* and *The Camera Always Lies* dealt respectively with the problems of a painter and a group of film-makers. It is the seeing-into-things, the capacity for meditative abstraction, that interests me about philosophy, the arts and religious practice. I love most in painting an art which exhibits the transcendental element dwelling in living things. I think of this as true *super-realism*. And I think of Vermeer, or among American artists of Edward Hopper, whose paintings of ordinary places, seaside cottages, a road-side snack bar and gasoline station, have touched some level of my own imagination which I can only express in fictional images. In my story "Getting to Williamstown" there is a description of a roadside refreshment stand beside an abandoned gas pump, which is pretty directly imitated from a painting of Hopper's. I see this now, though I didn't when I wrote the story. That is what I mean by the unconscious elements in my work which co-operate with my deliberate intentions.

I have to admit at this point that my Ph.D. thesis discussed the theory of the imagination of the Romantic poets and its background. The argument of the thesis was that Romantic imagination-theory was fundamentally a revision of the theory of abstraction as it was taught by Aristotle and the mediaeval philosophers. The kind of knowing which Wordsworth called "reason in its most exalted mood" and which Coleridge exalted as creative artistic imagination, *does the same thing* as that power which Saint Thomas Aquinas thought of as the active intellect. I do not think of the imaginatin and the active intellect as separate and opposed to one another. No more are emotion and thought *lived* distinct and apart. The power of abstraction, in the terms of traditional psychology, is not a murderous dissection of living beings; on the contrary it is an intimate penetration into their physical reality. "No ideas but in things," said William Carlos Williams. I believe that Aquinas would concur in that—the idea lives in the singular real being. The intellect is not set over against emotion, feelings, instincts, memory and the imagination, but intimately united to them. The artist and the metaphysician are equally contemplatives; so are the saints.

Like Vermeer or Hopper or that great creator of musical form, Joseph Haydn, I am trying to concentrate on knowable form as it lives in the physical world. These forms are abstract, not in the sense of being inhumanly non-physical, but in the sense of communicating the perfection of the essences of things—the formal realities which create things as they are in themselves. A transcendentalist must first study the things of this world, and get as far inside them as possible. My story "The Hole" tries to show a philosopher working out this idea in his own experience. Here, as everywhere in my writing, I have studied as closely and intensely as I can the *insides* of things which are not me. The great metaphor in human experience for truly apprehending another being is sexual practice. Here, perhaps only here, do we get inside another being. Alas, the entrance is only metaphorical. In plain fact no true penetration happens in love-making. It is not possible for one physical being to merge into another, as D.H. Lawrence finally realized. Bodies occupy different places; there is nothing to be done about this. Sex is a metaphor for union, not itself achieved union.

What we are united to in this world is not physical insides of persons or things, but the knowable principle in them. Inside everything that exists is essence, not in physical space and time, but as forming space and time and the perceptions possible within them. What I know, love, and desire in another person, isn't inside him like a nut in its shell, but it is everywhere that he is, forming him. My identity isn't inside me—it is *how I am*. It is hard to express the way we know the forms of things, but this is the knowing that art exercises.

Art after all, like every other human act, implies a philosophical stance: either you think there is nothing to things that is not delivered in their appearances, or you think that immaterial forms exist in these things, conferring identity on them. These are not the only ontological alternatives, but they are extreme ones, and they state a classical ontological opposition. The bias of most contemporary thought has been towards the first alternative, until the very recent past. But perhaps we are again beginning to be able to think about the noumenal element in things, their essential and intelligible principles, what Newman called the "illative" aspect of being. The danger of this sort of noumenalism is that you may dissolve the hard, substantial shapes of things, as they can be seen to be, into an idealistic mish-mash—something I'm not inclined to do. I'm not a Platonist or a dualist of any kind. I think with Aristotle that the body and the soul are one; the form of a thing is totally united to its matter. The soul is the body. No ideas but in things.

That is where I come out: the spirit is totaly *in* the flesh. If you pay close enough attention to things, stare at them, concentrate on them as hard as you can, not just with your intelligence, but with your feelings and instincts—with your prick too—you will begin to apprehend the forms in them. Knowing is not a matter of sitting in an armchair while engaged in some abstruse conceptual calculus of weights and measures and geometrical spaces. Knowing includes making love, and making pieces of art, and wanting and worshipping *and* calculating (because calculation is also part of knowing) and in fact knowing is what Wordsworth called it, a "spousal union" of the knower and the known, a marriage full of flesh.

I want to propose the Wordsworthian account of the marriage of the mind and the thing as a model of artistic activity. I don't think that the Romantic movement failed. I think we are still in the middle of it. Of the Romantic masters, Wordsworth seems to me to have understood

236

best how things move in themselves, how they exist as they are when they are possessing themselves, having their identities, living. Wordsworth has an extraordinary grasp of the movement, the running motion, of the physical, the roll of water or sweep of wind, changing textures of fog or mist, all that is impalpable and yet material. In this fleeting, running movement of physical existence, for Wordsworth there is always the threat of an illumination, "splendour in the grass, glory in the flower". Things are full of the visionary gleam.

The illuminations in things are there, really and truly *there*, in those things. They are not run over them by the projective intelligence, and yet there is a sense in which the mind, in uniting itself to things, creates illumination in them.

> The clouds that gather round the setting sun
> Do take a sober colouring from an eye
> That hath kept watch o'er man's mortality;

This is a triple eye, that of the setting sun which colours the clouds, and that of the sober human moral imagination, and finally that of God as brooding, creative Father of all. The colouring of the clouds is given to them by the Deity in the original act of creation. Every evening the sun re-enacts the illumination. The moral imagination operates in the same way, though it is not originally creative; it projects colouring into things, true, but the colouring has already been put there by the divine creation. The act of the human knower is an act of reciprocity. It half creates, and half perceives "the mighty world of eye and ear".

"I have at all times endeavoured to look steadily at my subject," said Wordsworth, very justly. His regard to things is concentrated and accurate; he insists everywhere on the utter necessity of the sensory process, of seeing and hearing, of taking in the sensible world and transforming it. He proposes "to throw a certain colouring of the imagination over incidents and situations taken from common life." This is the same metaphor as that of the final stanza of the "Intimations Ode". The eye in seeing gives colour to things; but the colour is there.

The poetry of Wordsworth supplies us again and again with examples of this colouring of imagination spread over incidents and situations from common life. The figure of the old Leech-Gatherer in "Resolution and Independence" is perhaps the most overwhelming example of this capacity of very ordinary persons and scenes to yield, on close inspection, an almost intolerable significance.

> In my mind's eye I seemed to see him pace
> About the weary moors continually,
> Wandering about alone and silently.

The concentrating eye, interior/exterior, giving to things their sober hues, is constant in Wordsworth. I have imitated it from him in my work. In the deliberately paired stories "Socks" and "Boots" I have chosen incidents from ordinary life and characters such as may be met with everywhere, and I have attempted to look steadily at these persons in the hope that something of the noumenal will emerge.

These stories are, to begin with, political; they are about the ways in which living in society modifies our personal desires, a very Wordsworthian theme. Domenico Lercaro in "Socks" does not want to work so hard. Nobody wants to work that hard. He doesn't want to work on a garbage truck or do snow removal, but he is driven to it by the need to survive. The fictional "my wife" in the story "Boots" want to buy a certain specific kind of winter footwear, but the stores simply don't stock the boots she wants. We can buy only what we are offered, and our range of choice is surprisingly limited.

I have tried to move beyond the fiction of social circumstance by taking a very attentive look at my two main characters. In "Socks" poor Domenico sees the enormous, noisy, snow-removal machine turn before his eyes into a divine beast or Leviathan. Everyone who has seen these machines at work recognizes their intimations of violence, in their noise and in the sharpness of their rotary blades. They have actually killed and eaten people. Modern life is full of these mechanical beasts.

"My wife" in "Boots" feels trivialized by fashion; most women in middle-class circumstances do, I think. To wear high heels and a girdle is to enslave yourself—to adopt the badges of a humiliating subservience. This story tries to make its readers sense the galling limits on their activities felt by intelligent women in the face of the clothes which fashion and *chic* propose for them: the necessary sexual exhibitionism, the silly posturing, the faked little-girlishness.

The two stories insinuate larger issues than their subjects would suggest; they are following Wordsworth's prescription. I have at all times endeavoured to look steadily at my subjects. I hope that my gaze has helped to light them up.

1971

Robert Kroetsch
1922—

Born in Heisler, Alberta, Robert Kroetsch attended the University of Alberta and McGill University and later joined the Department of English at the State University of New York at Binghamton. His first novel, *But We Are Exiles*, was published in 1965, and he has since published literary criticism, a travel book and several volumes of poetry and fiction. His novels include: *The Words of My Roaring* (1966); *The Studhorse Man* (1969); *Gone Indian* (1973); *Badlands* (1975); and *What The Crow Said* (1978). "Unhiding the

Hidden: Recent Canadian Fiction" appeared in the *Journal of Canadian Fiction* in 1974. "Death Is a Happy Ending: A dialogue in thirteen parts" between Kroetsch and critic Diane Bessai was first published in *Figures in a Ground, Canadian Essays on Modern Literature Collected in Honor of Sheila Watson* (1978).

Unhiding the Hidden:
Recent Canadian Fiction

Margaret Atwood, **Surfacing:** *"Now we're on my home ground, foreign territory."*

Survival itself is the Canadian apocalypse. The Canadian cannot die and therefore writes fiction. He longs to be destroyed by America; in his wrath at America's failure he sets out to be the destroyer. It is his only hope.

At one time I considered it the task of the Canadian writer to give names to his experience, to be the namer. I now suspect that on the contrary, it is his task to un-name.

This necessity did not originate with Canadian writers. Heidegger says in his *Poetry, Language, Thought:*[1] *"Roman thought takes over the Greek words without a corresponding, equally authentic experience of what they say, without the Greek word.* The rootlessness of Western thought begins with this translation (23)."

The Canadian writer's particular predicament is that he works with a language, within a literature, that appears to be authentically his own, and not a borrowing. But just as there was in the Latin word a concealed Greek experience, so there is in the Canadian word a concealed other experience, sometimes British, sometimes American.

In recent years the tension between this appearance of being just like someone else and the demands of authenticity has become intolerable—both to individuals and to the society. In recent Canadian fiction the major writers resolve the paradox—the painful tension between appearance and authenticity—by the radical process of demythologizing the systems that threaten to define them. Or, more comprehensively, they uninvent the world.

The most conspicuous example is the novel, *Surfacing,*[2] by Margaret Atwood. In that novel the three *named* characters, Joe, David and Anna, live constantly in danger of becoming American. Waiting for the barbarians, they begin to become, in terms of the essential American paradox, the awaited barbarians. But the Canadian who borrows this posture as an account of his condition is metamorphosed into the inauthentic fool that David makes of himself with his speech and his camera, that Anna makes of herself with her mirror and her compact and her cunt.

Atwood's heroine must remove the false names that adhere to her experience. The terror of her journey is not that she, like her drowned father, like her drowned and revived antipodal brother, almost drowns; it is rather that she surfaces. The terror resides not in her going insane but in her going sane.

Atwood signals this very Canadian predicament when she has the narrator say early in the novel, "Now we're on my home ground. foreign territory (II)." The truth is disguised, hidden. Camouflage, the narrator says, "was one of my father's policies (32)." And she too is good at varieties of camouflage: she says of herself as commercial artist, "I, can imitate anything: fake Walt Disney, Victorian etchings in sepia. Bavarian cookies, ersatz Eskimo for the home market. Though what they like best [her Canadian publishers] is something they hope will interest the English and American publishers too (53)." And as she is able to imitate art, so she imitates marriage, imitates friendship. She can fake, has been taught to and forced to fake, not only a personal identity, but adherence to a social order: looking at school pictures she sees herself "in the stiff dresses, crinolines and tulle, layered like store birthday cakes; I was civilized at last, the finished product (108)."

But underneath this layering, this concealing, is a woman who still recognizes that something doesn't fit. Joe says. "Do you love me, that's all," and she thinks: "It was the language again, I couldn't use it because it wasn't mine (106)."

The Roman writer borrowed a Greek word into a Latin context. The Canadian writer borrows an English word into an English-language context, a French word into a French-language context. The process of rooting that borrowed word, that totally exact homonym, in authentic experience, is then, must be, a radical one.

Atwood's heroine burns the drawings and the typescript from which she works. She takes off the ring that signifies her sham marriage, drops it into the fire. But even that is only the beginning:

> Everything from history must be eliminated, the circles and the arrogant square pegs. I rummage under the mattress and bring out the scrapbooks, ripping them up, the ladies, dress forms with decorated china heads, the suns and the moons, the rabbits and their archaic eggs, my false peace, his/her brother's/wars, aeroplanes and tanks and the helmeted explorers . . . Even the guides, the miraculous double woman and the god with horns, they must be translated. The ladies on the wall too with their watermelon breasts and lampshade skirts, all my artifacts. . . .the map torn from the wall . . . When the paper things are burned I smash the glasses and plates and the chimney of the lamp. I rip one page from each of the books . . . When nothing is left intact and the fire is only smouldering I leave, carrying one of the wounded blankets with me, I will need it until the fur grows. The house shuts with a click behind me (176-77).

In the marvellous extravagance of this surfacing, this uninventing of the world, the narrator must finally deliver herself of the notion that she is a human being. Bare-assed she can become bear-assed—in accordance with the outrageous, seductive, fabulated contemporary female vision of what total freedom must be. At the end of *Surfacing* the narrator has achieved a state wherein she might—with minimal help from Joe, who has in him still a bit of the buffalo, a bit of the bear—give birth to her true identity. "The word games, the winning and losing games are finished; at the moment there are no others but they will have to be invented, withdrawing is no longer possible and the alternative is death (191)."

Atwood's heroine will not die; rather, she will give birth to herself. And, curiously, a similar version of parthenogenesis marks the end of another fine recent novel.

David Staunton, the hero of Robertson Davies' *The Manticore*,[3] like Atwood's heroine, must begin by confronting death and the father. For eastern Canadian writers, this matter of literal ancestors is paramount. And David, named after his father's hero, the Prince of Wales (43-44), compared to Absalom, must not so much learn as unlearn family history: be it in the form of a borrowed coat of arms, a family fortune, or the English origins of the family name. His father, like the father in Atwood's novel, must literally be brought back to the surface from death by water. And, quite literally, Boy Staunton (the father) is unmasked: the dentist-artist who would make a death-mask succeeds instead in removing the corpse's face.

Where the larger process of uninventing, in Atwood, becomes a journey into the wilderness, in Davies it is a journey to the old civilization, the sum of our ancestry. And yet, for both these novelists, the condition of pre-history is necessary to valid and authentic birth.

I cannot here examine Davies' skill in taking us on that journey: his use of theatrical devices of unmasking, his exploration of the theme of illusion, his concept of the role of the fool in the unhiding of the hidden, in the speaking of the unspeakable. Davies, the sophisticated novelist, works back to notebooks, to diaries, to confession, to psychoanalytic method, to Jungian archetypes.

What is central is that his hero, David Staunton, criminal lawyer, alcoholic, Oxford graduate, archetypal Canadian fucked virgin, literally goes back into the earth. High up in the mountains of Switzerland he crawls with a mysterious woman down into a cave. He goes back to the darkness, extinguishes the last light. He finds in that darkness, in that womb-like cave, the necessary connection between Felix, the stuffed bear that was his consolation at age four, and his bear-worshipping ancestors. The world has been uninvented: by this man, for this man who earlier was told, "You think the world is your idea (242)." And now, reunited with his infancy, with his animal nature, with his emotions—gone back beyond thinking (274)—he finds himself so close to death that in terror he shits himself.

At that "lowest ebb," the woman tells him: "Go on, you dirty brute, go on (275)." And Staunton, his anima recognized, his whole

241

ancestry acknowledged, is able at last to give birth to himself. He crawls out into the cold sunshine. It is Christmas eve. He is the newborn stranger ready to return to his "home ground, foreign territory." Like Atwood's heroine on her island, Davies' Staunton is ready to begin. Atwood's narrator hopes she is pregnant. Staunton is ready to look for a wife. Having uninvented the world, each is prepared—in the manner of the newly-wed couple at the end of the traditional comic novel—to invent a new one.

Atwood and Davies, using the established conventions of the novel, act out this process of decomposing the world in terms of individuals. Curiously, it has been left to western Canadian writers to act it out in a larger social context.

Grove is the paradigm of this larger mode. Felix Paul Greve he departed Europe; in mid-Atlantic he uninvented himself, unwrote his history, arrived in Canada a new self, Frederick Philip Grove, about to invent new ancestors. He is the true trickster in our prose tradition, as Layton and Birney are of the poetic. He is the fool-sage, the holy nut so pompously wise he could unlearn not just himself but a literary tradition, a civilization; he could discover the new form of *Over Prairie Trails*, the fictional reality of *In Search of Myself*. . . . And of his descendants, some of whom might not recognize their mysterious father, Rudy Wiebe is the most central to my thesis. But Robert Harlow's *Scann* is a reckless demolition of inauthenticity towards an Easter of recognition. And Dave Godfrey, that exiled westerner, has written a novel quite literally called *The New Ancestors*.

I choose to comment on Wiebe's *The Temptations of Big Bear*[4] because here a bear-inspired man acts out, not only mythologically, but historically as well, the uninvention of the world. By an act of imagination that approaches the complexity of Grove's own, Wiebe makes of a tribe of Crees the epitome of our Canadian selves being extinguished into existence by the British and American cultures. Hounded, tricked, robbed, cheated, shot at, starved—we prove they cannot capture us: and then voluntarily we reveal ourselves to the destroying elements. Big Bear is the poet-creator who must himself be uncreated in order to represent our necessary fate. He must resist temptations to be anything—farmer, politician, trading-post white man, Christian—other than his fated self. He must *talk* his way into his decreated and valid self; he must, dying, become the source and creator of the unimaginable new.

In his talking—in the language of the novel—he and Wiebe decreate the literary tradition that binds us into not speaking the truth. Wiebe and Harlow and Godfrey, like Grove before them, have a marvellous ability to keep the language clumsy, brutal, unbeautiful, vital, charged. Atwood makes a fine Canadian prose style of the run-on sentence. Davies distrusts any sentence that loses its connection with his newspaperman's background. But Wiebe is determined to destroy the sentence itself back to sense, back to its ground. He says in his dedication that he "unearthed" the story. He recognizes the problem of language: we learn that Corporal Sleigh "never read a book because people in them never walked in mud. . . . You never got the sense of anyone being downright dirty the way Territories' mud stuck to you in globs . . . (272)." He demonstrates how the problem of language becomes one of culture, society, identity: Peter Houri attempts to translate, to speak of the crime against, Queen Victoria's "crown and dignity." Big Bear responds:

. . . there is nothing true when they say I tried to steal her hat. How could I do that? Or knock it off, as Poundmaker said they told him, by throwing sticks at it. . . . I didn't know she had a hat and I never wear hats, what would I want it for to make me steal it, women's hats are nice but a man would be drunk—(387)

Where Davies invented documents, Wiebe quotes from existing sources, lets government records and legal debate and newspapers and memoirs and journals speak for themselves. The sheer failure of that language to confront reality is both comic and appalling. We discover, finally, why Wiebe is driven into complicity with the so-called renegade Indians. Like them, he must experience the de-composition of the world. He must, whatver the cost, go Indian himself.

It is possible that the old obsessive notion of identity, of ego, is itself a spent fiction, that these new writers are discovering something essentially new, something essential not only to Canadians but to the world they would uncreate. Whatever the case, they dare that ultimate *contra-diction:* they uncreate themselves into existence. Like Heidegger they will accept that the root meaning of the word truth is un-concealing, dis-closing, dis-covering, un-hiding. Or, to put it in prairie terms, they will, like Rudy Wiebe's Big Bear, even when locked up in the Stony Mountain pen, with the Archbishop generously in attendance—even then they will be loyal to their own first visions. Offered the consolation and pride of the old names, they will "decline to be christened."

1974

Notes

[1]Martin Heidegger, *Poetry, Language, Thought.* Translation by Albert Hofstadter. New York: Harper & Row. 1971. I am indebted to my colleague, William V. Spanos, for his illuminating discussions of Heidegger's use of the Greek word, *aletheia.*
[2]Margaret Atwood, *Surfacing.* Toronto: McClelland and Stewart, 1972.
[3]Robertson Davies, *The Manticore.* Toronto: Macmillan of Canada, 1972.
[4]Rudy Wiebe, *The Temptations of Big Bear.* Toronto: McClelland and Stewart, 1973.

Death is a Happy Ending: A dialogue in thirteen parts (with Diane Bessai)

I

R.K. One is struck, in reading Canadian fiction of the first half of the twentieth century, by the degree to which tradition writes the novel, form creates the author. Regardless of content, the Victorian prototype is apparent in works as seemingly different as the prairie novels of F.P. Grove and the urban novels of Hugh MacLennan. Concepts of character, theme, setting and structure derive from the great models of the nineteenth century. Canadian writers, like third-world writers elsewhere, confronting new materials, resorted to old methods. The author is not creator but created—by genre, history, convention.

D.B. *Should this be seen as a Canadian problem only? It is exactly that of the early moderns. Take Virginia Woolf's 'Modern Fiction' which certainly didn't lead to the minimal novel until her marvellous* Between the Acts. *Think of all those years she took working her way through the prototypes, including her own. Why not view the modernist examples from elsewhere as in some way a paradigm for patterns of Canadian literary history? It puts Canadian developments in the main stream, although the process is much slower here and I am inclined to favor your suggestion, in* boundary 2, *of a jump from Victorian to postmodern.*

R.K. I don't like to see it as a slower process in Canada; rather, as a different one. We went from agrarian to post-industrial in a leap that excluded high modern from our experience. Young men went from America to the end of the First World War to experience an urban world that was in a state of violent and exhilarating change. Young men went from Canada to the beginning of the First World War literally to die in the fields.

D.B. *It sounds so solemn and romantic—Flanders Fields, Beaumont Hamil and the rest. Some came back, however, and we cannot lament the unwritten. We are only beginning now to lament the colonial mind of those post-war days, which in the main was unreceptive to radical literary change. That is why* Settlers of the Marsh *was banned in public libraries. Of course writers such as Grove and Ostenso were so busy getting at the psychology of the agrarian society that they hardly had energy for breaking new formal ground. Thus we were long left awaiting. . .*

II

R.K. The necessary act of decreation: the exercise in minimal art: the writing of a skinny novel. Gertrude Stein: *Ida.* Joyce's Dedalus: 'The radiance of which he (Aquinas) speaks is the scholastic *quidditas,* the

244

whatness of a thing.' Gide, before Joyce, trying to define and write the pure novel. Robbe-Grillet, since, trying to free his contemporaries from the Balzacian model. Beckett, parodying even the basic assumptions of whatness. John Hawkes:

'I began to write fiction on the assumption that the true enemies of the novel were plot, character, setting, and theme, and having once abandoned these familiar ways of thinking about fiction, totality of vision or structure was really all that remained.'

D.B. *Explain how vision and structure are the same thing.*

R.K. James Potter: in order to begin: killing the old lady.

D.B. *Now we are getting close to home. A paradigm of the problem itself, that killing. Especially since the old lady won't really go away! . . . Decreation—going for whatness or disintegrating it. In Canadian terms you are back to your idea of unnaming, deliberately 'uninventing' the world that threatens to define in traditional colonial terms. The* Double Hook, *then, is a paradigm of decreation, of which one kind is a self-reflexive novel (in good company with several other important novels written in this country).*

III

R.K. James Potter. Killing. Beginning.

The current threat to the literary text: the critic as theologian who cannot permit deviation from the right reading. The critic who cannot allow that the work of art *acts out* just this—the play of possible meanings; the text not as artifact but as enabling act. Not *meaning,* but the possibility of meanings. The teacher who cannot offer the occasion, but rather the end.

But the question remains: Is it possible to define a Canadian novel, not in terms of content, but in terms of structure or form?

Killing. Beginning. But the questions remain.

D.B. *Before you get on to that question, permit a word about critics, as I understand your comments. Surely the* single-minded *critic is a marked man these days. There is a contemporary brand of reader-as-critic, however, who is on the rise. The novel as enabling act is, of course, tremendously important. If I ask whether you are feeling the special need to educate the Canadian reader at this particular stage of literary development, it is because I believe he may need it—he is accustomed to traditional form in* Canadian *fiction at least: to having his 'synthesis' so explained away by the novelist that the 'illumination' is cloudy. You are insisting on the right and need of the novelist to be duplicitous and that the reader must tune in. But the novelist ought to learn how to signal effectively and the reader how to recognize his signals. My suspicion is the current Canadian reader-as-critic invents his own—perhaps out*

of wishful thinking for good post-modern models to work from. The
number of such critics who have romanced away at Ross, or Grove, or
Mitchell, or Callaghan in recent years is truly astonishing. 'Collab-
oration' is the name of that game according to one. I wonder if the novelist
ever holds the reins any more in this process. Or is the critic turning
novelist himself now, just to meet his own standards? But the serious
artist. . .

IV

R.K. the artist him/her self:

in the long run, given the choice of being God or Coyote, will, most
mornings, choose to be Coyote:

he lets in the irrational along with the rational, the pre-moral along
with the moral. He is a shape-shifter, at least in the limited way of old
lady Potter. He is the charlatan-healer, like Felix Prosper, the low-
down Buddha-bellied fiddler midwife (him/her) rather than Joyce's
high priest of art. Sometimes he is hogging the show instead of paring
his fingernails. Like all tricksters, like Kip, like Traff, he runs the risk
of himself being tricked.

D.B. *Truth by concealment . . . or is it dressage? The danger is seduction*
by style, everything metaphoric: 'there are no truths, only correspon-
dences.' In fact you might say that the current extreme is over-signaling.
However, in what dimension does the common reader exist in all this?

V

R.K. the reader:

a character out of one of the novels the novelist is deconstructing. He
expects certain consolations: of plot, of motivation, of characterization,
of conclusion. The domesticated reassurances of the idyll, of the epic,
of Greek tragedy, of the modern world as waste land, of the western
movie—plus generous portions of both Testaments, Old and New.

Yet, when he meets on page one Coyote and his twelve apostles, the
reader should recognize that he has met the novelist as jester. Ultimately, as trickster. And he, the old reader, must slowly unlearn
concepts of character. Of motivation. Of plot and ending. He must, to
sum it up in one expression, acquire Negative Capability. He has
entered a world where possibilities not only co-exist but contradict.
Where thesis inspires antithesis. Where day and light of chapter one
become the night and darkness of chapter two, where the blind see and
the seeing are fooled, not only by the trickster and each other—but
by seeing.

But should not the dichotomies themselves be dissolved?

246

D.B. *Between reader and writer? Ideally so. But what if the reader's a fool critic? Or the novelist is leading him on? The post-modern voice is so often mysterious, secretive. Where is that voice coming from?*

VI

R.K. language:

For novelists like John Barth and William Gass and Robert Coover, the connection between word and world is gone. Beckett's Watt, muttering the word 'pot,' cannot connect word and object. Fiction becomes fiction.

For Sheila Watson, the situation is more blatantly ambiguous. A happier desperation pertains. She as author—like her characters—possibly like her readers—is both trapped in and saved by language. Like James Potter, who is robbed of the money that would buy him a train ticket out, we are somehow 'freed . . . from freedom.'

Her characters are trapped in language that is rooted in the oral tradition, a language that tends always toward the formulaic. Yet that same language enables them to get things said. Right at the edge of parody, the language becomes serious, becomes vehicle. At the edge of the general and the abstract, we are reminded of the ground:

'I've been thinking,' the [Wagner] boy said . . . 'Felix sits there like the round world all centered in on himself.'

'He drinks coffee like the rest of us,' William said. 'Though . . . I'd be hard pressed to know how he comes by the money to pay for it.'

D.B. *Certainly in the loss of connection between word and world, Beckett went about as far as he could before silence (or the scream). Yet the Canadian writer at present knows he can exploit a certain cultural immediacy; the radical urge for authenticity combines fittingly with the post-modern scorn for dependence on artifice. Of course, the drive to discover or forge his own language is intimately related to his sensitivity to the dictates of form. This in turn has its own inner compulsions.*

VII

R.K. James Potter, page one, is man fallen. He is upstairs murdering his mother. But downstairs his sister is turning hotcakes—and the kitchen stove is one of the centers of the novel—so that man the (murdering) animal can live.

Sheila Watson doubts that anyone can 'light out.' James Potter tries it—only to return. And when he returns, the house he left has been burned to the ground. By that same sister and that same stove.

The world of potters is a world of clay, of making and unmaking and making again. Of turning and turning and re-turning.

'He shut his eyes. In his mind now he could see only the seared and smouldering earth, the bare hot cinder of a still unpeopled world. He felt as he stood with his eyes closed on the destruction of what his heart had wished destroyed that by some generous gesture he ad been turned once more into the first pasture of things.'
'I ran away . . . but I circled and ended here the way a man does when he's lost.'

D.B. *You offer an easy temptation into a tidy generalization; the eternal return (certainly not 'lighting out') as defining structure. But that might lead us back to that marked man, 'the critic as theologian'; fortunately for the 'enabler,' the re-turn is where the true complexity lies—made so by the experience of loss itself.*

VIII

R.K. The hazard of the essential novel is in that implicit word, *essence.* With the dross burned away, the novel stripped, deconstructed—we have the final victory of form itself. A platonic form emerging as the *quidditas.*

John Barth:

'After [the silence of Beckett's *Molloy*] . . . it might be conceivable to rediscover validly the artifices of language and literature—such far-out notions as grammar, punctuation . . . even characterization! Even plot!—if one goes about it the right way, aware of what one's predecessors have been up to.'

One is tempted to rush out of the garden and into the bush.

D.B. *A reminder that we are not Huck Finns. Not even Margaret Atwood is Huck Finn. But the real point is that while there is a thin line between Barth's re-invention and the Canadian novelists' uninvention (such as Atwood in* Surfacing*), the difference is in the perspective. The best Canadian artist is confronting traditional cultural dependencies more than he is reacting to the inevitable reversals in fiction-making in general.*

IX

R.K. After the skinny novel of Sheila Watson, we witness a flowering of the expansive novel, the fat novel. Where American writers (Pynchon, Gardner, Heller) have written long books, and British novelists have written long series (*The Music of Time*), Canadians have turned to the trilogy. Robert Harlow, Austin Clarke, Robertson Davies, Mordecai Richler—they deal in developments of plot, character and theme that, for all their contemporary trappings, are curiously reminiscent of the Victorian.

D.B. *Some are: Robertson Davies, a novelistic Matthew Arnold. But the good post-modern novel is something else—perhaps* Scann, *which achieves its complexity without telling you how complex it is, or how*

248

much meaning is to be found in it all . . . and it reflects, quite delib-
erately, on the problems of its own creation.

R.K. In *Scann* we have art as overload, permitting origins, finding
the ground. Like Wiebe, in *The Temptations of Big Bear*, uninventing
himself back to Big Bear . . . We have come to the end of endings. The
existential posture—choose, choose—now seems too simple. It's hard
enough to get to a beginning.

D.B. *You've remarked elsewhere that we must 'not so much learn as*
unlearn family history.' Yet Margaret Laurence documents the family
in an ordinary—in my view, gynecological—way.

R.K. Maybe I'm only interested in the geology of the family.

D.B. *The same can be said of Rudy Wiebe. He literally documents the*
world. But behind Big Bear is Wiebe's vision of a Mennonite patriarch.
Behind the patriarch is his vision of the lost Old Testament world. . . .
Just as Sheila Watson synthesizes a lost New Testament world in her
Indians. And, incidentally, she did documentary research on the
Thompson Indians of B.C. We enlarge the family history. Maybe the
whole thrust of post-modern in Canada is in this direction—discovering
the forms for the hitherto hidden experience.

X

R.K. The expansive impulse has found its lengthiest expression in the
Manawaka stories of Margaret Laurence. They complete the binary
pattern occasioned by Watson's deconstructive originality, the finding
of shapes in the nuisance grounds. The old woman in *The Stone Angel*
(and again, the absolute opposition in the title) acts out the strength of
womanhood that is reduced to a few inferences in *The Double Hook*. Yet
in both we hear the lament of the archetypal Canadian family: The
Queen must die. Long live the Queen.

Both novelists write novels about writing. Old Mrs Potter, enigmat-
ically, must die so the child might be born. The literal writer, Morag
Gunn, in *The Diviners*, must have her specific destructive-creative
encounters with the scavenger, the professor, the singer, the snake-
dancer, the diviner—before she can return to the house and set down
the title of her book. Yet, in their different ways, each of these women,
one figuratively, one literally, must locate and confront the source of
energy, the trickster-god, the fish-phallus of her male muse.

D.B. *And what are we to make of this?*

XI

R.K. The opening chapter of Auerbach's *Mimesis*. He contrasts the
literary method of Book 19 of *The Odyssey* and the biblical account
of the sacrifice of Isaac.

'The two styles, in their opposition, represent basic types: on the one hand fully externalized description, uniform illumination, uninterrupted connection, free expression, all events in the foreground, displaying unmistakable meanings, few elements of historical development and of psychological perspective; on the other hand, certain parts brought into high relief, others left obscure, abruptness, suggestive influence of the unexpressed, "background" quality, multiplicity of meanings and the need for interpretation, universal-historical claims, development of the concept of the historically becoming, and preoccupation with the problematic.'

XII

R.K. Watson and Laurence believe that art is more than play, that language is more than a linguistic construct, that a novel is more than the evasion of reality. *De contemptu mundi* is not their phrase. Both feel that the problem is not how to get to heaven. Or even to hell. The problem is how to live: here: now. Individuals, alone, living together. Together, living alone.

The ultimate fall of man is the fall out of time.

The novelist must tell the sacredness and the profanity of existence.

D.B. *There may be other kinds of things here. I think Harlow throws out a lot of the trappings (does Laurence?) that you say Hawkes does, althougth I haven't actually thought about Scann as giving totality of vision—which seems rather pretentious an aim in any case these days. What he does do, in some sense, is put his feet back on the ground and give you the world in stories again as well as a semi-comic view of the problems of the creative vision attempting to make those stories in his time and place. Actually, the expansive novel may be a combination of skinny ones emerging into a total construct. Maybe this reflects a particular Canadian need. In Scann itself, of course, nobody believes the stories in any case! But that is a typical line going back to Susanna Moodie, who was accused of writing lies for a living. What does emerge, then, if even story is still suspect?*

XIII
R.K. The double hook. The total ambiguity that is so essentially Canadian: be it in terms of two solitudes, the bush garden, Jungian opposites, or the raw and the cooked binary structures of Levi-Strauss. Behind the multiplying theories of Canadian literature is always the pattern of equally matched opposites.

Coyote : God
Self : Community
Energy : Stasis

The balance, whatever the specifics, is always so equal that one wonders how paradigm can possibly issue into story.

D.B. *So much for* the critic *as theologian; you have replaced him with* the creator *as theologian.* . . .

1978

Margaret Laurence
1926—

Born in Neepawa, Manitoba, Jean Margaret Wemyss was educated at United College, an affiliate of the University of Manitoba. After her marriage to Jack Laurence in 1948, she lived in England and in Africa for several years, and her first novel, *This Side Jordan* (1960), is set in Ghana. Laurence's best known works are a series of linked stories and novels set in the mythical Manitoba town of Manawaka: *The Stone Angel* (1964); *A Jest of God* (1966); *The Fire-Dwellers* (1969); *A Bird in the House* (1970); and *The Diviners* (1974). A collection of essays, *Heart of a Stranger*, was published in 1976. "Ivory Tower or Grassroots? The Novelist As Socio-Political Being" was published in *A Political Art: Essays and Images in Honour of George Woodcock* in 1978.

Ivory Tower or Grassroots?:
The Novelist as Socio-Political Being

I do not have a great deal of affinity with the ivory tower writer whose work bears no reflection of the concerns of everyday life. In fact, I don't believe the ivory tower breed has ever been all that numerous. Writers of serious fiction are almost always, in some way or other, consciously or unconsciously, expressing their own times. This is true of historical fiction just as it is true of the writing of history itself, for our perceptions and therefore our interpretations are formed by the communities in which we grow up. This is not to say that we always agree with the prevailing views in our communities; for many writers the reverse is often true. But we are products of our own era all the same.

For me, fiction is primarily a matter of portraying individual characters as faithfully as I am able to do. These characters, however, do not live in a vacuum. They live in specific places, and any writing about them must of necessity include social commentary.

In one way, fiction may be viewed as history, just as recorded history may be viewed as fiction. They are twin disciplines, and they include biography and autobiography, for the perceptions, interpretations, and choices of material of particular writers give form to our past and relate it to our present and our future. All fiction is written about the past. Even if we write about this day, *now*, this hour, this moment, as we set down the words the moment becomes the past. Science fiction may be the one exception, but I don't think so. Our projections about the future arise out of our view of our own times, and the themes which occupied the SF writers in the forties are not the same themes which occupy them thirty years later.

Fiction also may be viewed as belief, and by *belief* I mean something that has connotations both of faith and of politics. Humans are social and spiritual animals; we are, in the broadest sense of the words, both religious and political, although many people may be neither in any conscious way. We stand in need of our gods, and we need links with our ancestors, partly in order to determine who and what we are, to decide what we hope to become, and to know what sort of society we will try to form. Fiction, in the political sense, both binds us to and frees us from our ancestors; it acknowledges our dilemmas; it mourns and rages at our inhumanity to one another; and sometimes it expresses our faith in growth and change, and honours our children and our trust in them.

What do I mean by "politics" in this context? The Concise Oxford Dictionary defines politics in this way: "n. pl. Science and art of government, political affairs or life; political principles . . . " Exactly what I mean. I am, of course, not talking here about so-called party politics. One says "Liberal with a small 'l'," which means something vastly different and importantly more vast than the group of persons who at this moment in our history are attempting to run what we call our government. In the same way, I say "Political with a small 'p'," meaning something wider than the often-moronic exchanges in our (or any other) parliament, meaning a social commentary at a grass-roots level. A novel can scarcely avoid being this kind of commentary. It may not be a helpful commentary, or even a particularly relevant one, but a social commentary it most certainly is.

In this commentary, in the re-creation on the printed page of a community of human individuals, the novelist usually does not and should not write in any polemical way. We are not dealing in propaganda. We do not presume to tell the reader how to think, nor can we offer any easy solutions. Nonetheless, no novelist writes in an objective way, if indeed there is anywhere such a mode of writing. The novelist takes a stand, and this is what makes us so vulnerable. The novelist asks that the reader should *see* these characters, these humans, both in their own minds and spirits and in their relationship with other humans. The novelist attempts (and it is always an uncertain attempt, for this is a humbling profession) to communicate to the reader, or at least some readers, the pain and struggle, the joy and anguish of characters who—although they are fictional—are felt by writers to be as real as anyone we know. The writer's life view, the way in which people and their dilemmas and their society are seen, permeate any work of fiction. Fiction, for me at least, then becomes a matter of the individual characters moving within a history which includes past, present, and future, and the emergence through these characters of beliefs which cannot be didactic but which in the most profound way are both religious and political.

To illustrate my views, I would like to look briefly at the work of two Third World novelists. One of them is Chinua Achebe of Nigeria. The other is a Canadian writer, namely myself.

Yes, *Third World* novelists is what I said. Are Canadian writers Third World writers? In a cultural sense, very definitely yes. Canadian artists in general can be said to be of the Third World. I was pleased to see in *The Canadian Forum* (December-January, 1976/77) an article by Peter Such on the Canadian League of Composers, in which he said "'International art' . . . means the cultural forms of the dominant imperial cultures of the times. And it is only as that dominance wavers or becomes suspect that independent artists of Third World countries like ours can assert their true voices even in their own society, let alone the world at large." That is a statement with which I wholeheartedly agree. Canadian writers, like African writers, have had to find our own voices and write out of what is truly ours, in the face of an overwhelming cultural imperialism.

In Nigeria, as in many parts of Africa, people lost their own self-value, their own distinctive voices, throughout three generations of colonialism. They were taught as children to despise their ancestors and the old gods, and the result was, of course, that they learned to despise themselves. Chinua Achebe's generation of writers (which includes very many writers of distinction such as Wole Soyinka, John Pepper Clark, Cyprian Ekwensi, T.M. Aluko, Elechi Amadi, Flora Nwapa, and Gabriel Okara) has drawn on their relatively newfound sense of self-worth and on their people's past, and has tried consciously to impart these values to their own people, to combat the psychic damage done during the years of domination by British imperialism. Their novels and plays have been published mainly in Britain, ironically enough, because of the lack of indigenous publishing houses (the same has been true for West Indian writers). At first, of course, English critics reviewed Nigerian writers because they were a curiosity; these same critics have often been surprised, or, at the opposite pole, indifferent when a Canadian novel appeared in England and made use of themes other than those involving Mounties and mad trappers. As the years have gone on, some of the English critics have conceded that maybe some of these writers do have something to say after all. The view of the English critics, however, is not what has mattered. Writers like Achebe found that they had an audience among their own people, and not just among upper middle class academics, either, but among a very wide range of people. I recall once reading an interview with Cyprian Ekwensi, who said that among the people who bought and read his books the Lagos taxi drivers ranked high.

In Canada, our delimma was perhaps more subtle. We ostensibly gained our independence in 1867, and yet we remained colonial in outlook for many years. In literary terms, our models remained those of Britain and more recently of America. We did have indigenous publishing houses, and that has been a great advantage for Canadian writers, although it has to be said that when Ernest Buckler's novel, *The Mountain and the Valley*, probably one of the best novels in English in this century, first came out in 1952, it was published by an American firm, and only in 1961 when McClelland and Stewart brought out the novel in their New Canadian Library paperback series was this book published at home. The case was not untypical. The Canadian writers just before my generation—Ernest Buckler, Sinclair Ross, Morley Callaghan, Hugh MacLennan, Ethel Wilson, W.O. Mitchell, Howard O'Hagan, Hubert Evans, and others—all laboured for many years with hardly any response from their own people and hardly any recognition unless it were first accorded in either England or America. The writers of that generation are our literary heroes. All of them would laugh at the mere mention of the word. All the same, they are, and we owe them more than we can possibly ever express. They kept on, alone and unaided, and they wrote out of what they truly knew, the things that were genuinely theirs and ours. They were the first generation of non-colonial Canadian writers.

My generation of novelists was probably the first—thanks chiefly to the previous sod-busters—who found we could not only write out of our own backgrounds and culture but also had a considerable audience among our own people. Times had changed by the time that Mordecai Richler, Adele Wiseman, myself, Alice Munro, Robert Kroetsch, Rudy Wiebe, Marian Engel, and all the rest came along. Younger writers such as Margaret Atwood, Dave Godfrey, Graeme Gibson, and many others have been from the start very much aware of these changing patterns in our culture.

There are still those in our country who talk about the uselessness of teaching CanLit because "there is no such thing," or "it doesn't accord with international standards," by which they mean that Canadian writing isn't the same as British or American. No, it isn't. Rudy Wiebe once told me that someone had asked him, "But, if you don't constantly apply international standards, how can you develop any standards at all?" (For "international" here, read "British.") Rudy replied, "I think we just make them up as we go along." Exactly. How else did Chaucer write? How else the writers of any culture? They simply wrote what they were compelled to write, as best they could, and those of their writings that struck deep chords among their own people and sometimes beyond their own people, endured. This is not to say that we remain untouched by literature elsewhere, or that we reject the great writings of the past, from whichever culture they have come. Anyone who writes in the English language is in some way an inheritor of Shakespeare and Milton, of Fielding and Jane Austen, of Dickens and Thackeray. Our task is not to reject the past but to assimilate it, to take the language and make it truly ours, to write out of our own familiar idiom and out of our deepest observations of our people and our place of belonging on this planet. I really do not think that as Canadian writers we have a great deal to learn from recent British fiction, in which I sense a widespread weariness, repetition, and even triviality. We would do better to go our own ways now and to make our discoveries, just as African writers are making theirs.

Chinua Achebe, for example, writes out of his own experience and out of the memories of his people. He grew up in the village of Ogidi, a few miles from the Niger River. He was born in 1930, and belongs to the Ibo, the largest group in Southeast Nigeria. His family was a Christian one, his father being one of the first Ibo to be a mission teacher. His grandfather, however, was a grown man when the British administration first took over that part of Africa. In his novels, Achebe writes of pre-colonial times, when the old Ibo society was still firm. He writes of the mission-oriented era of his parents, and of the emancipated and troubled era of his own generation. During the civil war in the late 1960's, Achebe worked for Biafra, the Ibo heartland, which wanted to secede, and although a majority of Ibo felt united on that issue, Biafra is not now a country. It was defeated in a civil war of terrifying proportions, a war which should never have taken place. Achebe now lives in exile in America, teaching at a university Perhaps some day he will be able to go home.

In his witing, the hatred of imperialism emerges, along with his sense of mourning and rage at the way the old Ibo society was broken by the colonialists. Achebe never writes simply or polemically. He has a sense of the reality of all people, and even his imperialist characters are complex and believable.

In *Things Fall Apart*, his first novel, he recreates the first impact of European invasion upon the old Ibo society in the late 1800's and shows how Okonkwo, the protagonist, changes. He moves from being a self-driving, proud, and respected man to committing suicide, which was a crime against Earth and therefore a complete alienation from his people. His fate is to be buried impersonally by strangers and never to be united with the spirits of his ancestors. Okonkwo, however, is portrayed as a man who suffers both from his own flaws (unbending pride, ambition) and from the terrible damage done to him by the external situation, the takeover of his land and the demoralization of his people.

In *Arrow of God*, Achebe's third novel and in my opinion one of the finest to have appeared anywhere in the past half century, we see

Ezeulu, the priest of Ulu, and we feel his anguish at his responsibility for his people, his bewilderment at the influx of the missions, his attempts to meet the newcomers on their own ground (he sends one of his sons to be educated at the mission, in order to know what the white men are about). Achebe portrays here the life of an Ibo village in the 1920's, with love, authenticity, and fairness. The old gods are respected and are presented as real and true. At the same time, Achebe acknowledges the faith which the missionaries feel in their god. The Ibo villagers are shown as highly individualistic, and the British are portrayed as men caught up in an historical process which they do not understand, just as they do not understand their own very mixed motives for being in Africa at all.

My feelings about Ezeulu, and about Achebe's writings, are summed up in my book, *Long Drums and Cannons*, essays on contemporary Nigerian literature:

> Underneath the restraint of the novel, there is an almost choking sense of rage and sorrow. Not that Achebe would have wanted the old Ibo society to go on unchanged, for he sees plainly the weaknesses within it. But the rage is because it broke the way it did, by the hands of strangers who had convinced themselves that they were bringing light to a dark place, and whose self-knowledge was so slight that they did not recognize the existence of darkness within themselves. The sorrow is for such a man as Ezeulu, broken by the violence of both the inner and the outer forces. Yet Achebe never allows his own emotions to sway the novel from its natural course. It is always the emotions of the characters that come across the most strongly, and beeause of this, the novel succeeds as few novels do.
>
> Ezeulu, man and priest, god's man, like Oedipus and like Lear, has the power to reveal not only moving and terrifying aspects of himself, but moving and terrifying aspects of ourselves as well. (pp. 116-17)

In *No Longer at Ease*, his second novel, Achebe deals with the story of Obi Okonkwo, grandson of Okonkwo in *Things Fall Apart*, and with Obi's inner conflicts between the contemporary world and the world of his Christian parents, and also between these two worlds and the further one of his ancestors, whom he has been taught to despise. In *A Man of the People*, the publication of which shortly preceded the first military coup in Nigeria, Achebe is perhaps more narrowly political, although Chief Nanga will remain for a very long time in our consciousness, as the seemingly simple and corrupt politician who is really a prey to his own fears.

Undoubtedly at some time it will become necessary for Achebe to write a novel out of the civil war, which will deal fictionally with the events of the Biafran holocaust. It will, I believe, be the most anguished work for him in his entire writing life. I also feel that if any novelist can write such a novel, with truth, strength, and integrity, that novelist is Achebe. He sees history in terms of people with names and conflicts and places of belonging. His sense of social injustice is like a white-hot sword wielded through his powerful irony. Yet he knows one of the most frightening facts of life, the thing every novelist must come to know—the enemy is also within, and the external enemy is also human and feels pain as real as anyone's.

At the heart of Achebe's writing there is also, I sense, a profound belief that the whole order of things could be different. Mankind need not forever inhabit a world where, in the words of Matthew Arnold, "ignorant armies clash by night." Understanding, respect, communication—these are possible among individuals as among nations, although a novelist frequently must define these possibilities by their absence.

My own first two books of fiction were set in West Africa, although of course I could never write about Africa from the inside, but only as a concerned and involved outsider. Only about one's own people may one really write from the inside. Incidentally, I never read Achebe when I lived in West Africa. I returned to Canada in 1957. His first novel was published in 1958, and I read it about 1961, when I had completed the first draft of *The Stone Angel*, although that novel was not published until 1964. The rest of Achebe's writing I have read as it has come out, feeling about it the kind of kinship that one does feel with another writer who is working within some of the same broad human territories that one is attempting to work in, and with a similar sense of specific place and particular people that I discovered when I began at last to write out of my own cultural background.

I had come back home to Canada via Africa, both physically and spiritually. In writing my first novel, *This Side Jordan*, set in Ghana, it had finally become clear to me why I had chosen the theme of an independence which was both political and inner. I was from a land that had been a colony, a land which in some ways was still colonial. My people's standards of correctness and validity and excellence were still at that time largely derived from external and imposed values; our view of ourselves was still struggling against two other cultures' definitions of us. A joke when I was at college had been: "Ask a Swede what's the best country in the world, and he'll say Sweden; ask an Englishman and he'll say England; ask an American and he'll say America; ask a Canadian and he'll say—any damn country in the world except Canada."

Who on earth taught us to think of ourselves that way? A whole history of imperialism, of being defined in others' terms, not our own. The ironic thing is that while we went on knocking ourselves down and speaking in self-deprecating voices, *we knew it wasn't true.* Somewhere inside ourselves we knew our own value, and it was not low. Somewhere inside there was a deep anger and resentment at our betrayal and self-betrayal.

Our situation at the time, like that of all peoples with colonial mentalities, was not unlike that of women in our society.

Perhaps I interpret it in this way simply because I am a woman, but to me the parallels seem undeniable. These parallels, in my own mind, I may say, pre-dated the contemporary women's movement, although of course I was aware of the earlier women's suffragette movement in Canada and elsewhere. The upsurge of the new women's movement in the 1960's, however, served to confirm my own perceptions and gave me a much-needed sense of community, of not being isolated. I have not taken an active or direct part in the women's movement, just as I have not taken an active or direct part in any party politics, simply because my work resides in my fiction, which must always feel easy with paradox and accommodate contradictions, and which must, if anything, proclaim the human individual, unique and irreplaceable, and the human spirit, amazingly strong and yet in need of strength and grace. But in making this statement of my own belief, I do not mean that I have been unaware or unsupportive of the women's movement. I have been aware and, I hope, supportive in my own way, and I have felt the warmth and support of many of my sisters, both those who are my contemporaries and those who are very much younger than my half century.

The growth of some of the themes in my writing—those themes which in the broadest sense I may define as political—took place in my mind in an intertwined and simultaneous way. My sense of social awareness, my feelings of anti-imperialism, anti-colonialism, anti-authoritarianism, had begun, probably, in embryo form in my own childhood; they had been nurtured during my college years and immediately afterwards, in the North Winnipeg of the old Left; they had developed considerably through my African experience. It was not very difficult to relate this experience to my own land, which had been under the colonial sway of Britain once and was now under the colonial sway of America. But these developing feelings also related very importantly to my growing awareness of the dilemma and powerlessness of women, the tendency of women to accept male definition of ourselves, to be self-deprecating and uncertain, and to rage inwardly. The quest for physical and spiritual freedom, the quest for relationships of equality and communication—these themes run through my fiction and are connected with the theme of survival, not mere physical survival, but a survival of the spirit, with human dignity and the ability to give and receive love. It will be obvious that these themes relate to Hagar, in *The Stone Angel*, who finally even in extreme old age can find something of that inner freedom; to Rachel in *A Jest of God*, who will remain nervous and neurotic to some extent but who does succeed in freeing herself from her mother's tyranny and from her own self-doubt and self-hatred; to Stacey in *The Fire-Dwellers*, who comes to terms with her life and recognizes herself as a survivor; to Vanessa in *A Bird in the House*, who escapes from the authoritarian régime of her grandfather and who is ultimately able to be released from her hatred and fear of the old man; and finally, to Morag in *The Diviners*, who, more than any of the others, is able to assimilate her past and to accept herself as a strong and independent woman, able

258

to love and to create. The themes of freedom and survival relate both to the social/external world and to the spiritual/inner one, and they are themes which I see as both political and religious. If freedom is, in part, the ability to act out of one's own self-definition, with some confidence and with compassion, uncompelled by fear or by the authority of others, it is also a celebration of life and of the mystery at life's core. In their varying ways, all these characters experience a form of grace.

In a good deal of my fiction, and especially in *The Diviners*, the theme of dispossession is an important one. It is shown in Christie's tales of the Highland Scots, turned off their lands during the Clearances, and in the recurrence throughout my Canadian fiction of the Tonnerre family, descendants of the Métis, who were once the prairie horselords and who gradually were dispossessed of the lands which they and their Indian brothers had lived on and from and with, although not owned, for no man could own the land—the land was God's. Little did they know the concepts of the incoming European culture. They learned, however, in sorrow and pain.

Like love, like communication, like freedom, social justice must sometimes be defined in fiction by the lack of it. I believe this to be so in many instances throughout my fiction—the plight of the Métis; the town's scorn of such people as Lazarus Tonnerre, Christie Logan, Bram Shipley, Lottie Drieser, to name only a few; the depression years of the thirties; the way in which the true meaning of war comes to some of the town's men in the trenches of World War I, and again later to many of the townsfolk with the tragedy of Dieppe in World War II.

Fiction has many facets, and I have mentioned only a few. For myself, it encompasses both history and belief, both social and spiritual themes. It speaks first and foremost of individual characters, and through them it speaks of our dilemmas and our aspirations, which are always in some way or other those both of politics and of faith.

1978

Rudy Wiebe
1934—

Born near Fairholme, Saskatchewan, Rudy Wiebe was raised in a Mennonite community in Alberta. He was educated at Mennonite schools and colleges and earned an M.A. at the University of Alberta where he now teaches. Since the appearance of his first novel, *Peace Shall Destroy Many*, he has published short stories, anthologies, literary criticism and several novels, including: *The Blue Mountains of China*

(1970); *The Temptations of Big Bear* (1973); and *The Scorched-Wood People* (1977). "Passage By Land" first appeared in *The Narrative Voice* (1972) ed. John Metcalf. "On the Trail of Big Bear" was delivered as an address at the Western Canadian Studies Conference in 1974 and appeared in the *Journal of Canadian Fiction* in the same year.

Passage by Land

I have heard people say they can never tell one end of a poem from another and, what's more, they don't intend to bother finding out how to do it; I've never heard anyone say that about stories. There may not be anyone on earth who doesn't like stories. Certainly everyone at some time or another tells one, and the people who are most insistent that a story must actually have happened (i.e., be *true*) often care least about whether it has happened physically (ie., is true in the sense of *fact*) or largely in the mind (ie., is true in the sense of *fiction*).

When one thinks about it, it's soon clear that the best stories always emerge mostly as fiction; *Of a Fire on the Moon* is immeasurably better than the voice of Houston Control. Perhaps that's because the facts come to us through an organizing, imaginative, sometimes almost a transcendental intelligence. Who of us, unaided, can marshall all that overwhelming data; condense it; hammer it up to meaning?

All of which is general theorizing and, though I find it exciting, all the theorizing I wish to do about *why* people like stories has been done in another place.* Here it is enough to give some of my specific apprehensions about story writing. It would be useful to accept the whole of what follows as true even though I myself on any given day find it impossible at certain points to separate the layers of fact (the thing done) from the prisms of fiction (the thing made).

I never saw a mountain or a plain until I was twelve, almost thirteen. The world was poplar and birch covered; muskeg hollows and stony hills; great hay sloughs with the spruce on their far shores shimmering in summer heat, and swamps with wild patterns burned three and four, sometimes five feet into their moss by some fire decades before, filled with water in spring but dry in summer and sometimes smoking faintly still in the morning light where, if you slid from your horse and pushed your hand into the moss, you could feel the strange heat of it lurking.

In such a world, a city of houses with brick chimneys, telephones, was less real than Grimms' folk tales or Greek myths. I was born in what would become, when my father and older brother chopped down enough trees for the house, our chicken barn; and did not speak English

*Introduction to *The Story-Makers*, Macmillan, 1970.

until I went to school, though I can't remember learning it. Perhaps I never have (as one former professor insists when he reads my novels); certainly it wasn't until years later I discovered that the three miles my sister and I had meandered to school, sniffing and poking at pussy-willows and ant hills, lay somewhere in the territory Big Bear and Wandering Spirit had roamed with their warriors always just ahead of General Strange in May and June, 1885. As a child, however, I was for years the official flag raiser (Union Jack) in our one-room school and during the war I remember wondering what it would be like if one day, just as I turned the corner of the pasture with the cows, a huge car would wheel into our yard, Joseph Stalin emerge into the Saskatchewan air and from under his mustache tell my father he could have his farm back in Russia, if he wanted it. Then I would stand still on the cow path trodden into the thin bush soil and listen, listen for our cowbells; hear a dog bark some miles away, and a boy call; and wonder what an immense world of people—I could not quite imagine how many —was now doing chores, and if it wasn't for the trees and the curvature of the earth (as the teacher said) I could easily see Mount Everest somewhere a little south of east. Or west?

My first sight of the prairie itself I do not remember. We were moving south, leaving the rocks and bush of northern Saskatchewan forever, my parents said, and I was hanging my head out of the rear window of the hired car, vomiting. I had a weak stomach from having been stepped on by a horse, which sounds funny though I cannot remember it ever being so. Consequently, our first day in south Alberta the driver had me wash his car and so I cannot remember my first glimpse of the Rocky Mountains either. It was long after that that anyone explained to me the only mountain we could see plainly from there was in the United States.

But sometimes a fall morning mirage will lift the line of Rockies over the level plain and there they will be, streaked black in crevices under their new snow with wheat stubble for base and the sky over you; you can bend back forever and not see its edge. Both on foot and from the air I have since seen some plains, some mountains on several continents; jungles; the Danube, the Mississippi, even the Amazon. But it was north of Old Man River one summer Sunday when I was driving my father (he had stopped trying to farm and he never learned to drive a car) to his week's work pouring concrete in a new irrigation town, that we got lost in broad daylight on the prairie. Somewhere we had missed something; the tracks we were following at last faded and were gone like grass. My father said in Low German,

"Boy, now you turn around."

I got out. The grass crunched dry as crumbs and in every direction the earth so flat another two steps would place me at the horizon, looking into the abyss of the universe. There is too much here, the line of sky and grass rolls in upon you and silences you thin, too impossibly thin to remain in any part recognizably yourself. The space must be broken somehow, or it uses you up, and my father muttered in the car,

"If you go so far and get lost at least there's room to go back. Now turn around."

A few moments thereafter we came upon a rail line stretched in a wrinkle of the land—the prairie in Alberta is not at all flat, it only looks like that at any given point—white crosses beside rails that disappeared straight as far in either direction as could be seen. We had not crossed a railroad before but the tracks could no more be avoided here than anything else and some connecting road to the new town must be eventually somewhere beyond.

In that wandering to find it is rooted, I believe, the feeling I articulated much later; the feeling that to touch this land with words requires an architectural structure; to break into the space of the reader's mind with the space of this western landscape and the people in it you must build a structure of fiction like an engineer builds a bridge or a skyscraper over and into space. A poem, a lyric, will not do. You must lay great black steel lines of fiction, break up that space with huge design and, like the fiction of the Russian steppes, build giant artifact. No song can do that; it must be giant fiction.

The way a man feels with and lives with that living earth with which he is always laboring to live. Farmer or writer. . . .

1972

On the Trail of Big Bear

For the story teller there is only one problem of historical reconstruction; A.M. Klein has described it exactly in his poem, 'Portrait of the Poet as Landscape':

> Sometimes, depressed to nadir, he [the poet] will think all lost,
> will see himself as throwback, relict, freak,
> his mother's miscarriage, his great-grandfather's ghost,
> and he will curse his quintuplet senses, and their tutors
> in whom he put, as he should not have put, his trust.

Trusting the 'quintuplet senses'; the story teller, too, has been tutoring them, to be his guide through the maze of life and imagination. Through the smoke and darkness and piled up factuality of a hundred years to see a face; to hear, and comprehend, a voice whose verbal language he will never understand; and then to risk himself beyond such seeing, such hearing as he discovers possible, and venture into the finer labyrinths opened by those other senses: touch, to learn the

262

texture of leather, of earth; smell, the tinct of sweetgrass and urine; taste, the golden poplar sap or the hot, raw buffalo liver dipped in gall.

This trust of the wayward though beloved senses: that is the problem of the story teller. The facts: all the facts he will ever need to know, and many more besides, they are very easily and often pleasantly found.

For, unless they are very carefully handled, facts are the invariable tyrants of story. They are as inhibiting as fences and railroads, whereas the story teller would prefer, like Big Bear, 'to walk where his feet can walk.' A hundred years ago Henry James said of story telling: 'What is character but the determination of incident? What is incident but the illustration of character?' In terms of history I suppose that means that if we knew absolutely everything a person ever did, we could know his character absolutely. This theory has helped beget in literary circles the so-called 'laundry-bag-slip' school of biographers (as you might expect, its finest example is Leon Edel, biographer of Henry James), and it may have begotten similar historians and, taken with temperance, such theory may even be useful. However, since not even laundry bag receipts can reveal everything a person ever did, leave alone thought, it is obviously silly to hope by the simple massing of facts to arrange for art. Daily life is choked with facts, and these facts mean mostly nothing; some incidents are more revealing of character than others. A profounder observation on story telling was made by Edith Wharton: 'The possibilities of a given subject [i.e. the actions of a particular character] are whatever a given imagination can make of them.'

Therefore, when I decided to stick to historical incidents and characters in writing this novel about Big Bear—but it is impossible for me to speak of writing a novel that way. For I believe in 'story' as a fact beyond and outside the entity of its maker. Michelangelo's beautiful (perhaps apocryphal but no matter) statement that he studied the rock for the shape that was inside it and then used his chisels not to create that shape out of the rock but rather to release the shape from all encumbering rock around it—that has always seemed to me profoundly true to the storymaker's art also. At least of my own attempts. In the summer of 1968 I was working on one of the final versions of *The Blue Mountains of China*, but I was already probing about, wherever, for large story beyond that novel. Somewhere during the winter of 1967-8 (we had returned to Canada in the summer of '67 after four years and I was feeling the goodness of the land where I belong) I had stumbled on William Fraser's 15-page monograph *Big Bear, Indian Patriot* (1966). This revived something begun in the later '50s when, while I was writing *Peace Shall Destroy Many*, I first read William Cameron's *The War Trail of Big Bear*. [It may be that I was again looking up Cameron's book and discovered Fraser's new publication in the card catalogue with it.] Anyway, it was from reading Cameron in the '50s that I first realized the bush homestead where I was born in northern

Saskatchewan probably was traversed in June, 1885, by Big Bear and his diminishing band as among the poplars they easily eluded the clumsy military columns of Strange and Middleton and Otter and Irvine pursuing them; that I first realized that the white sand beaches of Turtle Lake, where Speedwell School had its annual sportsday with Jackpine and Turtleview Schools, right there where that brown little girl had once beaten me in the grade four sprints, a race in which until then I was acknowledged as completely invincible: perhaps on that very beach Big Bear had once stood looking at the clouds trundle up from the north. Of course, thanks to our education system, I had been deprived of this knowledge when I was a child: we studied people with *history*—like Cromwell who removed a king's head, or Lincoln who freed slaves—but I can see now that this neglect contained an ambiguous good. For in forcing me to discover the past of my place on my own as an adult, my public school inadvertently roused an anger in me which has ever since given an impetus to my writing which I trust it will never lose. *All* people have history. The stories we tell of our past are by no means merely words: they are meaning and life to us as *people*, as *a particular* people; the stories are there, and if we do not know of them we are simply, like animals, memory ignorant, and the less are we people.

Anger, even anger at one's own ignorance, is hardly enough emotion to sustain years of work. One of the first things I noticed about the person of Big Bear was the contradictory feelings he aroused in people; this was true for whites as well as Indians. To William Cameron and Teresa Gowanlock, his prisoners for two months, he is an admirable old man, yet to Commissioner Irvine of the Mounted Police he is simply a trouble maker, always demanding and never agreeing. Vankoughnet of Indian Affairs orders him either to take a reserve or starve, yet Edgar Dewdney gives him a character reference (albeit carefully unofficial) at his trial. He is spoken of as 'the heart and soul of all the plains Indians' and has a personal following of over one thousand, an incredible number among the buffalo-hunting Crees, yet at Frog Lake this orator, this leader who has a power bundle given him by the Great Parent of Bear himself, has no influence at all over a small group of his own Rattlers, led by his own son. He stands helpless, his great words falling into nothing as the white men he has personally pledged to protect are disarmed, sported with, and slaughtered before his eyes. Big Bear I found, lived these contradictions, contained these extremes of greatness and of pathos. Beneath the giant slag heap left by the heroic white history of fur trader and police and homesteader and rancher and railroad builder (oh, the heroism of that 19th century computor Van Horne as sung by that 20th century computor Pierre Berton Incorporated!), somewhere, under there, is the story of this life. Can I dig it out? Will I dare to look at it once I have, if I dare, unearthed it?

When my mind is tumbling story possibilities about, a process which inevitably takes years sometimes even for short stories, I write down nothing except very occasional notes to myself. A note dated January 19, 1969, begins:

"'Themes for a novel / setting Edmonton, possibly Klondike days ...'"

and ends:

"People: modern business man? triangle? just fucking around?"

Evidently that didn't hook very deep (I can still see why) because the next note is dated just over a month later (Feb. 28, 1969) and this one I'll give completely:

'Big Bear. A novel of historical Big Bear, the greatest chief of the Plains Cree—defied whites and their treaties for the longest time—treated in tragic-farcical manner and tone—there is undoubtedly farce in it (especially re attack at Frog Lake)'

But I find the next note dated a year and a half later, September, 1970, and after two summers working on the historical Big Bear it still begins

'—novel: present day Indian ...'

and ends

'... just out of jail, as Big Bear is heading into jail—they live out each others lives [apparently some ninety years apart] in a kind of reverse?'

Apparently I am still, in September 1970, struggling to get Big Bear's story unearthed so I can face it, so it will not disintegrate in our polluted modern atmosphere. But seven months later I seem to have reached some conclusions. The page is almost empty, just marked,

'The Temptations of Big Bear,'

and underneath a line in brackets

'title thought of on my way home from U of A—passing Aberhart San March 8, 1971'

To take the problems of following Big Bear's story to its final version, I can do no better than to quote here from an original introductory chapter, since dropped. It contained a sort of Henry Fielding narrator-type who hints at explanations in case his readers (whom I think he basically does not trust) don't catch on. This sometimes coy narrator was one of the reasons the chapter did not survive, but there are a few things in it I very unwillingly let—well—here are the relevant passages:

"There are some stories into which the reader should be led gently, and I think this may be one of them".

I quote Hugh MacLennan's opening line, with thanks, because it says exactly what needs saying here. This story is another one of those that demands a gentle leading into. Factually, so that everyone is quite clear about some things, at the very beginning. Anyway.

To begin with, every individual who will appear in this story is an historic person. Not one name has been invented. Every person (and a fair number of the animals) who has a part was once, literally, a living being, and there is documentary historic evidence available for each, if you care to look for it. Of course, the evidence varies widely: books, sometimes several, by or about a person; three to four feet of letters and papers in archives; an 'X' at the bottom of a treaty or a courtroom confession; a name mentioned in newspaper gossip; a smudged face on a photograph with perhaps a pencilled name on its back followed by a question mark that could refer to the spelling of the name or the identification itself—or, more likely, both. Usually, there are a great many, but always there are at least two points of historic reference to help us believe that those people actually breathed; that they were once born and, after their allotted time, like us all, died.

The author—I hesitate to over-use the pronoun 'I' in the first short chapter of what promises to be a lengthy novel; the reader will understand the gentle circumlocution—the author, I say, has never physically met any of these people. (There is only one exception to that statement and it will be noted in its place, which is not this story.) That is so because this story's events all took place before January, 1888, and the more it emerged out of the vacuum called history, which in Western Canada is no vacuum at all but rather the great ocean of our ignorance as horizonless as the prairies themselves, the more it became impossible to invent a non-historic person to act as guide into and through it. For if one is once willing to understand that he is beyond doubt thoughtlessly treading water on his ancestral past, on the past of his place, and will dare to plunge in, reckless of life and eyes wide open, he finds in that ocean a teeming of wildlife and tamelife and every other kind of life that takes his ordinary breath away anyway; he drowns in happiness, into a new life altogether.

I believe: Let that life itself be its own guide.

That said, it remains clear that a certain minimum of historic 'facts' are needed to make comprehension, recognition, possible.

I then give paragraph summaries of the lives of the main persons appearing in Section One: There is Wee-kas-koo-kes-pay-yin, translated Sweetgrass, Alexander Morris, John Kerr, James McKay, Pakan and John McDougall, ending with:

'Mis-ta-ha-mus-kwa, translated *Big Bear*, Plains Cree chief whose vital statistics in the Admittance Record Book of Manitoba Penitentiary are given as "Prisoner #103, *Received:* Sept. 29, 1885 *Born:* Northwest Territories *Age:* 60 *Race:* Native Canadian *Religion:* None *Married:* Yes *Height:* 5 ft. 5¼ *Complexion:* Dark *Eyes:* Black *Hair:* Black *Trade:* None *Crime:* Treason-Felony." He may have been born near Fort Carlton. In the summer of 1875 he was warned in a letter by the Reverend William Newton, first Anglican missionary ever to venture into the Saskatchewan

266

country and as soon as he arrived there: "To the Cree Chief, Big Bear: I am a priest of the Queen's religion. I have learned that thou art a turbulent and seditious fellow and I admonish thee to put aside such vain practises, etc.'

So far my dropped introduction; I have concentrated on these imaginative problems in finding Big Bear's story, which is what being 'on the trail of Big Bear' means to me, because that is the novelist's largest concern. The question for the novelist is not 'Will I find the facts?', it is rather, "Will I dare to fully contemplate with all my quintuplet senses the facts that I do find?

For the facts themselves I go to mostly the same places as historians:

— *people:* if there are any, matching one muddled memory against another; there was only Duncan Maclean left, 94 in Winnipeg when I met him, and now he too is dead;

— *books and pamphlets:* always trying to recognize the personal biases of writers, even those biased by their seemingly unbiased scholarliness. The list is long, and includes George Stanley, William Fraser, Joseph Kinsey Howard, John P. Turner, Wm. Bleasdell Cameron, Robert Jefferson, David Mandelbaum, Leonard Bloomfield, Alexander Morris, John Donkin, John McDougall, Charles Mulvaney in total, and many others in bits;

— *the Sessional Papers of the Parliament of Canada:* which include the annual Mounted Police and Indian Affairs reports, and the 1885 trials (but not, strangely enough, Big Bear's address to the court at his sentencing, although all the other major chiefs' responses are there. So, with the help of Cameron's summary, I have to write that one myself),

— *the diaries, notes, speeches, personal letters, memoirs, interviews:* all those miscellaneous treasures to be found in archives in Ottawa, Winnipeg, Regina, Saskatoon, Calgary, Edmonton—and even in Duck Lake or the cemetery at Ft. Qu'Appelle or Batoche or the marker at Frog Lake or the depressions in the soil on the Poundmaker Reserve, Battle River, Saskatchewan. And best of all, Big Bear's power bundle itself, intact in a canvas bag and tied with binder twine, in a place where one would expect it to be. Not anywhere in Canada of course, but in New York City. That's a complete story in itself which I cannot tell here.

It is in these searches that I discover those details which make the past sing in my ear with sweet songs, and wild songs, and with the contradictions which all historians I am sure must, when they discover them, love. A small example: even at the Indian trials only four months after the fact not one of the witnesses who was at the sacking of Fort

Pitt can agree on what day it took place. Four possible dates are suggested, I believe; yet men are hung for their actions there.

But in my idiosyncratic and certainly unscientific approach to historical research there are a few points I must emphasize.

— *The necessity of calendar:* In writing this novel I found myself becoming almost pyschotic about dates; I had to know whether something happened on Monday or Tuesday! In the 1970 Fraser Valley Telephone Directory (I had retreated to the seclusion of a BC. hillside to write) I found the page that saved my life: it was called 'Calendars 1776-2000' and contained all 14 possible calendars plus an index for any year from 1776 to 2000. Marvelous.

— *Newspapers:* often not too helpful with absolute facts but beyond peer in presenting contemporary opinion. *The Saskatchewan Herald,* 1879-88, with its outspoken editor Laurie, and the *Regina Leader,* beginning in 1883, are beyond price. One example will suffice. As I mentioned, the Sessional Papers do not record Big Bear's defence before his sentencing and though I spent a week in Ottawa doing little else, I could find no trace of his defense in either the Archives or the Department of Justice. So there is nothing left but William Cameron's summary of what Big Bear said, and he concludes with Richardson's answer.

> "Big Bear," said Justice Richardson, and his tone was not unkind, "you have been found guilty by an impartial jury. You cannot be excused from all responsibility for the misdoings of your band. The sentence of the court is that you be imprisoned in the penitentiary at Stony Mountain for three years."

That's recorded forty years after the fact; this is Nicholas Flood Davin's report in *The Leader,* Oct. 1, 1885:

> First came Big Bear, who made a long address to the Court, in the course of which he frequently used such language as, "when we owned the country" and he drew the Court's attention to the fact that he being in prison who was to protect his people.
>
> Judge Richardson in sentencing him told him that they never owned the land [,] that it belonged to the Queen, who allowed them to use it, that when she wanted to make other use of it she called them together through her officers, and gave them the choicest portions of the country and that, as to his people, they would be looked after as though nothing had occurred. He was then sentenced to three years in the Penitentiary.

How time smears edges; how it liberalizes, softens our motivations!

— *Pictures:* I don't really need to tell any researcher the value of pictures; how, far clearer than the sharpest observer, they give so much of certain kinds of information, as it were, quite incidentally. For a fiction writer working on a convincing illusion of life, it is often their tiny details that make his story work.

— *Maps and places:* Old maps, with the Indian names for topographical features, and what remains of those old places to this day. Strangely, considering the decades of industrious pioneering, some bits of the world crucial to Big Bear can still be seen, a few are not even greatly disturbed. One of the most enjoyable experiences of writing that novel for my whole family was visiting every place where it was recorded Big Bear had been. His life was lived approximately along what is now the Alberta-Saskatchewan border, from Cold Lake to the Missouri River, west and mostly east of that line several hundred miles. It is an immense world, especially when you think of walking and riding it.

As we travelled this world, we took such pictures of it as we could, and sometimes I would look at them again as I was writing: the North Saskatchewan near Carlton where Big Bear was born; the buffalo lands at Sounding Lake and Cypress Hills and Milk River; The Forks of the Red Deer and South Saskatchewan where the Great Spirit of Bear gave him his vision, his song, his power bundle; and then the sad sequence of Frog Lake and Fort Pitt and Frenchman Butte and Loon Lake Crossing, and Regina and Stony Mountain Penitentiary; then to the bank of the Battle River, where we met Mary Peemee, Horsechild's wife now 89, and John Tootoosis showed us Big Bear's grave which seems more or less exactly on the site of his last thirst dance held that summer of 1884 when his power was still too strong to permit his young men to wipe out Crozier and his police, but no longer strong enough to unite his People. And finally, the Great Sand Hills. Simply seeing these few pictures, I think, you would recognize how necessary it was for me to see this world in order to find his story.

In the National Archives I discovered some cryptic notes in English of a Cree speech made by an unnamed chief in the summer of 1884. From the internal evidence I feel certain that the chief was Big Bear, and I found out later that George Stanley, who saw the notes long before I, had come to the same conclusions. Anyway, I used those sketchy notes to construct Big Bear's speech to the Carlton chiefs in Part III of the novel, and I would like to conclude with a paragraph of it here. He is speaking particularly of his People and the buffalo, but in a strange way it seems to me I have to understand what he is saying, understand it for myself, if I am to truly follow his trail, if I am to dare contemplate his story.

"My brothers!" Big Bear's deep voice lifted to a great shout that shivered the lodgeskins and rolled out into the afternoon heat, "the White-skins have brought all this evil on us, but we trust them. Who does not have a white friend? Who has not received good things from them? What Person was ever shot by police? The buffalo has been taken from us. On this earth he was our life, and how can he return except The One who took him from us return him again? I see his track in the deep paths he wore to sweet water, and at river crossings where wind moans through his wool hung on the low bushes, I see his shape in the wallows, the print of his tongue where salt gleams like frost in the Scattering Moon, I hear the thunder of his running under the Tramping Lakes, and at Sounding where the Giver of All runs the great herds still and they graze the soft spring grass and lick their little calves. Eiya-eiya-a-a-, where have we gone, where, where."

1974

Margaret Atwood
1939-

Margaret Atwood, born in Ottawa, graduated from the University of Toronto in 1961 and from Radcliffe College in 1962. She has worked as an editor with the House of Anansi Press and has taught at several Canadian universities. Since the appearance of her first book of poems, *Double Persephone* (1961), Atwood has published several other volumes of poetry; a thematic study of Canadian writing; a collection of short stories and four novels—*The Edible Woman* (1969), *Surfacing* (1972), *Lady Oracle* (1976), and *Life Before Man* (1979). "The Curse of Eve—Or, What I Learned in School" was delivered as an address in The Gerstein Lecture Series at York University and appeared in *Women on Women* (1978), edited by Ann Shteir.

The Curse of Eve—Or, What I Learned in School

. . . I'll begin with a simple question, one which confronts every novelist, male or female, at some point in the proceedings and which certainly confronts every critic.

What are novels for? What function are they supposed to perform? What good, if any, are they supposed to do the reader? Are they supposed to delight or instruct, or both, and if so, is there ever a conflict between what we find delightful and what we find instructive? Should a novel be an exploration of hypothetical possibilities, a statement of truth, or just a good yarn? Should it be about how one ought to live one's life, how one can live one's life (usually more limited), or how most people live their lives? Should it tell us something about our society? Can it avoid doing this? More specifically, suppose I am writing a novel with a woman as the central character; how much attention should I pay to any of the above questions? How much attention will I be *forced* to pay through the preconceptions of critics? Do I want this character

270

to be likeable, respectable, or believable? Is it possible for her to be all three? What are the assumptions of those who will do the liking, the respecting, or the believing? Does she have to be a good "role model"?

I dislike the term "role model" partly because of the context in which I first heard it. It was, of course, at university, a very male-oriented university which had a female college attached. The female college was looking for a Dean. My friend, who was a sociologist, explained that this person would have to be a good role model? "What's that?" I asked. Well, the future Dean would not just have to have high academic credentials and the ability to get along with students, she would also have to be married, with children, good-looking, well dressed, active in community work, and so forth. I decided that I was a terrible role model. But then, I did not want to be a role model, I wanted to be a writer. One obviously would not have time for both.

It may be just barely acceptable for prospective Deans to be judged as role models, but as this is also a favourite technique of critics, especially when evaluating female characters in books and sometimes when evaluating the writers themselves, it has to be looked at quite carefully. Let me cite an example: several years ago, I read a review of Marian Engel's *The Honeymoon Festival*, written by a female reviewer. The heroine of this novel is Minn, a very pregnant woman who spends a lot of time reminiscing about the past and complaining about the present. She doesn't have a job. She doesn't have much self-esteem. She's sloppy and self-indulgent and guilt-ridden and has ambiguous feelings about her children, and also about her husband, who is away most of the time. The reviewer complained about this character's lack of initiative, apparent laziness and disorganization. She wanted a more positive, more energetic character, one capable of taking her life in hand, of acting more in accordance with the ideal woman then beginning to be projected by the women's movement. Minn was not seen as an acceptable role model, and the book lost points because of this.

My own feeling is that there are a lot more Minn-like women than there are ideal women. The reviewer might have agreed, but might also have claimed that by depicting Minn and only Minn—by providing no alternative to Minn—the writer was making a statement about the nature of Woman that would merely reinforce these undesirable Minnish qualities, already too much in evidence. She wanted success stories, not failure stories, and this is indeed a problem for the writer of fiction. When writing about women, what constitutes success? Is success even plausible? Why, for instance, did George Eliot, herself a successful female writer, never compose a story with a successful female writer as the central character? Why did Maggie Tulliver have to drown for her rebelliousness? Why could Dorothea Brooke find nothing better to do with her idealism than to invest it in two men, one totally unworthy of it, the other a bit of a simp? Why did Jane Austen's characters exercise their wit and intelligence in choosing the proper man rather than in the composition of comic novels?

271

One possible answer is that these novelists concerned themselves with the typical, or at least with events that would fall within the range of credibility for their readers; and they felt themselves, as women writers, to be so exceptional as to lack credibility. In those days, a woman writer was a freak, an oddity, a suspicious character. How much of that sentiment lingers on today, I will leave you to ask yourselves, while at the same time quoting a remark made to me several years ago by a distinguished male writer. "Women poets," he said, "always have a furtive look about them. They know they're invading male territory." He followed this with a statement to the effect that women, including women writers, were only good for one thing, but since this lecture is going to be printed, I will not quote this rather unprintable remark.

To return to my problem, the creation of a fictional female character . . . I'll come at it from a different angle. There's no shortage of female characters in the literary tradition, and the novelist gets her or his ideas about women from the same sources everyone else does: from the media, books, films, radios, television and newspapers, from home and school, and from the culture at large, the body of received opinion. Also, luckily, sometimes, through personal experience which contradicts all of these. But my hypothetical character would have a choice of many literary ancestresses. For example, I might say a few words about Old Crones, Delphic Oracles, the Three Fates, Evil Witches, White Witches, White Goddesses, Bitch Goddesses, Medusas with snaky heads who turn men to stone, Mermaids with no souls, Little Mermaids with no tongues, Snow Queens, Sirens with songs, Harpies with wings, Sphinxes, with and without secrets, women who turn into dragons, dragons who turn into women, Grendel's mother and why she is worse than Grendel; also about evil stepmothers, comic mothers-in-law, Earth Mothers, the earth as mother, virgin mothers, teeth mothers, fairy godmothers, unnatural mothers, natural mothers, Mad Mothers, Medea who slew her own children, Lady Macbeth and her spot, Eve the mother of us all, the all-mothering sea, and Mother, what have I to do with thee? Also about Wonder Woman, Superwoman, Batgirl, Mary Marvel, Catwoman and Rider Haggard's She with her supernatural powers and electric organ, who could kill a mere mortal man by her embrace; also about Little Miss Muffet and her relationship with the spider, Little Red Riding Hood and her indiscretions with the wolf, Andromeda chained to her rock, Rapunzel and her tower, Cinderella and her sackcloth and ashes, Beauty and the Beast, the wives of Bluebeard (all but the last), Mrs. Radcliffe's persecuted maidens fleeing seduction and murder, Jane Eyre fleeing impropriety and Mr. Rochester, Tess of the D'Urbervilles seduced and abandoned; also about the Angel in the House, Agnes pointing upwards, the redemptive love of a good woman, Little Nell dying to the hypocritical sobs of the whole century, Little Eva doing likewise, much to the relief of the reader, Ophelia babbling down her babbling brook, the Lady of Shalott swansonging her way towards Camelot. Fielding's Amelia snivelling her way through hundreds of pages of gloom and peril and Thackeray's Amelia doing likewise but with less sympathy from her author. Also about the rape of Europa by the bull, the rape of Leda by the swan, the rape of Lucretia and her consequent suicide, miraculous escapes from rape on the parts of several female saints, rape fantasies and how they differ from rape realities, men's magazines featuring pictures of blondes and Nazis, sex and violence from *The Canterbury Tales* to T.S. Eliot . . . and I quote . . . "I knew a man once did a girl in. Any man might do a girl in. Any man has to, needs to, wants to, once in a lifetime do a girl in." Also about the Whore of Babylon, the whore with the heart of gold, the love of a bad woman, the whore without a heart of gold, the Scarlet Letter, the Scarlet Woman, the Red Shoes, Madame Bovary and her quest for the zipless fuck, Molly Bloom and her chamber pot and her eternal yes, Cleopatra and her friend the Asp, an association which casts a new light on Little Orphan Annie. Also about orphans, also about Salome and the head of John the Baptist, and Judith and the head of Holofernes. Also about True Romance magazines and their relationship to Calvinism. Unfortunately, I have neither the time nor the knowledge necessary to discuss all of these in the depth and breadth they deserve, and they do deserve it. All, of course, are stereotypes of women drawn from the Western European literary tradition and its Canadian and American mutations.

There are a good many more variations than those I've mentioned, and although the Western literary tradition was created largely by men, by no means all of the female figures I have mentioned were male-invented, male-transmitted or male-consumed. My point in mentioning them is to indicate not only the multiplicity of female images likely to be encountered by a reader but especially the range. Depictions of women, even by men, are by no means limited to the figure of the Solitary Weeper (that creature of helpless passivity who cannot act but only suffer), which seems to have been encouraged by the dominant philosophy about women up until the nineteenth century. There was more to women, even stereotypical women, even then.

The moral range of female stereotypes seems to me to be wider than that of male characters in literature. Heroes and villains have much in common, after all. Both are strong, both are in control of themselves, both perform actions and face the consequences. Even those supernatural male figures, God and the Devil, share a number of characteristics. Sherlock Holmes and Professor Moriarty are practically twins, and it is very difficult to tell by the costumes and activities alone which of the Marvel Comics' supermen are supposed to be bad and which good. Macbeth, although not very nice, is understandable, and besides, he never would have done it if it hadn't been for the Three Witches and Lady Macbeth. The Three Witches are a case in point. Macbeth's motive is ambition, but what are the witches' motives? They have none, except to delight in evil, and this is true of a number of female stereotypes. They have no motives. Like stones or trees, they simply are: the good ones purely good, the bad ones purely bad. About the closest a male figure can come to this is Iago or Mr. Hyde, but Iago is at least partly motivated by envy and the other half of Mr. Hyde is the all-too-human Dr. Jekyll. Even the Devil wants to win, but the extreme types of female figure do not seem to want anything at all. Sirens eat men because that is what Sirens do. The horrible spider-like old women in D.H. Lawrence's stories—I am thinking especially of the grandmother in "The Virgin and the Gypsy"—are given no motives for their horribleness other than something Lawrence called "the female will." Macbeth murders because he wants to be king, to gain power, whereas the Three Witches are merely acting the way witches act. Witches, like poems, should not mean, but be. One may as well ask why the sun shines.

This quality of natural force, good or bad, this quality of thinghood, appears most frequently in stories about male heroes, especially the travelling variety such as Odysseus. In such stories, the female figures are events that happen to the hero, adventures in which he is involved. The women are static, the hero dynamic. He experiences the adventure and moves on through a landscape of women as well as one of geographical features. This kind of story is still very much with us, as anyone who has read the James Bond stories, Henry Miller or, closer to home, Robert Kroetsch's *The Studhorse Man* can testify. There are few female literary adventurers of this kind. One might call them adventuresses, and the connotation alone indicates how they differ from the male variety. A man who recites a catalogue of women, such as Don Giovanni, is held to be a rogue, perhaps, but a rather enviable one, whereas female characters, from Moll Flanders to Isadora Wing, of Erica Jong's *Fear of Flying*, are not allowed to do the same without a great deal of explanation, suffering and guilt.

I have mentioned the Solitary Weeper, that passive female victim to whom everything gets done and whose only activity is running away. There are male figures of a similar type but they are usually children, like Dicken's Paul Dombey, Oliver Twist and the suffering pupils of Dotheboys Hall. For the grown-up male to exhibit these characteristics —fearfulness, inability to act, feelings of extreme powerlessness, tearfulness, feelings of being trapped and helpless—he has to be crazy or a member of a minority group. Such feelings are usually viewed as a violation of his male nature, whereas the same feelings in a female character are treated as an expression of hers. Passive helpless men are aberrations; passive women within the range of the norm. But powerful, or at any rate active, heroes and villains are seen as the fulfilment of a *human* ideal; whereas powerful women, and there are many of them in literature, are usually given a supernatural aura. They are witches, Wonder Women or Grendel's mothers. They are monsters. They are not quite human. Grendel's mother is worse than Grendel because she is seen as a greater departure from the norm. Grendel, after all, is just a sort of Beowulf, only bigger and hungrier.

Suppose, however, that I want to create a female character who is not a natural force, whether good or evil; who is not a passive Solitary Weeper; who makes decisions, performs actions, causes as well as endures events, and has perhaps even some ambition, some creative power. What stories does my culture have to tell me about such women? Not very many at the public school level, which is probably the reason why I can remember nothing at all about Dick and Jane, although some vague imprints of Puff and Spot still remain. But, outside school hours, there were the comic books: Batman and Robin, Superman (and Lois Lane, the eternal dumb rescuee), the Human Torch and Zorro and many others, all male. Of course, there was Wonder Woman. Wonder Woman was an Amazon princess who lived on an island with some other Amazons but no men. She had magic bullet-deflecting bracelets, a transparent airplane, a magic lasso, and super skills and powers. She fought crime. There was only one catch—she had a boyfriend. But, if he kissed her, her superhuman strength disappeared like Samson's after a clean shave. Wonder Woman could never get married and still remain Wonder Woman.

Then there was *The Red Shoes*—not the Hans Christian Andersen fairy tale but the movie, starring Moira Shearer, with beautiful red hair. A whole generation of little girls were taken to see it as a special treat for their birthday parties. Moira Shearer was a famous dancer but alas, she fell in love with the orchestra conductor, who, for some reason totally obscure to me at the time, forbade her to dance after they got married. This prohibition made her very unhappy. She wanted the man, but she wanted to dance as well, and the conflict drove her to fling herself in front of a train. The message was clear. You could not have both your artistic career and the love of a good man as well, and if you tried, you would end up committing suicide.

Then there were Robert Grave's poetic theories, set forth in many books, especially *The White Goddess*, which I read at the age of 19. For Graves, man does, woman simply is. Man is the poet, woman is the Muse, the White Goddess herself, inspiring but ultimately destroying. What about a woman who wants to be a poet? Well, it is possible, but the woman has to somehow *become* the White Goddess, acting as her incarnation and mouthpiece, and presumably behaving just as destructively. Instead of "create and be destroyed," Grave's pattern for the female artist was "create and destroy." A little more attractive than jumping in front of a train, but not much. Of course, you could always forget the whole thing, settle down and have babies. A safer course, it would seem, and that was certainly the message of the entire culture.

The most lurid cautionary tales provided by society, however, were the lives of actual female writers themselves. Women writers could not be ignored by literary history, at least not nineteenth-

275

century ones. Jane Austen, the Brontë sisters, George Eliot, Christina Rossetti, Emily Dickinson, and Elizabeth Barrett Browning were too important for that. But their biographies could certainly emphasize their eccentricities and weirdness, and they did. Jane Austen never got married. Neither did Emily Brontë, who also died young. Charlotte Brontë died in childbirth. George Eliot lived with a man she was not married to and never had any children. Christina Rossetti "looked at life through the wormholes in a shroud." Emily Dickinson lived behind closed doors and was probably nuts. Elizabeth Barrett Browning did manage to squeeze out a child but did not bring him up properly and indulged in seances. These women were writers, true, but they were somehow not women, or if they were women, they were not *good* women. They were bad role models, or so their biographies implied.

"I used to have a boyfriend who called me Wonder Woman," says Broom Hilda, the witch, in a recent comic strip.

"Because you are strong, courageous and true?" asks the Troll.

"No, because he wondered if I was a woman."

If you want to be good at anything, said the message, you will have to sacrifice your femininity. If you want to be female, you'll have to have your tongue removed, like the Little Mermaid.

It's true that much was made of Poe's alcoholism, Byron's incest, Keats's tuberculosis, and Shelley's immoral behaviour, but somehow these romantic rebellions made male poets not only more interesting, but more male. It was rarely suggested that the two Emilys, Jane, Christina and the rest lived as they did because it was the only way they could get the time and develop the concentration to write. The amazing thing about women writers in the nineteenth century is not that there were so few of them but that there were any at all. If you think this syndrome is dead and buried, take a look at Margaret Laurence's *The Diviners*. The central character is a successful woman writer, but it becomes obvious to her that she cannot write and retain the love of a good man. She chooses the writing and throws an ashtray at the man, and at the end of the book she is living alone. Writers, both male and female, have to be selfish just to get the time to write, but women are not trained to be selfish.

A much more extreme version of the perils of creativity is provided by the suicides of Sylvia Plath and Anne Sexton and the rather ghoulish attention paid to them. Female writers in the twentieth century are seen not just as eccentric and unfeminine, but as doomed. The temptation to act out the role of isolated or doomed female artist either in one's life or through one's characters, is quite strong. Luckily, there are alternatives. When hard pressed, you can always contemplate the life of Mrs. Gaskell, Harriet Beecher Stowe or even, say, Alice Munro or Adele Wiseman or the many other female writers who seem to have been able to combine marriage, motherhood, and writing without becoming more noticebly deformed than anyone else in this culture.

276

However, there is some truth to the *Red Shoes* syndrome. It *is* more difficult for a woman writer in this society than for a male writer. But not because of any innate mysterious hormonal or spiritual differences: it is more difficult because it has been made more difficult, and the stereotypes still lurk in the wings, ready to spring fully formed from the heads of critics, both male and female, and attach themselves to any unwary character or author that wanders by. Women are still expected to be better than men, morally that is, even by women, even by some branches of the women's movement; and if you are not an angel, if you happen to have human failings, as most of us do, especially if you display any kind of strength or power, creative or otherwise, then you are not merely human, you're worse than human. You are a witch, a Medusa, a destructive, powerful, scary monster. An angel with pimples and flaws is not seen as a human being but as a devil. A character who behaves with the inconsistency that most of us display most of the time is not a believable creation but a slur on the Nature of Woman or a sermon, not on human frailty, but on the special frailer-than-frail shortcomings of all Womankind. There is still a lot of social pressure on a woman to be perfect, and also a lot of resentment of her should she approach this goal in any but the most rigidly prescribed fashion.

I could easily illustrate by reading from my own clipping file: I could tell you about Margaret the Magician, Margaret the Medusa, Margaret the Man-eater, clawing her way to success over the corpses of many hapless men. Margaret the powerhungry Hitler, with her megalomaniac plans to take over the entire field of Canadian Literature. This woman must be stopped! All of these mythological creatures are inventions of critics; not all of them male. (No one has yet called me an angel, but Margaret the Martyr will surely not take long to appear, especially if I die young in a car accident.)

It would be amusing to continue with these excerpts, but it would also be rather mean, considering the fact that some of the perpetrators are, if not in the audience, employed by this university. So instead of doing that, I will enter a simple plea; women, both as characters and as people, must be allowed their imperfections. If I create a female character, I would like to be able to show her having the emotions all human beings have—hate, envy, spite, lust, anger and fear, as well as love, compassion, tolerance and joy—without having her pronounced a monster, a slur, or a bad example. I would also like her to be cunning, intelligent and sly, if necessary for the plot, without having her branded as a bitch goddess or a glaring instance of the deviousness of women. For a long time, men in literature have been seen as individuals, women merely as examples of a gender; perhaps it is time to take the capital W off Woman. I myself have never known an angel, a harpy, a witch or an earth mother. I've known a number of real women, not all of whom have been nicer or more noble or more long-suffering or less self-righteous and pompous than men. Increasingly it is becoming possible to write about them, though as always it remains difficult for us to separate what we see from what we have been taught to see. Who knows? Even I may judge women more harshly than I do men; after all, they were responsible for Original Sin, or that is what I learned in school.

I will end with a quote from Agnes Macphail, who was not a writer but who was very familiar with at least one literary stereotype. "When I hear men talk about women being the angel of the home, I always, mentally at least, shrug my shoulders in doubt. I do not want to be the angel of the home. I want for myself what I want for other women: absolute equality. After that is secured, then men and women can take their turns at being angels." I myself would rephrase that: "The men and women can take their turns at being human, with all the individuality and variety that term implies."

1978

Matt Cohen
1942-

Born in Kingston, Ontario, Matt Cohen was educated at the University of Toronto. Since the appearance of his first novel, *Korsoniloff* in 1969, Cohen has published two collections of stories, *Columbus and the Fat Lady* (1972), and *Night Flights* (1978); and several novels, including *The Disinherited* (1974), *Wooden Hunters* (1975), and *The Sweet Second Summer of Kitty Malone* (1979). "The Rise and Fall of Serious CanLit" appeared in *Saturday Night* in May, 1979.

The Rise and Fall of Serious CanLit

In the past ten years the writing and publishing of Canadian fiction has become a true industry: plentiful, unpredictable—and now depressed.

Although there had been previous periods, most notably the 1930s, when Canadian fiction enjoyed wide public support, the most recent splurge came at an unexpected time. In the mid 1960s Canadian publishing, like publishing the world over, was beginning to suffer from the popularity of television and the movies. It was a time when people were asking why Canadian novelists were cursed with the one-book syndrome. To add to their woes, Canadian publishers were beginning to lose, to the American branch plants, the educational markets that had once supported them.

But during the same period, buoyed by the first major wave of nationalism since the Second World War, there were small presses starting up to publish political books and novels that weren't sufficiently conventional or international to attract the attention of the more established houses.

In the spring of 1969 one of these new houses put out a novel called *Five Legs*, by Graeme Gibson. It was, even in the quirky canon of Canadian literature, a strange book. Dense and complicated, with large debts to James Joyce and Malcolm Lowry, it did to syntax what winter does to flowers.

Some called it genius, other labelled it pretence. But as the sales began to mount up it became clear that *Five Legs* had achieved the impossible—carried by a new interest in things specifically Canadian, a difficult novel from an unknown press had achieved both critical and commercial success.

Immediately Anansi and other small presses began to publish in quantity. Novels, mostly first novels, suddenly began to appear on bookstore shelves. Where the crop had been a few novels a year, it now became dozens. And they proved, by their very multiple and flawed existence, that novels—highbrow, literary, and even unreadable novels—had a market in English Canada. It was not, to be sure, a very large market, but it was large enough to meet the costs of production, given a little help from the Canada Council.

In the fall of 1970, the rising nationalist sentiments were crystallized in publishing by two events; W.J. Gage sold its educational division to an American firm, and Ryerson Press, Canada's oldest and most respectable publisher, let itself be bought out by the American-owned McGraw-Hill.

The arts community protested loudly and demanded support from the Canada Council before the whole publishing industry met a similar fate. Fortunately, the Liberal Party was in a spending mood. Writers' tours, writers-in-residencies, block grants for publishing programmes, new national organizations for publishers and writers sprang up like little voters across the land.

But despite the marvellous growth of infrastructure, and a whole new battalion of cultural bureaucrats, the explosion of new fiction writing continued. And its acceptance widened. Books by such writers as Alice Munro and Margaret Laurence became popular successes. In 1970 a best-selling novel was considered one that sold 5,000 copies. In the spring of 1974 *The Diviners* was published, and a few months later more than 20,000 copies were in print.

The very successful books also increased the audience for the more ordinary sellers, and along with the expanded market for hardcover books came increased paperback sales. For these the prime target was university courses, where a burgeoning interest in cultural nationalism was bringing students to Canadian literature almost faster than the often reluctant (and American-staffed) English departments could handle.

The combination of the college market and the wider public enthusiasm for things Canadian brought this new phase of the Canadian fiction industry to its prime: during this period the normal successful book was a serious literary work which would receive good reviews and achieve sufficient sales in hardback to get into paper and finally onto college courses.

Canadian writers found themselves in a surprising situation. They were writing the kind of books that would have once guaranteed perpetual oblivion, but they were gaining an interested and often demanding audience.

The older publishing houses, especially McClelland and Stewart, with its ubiquitous New Canadian Library series, were quick to take advantage of this trend. And some of the newer ones, like Anansi, Oberon, and Talonbooks, were equally astute—often printing even their first editions in paperback to assure instant access to the educational market.

Writers had stumbled into a fortunate time. They were encouraged by an expanded Canada Council, their royalties were often augmented (in Ontario) by Arts Council grants, and their rejected manuscripts and embarrassing love letters were snatched up by eager libraries and archives. Thanks again to the Canada Council, even their personal appearances became a valued commodity.

While younger writers happily multiplied, major writers long silent—Irene Baird, Adele Wiseman, Robertson Davies, Morley Callaghan—surfaced with new books, books so good that the silences seemed all the more regrettable. Even some expatriate writers began to return to Canada, including Margaret Laurence and Mordecai Richler.

Between the older writers and the new, a remarkable outpouring of fiction commenced, a cornucopia of work in which anything was possible, books both excellent and terrible in absolutely unpredictable ways. While the rest of the world was breeding novelists who wrote about disasters, Canada was enjoying a flowering of Victorian sensibilities. Beautiful and baroque novels like *Fifth Business*, *Lives of Girls and Women*, *Lord Nelson Tavern*, *Bartleby*, *Arkwright*, *Farthing's Fortunes*, *Scann* were published. And while they were being read with interest, classics that had never really found their audience—books like *As For Me and My House*, *The Mountain and the Valley*, *The Stone Angel*, *The Double Hook*—were becoming popular in quality paperback editions.

Why, people were starting to ask, were there not more Canadian books in the really cheap and available mass-market lines? Like many industries in Canada, book publishing was dominated by foreign firms, but while government-funded organizations were still lobbying the government about foreign control of distribution, General Publishing made a surprise move.

From its low-profile, mass-market subsidiary, PaperJacks, it sent out a blizzard of contracts to an amazingly wide variety of writers. And then went one step further and bought the Canadian franchise for Pocket Books—distribution system and all. Within a couple of years, both McClelland and Stewart and Macmillan were also to announce joint ventures with American-owned paperback lines, Seal Books and Macmillan-NAL.

It is this development—the existence of several mass-market publishing lines—that will revolutionize the writing of Canadian fiction. For the first time it is economically feasible for large quantities of novels to be widely distributed. But this is happening when the ten-year boom in literary publishing is starting to slacken. The major houses, beset by rising production costs and a static market, have been cutting back. The small presses, while they introduced new writers and new styles of writing, never succeeded in increasing their cash base; and they are having, in face of the disappearing gap between costs and potential market, to publish in a more conservative way. Good books and new writers are still being published, but they are no longer centre stage.

Because, as the literary boom falters, it is clear that a new phenomenon is beginning to appear. With the support of mass-market paperback lines, international connections, a budding marketplace for Canadian agents, lawyers specializing in contracts, even the occasional film and television adaptation, it has become clear that there is a place for the *intentional* Canadian best-seller.

By the fall of 1978 the fiction lists of most major houses were heavy with these "commercial" novels. There are books being originated for Seal and PaperJacks. There are book packagers in Toronto specializing in putting books together with assured subsidiary and international sales. There are the Alberta fiction and non-fiction awards, and now there is the all-time leader in glitz, the Seal Books $50,000 first-novel award.

The kind of money involved in these commercial novels dwarfs the potential returns from a literary novel, and once again that kind of novel is becoming an economic dinosaur. The 5,000-copy printing that could be such a happy success just a few years ago now seems uneconomical.

Meanwhile, the campus boom has moderated. And the wave of nationalism that carried Canadian culture to such prominence is beginning to recede. It seems that Canada, with its incredible political and economic problems, can't bear to look itself in the face.

Even bookstores are in difficulty. The old-fashioned store, with its huge stock and excellent service, is becoming the well-loved but archaic exception. Chain bookstores have taken over almost half the market, and their share continues to increase. Most are leery of short stories, first novels, experimental novels—anything that might not sell. And for the small presses, chains are a total disaster, often refusing even to speak to small-press salesmen.

After ten years of excitement, the publishing industry is in many ways back where it started, and back in tune with the international publishing world. There are a few large companies—all of them in terrible financial condition—and a lot of equally beleaguered small presses. What can be expected for the future? Will the big companies overcome their fiscal problems? Will the small publishers find new markets for their books?

According to most observers, the answer to both questions is a qualified yes. The big publishers may survive—but they will be rescued by suicidal investors and government loans only on the condition that they trim their costs. And the literary publishers, with their lists shrunken and made conservative by aiming for wider sales, will struggle through hard times by cutting costs and salaries.

But the new wave in publishing, the place where the money and the energy is located, will be book packagers and small publishers doing solely commercial books: coffee table books for the carriage trade, and commercial fiction and non-fiction for the international market.

We had ten anomalous years of bizarre and wonderful books. Much of what was done was silly, vain, pompous, forgettable, but nevertheless that decade was the time when the publishing of Canadian fiction came of age. Now, when a new group of writers and editors must be expected to make their mark, the industry is in trouble and its possibilities are narrowing.

Will the new-style commercial publishers be able to afford the virtues that crippled the old? In shaping books for the best-seller and international market, the publishers may have to de-emphasize the books about Canada, about ourselves, in favour of books that blur cultural and national differences. Will they support writers through bad times, publish fiction that might not sell, publish poetry at all?

As the makeshift arrangements of the last decade collapse under the pressure of more conservative and stringent times, everyone agrees that large-scale changes are coming. The next year or two in the publishing industry will be interesting and dangerous.

1979

Acknowledgements

The editors wish to express their appreciation to Mary Joan Lozon, Mary Rubio, Clara Thomas and the secretaries of the Department of English at the University of Guelph for their assistance and cooperation. We also wish to acknowledge a grant in aid of publication generously provided by the University of Guelph. Finally, we thank our wives for their encouragement and support.

Care has been taken to locate the ownership of copyright material, but the editors will gladly receive any information that will enable them to correct any acknowledgement.

Graeme Mercer Adam. "An Interregnum in Literature", *The Week*. I, 28 (12 June, 1884), 438-9. "Some Books of the Past Year", *The Week*. II, 7 (15 January, 1885), 103.

Margaret Atwood. "The Curse of Eve" was first published in *Women on Women*, edited with an Introductory Essay by Ann B. Shteir. Gerstein Lecture Series. Toronto: York University, 1978. By permission of York University and the author.

Bertram Brooker. "The Future of the Novel in Canada", *Association of Canadian Bookmen's Literary Bulletin*. I (Winter, 1937-8), 9-11.

Ernest Buckler. "My First Novel" in *Ernest Buckler, Critical Views on Canadian Writers*, ed. Gregory M. Cook. Toronto: McGraw-Hill Ryerson, 1972. By permission of the author.

Morley Callaghan. From *That Summer In Paris*. Toronto: Macmillan 1963. By permission of the author. "The Plight of Canadian Fiction", *University of Toronto Quarterly*. VIII, 2 (1 January 1938), 152-161. By permission of the author.

Philip Child. "Fiction". Reprinted from *Canadian Literature Today* by permission of University of Toronto Press. Copyright, Canada, 1938 by the University of Toronto Press.

David Chisholme. [*St. Ursula's Convent. The First Canadian Novel*], *Canadian Review and Literary and Historical Journal. I*, 1 (July, 1824) 49-53.

Matt Cohen. "The Rise and Fall of Serious CanLit", *Saturday Night*. XCIV, 4 (May, 1979), 39-42. ©1979, Matt Cohen.

Robertson Davies. From *A Voice from the Attic*. Toronto: McClelland and Stewart, 1960. Reprinted by permission of The Canadian Publishers, McClelland and Stewart Limited, Toronto. Excerpts from *One Half of Robertson Davies*. Toronto. Macmillan, 1977. Reprinted by permission of Macmillan of Canada.

William Arthur Deacon. "The Canadian Novel Turns The Corner", *The Canadian Magazine*. XXXVI, 4 (October, 1963), 16, 38-40. By permission of the Estate of William Arthur Deacon.

James De Mille. From *Elements of Rhetoric*. New York: Harper and Brothers, 1878.

Sara Jeannette Duncan. "Saunterings", *The Week*. III, 28 (28 October, 1886), 771-2. "Saunterings", *The Week*. IV, 7 (13 January, 1887), 111-12. "Outworn Literary Methods", *The Week*. IV, 28 (9 June, 1887), 450-1. "Saunterings", *The Week*. V, 36 (2 August, 1888), 574.

John Galt. From *The Autobiography of John Galt*. London: Cochrane and M'Crone, 1833.

Charles Gordon. From *Postscript to Adventure*. Toronto: McClelland and Stewart, 1938. By permission of The Canadian Publishers, McClelland and Stewart Limited, Toronto.

Gwethalyn Graham. "Why Books Cost Too Much", *Maclean's Magazine*. LX (15 September, 1947), 22, 39-43.

Frederick Philip Grove. From *It Needs To Be Said*. Toronto: Macmillan, 1929. By permission of A. Leonard Grove, Toronto.

Thomas Haliburton. From *Nature and Human Nature*. London: Hurst and Blackett, 1855.

Julia Catherine Hart. From *St. Ursula's Convent; or The Nun of Canada*. Kingston: Hugh C. Thomson, 1824. From *Tonnewonte; or The Adopted Son of America*. Watertown, New York: James Q. Adams 1825.

Hugh Hood. "Sober Colouring. The Ontology of Super-Realism", *Canadian Literature*. XLIX (Summer, 1971), 28-34. By permission of the author.

William Kirby. [Letters] Kirby Papers. Archives of the Province of Ontario. "Canadian Literature and Copyright", *The Morning Chronicle* (Quebec). February 1, 2, 4, 1884.

Robert Kroetsch. "Unhiding the Hidden". Reprinted from *Journal of Canadian Fiction* (2050 Mackay Street Montreal, Quebec H3G 2J1), Vol. III, No. 3 (1974), pp. 43-45. By permission of *Journal of Canadian Fiction* and the author. "Death Is a Happy Ending: A Dialogue In Thirteen Parts" by Robert Kroetsch and Diane Bessai, from *Figures In A Ground: Canadian Essays On Modern Literature Collected In Honor of Sheila Watson*, edited by Diane Bessai and David Jackel, published by Western Producer Prairie Books, 1978. By permission of the publisher and the authors.

Margaret Laurence. "Ivory Tower or Grassroots? The Novelist As Socio-Political Being" in *A Political Art*, ed., W. H. New. Vancouver: University of British Columbia Press, 1978. By permission of the author.

Stephen Leacock. From *How To Write*. New York: Dodd, Mead and Co., 1943. By permission of The Canadian Publishers, McClelland and Stewart Limited, Toronto.

Hugh MacLennan. From *The Other Side of Hugh MacLennan*. ed. Elspeth Cameron. Toronto: Macmillan, 1978. By permission of the author. From *Scotchman's Return and Other Essays*. Toronto: Macmillan, 1960. By permission of the author.

Edward McCourt. "The Canadian Historical Novel", *Dalhousie Review*. XXVI, 1 (April, 1946), 30-36. By permission of *Dalhousie Review* and Margaret McCourt. From *The Canadian West in Fiction*. Copyright 1949. Reprinted by permission of McGraw-Hill Ryerson Limited.

Lucy Maud Montgomery. From *The Green Gables Letters*. Copyright 1960. Reprinted by permission of McGraw-Hill Ryerson Limited. "I Dwell Among My Own People". By permission of Dr. Stuart MacDonald.

Susanna Moodie. "A Word for the Novel Writers". *The Literary Garland*. New Series. IX (August, 1851), 348-51. From *Mark Hurdlestone or The Gold Worshipper*. London: Bentley, 1853.

Desmond Pacey. From *Essays in Canadian Criticism*. Copyright ©1969. Reprinted by permission of McGraw-Hill Ryerson Limited.

Gilbert Parker. "Fiction — Its Place in the National Life", *The North American Review*. CLXXXVI, 525 (December, 1907), 495-509.

Thomas Raddall. "The Literary Art", *Dalhousie Review*. XXXIV, 2 (Summer, 1954), 138-46. By permission of the author.

John Richardson. From *Eight Years in Canada*. Montreal: Cunningham, 1847. From *Wacousta; or The Prophecy*. New York: DeWitt and Davenport, 1851.

Mordecai Richler. From *Shovelling Trouble*. Toronto: McClelland and Stewart, 1972. Reprinted by permission of The Canadian Publishers, McClelland and Stewart Limited, Toronto.

Charles G.D. Roberts. From *The Kindred of the Wild*. Boston: Page, 1902. By permission of The Canadian Publishers, McClelland and Stewart Limited, Toronto.

Goldwin Smith. From *Lectures and Essays*. Toronto: Printed for the Author, By Hunter, Rose & Co., 1881.

Rudy Wiebe. "Passage by Land" in *The Narrative Voice*, ed. John Metcalf. Toronto: McGraw-Hill Ryerson, 1972. First published in *Canadian Literature*, Spring, 1971. ©Rudy Wiebe, 1971. "On the Trail of Big Bear". Reprinted from *Journal of Canadian Fiction* (2050 Mackay Street, Montreal, Quebec, H3G 251), Vol. III, No. 2 (1974), pp. 45-48. By permission of the *Journal of Canadian Fiction* and the author.

Ethel Wilson. "The Bridge of the Stokehold", *Canadian Literature*. V (Summer, 1960), 43-7. By permission of the Estate of Ethel Wilson.

George Woodcock. "Don Quixote's Dilemma, or The Future of Fiction" originally appeared in *Canadian Fiction Magazine*. XXII (Summer, 1976), 65-73. By permission of the author.

284